D0758691

PHILIPPINE SANCTUARY

PHILIPPINE SANCTUARY

A HOLOCAUST ODYSSEY

Bonnie M. Harris

THE UNIVERSITY OF WISCONSIN PRESS

The University of Wisconsin Press
728 State Street, Suite 443
Madison, Wisconsin 53706
uwpress.wisc.edu

Gray's Inn House, 127 Clerkenwell Road
London EC1R 5DB, United Kingdom
eurospanbookstore.com

Printed in the United States of America

This book may be available in a digital edition.

Library of Congress Cataloging-in-Publication Data

Library of Congress Cataloging-in-Publication Data
Names: Harris, Bonnie Mae, author.
Title: Philippine sanctuary: a Holocaust odyssey / Bonnie M. Harris.
Other titles: New perspectives in Southeast Asian studies.
Description: Madison, Wisconsin: The University of Wisconsin Press, [2020]
| Series: New perspectives in Southeast Asian studies
| Includes bibliographical references and index.
Identifiers: LCCN 2019011672 | ISBN 9780299324605 (cloth)
Subjects: LCSH: Cysner, Joseph, 1912-1961. | Jews—Philippines—Manila—History—
20th century. | Jewish refugees—Philippines—Manila—Biography.
| World War, 1939-1945—Jews—Philippines.
| World War, 1939-1945—Jews—Rescue.
Classification: LCC DS135.P45 H37 2020 | DDC 940.83/18092 [B]—dc23
LC record available at https://lccn.loc.gov/2019011672

DEDICATED TO MY FAMILY:

To my mom
Annie Ella, whose quiet dignity and fortitude
always inspired me to keep going

To my husband
Scott, who, with quiet words of kindness,
always found ways to have my back

To my daughters
Annie Laurie, Bonnie Jean, and Jennie Malinda,
whose combined love lit my way when life's storms covered my path

To my siblings and their spouses
Barbara and Carl, Robert and Liz, Rex and Judy,
who kept me laughing when I wanted to cry

and most of all,
To my grandchildren
who are my joy and the reason for any good I may accomplish in life

From the time Cantor Cysner arrived in the Philippines in 1939, until the liberation of Manila in 1945, Joseph Cysner was a cornerstone of our Jewish lives.

Margot (Cassel) Pins Kestenbaum,
Manilaner refugee and Holocaust survivor

Joseph sent this photograph of himself taken inside Temple Emil in 1941 to his brother in New York. He wrote: "Dearest Poldi and Herta! I am glad to have the chance of sending you a picture made in 1941 when we still had our lovely Temple. Things have changed ever since. Mother is fine! Hope to hear soon from you about evacuation. Love Joe." Cantor Joseph Cysner Collection. Courtesy of the Jewish Historical Society of San Diego.

CONTENTS

ILLUSTRATIONS

PREFACE: UNLIKELY JOURNEYS

In the summer of 2003, I embarked on a new journey in my life that I had never imagined possible—becoming a historian of the Holocaust and, more particularly, a chronicler of Philippine rescue operations intended to save tens of thousands of Jewish refugees terrorized by the Nazi regime. While I had a better than average knowledge of the history of the Jewish people, being a longtime instructor of biblical history and literature in the Church Education System of the Church of Jesus Christ of Latter-Day Saints (Mormons), my prior scholarship focused on the ancient Near East and classical Greek and Roman histories. I had never entertained the idea of pursuing modern Jewish studies and the diaspora of Germany's Jews until I was working as a public historian. It was at that time that I met a gentleman who had been dead for more than forty years.

I met Joseph Cysner in spring 2003 when Sylvia Cysner, Joseph's widow, donated his personal papers to the Jewish Historical Society of San Diego (JHSSD), where I worked as an archivist. My job of handling and organizing personal documents, photographs, and other minutia of people's lives contributed to the preservation of communal and institutional histories. That spring, I planned to write a regional history of Jews in San Diego. However, no sooner did I begin to process the newly accessioned collection of Cantor Joseph Cysner at the JHSSD then I knew those plans had changed forever. I had just found the story of a lifetime—the World War II odyssey of a victim of both Nazi and Japanese imprisonments.

I now literally had in my hands a Holocaust survivor's story, fragmentarily preserved at best, that crossed several fields of Holocaust scholarship. Questions flooded my mind as I contemplated documenting Joseph's story. Where do I start? What comes next? My fifteen-year research journey had begun.

In an effort to understand the broader historical context of Joseph's story that I intended to write, I filled my home office with films, books, and journal articles—titles on both Philippine histories and Jewish histories; titles on antisemitism, refugees, genocide, Diaspora; titles on the Holocaust, testimonies of survivors, histories of the events, stories of rescue and escape, and even psychological studies on the effects of Holocaust-related trauma. I also assembled works on Holocaust memory—memorials, museums, and witnesses. As my research progressed, I found that I could explain the enormity of the Holocaust—historically, academically, psychologically, geographically, and even historiographically—but I could not explain it rationally or morally, and certainly not emotionally. The closer I got to it on a human level, the more transient it grew and the more detached from it as a human being I became. Time and distance held up barriers and kept me out. The effects scared me. I felt myself becoming desensitized to its horrors. I knew, to a certain extent, that this had to happen in order to preserve my own sensibilities along with the objectivity of a historian; but that made me feel guilty. I started to question whether I, as a non-Jew, as one whose family never suffered generations of antisemitism, and as one who did not have a personal connection to the atrocities of the Holocaust could even be a Holocaust historian. Would my work be accepted in spite of what I thought were my limitations? Perhaps it was something I could only aspire to and never achieve, like being on a journey that never reached a final destination. Within it all, I was plagued with this one overarching question—where does one so unqualified as I begin a quest to become the Holocaust historian that Joseph Cysner's story deserved?

To find answers to these questions, I retraced Joseph's journeys and visited Holocaust sites of commission and memorialization; I followed Joseph's life, finding the places where he had been, in Europe and in the Philippines; I searched through repositories all over the world for the ever-elusive single piece of paper that would make it worth all the time and money spent in finding it. The journey I embarked upon to find Joseph reversed the steps he took in his own journey, with the last port of call bringing me to Hamburg, Germany. Once I found his tax record from the Staatsarchiv in Hamburg, I now had in my hand his actual last known address before his expulsion by the Nazis. I purchased a detailed street map of the area, walked around his neighborhood, and took pictures there, including several of his home at 65 Isestrasse. As I walked the long boulevard of multistoried apartment complexes, not wanting to leave the environs in which he had lived, I noticed the glowing golden surfaces of brass plaques, each stamped with the name of a Holocaust victim and the phrase "*hier wohnte* (here lived) . . ." embedded in the sidewalks. These plaques, *Stolpersteine* (stumbling stones), are the result of the Stolperstein Project, which began in 1992 by the sculptor Gunter Demnig of Cologne, who crafted each one personally and had them installed all over Europe. Also etched into the 10 x 10 cm (almost 4 in.) metal is the birthdate of each Holocaust victim, if known, where they were deported to, and when and where they died. These plaques are then set into the sidewalk, whether cement or cobblestone, in front of the residence where the victims last lived. Demnig has sought to preserve a memory of every known victim of Nazi persecution, whether Jew, intellectual, political prisoner, Gypsy, Jehovah Witness, or homosexual. Thousands of these Stolpersteine have been set into the sidewalks in Hamburg, Berlin, Bonn, Bremen, Essen, Cologne, and Frankfurt, just to name a few of the many German cities embracing this program.

Set into the walkways in front of the entrances of nearly every apartment complex on Isestrasse were several of these shining plaques. I tried to read them all, especially those at the address where Joseph had lived before his deportation to Zbaszyn. I watched as people walked along the sidewalks, and I noticed that no one else looked down to read the plaques. As I gazed back along the walkway, the setting sun glinted off the brass markers, making it impossible not to notice them. Each radiant, glowing stone bore the name of one remembered victim and in that brief, seemingly inconsequential moment, my quest to comprehend the enormity of the Holocaust came into piercingly sharp focus for me. Such a quest to understand it all was an exercise in eternal futility. At that moment I realized I was there to understand the enormity of just the one—the uprooted life and wartime experiences of Cantor Joseph Cysner. As I stood on that sidewalk in Hamburg, watching as the plaques turned golden under my feet, I knew I was there for him, not for me. I was there to connect with his past so that I could restore his lost life to his family and to his congregants, and to the larger field of Holocaust studies in general. Because of the successful rescue efforts of the Philippine community in Manila to save Jewish lives, Joseph's name was not among the shining epitaphs set in stone to those who had died in the Holocaust.

For more than fifteen years I have been consumed with Joseph's story, which began as an academic exercise of precision research and analysis that has matured into a lifelong commitment of remembrance and celebration.

What I had once perceived as personal limitations had become my strengths. Through them I came to know Joseph Cysner, his noble character, his warm personality, and his devotion to children, thanks to the constancy of his widow, Sylvia. Although I never met Joseph, I know I would have liked him very much.

ACKNOWLEDGMENTS

How does one begin to thank all the people behind the scenes who have helped in some way or another over the many years in bringing this book to completion? Such an acknowledgment would include historians, archivists, professors, colleagues, students, family, and friends, along with countless others who offered me insights and directions along the way. However, particular appreciations must go out to a few select friends and associates: to filmmaker and colleague Noel Izon, for always championing my work on this project with his gentle persuasion to never give up; to my friend S. L. "Koba" Kay, researcher and editor extraordinaire, whose help in pulling it all together has been immeasurable; to UC Santa Barbara professors Randy Bergstrom and Harold Marcuse, who exhibited unfaltering faith in my ability to succeed; and to Michele Thompson, my "handler" and travel buddy who from the beginning journeyed with me all over the world, keeping me together as we traced Joseph's story. But had it not been for Stanley and Laurel Schwarz, respectively, the president and archives manager of the Jewish Historical Society of San Diego (JHSSD), and Dr. Lawrence Baron, professor emeritus of modern Jewish history and director of the Lipinsky Institute for Judaic Studies, who offered a work study job to a lowly grad student at San Diego State University, I would never have met Sylvia Cysner, nor would I have discovered the wonderful documentary legacy of her husband's life that she had retained for posterity. These personal papers became the Cantor Joseph Cysner Collection in the Archives of the JHSSD, in affiliation with the Jewish Studies Department at San Diego State University. My very special thanks go to Lawrence Baron, Stan and Laurel Schwarz, and the Cysner family for giving me the opportunity to document the life story of Joseph P. Cysner and his Holocaust odyssey from Germany to Poland to the Philippines.

ABBREVIATIONS

IGCR   Intergovernmental Committee on Refugees

JDC   American Jewish Joint Distribution Committee

JHSSD   Jewish Historical Society of San Diego

JMA   Japanese Military Administration

JRC   Jewish Refugee Committee (Manila)

JWB   Jewish Welfare Board

NDC   National Development Company

REC   Refugee Economic Corporation

STIC   Santo Tomas Internment Camp

PHILIPPINE SANCTUARY

Introduction

OPEN DOORS TO THE PHILIPPINES

In the 1930s, when nations of the world were closing their doors to refugee Jews fleeing the growing horror of Hitler's Germany, one small island nation in the Pacific chose to do what others would not—save those lives. On July 6, 1938, eighty delegates from thirty-two countries around the world met at a French resort in Evian-les-Bains at the behest of President Franklin D. Roosevelt to address the growing Jewish refugee crisis in Hitler's "Greater German Reich." More than two hundred international journalists and representatives from Jewish relief organizations recorded ten days of deliberation by the delegates that ultimately failed to perform the task for which they were assembled—to save imperiled Jews via increased immigration plans. Characterized as one of the greatest diplomatic and humanitarian failures of the twentieth century, not one of the attending delegations voiced a commitment to either lift or suspend their nation's quota restrictions within their immigration laws or vowed to increase the numbers of Jewish refugees entering their country by offering them political asylum. But while these relatively low-level diplomats from Western Europe, the United States, and Latin America lamented the plight of the refugees, the small Asian nation of the Philippines had already set a rescue plan into operation.

Heroes in the form of officials from the Philippine Commonwealth, President Manuel Luis Quezon y Molina, and the US High Commissioner

Paul V. McNutt made the deliberate decision to rescue Germany's stateless Jews from the uncertain future of a world on the brink of war. One of those rescued was Cantor Joseph Cysner, one of many German Jews of Polish descent who was in the first wave of forced emigration (Polenaktion, or Polish Action) instigated by the Nazi government in October 1938. He was also one of the few who would eventually find refuge in East Asia. Documents and memoirs in the archives of the Jewish Historical Society of San Diego (JHSSD), donated by Joseph's widow, Sylvia Cysner, relate the unusual odyssey of her late husband's exile to the Polish border town of Zbaszyn and his rescue in the Philippines. Joseph's archival collection comprises two boxes of documents he gathered from Germany, Poland, and the Philippines, along with those from San Francisco and San Diego. These documents detail his expulsion by the Nazis and his incarceration by the Poles and the Japanese before and during World War II. Some of the most important items describe his deportation experiences in Zbaszyn from 1938 to 1939, his rescue by the Commonwealth officials and the American-led Jewish community of the Philippines in 1939, and his confinement at the Santo Tomas Internment Camp (STIC) in Manila in 1942.

Joseph's memoirs recount the expelled Jews' destitution and trials in the no-mans-land between Germany and Eastern Europe. Acting on a telegram offering employment in Manila, Joseph joined 1,300 fellow Jews in finding a sanctuary in that Pacific Island nation. Influential Jewish businessmen, whom President Quezon had empowered to form an interim Immigration Department of the Philippines, also saved refugees of other faiths and nationalities who were fleeing war zones. This book illuminates the unique and unknown rescue plan that went on to become a template, one that Jewish relief organizations duplicated in other parts of the world to better facilitate the rescue and relocation of Jewish refugees. Those Philippine officials and businessmen overcame limits imposed by the United States and other countries during the refugee crisis, and they heroically saved as many souls as they could before war intervened. They demonstrated what could be accomplished when leaders put aside political agendas to act in the universally noble cause of saving human lives.

Many in the field of Holocaust research and studies may ask if another treatise discussing the fate of the Jews of Europe during World War II is really necessary. What more can be said that hasn't been written in literally hundreds if not thousands of volumes of literature on the subject already? Recent publications in Holocaust literature have focused on rediscovering the few episodes of rescue and deliverance for the victims of Nazi Germany.

There are far more stories of failed rescue attempts or missed opportunities in rescuing the persecuted than there are stories of those that were successful. And while this story of the timely rescue of Cantor Joseph Cysner, who had survived both Nazi and Japanese imprisonments, is of deep import, it is yet so much more: it is the story of how one small Asian territory did what larger nation-states of the world declined to do in order to save Jewish lives while overcoming political constraints, economic limitations, racial prejudices, and religious differences.

While processing the archival collection of Joseph Cysner in 2003, I recognized that there was an incredible life story in my hands as Joseph's odyssey unfolded. It was the story of a Holocaust refugee who had endured a cruel expulsion by the Nazis, held in a Polish detention camp, incarcerated by the Japanese, and lived to tell about them all. When I dove deeper into the historiography of these episodes, I realized that Joseph's story offered a unique perspective within the genre of Holocaust survivor studies. To date, only one other narrative of rescue in the Philippines exists, in a book written in 2003 by one of the child survivors of the Manila experience, the German refugee Frank Ephraim. His monograph, *Escape to Manila: From Nazi Tyranny to Japanese Terror*, helped open up other contiguous examinations by historians in Asian studies as well as Holocaust studies.[1] Many of these writings are limited in scope, so there are no existing publications today that give the full documentary history of the three distinct rescue plans in the Philippines, their geneses, and the details of how these rescue plans operated. I also give important historical insights into the Polenaktion and the experiences of those deported refugee Jews who lived as exiles in Zbaszyn, one of the towns along the Polish border, which were forced to accept these expatriated Jews. Joseph's story is the unique vehicle that ties together these dual episodes of persecution and rescue, while restoring and preserving the historical record of successful feats of rescue in a world growing more ambivalent to the need. Few, if any, studies exist that discuss refugee rescue in the Philippines, and which have adequately posed the historical questions regarding the US response to the refugee crisis in general. This book situates the significance of these operations within the larger historiography and analysis of America's response to the Holocaust.

In all the existing literature on this subject since World War II, not one sufficiently acknowledges the role Paul McNutt played in the successful rescue of refugee Jews in Manila and his positioning of the Philippines as a successful site for possible mass resettlement under American auspices.[2]

This present book, however, chronicles in more meticulous detail McNutt's role in the efforts of the American-held Commonwealth of the Philippines and its Jewish community in Manila to devise programs that saved 1,300 refugees from between 1937 through 1941. High Commissioner McNutt and President Quezon, along with members of the Jewish agency in Manila, also formulated plans in late 1938 and early 1939 to resettle tens of thousands more on the southern island of Mindanao. Successful refugee rescue in Manila was already well known within the State Department and by President Franklin D. Roosevelt himself by late 1939, yet FDR was mostly silent about those efforts. The reasons for his silence have everything to do with his relationship with his political rival, Paul McNutt, and his own desire to distance himself from any activity that might favor McNutt and backfire on himself. Current scholarship is filled with FDR's reluctance to fuel the ire of anti-immigrationists within his political milieu: by ignoring McNutt's role with rescue in the Philippines, FDR could indeed protect his political backside. If successful rescue in the Philippines were to become public, it might bring adulation for McNutt. If it failed, it could be used by his critics to cast disparagement upon himself.

These Philippine rescue plans came at a time when American immigration laws had already been securely established with quotas that restricted the total numbers of immigrants entering the United States from specific parts of Europe. Those highly restrictive immigration laws and quotas had been written and passed as law in 1917 and 1924 and were immutable unless those laws were changed by Congress. It is ridiculous to suppose that FDR could have altered them in a political environment of both congressional and public opposition to foreign immigration, and "an entrenched State Department bureaucracy with a restrictionist viewpoint."[3] He proved unwilling to risk splitting the delicate Democratic Party coalition of Dixiecrats (southern Democrats), eastern Liberals, and western restrictionists, which had voted him into office based on his economic strategies, not on social reforms or foreign policies.[4] In an atmosphere of Depression-era economics, nativist nationalism, and congressional isolationism, peppered with antisemitism in nearly every American government agency, it was unrealistic to expect these laws to have been changed to facilitate an increase in immigration numbers of destitute aliens. However, those immigration quotas did not apply to the Philippines, which then was not an American territory but a Commonwealth Nation, with its own domestic autonomy and with full independence slated for July 4, 1946. Even though the Philippine Commonwealth officials had full power over their domestic affairs and a major part of their foreign relations, certain international issues still came under the purview of the American president and the State Department.

Did the State Department impede immigration of Jewish refugees into the Philippines? The answer is yes and no: no, with respect to the selection plan and sponsorship program that did rescue those refugees between 1937 and 1941; and yes, when we look at the documentary evidence concerning the resettlement plan for Mindanao Island. The selection plan came into being (which is fully explained in chapter 3) with the involvement of US State Department officials, Jewish Relief organizations in the United States and Europe, the Jewish Refugee Committee in Manila, President Quezon of the Philippines, and US High Commissioner McNutt. Past scholarship has failed to adequately comment on the role of the US consuls abroad, their interpretation of the restrictive immigrations laws, and their obstruction of immigration. This issue is addressed in the book by Bat-Ami Zucker, *In Search of Refuge*, in which she details how the consuls exercised autonomous power over those who received visas and those who did not, according to certain directives from the State Department to render a strict interpretation of the law in order to thwart Jewish immigration.[5] However, the successful selective immigration of Jews into the Philippines was taken out of the hands of the consuls and put directly into those of the Jewish Community of Manila itself, and neither the State Department nor the consuls could do anything to undermine that process. My book describes Cantor Joseph Cysner's story as the vehicle that drives those discoveries and their analysis.

By rescuing those refugee Jews, the small Asian Commonwealth Nation of the Philippines saved them from the fate of the 6 million Jews murdered in the Holocaust—and while those 1,300 Jewish lives when compared to the 6 million are not so many, to those hundreds who found sanctuary in Manila, each Jewish life rescued was a blessing. The greatest legacy of the Holocaust haven that Joseph helped create will always be that they healed wounds inflicted by the worst of times. As Joseph wrote in his memoir upon his departure from Zbaszyn: "My brothers and sisters I head for a new world."[6]

Joseph's story doesn't end after Zbaszyn and Manila. He immigrated to the United States after the war, and Sylvia, who had her own remarkable survival story, joined him in San Francisco, where they married and started a new life together.[7] Joseph served Congregation Sherith Israel in San Francisco until 1949, when, after their first daughter, Charlotte, was born, the Cysner family moved to San Diego. His last appointment as a cantor was at Tifereth Israel Synagogue in San Diego, until he passed away in 1961.

When Joseph died of a massive heart attack at the age of forty-eight on the eve of Purim in San Diego, Sylvia lost the love of her life. She kept his memory alive for their children and grandchildren by preserving his office intact and untouched for more than forty years; she then needed to close up their home and move closer to her children. It was at that time his donated papers found their way to me at the JHSSD. I feel privileged to have had the opportunity to restore these lost years of Joseph's life to his family while contributing to the larger field of Holocaust scholarship in general. I will be forever grateful to Sylvia for allowing me to know and love her husband, Joseph Cysner.

Joseph Cysner

FROM HAMBURG TO ZBASZYN TO MANILA

The advent of the twentieth century held great promise along with great uncertainty for the Jews of Germany. As will be seen in the life of Joseph Cysner, Germany's Jews realized a level of reception and tolerance in the early decades of the twentieth century that they had never before enjoyed, assimilating into the schools, businesses, professions, the arts, and the military. The paradox of the rise of the National Socialist German Workers' Party (Nazis) from the midst of this era of unprecedented social, religious, and political freedoms for Germany's Jews remains a topic of considerable discussion among historians.[1] As old religious notions of anti-Judaism succumbed to enlightened thoughts of the scientific era, a new modern-age racial slander against the Jews, labeled antisemitism, rose up suddenly at the very peak of Jewish emancipation and spread like a cancer throughout European society.[2] This was Joseph Cysner's world. He began his career as a cantor in Germany the same year that Hitler was appointed chancellor. As Joseph labored in the Jewish communities of Hannover and Hildesheim between 1933 and 1937, he witnessed the rising flood of antisemitic legislation marginalizing the political, economic, and social positions of Jews in Germany.

After accepting a lifetime appointment as cantor at the famous Hamburg Temple in 1937, Joseph embraced this hearth of Reformed Judaism in Western Europe, only to be violently ripped from that community through the actions predicated by the Polenaktion (Polish Action).[3] This was the first bureaucratically enforced mass expulsion in the history of the Holocaust, in which some twenty thousand Jews from Greater Germany were dumped at the Polish border between October 27 and 29, 1938. This event proved to be the trigger for Kristallnacht, the German pogrom known as the "Night of Broken Glass." The Polenaktion was almost immediately relegated to obscurity by the viciousness of the Reichkristallnacht pogroms against German Jews less than two weeks later on November 9, 1938; it overshadowed the fate of the expelled Polish Jews languishing at the border. Joseph was only one of nearly nine hundred Jews deported from Hamburg; he recorded a vivid description of the terrible scenes of chaos, suffering, and terror, leaving a poignant memoir as a rare testimony of this nearly forgotten episode in Holocaust history.

Joseph remained at the Polish refugee camp at Zbaszyn for six months, until his liberation by his Philippine rescuers in April 1939. Although born in Bamberg, Germany, in 1912, Cysner was classified as a Polish Jew because his mother, Chaja, née Rosenberg, was from Oswiecim (Auschwitz), Poland, although his father, Aaron Cysner, a shoemaker, was born in a small town near Prague, in the Czech lands of Bohemia.[4] Joseph's parents had come to Vienna from eastern Europe in the late 1880s, fleeing the Russian pogroms unleashed against the Ostjuden.[5] Six of their seven children were born in Vienna: Leopold, Ernst, Berthold, Charlotte, Henrietta, and another who died in infancy. Around 1910 the family moved to Bamberg, where their youngest, Joseph, was born. His was a typical religious Jewish Orthodox family who practiced a Judaism passed down to them by their ancestors. But Joseph was also a product of the age of Haskalah, the Jewish Enlightenment, enjoying a level of cultural adaptation and assimilation into non-Jewish society, which had apparently appealed to him.[6] He preferred a more modern, even dapper appearance over the traditional attire of the more orthodox practitioners of Judaism. And although he trained in the traditional study of the Jewish chazzan and excelled in classical performance, he loved all genres of modern music—musical theater, American jazz, and Big Band music.[7] Joseph had already adopted the new liberal Reform Judaism when he had received his appointment to the Hamburg Temple, one of the birthplaces of Reform Judaism. Key features of the liturgy of liberal Judaism were organ music and congregational choirs. Joseph was in his element when he was directing vocal ensembles, especially children's choirs. He was living the kind of life his parents had envisioned when they sought safety in Germany from anti-Jewish pogroms in eastern Europe. They could not have known that they had jumped from the frying pan into the fire.

FROM ASSIMILATION TO SOCIAL ANNIHILATION

An aberration in the escalating momentum of modern German antisemitism in the first part of the twentieth century occurred with the advent of the Great War in 1914. In order to rally all factions of the German population into supporting the war effort, the kaiser promised a civic peace that claimed all differences between classes, parties, and religions as nonexistent.[8] Well over one hundred thousand German Jews, including Joseph's oldest brother, fought as German soldiers in World War I.[9] In spite of an estimated twelve thousand Jewish soldiers losing their lives in defense of their German homeland, the battlefield failed to produce the universal postwar acceptance that many Jewish families had hoped for; instead, a scapegoat mentality in German society began to brand the Jews as the at-home enemy who precipitated Germany's defeat.[10] Instead of finding solidarity with their gentile co-combatants, Germany's postwar Jews forged stronger bonds with the Ostjuden, the tens of thousands of eastern European Jews who had moved into Germany between 1916 and 1920. This immigration of the Ostjuden transformed the culture of the westernized German Jews, who responded to the spiritual devotion of their eastern co-religionists in ways that encouraged a renaissance of Judaic culture within the now-secularized Jewish communities of the West. This new cultural solidarity succeeded only in further defining Jewish exceptionalism in the eyes of Germany's antisemites.[11]

The armistice, signed on November 11, 1918, had profound effects on postwar Germany. The German society that entered the Great War did so with a nationalistic fervor fed by decades of imperial-driven prosperity. This was certainly not the society that emerged from those years: World War I had created a lost generation of German veterans whose lives, once defined by violence and comradeship, now formed extremist paramilitary groups, and decried their defeat with the infamous "Stab in the Back" betrayal theory. For these malcontents, the German politicians who signed the armistice became known as the "November Criminals."[12] For the next decade and a half, the political environment in the country expressed the extremes of nationalism, militarism, and Marxism. The Weimar democratic experiment, considered the most progressive government on paper, gave way to constant warfare among these extremes and never achieved

its liberal potential. Under the pressure of postwar political and economic collapse, accompanied by the harsh terms imposed by the Versailles
Treaty, the Weimar Republic never really had a chance to succeed. The
vacuum of authority and leadership in the aftermath of World War I increased the popularity of radical nationalist movements, which, once on
the fringe of society, moved rapidly into the center of political and social
acceptability.

Ironically, after five years of an intense antisemitic revival immediately following the war, German Jewry experienced an unprecedented
renaissance of Jewish culture. During this time, as Jews enjoyed the legal
protection of the laws of the Weimar Republic, they began to advance
their presence in German society beyond a marginally tolerated role. They
were free to contribute more to the politics and culture of the Weimar
Republic, redefine their Jewishness, and endeavor to repair the damage of
war as well as years of antisemitism.[13] However, with this increasing Jewish
presence came a new onslaught of antisemitic literature, epitomized by the
infamous *Protocols of the Elders of Zion*.[14] The growing numbers of Ostjuden in Germany furthered the image of Jews as the antithesis of the ideal
German citizen: some seventy thousand eastern European Jews arrived in
Germany as laborers during World War I. While their presence in German
society had culturally revitalized the German Jews, many non-Jewish
citizens saw the Ostjuden as the embodiment of a repulsive Jewish stereotype promoted in the rabid rhetoric of the antisemites. Such were the
political and cultural germs for the advent of National Socialism and the
rise of Adolf Hitler.[15]

Joseph was finishing up his cantorial studies in 1932 when the Nazi
party ascended to power, permitting Hitler to make his own personal antisemitic agenda official government policy. He incrementally increased
legislation to separate Jewish Germans from the rest of German society by
escalating his programs according to the threshold of acceptance that German society would allow. He introduced legislation in 1933 that excluded
Jews from academic professions, civil service, and judicial systems; the
Nazi regime eventually enacted more than two thousand anti-Jewish laws,
essentially excising the Jewish presence from German society between the
years of 1933 and 1938.[16]

As Germany ratified more and more edicts that deprived Jews of their
businesses, assets, properties, rights to education, and eventually their
citizenship, an increasing number of Jews tried to leave Germany, com-
pelling nations on every continent to impose tighter and more restrictive

immigration policies. Owing to the Great Depression and growing anti-immigrant sentiment, most countries severely restricted any and all foreign immigration. This further emboldened Hitler, who saw an international community unwilling to aid his unwanted Jews. After the Anschluss (joining) of Austria with Germany in March 1938, and the attendant organized violence against Austria's Jews that ensued, a delegation of eighty diplomats from thirty-two nations convened in France for the Evian Conference on July 6, 1938, at the behest of FDR. The unproductive gathering further demonstrated to Hitler that other countries would take no action to either counter his antisemitic actions or accept the growing number of Jewish refugee immigrants.[17]

Polish politicians feared that Germany's anti-Jewish policies would propel a massive return of its unwanted Polish-Jewish citizens. In response to the oncoming crisis, the Polish government passed new decrees that would rescind citizenship from all Polish nationals who had been out of the country for more than five years, deliberately targeting its out-of-state Jewish citizens. Hitler responded to the decree by ordering a highly organized and well-coordinated deportation of nearly seventeen thousand Polish Jews living in Germany, Austria, and the Sudetenland in a mass expulsion: the Polenaktion. Among those affected by the new decree was a German-born son of Ostjuden parents, Joseph Cysner.

DIASPORA OF GERMANY'S JEWS

Thousands of German Jews found ways to escape during their Diaspora in the Hitler years from 1933 to 1945. The first phase of Jewish emigration, from 1933 to 1938, began with Hitler's assumption of power and ended with the Anschluss in 1938. The second phase, from 1938 to 1941, began immediately following the Anschluss and the other disastrous events of 1938 and ended with Hitler's reversal of his forced emigration plans for Jews by sealing off Germany's borders and stifling any future escape from Europe in 1941. The third phase, from 1941 to 1945, entailed the deliberate annihilation of Jews during the height of the war years until the defeat of Nazism by the Allies.

The first period of emigration, the period just prior to Cysner's expulsion to Zbaszyn, can be divided into subperiods that correspond to the episodes of antisemitic actions taken by the Nazi regime from 1933 to 1938. In order to better understand the Jewish diaspora at this time, which included Cysner and the hundreds of Jewish refugees who fled to the Philippines, we must understand the international climate with respect to immigration policies for foreign aliens in general, and Jewish immigrants in particular.

Migrations were normal occurrences for populations in the industrialized age, and indeed the United States received significant numbers of European immigrants from the mid-1800s to the 1920s, totaling approximately fifty million immigrants in a one-hundred-year period.[18] Wars, economic downturns, and political turmoil are usually the main causes for mass migrations, and the first decades of the twentieth century experienced many of these. Add to this a worldwide increase in nativist nationalism, sprinkled with anti-immigrant and antisemitic propensities, and an extremely unfriendly and unresponsive environment for any refugee crisis was likely to form.[19]

Immigration policies in the United States remained unreceptive to Jewish refugees throughout the 1930s, despite Germany's openly antisemitic Nuremberg Laws of 1935, which declared its half-million Jews to be stateless. When the Evian Conference convened in July 1938 to address the issue of German Jewish refugees, Poland implied that they would like to deport their three and a quarter million undesirable Jews as well. Any serious resolutions for Germany's Jewish refugees quickly evaporated under the daunting prospect of having to also rescue millions of Poland's Jews. This became another reason for the restrictive immigration policies of the western nations to remain unchanged.[20]

Emigration numbers show that with each year after 1933 until 1938, the number of Jews leaving Germany progressively decreased. Wealthy families did not want to give up the comforts of their homes and the security of their established businesses on the off chance that a lunatic would be taken seriously for very long. Families with older grandparents and young children found it was too cumbersome to flee and give up a sizable portion of their assets: 25 percent in what the Nazis called a "flight tax." But the wealthy waited too long, losing more time and assets to the ever-increasing antisemitic legislation and policies of the Third Reich, making it nearly impossible for them to leave.[21]

During this first phase of emigration, especially in the early years, most of the Jews who fled found refuge in other European countries. Those who had been targeted by Hitler's first anti-Jewish legislation were professionals, civil servants, intellectuals, artists, and political dissidents whose voices of warning might have swayed more of the complacent Jews to take the Nazi threat more seriously. But it was also from these countries that most of the displaced refugees would later be returned to Germany on their way to

concentration camps. As the countries of Europe began to feel overbur-
dened by the number of refugees seeking asylum within their borders,
the United States began to increase the numbers of immigrants allowed
within its quota system. But there were always more German Jews wanting
to leave Europe than there were places for them to go. When faced with
international inaction regarding their worsening situation, those remaining
in Germany chose to stick it out at home in hopes that the situation would
improve.[22]

The violence launched against Austria's Jews with the Anschluss and
the wholesale destruction during Kristallnacht in November 1938 shook
the two hundred thousand Jews of Austria and nearly three hundred
thousand Jews still in Germany out of their complacency and urged them
to take whatever steps necessary to leave Nazi-dominated territory. Some
nations, including Germany, sought an answer to the refugee crisis with
grandiose plans for mass resettlement projects around the world. Germany
tried to propose a mass relocation plan of its own to Madagascar in hopes
of shipping tens of thousands of its Jews to this East African island.[23]

At the Evian conference, Roosevelt had hoped to promote the possibility of mass resettlement throughout the world as being funded and
operated by private organizations. But the need became immediate, and
grand plans take time. He instead instructed American consuls abroad to
fill America's immigration quotas, which had gone only partially filled for
several years. This doubled and even tripled the number of refugees entering
the United States in 1938 and 1939. In contrast to and in spite of Britain's
restrictive enforcements when it came to immigration to Palestine, illegal
entry into the British Mandate there brought mostly Polish Jews before
Kristallnacht and German Jews afterward, with the Nazis going so far as to
forcibly expel Jews by either shipping them off to Palestine in rickety transport ships or by dumping thousands at borders and forcing them at bayonet
to cross international boundaries.[24]

During these years, German and Austrian Jews found alternative refuge
in Latin America and Asia. If visas could not be obtained for Latin American countries, people often left without proper papers in hopes that they
could find a port anywhere that would allow them entry. Argentina took
in the greatest number of refugees, about twenty-five thousand, with other
South American countries such as Brazil, Chile, and Bolivia offering havens
as well. In the Chinese International Community of Shanghai, nearly twenty
thousand Jewish refugees, mostly Germans, were admitted without visas.
Smaller numbers entered Japan, Singapore, and the Philippines. By 1940,

as many as five hundred thousand European Jews had found safe havens, and close to four hundred thousand from Germany and Austria alone.[25]

FROM GERMAN JEW TO POLISH REFUGEE

Although Joseph Cysner had been born, raised, and educated in Germany, he was designated a Polish Jew because of his mother's ethnicity as denoted on his German residency papers. He left Bamberg in 1929 to attend the Jewish Theological Seminary in Würzburg and graduated in 1933, the same year Hitler was appointed chancellor. Joseph then served as a cantor in Hildesheim and Hannover before accepting the lifetime contract offered him as cantor for the Hamburg Temple in 1937, the same year his father died. Between 1933 and 1937, Nazi anti-Jewish measures in Germany accelerated with the enactment of the Nuremberg Laws in 1935 and their implementation in the years that followed. Joseph's older brothers all emigrated in the early 1930s—Leopold eventually went to the United States, Ernst and Berthold became Zionists and went to Palestine. Joseph's sisters, Charlotte and Henrietta, married and moved to Berlin, with Henrietta making her way to London. Joseph shouldered the financial responsibility for his mother for the rest of his life. He never saw his brothers in Palestine again. His sister Charlotte and her husband, Henry Kahan, perished in Auschwitz.

The critical year of Joseph's story was 1938, as it was for Jewish refugees in general. Poland passed new legislation nullifying the passports of Poles living abroad, essentially making stateless the nearly sixty thousand Polish Jews living in Germany and the newly annexed Austria. In October 1938, Czechoslovakia was carved up, impelling even more Jews to run from the occupying German armies. The Anschluss and the annexation of Czech Sudetenland sent thousands of Jews fleeing to Polish consular offices, while Poland tried to halt the tidal wave of returning Jews. When Poland passed new laws revoking citizenship of its out-of-state Jews, Hitler ordered the German foreign ministry and the Gestapo to arrest all Polish Jews in Germany and Austria and to deport them en masse to the Polish border.

After being collected overnight in community centers, jails, parks, and other large facilities, the thousands of Ostjuden were packed onto passenger trains all headed east. Joseph was one of those nine hundred Jews from Hamburg deported that night; his mother, still in Bamberg, was spared, shielded by the careful actions of Bamberg's Jewish families. Joseph recorded the event and described the scenes of chaos, suffering, and terror at the border. German soldiers with fixed bayonets drove the Jewish masses across the no-man's-lands; Polish border guards fired rifles into the air to stop them. Joseph described a scene of mass panic in his diary.

THE POLENAKTION, OCTOBER 1938

Jews from eastern Europe began immigrating to Germany in the seventeenth century, but the largest exodus of the Ostjuden occurred in the early 1880s following government-directed violence by the Russian Empire, which held territory in Poland and Eastern Europe. Although most eastern refugees merely passed through Germany on their way to the United States, tens of thousands stayed and settled in the territories of the Prussian and Austro-Hungarian empires, as did Aaron and Chaja Cysner. In 1925, nearly half of the more than one hundred thousand Jewish foreigners living in German-speaking lands held Polish passports. In the census of June 16, 1933, nearly one-third of the Jewish foreigners in Germany were of Polish origin, 40 percent of whom had been born in Germany.[26] The rise of the Nazi regime at that time did little to comfort Polish Jews who were as unwelcome as their German co-religionists.

A change in political leadership in Poland in 1935 brought about similar repressive laws against their own Jewish citizenry.[27] The Polish government encouraged their mass emigration from 1936 on; as more Jews attempted to leave Poland, they found more countries closing their doors to them. Hopes for escape faded fast for the millions of Jews suffering in Poland, along with their seventy thousand fellow Polish Jews in the Greater German Reich.[28] Worse yet, Poland was not included in the deliberations at Evian and voiced its own desire to rid itself of Jews. Strained economies resulting from the Great Depression convinced the Western world that it simply could not, or would not, make room for that many more destitute people.[29] The Polish Jews in Germany found themselves between the proverbial rock and hard place, as neither Germany nor Poland wanted them, and there were virtually no places to emigrate elsewhere. Coupled with the deteriorating diplomatic relations between Germany and Poland as each vied for regional recognition as the purveyor of power in eastern Europe, the events of the Polenaktion and the expulsion of thousands of Polish Jews from Germany seemed inevitable.

In an effort to stave off the mass return of its foreign resident Jews following the Anschluss, Poland revoked citizenship rights for its people living abroad with new statutes. Months of heated negotiations followed as Germany demanded that Poland rescind the edicts as they applied to Polish Jews in Germany and Austria. The Nazi government waged violent means against their resident Polish Jews in an effort to drive them out before the decrees went into effect. German ordinances targeting these Jews—Joseph Cysner being one—pronounced that all foreign residents who had lost their citizenship in their home countries could be summarily deported without notice.

Following the implementation of Germany's regulations against its foreign Jewish residents in September 1938, Poland's Interior Ministry announced a new ordinance of its own, augmenting its already legislated renouncement of citizenship statute. Poland hurriedly passed measures that required all passports to have validation stamps by October 30, 1938—giving Polish citizens abroad only days to acquire the stamp before they became stateless. According to the ordinance, without the stamp the bearer of the passport would lose all Polish citizenship rights immediately and be refused entry into Poland. As Polish Jews presented their passports at Polish embassies across the Reich, Polish consular officials confiscated the passports, thus insuring a de facto stateless condition on its Jews abroad before the target date of October 30, 1938. This enraged Hitler.

On October 26, 1938, the German Foreign Ministry instructed the German Embassy in Warsaw to demand that the Polish government issue a binding statement permitting Polish passport holders in Germany admittance into Poland, even if the passports did not bear the newly required validation stamp. This message further declared that Germany had no other recourse than to initiate the immediate expulsion of Jews of Polish nationality from Germany as a precautionary action. The Reich would refrain from the expulsions only if Poland guaranteed not to enforce its own decrees as they pertained to Germany.

An urgently marked Schnellbrief (express letter) from Berlin dated October 26, 1938, from the Office of the Reichsführer SS sent throughout the Reich gave implicit instructions that the state police immediately initiate a large-scale operation to terminate residency rights of all Polish Jews living within their jurisdictions. All Polish Jews were to be expelled from Germany on or before October 29, 1938, prior to their Polish citizenship being revoked by the Polish government's new statutes.[30]

Locating Jews through the centralized files created by German census records and residence registry cards, the Gestapo, as directed by the German Foreign Ministry, arrested nearly seventeen thousand Jews of Polish national origin throughout Germany and Austria on October 27, 28, and 29, 1938, and transported them en masse to the Polish border. The Polish government then issued reprisal directives to immediately expel German citizens from western areas of Poland. Immediate negotiations between the German Foreign Ministry and the Polish government halted any further deportations, on either side. The remaining Polish Jews in Germany, who were in the process of expulsion from Germany when the agreement was reached, returned to their homes. Several thousand deportees, however, still remained at the border, detained by armed personnel in the no-man's-lands on both sides of the zone. The Gestapo, who insisted that the ministry accept responsibility for the deportations, inquired what they were supposed to do with the human masses in their charge at the border.

Poland refused to allow the refugees to enter their country, and the German secret police rejected the idea of sending them back to their homes in Germany. Polish authorities estimated that seven thousand Polish Jews from Germany had entered the country already, and they felt obliged to deport the same number of German citizens from Poland back into Germany. Resident non-Jewish Germans living near the border in Poland, deported in a reprisal action by the Poles, found comfortable accommodations in towns in Germany while the Jewish Poles, victims of the Polenaktion, lived in fear and varying degrees of deprivation in makeshift camps.[31]

These stateless Jews sought shelter all along the border in tent camps until some were sent on to Warsaw. Joseph and about eight thousand others faced a forced detention in Zbaszyn, a Polish border town. Later, Joseph wrote about his experiences during the months he spent there. Part of those group deportations that ended up in Zbaszyn included Jews from Hannover, where Joseph had once lived and worked. The Grynszpan family, also from Hannover, ended up in Zbaszyn as well. From there they cabled their son, Herschel, who was at school in Paris, telling him of their terrible expulsion. With a postcard from his sister in his pocket, Herschel entered the German Embassy in Paris and fatally shot a German consular official, Ernst vom Rath. This act was used by members of Hitler's inner circle to trigger Kristallnacht, which many historians designate as the beginning of the Holocaust. The Polenaktion not only precipitated Kristallnacht but was also the first mass expulsion of Jews from Nazi Germany: a foreshadowing of later deportations to sites of mass murder. It was an act that required the coordination of several bureaucratic agencies to accomplish—all precursors to the well-organized expulsions conducted during the war years. After hearing about Kristallnacht while being held at Zbaszyn, Cysner knew that he and the thousands of other displaced Jewish refugees at the border would never be able to return to Germany.

THE EXPULSION AND JOSEPH'S MEMOIR

Although the why and when of the Polenaktion expulsions were fairly universal, there were disparities of where, who, and how it was conducted throughout the many communities of the Third Reich. While some city authorities only arrested and deported the men, as in Baden, others arrested and deported entire families, as was done in Frankfurt am Main and Württemberg. In Nuremberg, the Gestapo arrested families, some of whom became separated when the police transported the men two days before the rest of their families. Women and children faced expulsion from Saxony, Hamburg, and Munich. Armed men seized school children in Berlin and deported them to the border without their parents, who were later arrested and sent on different transports to different border locations. Jews in Leipzig, forewarned by Jews in Halle, sought protection from the Polish consulate, while others fled arrest via other means. Consequently, only 50 percent of Leipzig's Polish Jews experienced deportation, while Dresden expelled nearly 90 percent of its Polish Jewish population. Some victims, roused from sleep and arrested in the middle of the night, were given only enough time to pack one bag. Still others, arrested at their places of business in broad daylight, were sent immediately to transports; their only possessions were whatever they happened to have with them at the time. Nazi officials set up collection points in places large enough to assemble several hundred people. Trucks and automobiles were used to transport the deportees from schools, restaurants, or auditoriums to the nearest train depots. Major cities with train lines running directly to the Polish border became transit stops for sending the collected human cargo east. Although Germany had carried out other deportations prior to the Polenaktion, this was by far the largest yet attempted. Ironically, witnesses to the expulsions thought it the most horrific act of injustice they had ever witnessed, unaware that it was only foreshadowing what was to come.

In the early days of October 1938, upon completion of the Munich Pact in September and the invasion of the Sudetenland, the Nazis had deported about 3,000 Czech Jews and abandoned them in impoverished camps inside the border zones. In comparison, nearly 17,000 Polish Jews were deported in the Polenaktion in the final days of October 1938.[32] Approximately 4,000 to 6,000 refugees crossed the border between Beuthen and Kattowitz, in the southernmost border area of Poland and Germany. Another 1,500 exiles from Berlin and Königsberg in the north sought refuge at Chojnice (Konitz) and at the frontier town of Dworsky-Mlyn. From October 30 to November 10, 1938, refugee camps sprang up along the borders of Slovakia, the Sudetenland, and Hungary, holding between 50 and 2,000 deportees each. By far, the largest concentration of Polish refugee Jews, more than 8,000, descended upon the border town of Zbaszyn, the westernmost Polish city of the Poznań district, just across the German-Polish border from Neu Bentschen. This sudden influx of displaced persons at Zbaszyn more than doubled its population, whose original Jewish population consisted of only 52 people in an overall population of just over 5,000. The city received its refugees primarily from Berlin, Hamburg, Hannover, Hildesheim, and Leipzig in the north and from the Rhineland cities of Düsseldorf and Cologne.

The Altona District of Hamburg, with its Platz der Republik, a large square in front of the Old Altona train station, became a perfect gathering place for the nine hundred Jews arrested there and marked for deportation during the Polenaktion.[33] Joseph was one of those victims, and his experiences depicted how the Nazis implemented the deportations. The process involved several typical steps. First, the victims had to be identified through census and residency records, and once the Gestapo obtained their identifications, they made the arrests.[34] The behavior of the arresting officers varied as much as their victims. Some allowed their Jewish charges to take their time packing, affording them a chance to change and pray, as it was the Jewish Sabbath; others employed various means of humiliation and force to segregate men from their families.[35] Sometime during his deportation and confinement experience, Joseph began writing down his memoir.

Joseph's original German manuscript has no dates, but from the paper, the language, and the penmanship, we can deduce that he began the memoir while he was detained at Zbaszyn and shortly after his arrival there. Paper type, ink, and handwriting demonstrate that the memoir was written on at least three different occasions, possibly more.[36] Also, a typewritten German letter, dated November 6, 1938, with Zbaszyn in its title and signed by Joseph, reads as an encapsulation of his handwritten notes.[37] Joseph starts the letter by stating that it has been eight days since he has been in Poland as part of the expulsion of thousands of Jews from Germany. The date suggests the handwritten memoir began before this date. A typewritten English version was composed by Joseph from the German memoir and the German letter while he was in Manila, possibly with the aid of a translator and probably after the city's liberation by US Armed Forces as Joseph alludes in his English version to the heroes of the Warsaw Ghetto Uprising that occurred in April and May 1943. Joseph's English version recounts his experiences of October 28 and 29, 1938, replete with personalized detail.

A well planned action seals the fate of thousands of polish Jews in Germany, a cruel and barbaric deportation brings sorrow and unhappiness to thousands of jewish families. Over night comes the command of the Gestapo and immediately are the polish Jews rounded up and marched into a dark future, taken away from their houses and property, pushed around like animals by inhuman beings! Hamburg's Jewry is full of anxiety and excitement! Word spreads around as all the polish Jews are rounded up and coming home from the Temple I hear the shocking news from our neighbor. Not knowing what to do, as a policeman called for me in my absence, I go fearfully to the Temple and pray . . . hoping, that my Mother will be save and well! In my restlessness I go to the Consulate, where crowds await an answer from the Consul and not achieving anything there, I hasten to Dr. Italiener [chief rabbi at the Hamburg temple], who advised me to report to the policestation and who assures me to work for my early release. Being convinced to go this straight way I return home, took my Tefillin and a prayerbook and go the heartbroken way to the police. Like a prisoner I was taken to Altona into a big hall where already hundreds of Jews are gathered, crying, praying, fearful what is going to happen next. A sorrowful picture! Old and sick people, children and babies are jammed into this hall awaiting their fate from the hands of the Nazis. . . . It is EREV SHABBOS [Sabbath eve, Friday night], and a tragedy of being dragged away from the places of worship into a place of horror. Everybody is guessing what will happen . . . the chance of being freed in a few hours dwindles more and more. . . . The hour of service approaches and here and there are groups of Jews formed to receive the Sabbath with prayer and song in the midst of affliction. The prayers are full with tears and cries—a heartbreaking picture of jewish suffering! Rough policemen force us to line up for registration and beat the Jews in their savage manner. Every hope of being released is gone when the darkness comes, and we are loaded like animals into policewagons, which move fast through the streets of Altona, heading for the station. There we were unloaded, lined up again and with four dry pieces of bread in our hands we were packed into compartments. The cries and weeping increase as we all feel the uncertainty of that trainride, the fateful hour in our life, which is in the hands of the Gestapo. . . . We did not know where we go . . . we only guess . . . to Poland, to the border! Our train passes numerous other trains moving in the same direction and tears roll down my cheeks when I see frightful faces pressed towards the windows . . . and suddenly my name sounds out of the darkness: Mr. Beim from Hildesheim recognizes me from another train and his voice trembles with fear.[38]

In Joseph's Zbaszyn letter, addressed to "my dear ones," no doubt unnamed siblings as he mentions their mother, Joseph compared the flight of the Jews from Egypt with this expulsion of Jews from Germany and believed the latter to be the more tragic, as they were ripped from their beds and their lives in a most inhumane manner.[39]

As his train sped eastward, Joseph saw other trains filled with deportees who would call out the names of their hometowns to each other. This important main transport line, running from Berlin through Poznań to Warsaw, took the exiles of the northern cities to the German border town of Neu Bentschen, where police and officials unloaded the trains and force-marched the refugees on the last 4.3 miles (7 km) of the journey at gunpoint in full view of the local residents. Stragglers on this arduous trek risked bodily harm as well as losing their luggage, as the armed troops beat any who fell behind.[40] Other witnesses to the mass expulsions included newspaper correspondents from other countries who wired in their eyewitness accounts for the rest of the world to read. The October 29, 1938, issue of the *New York Times* reports how the "raids" began in Berlin at 5:00 a.m.: "Men were hauled out of bed and taken to police stations. Their panic-stricken families followed them, and all-day weeping women and children stood around the police stations anxiously questioning everybody leaving them as to the whereabouts of their menfolk. Nobody knew any answer."[41]

According to the *New York Times* correspondents in Frankfurt am Main, trains with seven hundred to eight hundred deportees passed through the city every hour, along with trucks crammed with more refugees being transported to the border via the highways. Munich's police officials stood around taking pictures of the trains loaded with "700 Jews, including eleven women with babies in their arms and more than a hundred children." In Vienna, "brown-shirted Storm Troopers in groups of six raided homes, loaded foreign Jews, including Czechoslovaks and Romanians, into trucks and hauled them off to police stations." Once their non-Polish status was confirmed, they were freed. When officials released hundreds of Polish Jews in Vienna because the detention sites were full, they also redirected a train of two thousand deportees to the new Mauthausen concentration camp.[42] The articles further reported how refugees' neighbors back home had cleared out or boarded up the Jewish businesses and marked the goods for sale. These accounts confirm that the Nazis made no attempts to hide the action from the eyes of the German public or from the world. This aspect of the Polenaktion demonstrated that the "conditioning" of the German people and observers worldwide as bystanders to Nazi atrocities had progressed far enough that hiding this brutality was no longer necessary. It established a precedent for future deportations and Nazi actions against Jews.

REFUGEES AT THE BORDER

The train station at Zbaszyn was built in the 1920s to accommodate passengers arriving for the Polish trade expeditions.[43] Until 1939, it had been a point of respite for travelers passing through to other destinations. As soon as eastward traveling passengers crossed the border, Poland officially began at the train station in Zbaszyn. "Crowned heads and foreign dignitaries were greeted with luxurious saloon carriages, flowers, and orchestras. Common passengers could rest in the spacious interiors of the modern station."[44] As a result of the Polenaktion, the purpose of the Zbaszyn train station changed forever: it became a site of banishment and despair as hundreds departed from their incarceration at Zbaszyn over the ensuing ten months to unknown futures in exile.

The first transports of refugees arrived at the border on October 28 and crossed without incident into Poland, taking the Polish officials by complete surprise. "Fearing difficulties with the next load there, the Germans emptied the trains on German territory and drove refugees [on foot] across fields into Poland."[45] Polish passport officials in Neu Bentschen, a German town built just west of the border, tried to prevent or delay the transport of the Jewish refugees into Poland, but according to the *New York Times*, German officials carefully boarded those on the trains who held valid Polish passports. This left no other option for the Polish officials but to allow their passage across the border to the next depot, Zbaszyn. According to the Polish passport decree, those Jews could not be refused safe passage into Poland. By that night, not one refugee remained in the German border town of Neu Bentschen.[46] Joseph recounts the scene that unfolded when he arrived following this first wave.

In the early morning we reach [Neu] BENSCHEN, the city on the Polish border. We are told to leave the train and again lined up, searched if we have more than 10.00 Mark with us. For hours we stand around and while we shiver in the cold the endless column of Jews were forced to march, escorted by the military police with fixed bayonets. . . . Children could hardly walk anymore . . . old people collapsed on the way . . . but on went the column of polish Jews, driven by the Nazi beasts and beaten and threatened with the bayonets if they refused to move on! Left and right were fields and woods . . . it was evident that we were to be driven and expelled to Poland! Turning around I saw the suffering of a persecuted people, defenseless and weak, exposed to the cruelty of the Nazis . . . another wandering in history. . . . Ad Matai [for how long], I thought . . . how long will we be the scapegoat of the nations? For hours and hours we drag ourselves along through the rough highways and we approach a little house that stands right before the border—we reached NOMANSLAND. The soldiers shout their orders and stand in groups, ready to do their job of chasing us with their bayonets over the border. On the other side you could clearly see the polish border police, few men that were quite puzzled to see such a mass facing them. The following phase is the most tragic one of that historic event. The soldiers amused themselves pushing us into Nomansland, making pictures while we passed them and threatened to kill everyone who retreats. VORWÄRTS IHR JUDENPAK!!! [Keep marching, Jewish rabble]. There was no alternative than to cross the polish border, but we were between two rows of bayonets and nobody dared to move forward or backward. Men and women, children and babies cried and screamed at this moment of despair, polish speaking Jews showed their passport to the guards . . . without chance of crossing the border. A wall of people was moving back and forth, a terrific screaming filled the air and the SHMA was uttered in this hour of danger.[47] The pressure from the Germans increases more and more and the prayers of desperate Jews are filled with tears and pleading. . . . Suddenly the Poles raise their guns and we were all told to lie down . . . then to stand up . . . and confusion made the people more afraid and frightened. The minutes of that pushing and pressing seemed like hours! I observe people looking for a place to run over and suddenly inspired by an inner voice I take a chance and take my little baggage and the violin of Dr. Broches and run . . . run . . . run . . . right through the space between two guards into the woods.[48]

Joseph told how a young girl, one of his former students from Hamburg, recognized him and ran with him, having been separated from her parents in their initial expulsion. Both Joseph and his young student ran "several meters" through the woods to a road, evading a policeman searching the area on a bicycle. Joseph noticed a vehicle approaching on the roadway and called out for help. He and his young student joined this transport of Hannover refugees headed for the Polish border town of Zbaszyn. Those whom Joseph left at the border with his flight through the woods remained there for another twenty-four hours before police allowed them to travel farther into Poland and find shelter from the weather.

Polish authorities forced the internment of the hastily deposited Jewish refugees at Zbaszyn because of its proximity to the border. They hoped that the Jews' temporary status would facilitate negotiations for their return to Germany. Nearby abandoned barracks provided scant protection from the advancing winter weather. Discarded in obscurity and nearly destitute, the refugees struggled to find shelter and provisions. In many cases, the only accommodations available were barns, stables, and pigsties. Escape attempts could end in death.[49] Joseph's memoir records the dismal scene at Zbaszyn when he arrived.

> Thousands of Jews from all over Germany are already assembled and the picture I saw was a typical page of jewish history: Galuth [exile], deportations, suffering . . . Emek Habacha . . . a valley of tears!!!! Barracks were all around a desperate crowd . . . here and there trunks and blankets were lying around. Bearded Jews are praying fervently and the expression in their faces tell of their sorrows and hope. Hungry and thirsty we moved around the big compound, looking for friends, inquiring what cities are represented. . . . And while we err around that place of distress [the] few Jews of that village walk around with buckets of tea and refresh us. They work day and night and try to encourage us and to give us whatever they could. 10000 Jews were made homeless overnight, expelled by barbaric Nazis.[50]

Once the expulsions stopped, Warsaw was forced to deal with the thousands of displaced persons still abandoned at various border locations. Evacuations of these border camps by the Jewish Joint Distribution Committee (JDC) in Warsaw allowed hundreds of refugees to find shelter with relatives in Poland. The JDC and other relief organizations provided accommodations for a thousand refugees who were received at assembly sites in Warsaw. For the more than twelve thousand refugees at Zbaszyn and other smaller sites of detention along the border, no rescue from their forced incarceration materialized as they awaited further negotiations between Germany and Poland.[51] Joseph relates more details about his own experience at Zbaszyn.

> For days and nights registration is going on, everytime somewhere else and everytime by another polish official. Few people escape into the interior of Poland . . . but the majority are concentrated in Zbaszyn. After a few days a strict order forbids any move out of the village. We sleep in barracks like horses, crowded in stalls and resting on straw, living on a little bread and butter. The Hildesheimer Family Beim take good care of me and whenever there is somewhere something to eat they share it with me. Hundreds are sleeping in our barracks and try to get some rest while voices are whispering and babies are crying. Thousands of polish Jews have only one thought this historic night: Justice to those who did injustice to mankind!! Not being able to sleep in this unbearable atmosphere I stroll around the camp, move over resting bodies, stumble over trunks. I get some fresh air and pass by the railway station, where a great number of Jews warm themselves and lie all around the halls. You hardly could find your way through . . . such a mass of unhappy people.[52]

Although Poland expressed its position that the refugees be allowed to return to Germany, Germany made it clear that if Poland did not rescind its revocation of citizenship decree, many more thousands of Polish Jews still residing in Germany would be deported as well. While a political solution to the plight of the refugees appeared to be hopeless, Polish Jewish relief organizations eventually arrived in Zbaszyn with food and supplies.

Four days passed before that help came. A November 4 *Jewish Chronicle* article noted, "as the American Joint Distribution Committee was busy organizing help for the Jews expelled through Chojnice, Beuthen, and one or two other places, Zbonszyn [*sic*] had to wait until Monday."[53] The correspondent reported on the horrible conditions he found there when he arrived, describing rodent-infested stalls and pigsties where women and children suffered, most crying from hunger. He also described the dismal sanitary conditions, relating how two hundred refugees had fallen ill and were being hospitalized in Poznań and elsewhere. As the journalist walked through the camps, he heard and witnessed tales of terror and agony from the countless crowds.

The tragedy I saw is almost beyond description. . . . Several people have gone mad. I myself saw one of them—a woman. Eyewitnesses told me that near the frontier she started screaming and weeping and would not move any farther. Two Gestapo agents dragged her for about two miles until Polish territory was reached. Aged Jews were kicked and beaten by Gestapo agents because they could not run as fast towards the frontier as ordered. . . . A father of three boys was arrested in Frankfort [sic] with his wife and only one boy. The other two were not at home when he received his expulsion orders, and he was weeping bitterly over their unknown fate. One young man was searching for his mother, whom he lost when crossing the frontier. He tried to search for her, but was not allowed to by the Gestapo, who beat him and forced him to move on. . . . I visited the temporary hospital in Zbonszyn [sic]. This was worse than any war hospital. The patients, men, women, and children lay on straw without any blankets. Their only covers were meager straw mattresses. Among the patients I saw an old woman of about ninety and a baby of eleven months.[54]

Once relief arrived and basic human needs began to be met, postcards and other forms of communication allowed the refugees to share their plight with family and friends back home in Germany.

By December, as many as four thousand letters and postcards to and from refugees were delivered daily by aid workers. And while messages brought much needed currency so that some refugees could pay for room and board at private locations in the town, other communiqués only seemed to heighten the fear and anxiety of the Jewish community at large. Joseph alludes to the tragic effects that the Grynszpan family's postcard had on their son, Herschel.[55]

Strange enough, but human, many Jews think that there is a chance of returning to Germany and many cables were received from there expressing the same hope. Rabbi Dr. Italiener sent me also an encouraging cable. Joy and happiness suddenly prevailes . . . optimism creates an atmosphere of hope . . . till the day of the killing of Rath by Grünspan, whose parents and sister are in the same camp.[56]

Any hope of freedom among the refugees from their confinement at Zbaszyn evaporated with the shooting on November 7, 1938, of the German Embassy official, Ernst vom Rath, by Herschel Grynszpan, the distraught son of Zbaszyn refugees.[57]

Nazi officials seized on the Grynszpan incident as justification for the mass destruction of Jewish property and synagogues throughout Germany known as Kristallnacht. A previous incident in 1936, the assassination of Wilhelm Gustoff, head of the Swiss Nazi Party, by David Frankfurter, a Jewish medical student from Yugoslavia, was linked by Nazi officials to the shooting of vom Rath and was promoted by the German press as examples of a worldwide Jewish conspiracy. Violence erupted spontaneously on November 8 as a result of these inflammatory editorials, but once vom Rath died, the Germans used this incident as a means to promote government-sanctioned statewide violence against the Jews on the evening of November 9.[58] The violence of the Kristallnacht pogroms left 267 synagogues destroyed, and an estimated 7,500 Jewish businesses burned or looted. By November 30, 1938, approximately 30,000 German Jews began to fill the new network of concentration camps. According to Nazi estimates, nearly 100 died that first night—along with the victims of the Polenaktion, they were some of the earliest casualties of the Holocaust.[59] Joseph, not knowing the fate of his mother or of his own hometown of Bamberg, records the despair in Zbaszyn over the news.

> The jiddish papers report the destruction of the synagogues in Germany and the rounding up of all Jews and we know that the return is impossible. . . . Not even into Poland we are allowed to travel . . . they have enough Jews there, the Poles do not like anymore! And Zbaszyn develops into a jewish center, a community of its own with all its organizations. A polish village turns overnight into a lively city of active Jews, who try to help each other and uplift each other in the hour of grief.[60]

While Jews throughout Germany and Austria quivered in the cellars of their businesses, fearing the destruction taking place above them, their one-time neighbors were stranded in the border town of Zbaszyn, each oblivious to the circumstance of the other and yet inevitably linked by the events they suffered.

THE COMMUNITY OF ZBASZYN

Zbaszyn lay some forty-four miles (70 km) due west of Poznań, the capital city of the westernmost province of the same name in Poland. Zbaszyn, a rather insignificant agricultural township, was the first railway stop heading east once you crossed the German-Polish border on the important line that connected Paris to Berlin to Warsaw to Moscow. The history of this border town is inseparably linked to the history of Prussian and German hegemony in the region. From 1795, when the imperial powers of Eastern Europe had finally partitioned the nation of Poland into political nonexistence, until 1918 Zbaszyn, then known by its German name Bentschen, had been ruled first by the kingdom of Prussia and, from 1871, by the Second German Reich.[61] For more than a century, Bentschen was home to a mixed German-Polish ethnicity. By provisions detailed in the Treaty of Versailles that ended World War I, the Poznań Province once again became the westernmost territory of the new Second Republic of Poland, and German Bentschen changed hands and again became a Polish town. Little did Zbaszyn's population of five thousand realize that their community would change hands yet again in a mere twenty years.

Various accounts number the total population of Zbaszyn in 1938 at around 5,400 people, with fewer than 400 Germans. More significant demographics at this time concern the Jewish population numbers. Between 1921, the year of the first census of the new Second Republic of Poland, and Germany's invasion of Poland in 1939, Jewish population numbers in the Poznań region had undergone a steady decline. In the ten-year period between the 1921 census and the 1931 census, the Jewish population in the entire Poznań district decreased by more than 80 percent. While many factors offer explanation for the steady exodus, one significant cause can be attributed to the liberal ideals of the German Weimar Republic, which attracted many Jews in the border regions to choose Germany over Poland during the interwar years.

We know very little about the small Jewish community of Zbaszyn, which numbered about 52 persons in 1938. Tax records of the Jewish district reveal that the entire district numbered 156 members, but only 9 of those actually paid taxes. District tax laws exempted the poor with insufficient incomes from contributing. The majority of those who did pay taxes were merchants, some who owned houses, and craftsmen.

In Zbaszyn, ten Jewish families depended on subsistence farming and suffered impoverished lives, as did most of their non-Jewish counterparts in similar small, provincial Polish towns. When the deported Polish Jews of Germany were foisted upon the township of Zbaszyn, most of them had come from more comfortable lifestyles than their fellow Jews along the border. The infrastructure of this little town simply could not handle the burden of its population nearly tripling overnight. And the refugees themselves, mostly affluent people left virtually penniless, had no immediate means with which to care for themselves and their families. Both the townsfolk and the refugees needed outside help to cope.[62]

REFUGEE SURVIVAL IN ZBASZYN

Survivors and rescuers all depict terrible scenes of deprivation and want during those days, weeks, and months of incarceration, despite the valiant efforts of both the small Jewish community of Zbaszyn and the township's Polish citizens. The memoir of Gerd Korman describes how relief trucks loaded with bread, butter, and eggs arrived and the way workers in the trucks hurriedly broke loaves in half, slapped hunks of butter on the fragments, and tossed them over the sides of the trucks into the crowd. He recalled how refugees frantically grabbed for the buttered loaves and caught tossed eggs before they fell to the ground.[63] Joseph's memoir attests to the relief work as well and also disclosed his observations on the mood of the community that developed in those early weeks.

> Polish Jews prove their Jewish heart and their traditional spirit of helping the brother in need by sending immediately food, medicine, and clothes to the refugees. Community leaders from nearby Posen encourage us and give us hope. "Gulaschkanonen" [soup wagons] roll after days into the camp and hungry Jews line up to get their ration. A post office is quickly organized and one of the most important activities of the day becomes the patient waiting for the mail. Cables and money orders are coming in and after days I am also lucky to get a few Zlotys, after I find out the "Eisner" must be "Cysner." Money makes everything easier and even in sorrow it helps to forget. The atmosphere in the barracks grows more and more tense and unbearable so that Beims and I decide to look for a room. We succeed to get one room from a polish railway worker, who enriched himself pretty much during that time. At last, you can take off your clothes after one week, at last you have four walls around you again and you can eat homelike food. We are 12 people in one room, the women and girls sleep in the 2 beds, while we men and some boys have straw and blankets as our beds.[64]

The refugees continued to try any means available to them to contact family and friends in Poland and Germany in order to secure more help.

Aid from Poznań and Warsaw was slow in coming, owing in part to the fact that neither the Polish press nor the Jewish press could publish details about the expulsion due to the efforts of the Polish authorities to minimize the deportations' overall importance in the greater scheme of relations with Germany. As previously mentioned, they had also hoped to force the international community through the directed efforts of the Evian Conference to respond to Poland's Jewish problem.[65] What news did manage to get out prompted the formation of the Central Jewish Aid Committee (Tsentraler Yidisher Hilf-Komitet), led by Rabbi Moshe Schorr, professor and senator in Warsaw. The Bund Party and Jewish trade unions provided assistance through a specially established "Actions Committee," which brought in representatives from Polish workers' organizations. The most immediate needs that the committee addressed concerned special aid for the seven hundred children in the camp, along with food, material, and legal assistance as needed. Emanuel Ringelblum, who worked for the JDC in Warsaw, was one of the first to arrive on the scene with much-needed aid.[66] The greatest service Ringelblum rendered was his foresight in orga-nizing the hordes of refugees into groups of medical professionals, legal advisors, craftsmen, teachers, and others so that the refugees could be self-sufficient, doing as much as possible for themselves, while relieving the local citizens and the many relief organizations to do other things.[67] Ringel-blum related how they set up the Zbaszyn Township with "departments for supplies, hospitalization, carpentry workshops, tailors, shoemakers, books, a legal section, a migration department, and an independent post office . . . a welfare office, a court of arbitration, an organizing committee, open and secret control services, a cleaning service, and a complex sanitation service."[68] Ringelblum further described the formation of cultural activities, including classes in Yiddish and Polish, as well as establishing educational facilities such as a reading room, a library, and a Talmud Torah religious school. Joseph also relates how important these activities became for the refugees.

> Life in that isolated place became more contented when the cultural ac-
> tivities were emphasized. The moral was in danger as people had nothing
> to do and children were lingering around in the community houses.
> Under the leadership of experienced social workers from Poland and from
> Germany committees were formed to activate the camp. One of the first
> activities and the most impressive ones were the services held in the Syna-
> gogue and in the Schützenhaus [clubhouse] as well as in the Mühle [mill].
> Wherever there are polish Jews there are Chasonim—and there were a
> number of good ones right in the camp.[69] We alternated in different

places and it was quite an experience to pray in the midst of the Zores [trouble] in the halls of the refugees. I recall the Chanukah days when I officiated in the Hospital where my eyes saw the whole cruelty of the Nazis, dragging away sick and lame people!!!! The tears of the poor people touched me immensely and I prayed for light, for help of this poor and helpless Jews.[70]

The refugees themselves manned the newly created infrastructure of social organizations, which numbered about twenty.

The internees also enjoyed concerts and the formation of a choir, assisted by Joseph, who taught singing classes in camp and helped care for the children.

Our noble duty was to take care of the children and to give them an education to prevent demoralization. Courses of all subjects were introduced and I was very successful with my music classes. The kids liked to sing and forgot all their worries and at the same time learned music and its moral and ethical value. Those children whose parents could not take care of them were sheltered in a big stadium under the supervision of young and experienced teachers employed by the miracle-doing Joint [JDC]. They had good food and all the privileges they needed and plays and other programs proved the good job that was done in such a short period. One of the most impressive features was also an ONEG SHABBAT on the 6th floor of the Mühle [mill], where hundreds were housed.[71] While a dim light was burning girls and boys gathered around, sitting on the floor and singing spirited and inspiring jewish songs. A discussion about current problems gave that evening a high level. All different organizations united in that affair and one could feel the spark of Chaverut, of brotherhood![72]

But all the social and medical dangers of overcrowded, overtaxed living conditions still caused great hardships for Zbaszyn's townsfolk and refugees alike, as outbreaks of typhus claimed more and more lives and Poland's bitterly harsh winter weather rolled in.

The task of feeding, clothing, nursing, and housing eight thousand extra bodies over an extended period of time was not an easy venture. Most of the refugees spent the first week in Zbaszyn in deplorable conditions. Eventually two thousand refugees took up permanent shelter in the long-abandoned army barracks on the outskirts of town that had originally been converted horse stalls. One letter from Zbaszyn, printed in a local newspaper, reported 107 persons living in barracks #1 alone. More than five hundred refugees occupied the Old Flour Mill in town, which had five levels of bare concrete floors strewn with damp straw, on which people slept in their clothes, lined up like sardines.[73] Joseph mentions a stadium in his English memoir, where hundreds of children were placed who had been separated from parents, deported without parents, or whose parents or guardians could not care for them. Refugees, who either smuggled in money, jewels, or other negotiable items or had procured money via post from family and friends, rented single rooms in homes or entire apartments from the local non-Jewish townsfolk. Nearly every house in the town harbored one or more Jewish refugees.[74] About one-third of the total number of refugees in Zbaszyn relocated to private homes.[75] Joseph's memoir recounts his various housing situations during his first few months at Zbaszyn, when he left the Old Mill to find other accommodations.

> I was very lucky to be with a family I knew well as they did everything possible to make life bearable. A Friday evening was just like home and there was no food lacking as we got our daily rations from the Mühle [mill] and we were able to buy food at exorbitant prices. After weeks I moved from that crowded place and rented a bed in a small room—but my friend and I moved soon again as the Polish "Trefniak" came shikker [drunk] from the village and it was pretty dangerous for us.[76] The room we rented with four others afterwards was very comfortable and clean, very beautifully located at a vast lake. At last I had my own bed and that was a luxury for Zbaszyn.[77]

Money donated to the refugees from local, national, and international relief organizations made only a small dent in the daily cost of supporting them, which Ringelblum estimated at about $2,000 to $2,500 per day.[78]

Meeting the most basic of human needs for the refugees, which involved supplying adequate food, water, and clothing, became a constant struggle. When winter set in, a reporter from the *Jewish Chronicle* related how Zbaszyn's refugees had to battle the freezing weather, making survival impossible for many.

> Among the Polish Jews deported by the Nazis and now encamped in Zbonszyn [*sic*], on the Polish frontier, the cold weather is causing unspeakable misery. An eleven-day-old child was frozen to death this week,

and twenty-seven other children are said to have lost limbs owing to frostbite. According to the *News Chronicle*, about 2,000 people are crowded in an old stable with only one stove to keep them warm. Five hundred are living in an old mill with no heating facilities whatever. As most of the deportees were driven from Germany without proper clothing, many are unable to leave their tents and stables to fetch food from the field kitchen. A number of them have been frozen while waiting in the long queues for food.[79]

After five weeks of relief work performed almost exclusively by local Jewish organizations, Emanuel Ringelblum and his companions left Zbaszyn, commenting that there had "never been so ferocious, so pitiless a deportation of any Jewish Community as this German deportation."[80] As conditions for refugees worldwide worsened, funds and assistance for the refugees in Zbaszyn waned. In May 1939, the *Jewish Chronicle* reported that the deportees instituted one fasting day per week "in order to be able to live a day longer on the verge of starvation."[81]

By the middle of May 1939, about 3,500 refugee Jews still lay encamped at Zbaszyn, most living in the poorest conditions. Relief funds dried up when the Polish government stopped all nationwide fund-raising operations for any purpose except for the Anti-Aircraft Defense Fund. Germany threatened more expulsions. On May 8, 1939, the Nazi security chief Reinhard Heydrich ordered all Polish Jews still residing in the Reich to leave the country by July 31, 1939, or be interned in concentration camps and later forcibly expelled to Poland.[82] The futile negotiations between Germany and Poland finally ceased in June 1939, putting an end to the initial agreement between the two nations, leaving 3,000 to 4,000 women and children, families of deported husbands and fathers, stranded in Germany waiting for exit visas.[83] When the Nazis arrested another 3,000 Polish Jews and secretly pushed them across the border near Zbaszyn in early July 1939, Polish military guards forced the groups to return.[84]

In the summer of 1939, many stateless Jews remaining in Reich territories tried to bribe border guards to let them into Poland, while any refugees still left in Zbaszyn who could confirm that they had either secured a job in Poland or a visa to emigrate left the camp and moved into the interior. The unfortunates who remained at Zbaszyn, those whose numbers were slowly augmented by more refugees crossing the border, fought worsening conditions of poverty in order to survive.[85] By the middle of that summer,

16,000 Polish Jews who had been summarily banished from Germany now resided in Poland, 12,000 of whom were in need of assistance. The Polish government disbanded the refugee camp of Zbaszyn just days before Germany invaded Poland: "The last group left immediately before the German invasion of Poland; the train on which they were going to Warsaw was bombed at dawn on 1 September 1939."[86] The final chapter of Zbaszyn marked the beginning of World War II and the subsequent acceleration of Nazi-led terror against the Jews of Europe.[87]

Joseph stands as one among a relatively select group of recorded testimonies to the events of the Zbaszyn deportation and internment. Another who shared the experiences of the camp, as well as escape to the Philippines, was Norbert Propper. His parents, also Ostjuden as were Joseph's parents, and who came to Germany after World War I, lived an assimilated lifestyle in Hannover, Germany, where Norbert was born on January 21, 1920. Unlike the Cysners, however, the entire Propper family were deported to Zbaszyn in the Polenaktion. Norbert, who had trained in a gardening apprenticeship since the age of fourteen, received word from a German Jewish mentor that an opportunity existed for immigration to the Philippines. Unbeknownst to each other, Joseph and Norbert both received permission to immigrate to that distant island nation. When asked by his interviewer about his time in Zbaszyn and his association with Joseph, Norbert related, "I was aware of Cysner before I got to Zbaszyn. Cysner . . . was a chazzan in Hildesheim, which is a suburb of Hannover. I had met him before we went to Poland. . . . Suddenly he appeared and told me he had heard about my visa and told me that he was going to be the chazzan there. Anyways, when I got to Manila, he was there, just like a guarding angel to welcome me."[88]

While most refugees faced detention at Zbaszyn for up to a year, Joseph and Norbert found an escape from their confinements and the impending Holocaust after only six months. Joseph records his reprieve:

> Half a year passed quickly and every week had another attraction, another experience that formed our personality. Naturally everybody was working to be released soon and emphasizing his immigration. Numerous Chaverim went illegally to Palestine, led by Shelichim, who came from Palestine to liberate them.[89] The news that I was called to Manila as cantor gave me more confidence and hope. The formalities for getting the visa gave me a chance to see Warsaw for a few days and—imagine—all by myself without

a guard as originally planned . . . but I had to make a number of pictures . . . just in case I run away. The few days I spent there gave me a good impression of the jewish status in POLAND and I never forget the uplifting service in the Klomatzki synagogue and the jewish life in the Ghetto. The Jewish patriarchs that roamed the street . . . the sweating Jew carrying heavy loads . . . the carefree children playing on the streets or in the dark Ghettoyards . . . and the frightened look of many a Jew. . . . I cannot forget you.[90]

Joseph left his refugee camp imprisonment at Zbaszyn and found a new world of freedom in the Philippines. He and Norbert were but two of a small number of Zbaszyn deportees who were able to obtain papers for non-European immigration. Those who found refuge in other countries of Europe faced futures of escalating persecution, incarceration, and, ultimately, extermination.

As a cantor in Hamburg, Joseph had been beloved of his congregants, especially by the children. He was the Jewish Pied Piper with a violin. Children and adults alike seemed to gravitate to him. He taught Hebrew and prepared the young boys for their bar mitzvahs. He organized music classes and choirs, and seemed to have a natural, gentle way with all people. While confined at Zbaszyn, he transliterated folk songs that were sung at the camp, so the music of the people could be preserved.[91] He especially sought after and nurtured the children who were alone, separated from their families, or whose parents were too distressed to care for them. He brought them into classes and taught them music and how to sing, so that in their singing they could express hope for a better future. He tried to bring a calming, healing influence into scenes of chaos and pain; what he did in Zbaszyn, so would he do again in Manila.

> In the middle of April [1939] I had all my papers fixed and was permitted to stay four weeks in Germany to arrange my transportation. The committee for the refugees as well as all the teachers gave me a fine farewell party, handing me a precious certificate for the services I rendered. Teachers and children accompanied me to the railway station, and I felt honored and proud to have worked successfully and to have given to my students and to the Jews in distress ideas that strengthen, prayers that uplift, songs that enlighten. The train rolls out of the station and Hundreds wave their hands with Shalom and Beracha [Peace and Blessing] on their lips . . . and we

passed that thornful and tearful road that we walked months ago . . . and with prayers of gratefulness and gratitude for my salvation and those of my brothers and sisters I head for a new world.[92]

Joseph had received a telegram while in Zbaszyn from his friend Rabbi Joseph Schwarz, who had immigrated to Manila in September 1938. Schwarz had convinced the leaders of the Jewish Community in Manila that the growing population of diverse refugee Jews needed a cantor to help unify it. When he sent the telegram to Cysner, he did not know that Joseph was no longer in Hamburg. But the telegram, through the ever-efficient German bureaucracy, eventually found him in Zbaszyn. Joseph accepted the job offer and left Zbaszyn in April 1939, arriving in Manila in May 1939. Joseph was met by other refugee Jews who had escaped from Europe through the efforts of a rescue plan engineered by the Commonwealth officials and implemented by wealthy American merchant Jews in Manila. Between 1937 and 1941, approximately 1,300 refugees from Europe would find a safe haven from Nazi tyranny in the Asian Pacific archipelago of the Philippines.

As I investigated the life story of Joseph Cysner and traced his steps through Europe to his eventual immigration to the Philippines, I discovered that historians at the Hamburg Temple, where Joseph held a lifetime appointment as cantor, knew nothing of his arrest and deportation to Zbaszyn. They had merely listed his fate as unknown. And even though the fate of the vast majority of the victims of the Polenaktion and the Zbaszyn internment still is and always will be unknown, the recovered memoir of Joseph Cysner, his sufferings, his service, and his rescue, stands as a witness for them all.

JOSEPH'S ODYSSEY TO THE PHILIPPINES

The necessary documentary evidence for re-creating Joseph's travels once he left Zbaszyn until he finally arrived in Manila was missing as Joseph related few details, leaving a blank spot in the research. He states in his memoir that "in the middle of April I had all my papers fixed and was permitted to stay four weeks in Germany to arrange my transportation."[93] We can only assume that during this time he also visited his mother in Bamberg, assuring her that he would send for her to join him in the Philippines as soon as possible.[94] The next piece of his documentary record shows that he arrived in Manila via the SS *Scharnhorst* on May 15, 1939.[95] He gives no details of his experiences while in Germany securing his passage on the

German luxury liner or from which port he sailed. That information can be deduced from other sources.

The SS *Scharnhorst* was one of three new German passenger luxury liners built by the Norddeutscher Lloyd shipping company in 1934. She was the second passenger liner named after the Prussian military theorist General Gerhardt von Scharnhorst, the first having been launched in 1904 and later seized by the French in 1919 after serving in the Imperial German Navy as a troop transport on the Baltic Sea during World War I. After ten years as a transatlantic French passenger liner, the first SS *Scharnhorst* was dismantled in Genoa in 1934, the same year the second SS *Scharnhorst* was launched along with her sister ships the SS *Gneisenau* and the SS *Potsdam*. Nazi-built German battleships clearly breached the restrictions of the Treaty of Versailles; however, the new Kriegsmarine was testing new engines and mechanics on "test-bed" passenger ships. The *Scharnhorst* was shaking down new high-pressure, high-temperature boilers with electrically driven propellers from AEG turbines. The luxury passenger liner had a relatively short and but active existence because it was trapped in Japan at the beginning of the war in 1939 and sold to the Imperial Japanese Navy.[96]

The *Scharnhorst* made its maiden voyage on May 3, 1935, as the first of the three German express steamers that sailed between Europe and the Far East via a route that took them through the Suez Canal. Lauded as the fastest passenger liners of their time, at an impressive twenty-one knots, a voyage on the SS *Scharnhorst* from Genoa, Italy, to Manila in the Far East took about three weeks—five to six days shorter than its competitors. The *Scharnhorst*'s home port was Bremen, and her voyages to the Far East took her to Hamburg, Rotterdam, Southampton, Palma, Genoa, Port Said, Colombo, Penang, Singapore, Manila, Hong Kong, Shanghai, Yokohama, with her terminus at Kobe, Japan. Other ports were added on the return voyage, such as Belawan, Marseilles, and Barcelona.[97] For Joseph to have arrived in Manila on May 15, he would have had to have sailed out of Genoa in the last week of April. The recently discovered story of Peter Nash, whose parents and other family members had purchased "tickets for sailing on the Norddeutscher Lloyd's 'SS *Scharnhorst*' . . . boarding in Genoa, Italy" supports this deduction: "With my parents, my mother's parents and her brother, we finally left Berlin in April 1939."[98] The final destination for Peter Nash and his family was Shanghai; he recounts that it took them twenty-four days to sail from Genoa to Shanghai, having left Genoa on April 26, 1939, and arriving in Shanghai on May 19, 1939. His passport stamps show they disembarked on May 17 at Hong Kong before continuing onto Shanghai. Joseph would have disembarked earlier, as the ship's route included a stop at Manila before going on to Hong Kong and Shanghai.

These express passenger liners, which sailed between Europe and the Far East, were luxury liners; Nash tells of the first-class amenities they enjoyed aboard the SS *Scharnhorst*, including table tennis and a pool. No doubt Joseph was on this same voyage of the *Scharnhorst* as Peter Nash and his family. Sadly, the Bremen passenger lists at the city's Staats Archiv show lists for 1939 only for a departure on January 24 with voyages resuming from that port on July 10. Either passenger lists for voyages from February through June 1939 were lost or destroyed, or the *Scharnhorst* ran between Genoa and its eastern ports only during those months. The former is very likely because advertisements in the *Strait Times* from February 14, 1939, promoted the sale of passages aboard the *Scharnhorst* on its return voyage to her European ports in Genoa, Rotterdam, Hamburg, and Bremen, leaving Singapore on March 14, 1939. Therefore, it can safely be assumed that Joseph either sailed out of Bremen in mid-April, shortly after he arrived back in Germany from Zbaszyn, passing through Genoa on April 26 and arriving in Manila on May 15, 1939, as indicated by the list of passengers disembarking in Manila according to the *Manila Bulletin*, or he boarded the *Scharnhorst* at one of its other ports of call either at Hamburg, Rotterdam, or Genoa before passing through the Suez Canal. In either scenario, he would have been in the company of dozens of other refugees fleeing the Third Reich to ports of anticipated rescue in Shanghai, Singapore, Yokohama, and his own destination, Manila.[99]

The Jewish community in Manila finally had its first official cantor in the person of a refugee from the Nazi nightmare, Joseph Cysner. Frank Ephraim recounts the first Shabbat services in Temple Emil conducted by Cantor Cysner just a few days after he arrived.

> On the following Friday evening he made his first appearance on the bimah, the raised platform at the front of the synagogue. Seemingly shy at the beginning, he walked slowly to the center of the pulpit, faced the Torah scrolls in the cabinet, and slowly, in a rich baritone, intoned the hymn "Ma Tovu" that traditionally began the Friday evening Sabbath services. The audience was completely quiet, but as he continued one could sense the rising emotion because the hymn begins with the words, "How goodly are your tents, O Jacob; your dwelling places, O Israel." To many it reminded them of their modern Exodus and the indomitable spirit of

the Jewish people as they once more drove their tent pegs into the soil of another new "dwelling place." Cysner continued to chant the service with the melodies of middle-European Jewry—sung in the great synagogues of Berlin and Vienna that were now no more. But whose legacy would carry on, even in the most remote places on earth.[100]

A real chazzan had finally arrived to serve the growing Jewish community of Manila, in which he would conduct religious services, organize Hebrew school for the children, prepare boys for their bar mitzvahs, and in general promote a revival of Jewish religious culture among a diverse congregation of Jews from all over the world, who were now making a new life for themselves in eastern Asia.

FDR, Evian, and the Refugee Crisis

The symphony of circumstances that delivered Joseph from Zbaszyn and set him on his voyage of rescue to the Philippines makes up the bulk of this story. But in order to fully comprehend its significance as it relates to the many genres of Holocaust studies, it must be understood within the scholarship that discusses and analyzes America's role in the Holocaust. Over the decades, literally dozens of Holocaust historians have debated America's reactions to the persecutions levied against the Jews of Europe, and more particularly the actions or inactions of President Franklin Roosevelt in saving them. They have weighed him and other politicians, religionists, journalists, and even Jewish relief agencies in the balance and have found them all wanting to some degree or another. Not one of these scholars has examined the facts surrounding the Philippine rescue of refugee Jews or asked how the efforts of this Philippine-led rescue in an American-governed Commonwealth nation in Asia should be situated in the bigger context of America's response to the Holocaust. This story does just that. Understanding the voluminous literature on FDR, with both its indictments and adulations for his actions during World War II as concerning the Jews, provides necessary context for weighing the efforts of those who successfully orchestrated Jewish rescue in the Philippines.

FDR AND THE JEWS—A SCHOLARLY REVIEW

David Wyman admits in his 1984 best seller, *Abandonment of the Jews*, that his arguments concerning America's response to the worldwide refugee problem have been around for a while.[1] His first book, *Paper Walls*, published in 1968 on the heels of another work by Arthur Morse, *While 6 Million Died*, expounds on the failure of FDR's administration to act decisively in response to the persecution of Jews and went so far as to accuse the State Department of antisemitic practices purposefully aimed at preventing Jewish immigration into the United States.[2] Morse was the first to publicly denounce FDR for duplicity in his responses to the plight of Europe's Jews and accused Roosevelt of obstructionism when it came to opportunities for rescuing them.[3] These early publications open wide the door of scholarly research that offers both consensus and rebuttal to their accusations, this monograph included.

Henry Feingold, who wrote *The Politics of Rescue* in 1970, contextualizes the arguments of his literary predecessors, Wyman and Morse, within the political and social climate of the United States between 1938 and 1945. Feingold maintains that it was poor historical practice to morally judge the poor response of the FDR administration until one had sufficiently examined all aspects of the era to determine what, if anything, could have been done differently.[4] Several other works by other Holocaust historians followed. In 1973, Saul Friedman published *No Haven for the Oppressed*, in which he uses new evidence to show that opportunities existed wherein FDR and his administration, along with the Jewish leaders in America, could have done more to facilitate Jewish rescue.[5] Martin Gilbert's 1981 *Auschwitz and Allies* explores how the United States refused to take steps regarding the bombing of Auschwitz when it had plenty of chances to do so.[6] Monty Penkower published his work in 1983, *Jews Were Expendable*, in which he, too, uses newly recovered archival documents to show that several means were feasible to facilitate rescue of the Jews that the United States flatly refused to take.[7] With this already rich scholarly treatment of the failed opportunities to take action to save Jewish lives, David Wyman's 1984 best seller *Abandonment of the Jews* hit the scene at a full gallop.

Wyman maintains that the US State Department had no intention of ever saving Jewish refugees and did all it could to obstruct their immigration. He claims that FDR knew of the exterminations at an early date and made no attempt to address the situation until pressured by American

Jewish leaders to do so. Wyman felt that had the Jewish organizations in America challenged FDR sooner with a more united front, greater numbers of lives could have been saved. Wyman emphatically declares that FDR's failure to respond in a higher moral manner to the plight of Europe's Jews was the greatest failure of his presidency. Wyman's book was reviewed by renowned Holocaust scholars of the day, and it propelled Wyman into Hollywood-like stardom. Over the next decade Wyman gave more than four hundred lectures and made guest appearances on nationally syndicated talk shows. His work was revered by the public and championed by scholars, who praised him for dispelling the myth that the United States did not know about the Holocaust or was unable to rescue its victims. His work even affected national foreign policy when a copy was given to Vice President George H. W. Bush during the Ethiopian refugee crisis in 1985. Wyman's book influenced Bush's decision to facilitate the rescue of nine hundred Jewish Ethiopian refugees during his presidency in 1991.[8]

Wyman's attack on FDR brought a new upsurge of historical rebuttals. In November 1993, the Franklin D. Roosevelt Presidential Library at Hyde Park convened a conference of Roosevelt and Holocaust historians who presented papers discussing "Policies and Responses of the American Government toward the Holocaust."[9] The compiled articles of participants and nonparticipants were published in 1996 under the title *FDR and the Holocaust*. Hosts from the Franklin and Eleanor Roosevelt Institute organized the event to respond to the last twenty-five years of opinions professing that FDR and others "failed to rescue the Jews of Europe from the Holocaust and therefore bear some responsibility for the death of six million Jews."[10] The mission statement of the conference, which was closed to press and the public, asked if the controversy still roiled with issues that "defied scholarly resolution" or whether it could be rectified with further historical study.[11] While the debaters neither excused nor forgave all perceived issues of failure, many agreed that it was "unreasonable to expect leaders of one sovereign nation to intervene on behalf of the citizens of another nation . . . the Jews were not FDR's responsibility."[12] If historians of the past had been seeing the glass half empty, from this conference on, historians writing on FDR and the US response to the Holocaust began to see the glass half full. A pendulum was in the process of swinging back from one extreme of interpretation to another.

Henry Feingold, a noteworthy critic of Wyman's exposé and contributing presenter at the 1993 Hyde Park Conference, objected to Wyman's "historical morality tale" coming from his "outraged Christian con-science."[13] In his 1995 publication, *Bearing Witness: How America and Its Jews Responded to the Holocaust*, Feingold further criticizes Wyman for his overmoralizing of political intentions at a time of war. Feingold claimed that according to Wyman's moral standards, everybody was implicated, and all were guilty of gross negligence. He accuses Wyman of coloring the historical aspects with his own moralistic beliefs that did a disservice to true historical interpretation, calling it "retroactive investigative journal-ism."[14] In his introduction, Feingold comments on his closing statement in *Politics of Rescue* (1968), asking if it was fair to expect nation-states to be capable of moralistic human response during extreme times of economic depression and war.[15] But it is important to note that Feingold concurs that America's response to the Holocaust was weak, yet maintains that when looked at in the context of global economic conditions, the presence of a virulent antisemitism in the United States, and a disunited American Jewish community, what more could have realistically been expected in those circumstances? One would have had to change the circumstances in order to have altered the result, which is purely in the realm of speculation. After nearly three decades of an accelerating diatribe implicating various sectors of US society in the Holocaust by both Jewish and non-Jewish his-torians, along with journalists and filmmakers, the pendulum continued to swing back with new pedagogical thought throughout the 1990s.

To some, Wyman's accusations had gone too far, and the pendu-lum needed to be aimed in an entirely different direction. The historian and author William D. Rubinstein offers an impassioned rebuttal to Wyman's arguments in his 1997 publication, *The Myth of Rescue: Why the Democracies Could Not Have Saved More Jews from the Nazis*. Relying solely on selective secondary sources, Rubinstein challenges Wyman's in-terpretation of the documentary record while characterizing Wyman's conclusions as "historically inaccurate," asserting that the "Jews of Nazi-occupied Europe were prisoners, not refugees."[16] Objecting to Wyman's moralistic condemnation of the recalcitrant nations, Rubinstein emphati-cally opposed Wyman's position that the nations should have made the futile attempts at rescue, knowing that they would fail, not least for the moral victory the failed attempts would have offered. Rubinstein main-tains that "arguments used by historians to indict the Allied Govern-ments . . . are—invariably—specious, ahistorical and egregious."[17] Critics of Rubinstein's summations called his work "a polemic that will quickly fade," "a quest for sensationalism," and "counterfactual speculation."[18] These forceful rebuttals did not stave off forthcoming scholarship in support of FDR.

Robert Beir, a self-proclaimed "Rooseveltian" and Holocaust historian, maintains in his 2006 monograph, *Roosevelt and the Holocaust*, that FDR had done the best he could with the hand he was dealt, albeit ending his treatise on FDR with the lukewarm position that "great people are not great all the time."[19] A historian of American Judaism, Robert Rosen, experienced a similarly disturbing awakening to FDR's flaws when he researched his 2006 narrative, *Saving the Jews: Franklin D. Roosevelt and the Holocaust*. Rosen recounts the historiography that labeled FDR "a coward who was guilty of indifference and even complicity in the Final Solution."[20] However, Rosen claims that his research exposed documentary evidence, as yet uncited by prior historians, that acquitted FDR of any egregious indifference, inaction, or ineptitude. In fact, Rosen characterized Roosevelt as having saved Europe's surviving five million Jews instead of being passively complicit in the deaths of the six million, emphasizing his humanitarianism.[21]

Fifty years of historical exegeses have characterized Roosevelt from one extreme to the other—from being an apathetic bystander by Arthur D. Morse in 1968 to being a passive accomplice characterized by David Wyman in 1984, then to being seen as the singular world leader who stood in opposition to Hitler from the beginning and mobilized the world's forces to save the Jews of Europe as expressed at the 1993 Hyde Park Conference. Yet another historical treatment in *FDR and the Jews* sidesteps these arguments and pronounces them all valid. The senior Holocaust scholar Richard Breitman and the political historian Allan Jay Lichtman assert in their 2013 treatise that four distinct FDRs existed in terms of his dealings with the persecuted Jews of Europe. Breitman and Lichtman show an FDR whose position and actions changed with the political dynamics of the nation and the world, swinging from being a bystander in his first term as president to being a rescuer in his last term, with variations in between. In this manner, they adroitly avoid taking one side or the other in the decades-long debate, which they classify as "unforgiving, passionate" and "politically charged."[22] So then, how does this current research into the rescue of European Jewish refugees in Manila figure into this historiography? How do the Philippine rescue plans of selection, sponsorship, and mass resettlement defend or dispute critics of FDR and the American response to the Holocaust? While there are several historical discussions on these issues in this book, a quick look at the timing of the Evian Conference and refugee rescue in the Philippines is warranted.

EVIAN, FDR, AND PAUL V. MCNUTT

Whether critic or champion of FDR, one cannot effectively support either position while challenging the exegesis of the discourse without carefully examining the Evian Conference. Whether an advocate or an adversary, a consensus of historians agree that the Evian Conference did little or nothing to remedy the Jewish refugee crisis. But the differences in the debates, where Evian is concerned, lie in FDR's motivations for assembling the conference in the first place. Morse uses extensive documentary evidence to expose the concept for the conference as a US State Department ruse to derail attempts to have immigration laws "liberalized" with a shallow show of concern, which FDR approved. Morse further asserts that the Evian Conference did, in fact, achieve its real purposes—first of pacifying FDR's moral critics, and second, diverting refugee Jews to other nations.[23] Rosen, on the other hand, projects an FDR who took great political and personal risks when advancing any dialogue favoring refugee rescue. Rosen recites FDR's efforts, in conjunction with the Evian Conference, in which he urged unfilled German and Austrian quota numbers for immigration into the United States be given to Jewish immigrants. But even Rosen suggests that FDR realized that a failed Evian Conference would further anti-Nazi sentiment by highlighting "German barbarity."[24] Historians' analyses of FDR's intentions—with his show of concern expressed by empowering a powerless body of diplomats at Evian—range from projecting a facade behind which he could hide, to leading an altruistic charge against the growing fascist terror. One alternative argument explaining FDR's motivation for initiating the Evian Conference has been overlooked: an act of vanity in which he did not want to be outshown by Paul V. McNutt, a longtime political rival. In February and March 1938, McNutt had meetings with FDR, preceding his return to the Philippines in late March 1938, when he immediately put a process for rescue to the Philippines into operation. FDR's earliest protestations that an international rescue plan was warranted came just days following his February 1938 meetings with McNutt.[25] If timing is everything, then FDR may have wanted to get ahead of McNutt on the world stage as a benevolent benefactor.

President Roosevelt appointed Paul Vories McNutt as High Commissioner to the Philippines on March 1, 1937, and he served in this capacity for two years—the most crucial years in organizing Jewish immigration to the Philippines. McNutt's earlier professional ambitions had been strictly academic, having graduated from Harvard Law School in 1916 on the brink of America's entry into World War I. He enlisted and served as an officer in the US Army stateside during the Great War. McNutt's biographer, Dean J. Kotlowski, characterizes these two episodes of his early adult life as "pivotal experiences" that not only shaped his deep patriotism for his country but also set him on the path of political activism on both a national and a world stage.[26] After McNutt's discharge from active duty in 1919, he became a full professor of law at Indiana University in 1920 and went on to become the youngest dean of the Indiana University Law School in 1925.[27]

McNutt's first steps on the path of his political career occurred during his years spent in the American Legion, an influential veteran's organization, which he joined after his discharge from the armed forces. He was elected commander of the Legion's Indiana Department in 1926 and in 1927 was voted in as the National Commander of the Legion. Kotlowski details, in an earlier publication, that McNutt honed and projected an egalitarian idealism of "Americanism" during his years with the Legion that publicly championed racial, ethnic, and religious tolerance while advocating equality for all men "in rights, privileges, and immunities."[28] He also maintains that it led McNutt to take "serious political risks."[29] One of those undoubtedly was his unabashed political partnership with Jewish colleagues such as Jacob Weiss, with whom he developed a favorable professional relationship when Weiss became president pro tem of the Indiana State Senate during McNutt's governorship. This relationship was pivotal in advancing Jewish refugee rescue in the Philippines.

McNutt was elected governor of Indiana in 1932 as the first Democratic governor after a long line of Republicans.[30] Another McNutt biographer, I. George Blake, describes him during this time as a defender of all and "particularly of their civil rights. . . . The result of McNutt's stand was that the Jews, Negros, and the Catholics looked upon him as their champion."[31] In the foreign policy arena, Governor McNutt publicly and passionately condemned the Nazi agenda of targeting Jewish citizens. On March 27, 1933, McNutt addressed an overflow audience of thousands in an auditorium in Chicago where he characterized Nazi injustice as "outrageous against morality and humanity." He went on to pronounce that "for the second time in my life I rise to protest against acts of the German Government. I join in this prayer with you for the freedom of the world."[32] As the principle speaker at the event, he joined the call for adopting a resolution asking that the United States "refrain from further relations with Germany."[33] McNutt's anti-Nazi activism at this time stood in sharp contrast to FDR's first-term ambivalence on the matter of Jewish persecution by the German government. No doubt FDR took note of McNutt's passion when one considers their past political encounters.

Paul McNutt was, in physical appearance, everything FDR was not. He was tall and lanky with an athletic frame, a handsome chiseled face, with mesmerizing dark eyes under black eyebrows and a thick shock of graying hair.[34] He had risen quickly within the echelons of the Indiana Democratic Party, so much so that he wielded considerable sway at the Democratic presidential convention of 1932 that would eventually nominate New York governor Franklin Roosevelt as its candidate, in spite of the efforts of the "Stop Roosevelt" faction to push the nomination toward McNutt. The first time the two men met was in June 1931 when FDR attended the governor's conference in Indiana. McNutt, then chairman of the Indiana State Democratic Party, declined to give FDR public support at that conference as Indiana's top Democratic pick for the White House. This reluctance carried over into the 1932 Democratic Convention, as FDR came into the convention shy of the required number of delegates required to secure his party's nomination. McNutt, representing Indiana's caucus, voted against FDR's nomination three times, which held up the New York governor's candidacy. Whatever political positioning he had hoped to gain against Roosevelt was lost when the California and Texas delegations cast their votes for FDR on the fourth ballot. Kotlowski asserts that Indiana's fourth vote in Roosevelt's favor was "too little, too late" in FDR's mind; thus McNutt became known in the candidate's inner circle as "the platinum blonde S.O.B. from Indiana."[35] McNutt's loss at the 1932 national convention became a win at the state convention as he easily secured the party nomination for Indiana's gubernatorial race.

As governor, McNutt built a political machine dedicated to his presidential ambitions. The documentary record suggests that McNutt's quest for the presidency led Roosevelt to send him to the Philippines, on the other side of the world, as a way of neutralizing an up-and-coming political opponent. This is readily deduced from a conversation on February 15, 1937, between FDR, James Farley, his campaign manager-cum-postmaster general, and Vice President John Garner, which Farley recounted in his 1948 memoirs. The discussion centered on McNutt, who had recently accepted the proffered post as High Commissioner to the Philippines:

During the dinner, the President, Vice President Garner, and I chatted between courses. One exchange involved Paul V. McNutt, former governor of Indiana, and his impending appointment as United States High Commissioner to the Philippines.

"I'm not so sure," the President mused, "because McNutt is inclined to be dictatorial in his attitude and he might not be the right fellow to send out there. Maybe he ought to go on the Maritime Commission."

"I don't know him very well," Garner put in, "but I know he is a candidate for the Presidency in 1940 and it might not be a bad idea to send him out there."

The President smiled thoughtfully.

"Do you think the Philippines will be far enough?" I asked.

"Yes, yes," he laughed.[36]

It is within this competitive adversarial relationship between FDR and McNutt that the inception of the Evian Conference must be contextualized.

McNutt visited Washington, DC, in February and March 1938, while still serving as High Commissioner to the Philippines. William Baehr, the archives specialist for the Franklin D. Roosevelt Presidential Library, explains that their database of presidential appointments shows "four visits by High Commissioner McNutt to the White House: February 24, 1938, from 11:30–12:00; February 26, 1938, from 1:10–1:40; February 28, 1938, from 2:00 (his next scheduled event was dinner at 6:15, but he went to dinner after a dip in the pool, so it is unknown how long this meeting was, probably at least two hours); March 15,1938, from 11:15–11:30."[37] The probable two-hour meeting on February 28 is particularly noteworthy. When we pair this information with a Washington Associated Press article in the *Hutchison (KS) News* dated February 23, 1938, and an undated Jewish newspaper article from South Haven, Michigan, in the Paul V. McNutt papers at Lilly Library of Indiana University, a likely picture of the following scenario might be drawn: McNutt received an inquiry from Jacob Weiss about the potential of Jewish refugee rescue in the Philippines sometime prior to McNutt leaving Manila for his February/March visit to Washington, DC. McNutt responded that he would soon be stateside, and they could discuss it then. Just days after McNutt's arrival, an elaborate reception for McNutt was hosted by his Indiana colleagues on the afternoon of February 23, 1938, at the Mayflower Hotel in Washington, DC. Weiss and McNutt spoke for about ten minutes in the reception line, at which time McNutt told Weiss that he had several meetings to attend over the next few days with the "President, the Secretary of State, and a dozen other important government officials."[38] Over the next five days, McNutt would meet with FDR in the Oval Office on three separate occasions. When Weiss and McNutt met up again, presumably after at least one or maybe all three of these February appointments with the president, McNutt informed Weiss that "it's all arranged. The visas will be okayed by me and won't have to clear through the State Department."[39] A few important conclusions can be drawn from this scenario: that FDR and McNutt discussed McNutt's intentions to bring refugee Jews to the Philippines; that McNutt learned that the State Department did not need to be involved; and that McNutt could authorize the visas himself. How does this interface with FDR and his announcement for an international meeting to remedy the refugee dilemma triggered by the Third Reich?

McNutt returned to Manila on board the *Hawaii Clipper*, one of three Pan Am airboats making transpacific flights between San Francisco and Manila in 1938. The sixty-hour flight took six days with overnight stopovers at Pearl Harbor, Midway Atoll, Wake Island, and Guam. Various newspapers report that McNutt returned to Manila on March 24, 1938, so we can conclude that he had to have boarded the *Hawaii Clipper* out of San Francisco no later than March 18, and therefore left Washington, DC, for the West Coast sometime between March 15 and March 17, 1938, as we know he had a brief meeting with FDR on March 15. FDR made his earliest announcement alluding to the formation of an international committee "to facilitate and finance emigration of 'political refugees' from Germany and Austria" on March 22, 1938, as McNutt was on his way back to Manila with an agenda of pursuing refugee rescue in the Philippines.[40] Given the fact that FDR never once mentioned McNutt's objective to organize the rescue of Jews in the Philippines, which was already formulated and implemented before the Evian Conference convened in July 1938, one has to ask the questions: What influence did McNutt's intentions of furthering Jewish rescue in the Philippines have on FDR's plans for the Evian Conference? Did FDR deliberately remain silent on McNutt's rescue plans in the Philippines so as not to draw attention to his political rival?

McNutt resigned his office in the Philippines in 1939 and returned to Washington to head up FDR's new Federal Security Agency. When Franklin Roosevelt decided to forego the presidential custom of retiring from the presidency after two terms, McNutt had to stand aside at the peak of his political career while FDR won third and fourth terms as president. After his service as High Commissioner, McNutt filled other governmental posts in the Roosevelt administration and later returned to the Philippines as the first American Ambassador to the new republic in 1946.[41]

US IMMIGRATION LAWS

FDR's invitation to select countries requesting their participation in an international conference on the refugee crisis went out March 25, 1938. It read:

> The government has become so impressed with the urgency of the problem of political refugees that it has inquired of a number of governments in Europe and in this hemisphere whether they would be willing to cooperate in setting up a special committee for the purpose of facilitating the emigration from Austria, and presumably from Germany, of political refugees. Our idea is that whereas such representatives would be designated by the governments concerned, any financing of the emergency emigration referred to would be undertaken by private organizations with the respective countries. Furthermore, it should be understood that no country would be expected or asked to receive a greater number of immigrants than is permitted by its existing legislation. . . . It has been prompted to make its proposal because of the urgency of the problem with which the world is faced and the necessity of speedy cooperative effort under governmental supervision if widespread human suffering is to be averted.[42]

If the other countries of the world were not expected to take in any more refugees beyond their existing immigration policies, then surely that would apply to the United States as well. The Evian Conference was rendered impotent from its inception. In order to understand the significance of refugee rescue in the Philippines against the backdrop of the failed Evian Conference, it is important to be familiar with US Immigration Laws and their application to the US Commonwealth Nation of the Philippines.

The Americas had been the favored destination of colonists from around the world since its initial discovery and exploration in the sixteenth and seventeenth centuries. Settlers on the Eastern Seaboard on the Atlantic coast, which would become the United States of America, came mostly from northern and western Europe—a distinct majority from Great Britain—for the next two hundred years.[43] In 1873, nearly half a million immigrants, chiefly from Britain, Germany, and various places in northwestern Europe, flooded America's shores.[44]

A distinct change in the ethnic origins of immigrants to the United States began in 1880 and increased every year. More and more came from southern and eastern Europe, until 47 percent of the immigrants in 1892 could be identified from such countries as Italy, Russia, Poland, and Austria-Hungary, with a considerable number of the immigrants being "of the Hebrew race."[45] Not until 1896 did the numbers of immigrants from southern, central, and eastern Europe surpass the number of immigrants from the northwest. From 1880 until the implementation of the first US quota laws in 1921, immigrants from southern and eastern Europe exceeded half the total numbers of immigrants to the United States, which amounted to nearly twenty-five million.[46]

This increase in immigrants coming from various racial and ethnic parts of Europe raised objections across the country. In conjunction with the rise in Chinese immigration in California, this spurred the enactment of the first of many official immigration restrictions—the Chinese Exclusion Act of 1882, which prohibited entry to "any person unable to take care of him or herself without becoming a public charge."[47] The law also excluded other undesirables, including convicted criminals, the poor, and the mentally ill. Later laws in 1888 added contract laborers, beggars, importers of prostitutes, while racially targeting Chinese and Japanese. Nativists in the United States believed these "new" immigrants from the so-called racially objectionable nations were unsuitable for assimilation into American communities. The US census data between 1880 and 1920 reveals that eastern European Jews were one of the largest ethnic groups of this period.[48] The 1917 Immigration Act expanded definitions of "undesirables" that included "homosexuals," "idiots," "feeble-minded persons," "criminals," "epileptics," "insane persons," "alcoholics," "professional beggars," all persons "mentally or physically defective," "polygamists," "anarchists" and anyone over the age of sixteen who was illiterate. Following two centuries of unlimited immigration, the US State Department developed restrictionist policies spawned by economic decline, postwar isolationism, and nationalistic racism. In spite of these restrictions, an estimated twenty-five million immigrants disembarked at American ports between 1900 and 1920, making it the largest migratory flow of people in world history.[49]

On May 19, 1921, an alarmed Congress passed the Emergency Quota Act, followed by the Immigration Act of 1924. For the first time, the Emergency Quota Act put numerical limits on immigration from Europe that restricted the number of immigrants admitted from any one country annually to 3 percent of the number of residents from that country living in the United States as of the 1910 census.[50] By using the population totals of 1910, allowable immigration quotas favored northern and western European countries, since more immigrants from these locations arrived at the time of the 1910 census rather than the 1920 census.[51] Based on that formula, the number of new immigrants admitted fell drastically from 805,228 in 1920 to 309,556 in 1921–22. Followed by the 1924 Immigration Act, also known as the Johnson-Reed Act, the permanent immigration law of 1924 restricted even more the numbers from "the racial inferiority of Southeastern Europeans," as a contemporary writing in *Foreign Affairs* stated.[52] This new immigration strategy, in conjunction with the comprehensive immigration laws of 1917, governed American immigration policy until "the passage of the Immigration and Nationality Act (INA) of 1952 organized all existing immigration laws into one consolidated source."[53]

The Immigration Act of 1924, which superseded the 1921 Emergency Quota Act, had essentially formulated two quota systems. Until July 1, 1929, the Johnson-Reed Act limited the annual number of immigrants who could be admitted from any one country to 2 percent of the number of foreign-born residents of that country who were already living in the United States according to the 1890 census, not the 1910 census. This revised formula reduced total immigration from 357,803 in 1923–24 to 164,667 in 1924–25. By using the census of 1890 instead of the 1910 census, this formula favored western and northern European countries even more, whereas the largest population of "ethnically undesirable" immigrants who had inflated population numbers in the two decades between 1890 and 1910 were not factored in; the 1890 census got around those numbers.[54]

This act also established a new "Consular Control System" that mandated all visa requirements for applicants be reviewed at US Consular offices abroad before an immigrant left her or his home country. This provision provided a "culling" of undesirables by consular officials before the immigrants ever stepped foot onto American soil. This tactic was aimed at further restricting immigration from southern and eastern Europe, especially Jews, Italians, and Slavs, who had dominated immigration totals since the 1880s. Quotas for immigrants from Poland, Italy, Czechoslovakia, Russia, Romania, and Hungary totaled less than 10 percent of the overall total annual immigrant quota.[55] Added on July 1, 1929 to the 1924 Immigration Act, the National Origins Formula imposed a plan that no longer used a percentage system. Total immigration was then limited to a flat total of 150,000 per year, with the proportion of that number admitted from any country based on that country's "national origins" representation in the

US population according to the 1920 census. Using "national origins" instead of "foreign-born" allowed a redistribution of quota numbers that utilized population numbers of US-born ethnic citizens along with foreign-born residents, increasing quotas for "Old" style immigrants over "New" immigrants.[56] Whereas quotas for Britain and Northern Ireland between 1924 and 1929 allowed 34,000 immigrants annually, Germany's quota allowed more than 50,000. With this new redistribution calculus, Great Britain's quota increased to about 85,000 while Germany's numbers decreased to about 20,000.[57] Although originally slated for implementation in 1927, the difficult task of determining the national ethnic numbers required the postponement of the initiation of the national quota formula until 1929, which increased Germany's annual quota to 25,557.[58]

No alien could obtain entrance to the United States without an immigration visa issued by a US consular officer abroad. By joining the provisions of the Act of 1924 to the comprehensive immigration laws of 1917, US consuls in offices throughout Europe determined the eligibility of visa applicants according to an exhaustive list of exclusionary standards. This allowed consular officials to deny visas to applicants based on selective interpretation of the laws, especially to the one line of the 1917 law that excluded "persons likely to become a public charge."[59] Strict adherence to these new laws for the next decade resulted in the actual number of issued visas being far below the already reduced quota limits. Had these quotas been filled between 1929 and the advent of World War II on September 1, 1939, more than 275,000 German immigrants could have entered the United States during that decade, about half the entire population of Jews living in Germany at the time. These constraints, similar to those imposed by many countries, were not lifted as a result of the Evian Conference and that translated into disaster for the millions of Jews in Europe who faced worsening Nazi anti-Semitic practices, which demanded their "deportation"—a euphemism that soon translated into extermination.

US/PHILIPPINE RELATIONS AND IMMIGRATION POLICIES

The US Immigration Acts of 1917 and 1924 became the dual directives of immigration policies for the first half of the twentieth century.[60] However, only the Immigration Act of 1917, which outlined qualitative restrictions on potential immigrants, was applied to the Philippines during its time as a territory and then as a commonwealth nation of the United States. The opening section of the 1917 Act reads: "That this Act shall be enforced in the Philippine Islands by officers of the general government thereof, unless and until it is superseded by an act passed by the Philippines Legislature and approved by the President of the United States to regulate immigration in the Philippine Islands as authorized in the Act."[61] No such directive appears in the text of the US Immigration Act of 1924 that regulated immigration quantitatively into the United States. This is extremely important when discussing the rescue of refugee Jews in Manila, as the qualitative nature of the refugees came under scrutiny by virtue of the 1917 Act alone. However, no number restrictions on immigration into the Philippines existed in US Immigration Laws, as was prescribed for entrance into the United States by the acts of 1921 and 1924. Such numeric restrictions to the Philippines did not become law until the Commonwealth passed their own immigration regulations in 1940.

Most of the European refugees fleeing the Nazis and World War II were barred from coming to the United States due to these deliberately contrived systems that favored the "old" acceptable immigrant identity over the "new" undesirables. However, during the years of Jewish refugee rescue in the Philippines from 1937 to 1940, restrictive quotas did not apply, nor was there US State Department or consular oversight in approving the issuance of visas to refugee aliens immigrating to the Philippines. The Immigration Act of 1917 did impose numerous grounds excluding individuals as acceptable immigrants to the United States, and by extension, to the Philippines. While the US State Department supposedly could not restrict the numbers of Jewish immigrants going to the Philippines, it could, and did, demand a process that ensured that there was adequate financial support for the refugees.

As immigration policies of the 1930s remained hostile to Jewish refugees, a growing antisemitism infected all levels of American society, including such government institutions as the military, Congress, and the State Department.[62] In the face of Germany's openly antisemitic Nuremberg Laws of 1935 and America's social barriers to implementing rescue, the United States resisted accepting more immigrants than the quotas allowed, even after Hitler classified 500,000 German and Austrian Jews as stateless enemies in 1935. The conference at Evian, France, from July 6 to July 15, 1938, contrived for the purpose of facilitating opportunities for refugee rescue, was not expected to violate the quota systems. The Depression had strained economies, and the nations of the world declined to increase their immigration quotas.[63] When eastern European countries implied that they would like to deport their Jewish citizens as well, the manageable refugee numbers from Germany and Austria suddenly became augmented by more than three million potential refugees from Poland alone. This ended the possibility of any serious resolutions at the Evian Conference in favor of Germany's and Austria's refugee Jews. America's restrictive immigration polices remained unchanged, although Roosevelt urged the State Department in 1938 to allow immigration numbers to reach their fullest as granted by US Immigration Laws.[64] It is against this background that the collaborative effort of the Jewish community in Manila, empowered by McNutt and Quezon in rescuing Joseph and the 1,300 refugees from Europe's Holocaust, is so remarkable.

Appreciating the rescue of Joseph and other refugees of Nazism by the Philippine Commonwealth also requires some insight into the political relationship between the United States and the Philippines. Upon the acquisition of the territories ceded to the United States as a result of its victory over Spain in 1898, the US government created an agency on December 13, 1898: the Division of Customs and Insular Affairs within the Office of the Secretary of War. This agency oversaw all customs issues and civil affairs pertaining to the islands of Puerto Rico, Cuba, and the Philippines.[65] The name of the agency changed in 1900 to Division of Insular Affairs, and then changed again in 1902 to Bureau of Insular Affairs. This agency administered all civil governments of US island territorial possessions and came under the jurisdiction of the US War Department.[66] The Bureau of Insular Affairs administrated the civil government of the Philippines continuously for the entire forty-one years of its existence. It primarily served as an advisory liaison between the governments in the Philippines and the United States.

The US colonial era in the Philippines began January 20, 1899, when President McKinley created the First Philippine Commission, comprised of five appointees, to investigate conditions in the islands after the end of the Spanish-American War and make recommendations for future proceedings. The commission's report recommended establishing civilian government as soon as possible, with a bicameral national legislature and autonomous governments in the provinces and municipalities.[67] President McKinley established the Second Philippine Commission on March 16, 1900, also called the Taft Commission after its appointed head, federal judge and future US president William Howard Taft. With both legislative and executive powers, this commission enacted 499 laws that allowed the Filipinos an ever-increasing share in the operation of their own governments.[68] The July 1902 Philippine Organic Act authorized the creation of a bicameral legislature with a popularly elected lower house, known as the Philippine Assembly, and an upper house known as the Philippine Commission, whose members were appointed by the president of the United States. The chairman of the commission was the American governor-general of the Philippines, also appointed by the US president and regarded as the chief executive of the colonial administration. The Second Philippine Commission literally wiped away three hundred years of Spanish feudalism, while permitting the Filipinos guarded advancements in democratic self-rule.[69]

The Jones Act of 1916, which carried forward certain provisions of the Organic Act of 1902, provided for a twenty-four-member elected Philippine Senate to replace the appointed five-man Philippine Commission. The former ninety-member Philippine Assembly was renamed the Philippine House of Representatives. "The legislature's actions were subject to the veto of the governor general, and it could not pass laws affecting the rights of United States citizens."[70] The governor-general of the executive branch remained an appointed position by the US president until the establishment of the Philippine Commonwealth, which was inaugurated on November 15, 1935.[71]

The Tydings-McDuffie Act of 1934, also called the Philippine Independence Act, outlined the terms of the Philippine Commonwealth and its anticipated ten-year transition period into the fully independent Republic of the Philippines, which was predetermined for July 4, 1946.[72] The Tydings-McDuffie Act authorized the Philippine Legislature, now one body called the National Assembly, to draft a constitution for the government of the Commonwealth.[73] The executive power of the new government centered in an elected Filipino president, as stipulated by Article VII of the Commonwealth Constitution, which was ratified on May 14, 1935: "Laws passed by the legislature affecting immigration, foreign trade, and the currency system had to be approved by the United States President."[74]

Another important provision of the Tydings-McDuffie Act was the creation of the Office of the US High Commissioner to the Philippines. The office had no direct administrative powers in the Philippines but was primarily concerned with protecting American interests in the new commonwealth nation. This office superseded that of the American governor-general. The connection between these newly vested offices and the US War Department was never really clarified until the Philippine Supreme Court Justice George A. Malcolm composed an official statement to the High Commissioner's office on January 9, 1939. His official opinion clarified "the relationship of the office of the High Commissioner to the Philippine Islands and the War Department."[75]

Malcolm explained that the Tydings-McDuffie Act provided three agencies to act as representatives of the US president in the execution of his duties as the supreme commander over the islands of the Philippines. In the islands proper, that representative was the US High Commissioner to the Philippines. In Washington, all issues touching upon the foreign affairs of the Commonwealth were handled by the Office of Philippine Affairs within the State Department. Certain other affairs of the Philippines continued to be administered by the secretary of war through the Bureau of Insular Affairs. All three of these executive representative agencies played a significant role in the immigration of Jewish refugees to the Philippines.[76]

The Office of Philippine Affairs was created on December 12, 1936, for the sole purpose of carrying out the directives of the State Department pertinent to foreign affairs issues in the Philippines. Whenever situations demanded communication between the Philippines and the State Department, the practice was to transmit the message to the War Department via the Bureau of Insular Affairs, which then forwarded the message to the designated agency, whether that was the High Commissioner in the Philippines or the Office of Philippine Affairs in Washington, DC. In this manner, the secretary of state advised the High Commissioner of the Philippines on issues of foreign affairs, and "the views of the Secretary of State [were] accepted as conclusive."[77] This suggests that the High Commissioner was in a junior position of authority to the US Secretary of State, which was completely reversed by McNutt during his tenure in office when he facilitated Jewish rescue in the Philippines. Within a few months of Malcolm's official opinion, the functions of the Bureau of Insular Affairs were transferred to the Department of the Interior on July 1, 1939, and combined with those of the Division of Territories and Island Possessions.[78] For the first time in forty years, the Philippines were no longer under the jurisdiction of the US War Department. It was the US government's decision to grant more autonomy to the country between 1936 and 1941 that allowed for the execution of a rescue plan saving refugee Jews from approaching destruction.

REFUGEE JEWS IN ASIAN PORTS

The European Jewish refugee crises of the 1930s and 1940s produced an incredibly large forced migration of stateless, persecuted Jews from nearly every country in western, central, and eastern Europe, as fleeing Jewish families attempted to find safe havens from the accelerating antisemitic policies of Hitler and his expanding Third Reich. The Jewish population of Europe, numbering between nine and ten million, would, in the course of twelve years of Nazi terrorism, lose more than two-thirds of its members, some due in part to compulsory and voluntary emigrations but most because of fascist policies of harassment, torture, and extermination.

Jewish refugees began exiting Europe, specifically Germany and Austria, in 1933, reaching its highest emigration numbers in 1939, the year Joseph fled to the Philippines. While the majority of Europe's fleeing Jews headed west, a relatively small number of refugee Jews fled eastward in a significant new wave of Jewish migration to southern and eastern Asia, finding safe ports in existing Jewish diaspora communities in China, India, Singapore, Japan, Thailand, and the Philippines. Receiving these predominantly westernized Ashkenazi Jews presented extreme difficulties for the already long-established Jewish merchant communities of Mizrahi, Sephardic, and Russian origins.

Joseph's odyssey illustrates the obstacles tens of thousands of Jewish refugees endured in their quests to flee Europe and find safety in Asia. Having already suffered the loss of his citizenship rights, Joseph and more than half a million other Jews in Germany and Austria were left with no legal recourse. They endured confiscation of their property and assets, termination of their jobs, expulsions from schools, random acts of violence, arbitrary arrests, forced deportations, incarcerations, starvation, and other depravations. If one survived these hardships and managed to accrue the small fortune usually necessary to secure travel papers and passenger tickets, the actual journeys themselves could take anywhere from four to ten weeks. For several years, when international immigration quotas drastically inhibited refugees' chances in obtaining visas and other necessary travel permits to western countries, many refugees opted for more immediate travel opportunities to uncertain destinations in the distant East rather than risk their lives waiting for an immigration quota to open up in a western nation.

Depending on the time frame in which refugees left, there were two major routes refugee Jews could use from various points of departure in Europe to reach ports in southern and eastern Asia. From the early 1930s to the mid-1940s, the one route by sea carried fleeing refugees from ports mostly in Italy on to Alexandria, Egypt, and then through the Suez Canal to ports of call in Bombay, Singapore, Hong Kong, Manila, Shanghai, and Kobe and Yokohama, Japan. Other vessels leaving from seaports in the north, such as Bremen or Hamburg, usually sailed around the Cape of Good Hope in South Africa, extending the already four-week voyage time to East Asia by another six weeks.[79] Refugees often had to pay for first-class passage because those were the only berths still available, and shipping companies were known to charge exorbitant prices in times of extreme demand. Ships could be booked six months in advance and would carry as many as one thousand Jewish refugees per voyage. The other major route of transportation to the Far East was the land route across Russia and Siberia via the Trans-Siberian Railway and the Chinese Eastern Railroad that had once brought Russian Jews to Asia more than two decades earlier.

In 1940, when Denmark and Norway fell to the Germans in April and Italy entered the war in June, the Baltic and Mediterranean ports closed to commercial shipping so that refugees fleeing to Asia only had the land route by which to escape.[80] Thousands of Polish Jews as well as Jews from western Europe labored to secure travel documents and train tickets to Moscow, where many boarded the Trans-Siberian Railway for a six-thousand-mile journey to Harbin in Manchuria, and then on to either the port city of Dairen or to Vladivostok, where they hoped to secure papers to final destinations anywhere along the Pacific Rim. Jewish refugees disembarked at nearly every East Asian port—such as Bangkok, Singapore, and Manila—where already established Jewish communities hosted the new arrivals as best they could. But the largest colony of refugee Jews in Asia assembled in Shanghai, China.

After the first of the Opium Wars that China lost to Great Britain in the mid-1800s, Shanghai became a treaty port open to international trade, which attracted merchants from the Americas, Spain, Portugal, Italy, and France. The arrival of foreign traders and their families soon contributed to Shanghai developing into China's largest city by the late 1800s. Dozens of different nationalities eventually inhabited sections of the city that had been partitioned into territorial zones. The original British and American zones reorganized themselves into the International Settlement in the western part of Shanghai, with the French Concession operating next to it on its southern flanks. Exempt from Chinese laws, the national enclaves within these international zones imported their own western cultural norms into the social and professional lives of the local inhabitants.

As western ways spread, periodic Chinese opposition to the ever-growing foreign influence in Shanghai gained ground, culminating in the capture of the eastern Chinese section of Shanghai by the Nationalist army of Chiang Kai-shek in 1927. Although threatened, the foreign settlements remained unmolested by the revolutionary violence affecting the rest of the country. Shortly thereafter, in 1931, the Nationalists also initiated resistance to the ever-encroaching presence of the Japanese within China's territories, resulting in the second Sino-Japanese War in 1937. This time the conflict did not spare the foreign territories and large sections of Shanghai fell to the Japanese, one of those being the American-controlled Hongkew district in the Shanghai International Settlement. Violence ripped through large areas of its industrial sector, leaving piles of rubble in its wake. Into this already suffering war-torn city, nearly twenty thousand refugee Jews from Europe arrived.[81]

Shanghai had two distinct Jewish communities that predated the arrival of the refugee Jews from Europe by several decades. The earliest, the Mizrahi Jewish merchant class, remained relatively small and elite while the later, primarily Ashkenazi Jews were refugees from the wars and pogroms of the Russian Empire and the chaos of its revolutions in 1917. The Mizrahi community developed as a result of the migrations of Jews from Baghdad, via Bombay in India, from the latter half of the nineteenth century up to World War I. This group, which ultimately numbered about seven hundred, included a number of prominent business families, although most were employees of Jewish-owned-and-operated businesses. The Ashkenazi community of Jews from Russia and Eastern Europe had settled in Shanghai as a result of several waves of migration, beginning in 1895 and ending in 1939. During these decades, Jewish immigrants included ex-soldiers, political exiles, escapees from Siberian exile, adventurers, and refugees. The Ashkenazi and Mizrahi communities each had their own synagogues, cultural norms, and languages. With the massive influx of German and Austrian refugee Jews between 1938 and 1941, yet another type of Jewish community in Shanghai formed of a central European character.[82]

Jewish refugees escaping Nazi persecutions began arriving in Shanghai as early as 1933, following Hitler's ascent to power. Some jumped ship in Manila, seeking asylum in an American-run overseas colony rather than an Asian one. The increasing number of refugees fleeing to Shanghai and other Asian ports corresponded with the waves of increased antisemitic violence in Third Reich territories. In Joseph's flight to the Philippines, he shared quarters on the ship with many refugees bound for Shanghai. Following the Anschluss, the 1938 annexation of Austria by Nazi Germany, and especially in the aftermath of Kristallnacht, refugees from Austria and Germany "streamed in like a flood."[83] In just one year, the number of Jewish refugees in Shanghai grew from 1,500 near the end of 1938 to nearly 17,000 by the end of 1939. Stripped of their assets and property, refugee Jews added the already destitute population of Hongkew with its own similarly large numbers of impoverished people. Large-scale relief plans implemented by the existing Jewish communities of Shanghai collected funds and provided affordable lodging and food distribution centers. Much-needed aid also began to arrive from the foreign offices of US Jewish aid agencies such as the American Jewish Joint Distribution Committee, commonly known as the Joint or JDC, and the Hebrew Immigration Aid Society (HIAS).[84] It eventually became more difficult to fulfill the needs of the thousands of Jewish refugees in Shanghai and other Asian ports when a growing number of refuge locations around the world competed for the funds of these and other American and international Jewish relief organizations.

JEWS IN THE PHILIPPINES

The history of Jews in the Philippines bears many similarities to the story of the Jews in Shanghai specifically and of Jewish migration to Asia in general. Nevertheless, there were many more differences. In the late fifteenth and early sixteenth centuries, Portuguese vessels carried Sephardic Jewish merchants down the West Coast of Africa, around the Horn, up Africa's East Coast, and then across the Persian Gulf and Indian Ocean to India, China, the Spice Islands of Indochina, as well as to the yet-unnamed islands of the Philippines. These Crypto-Jewish merchants escaped the persecutions of their time by migrating from the Iberian Peninsula to commercial ports scattered throughout the world. Even before the arrival of these first Europeans to the Philippine archipelago, the sociopolitical fate of the islands was destined to be contested by the Spanish and Portuguese by virtue of the 1494 Treaty of Tordesillas, a papal decree that divided all New World discoveries between Spain and Portugal. Disputes between the Iberian kingdoms over the Philippines and its neighboring islands, the Moluccas, resulted in the 1529 Treaty of Zaragoza, in which Portugal ceded the Philippines to Spain, which would remain under Spanish control for nearly four hundred years. Moreover, the Portuguese enjoyed an economic advantage within the Spanish realm by virtue of Jewish merchants fleeing the Spanish Inquisition via Portugal to the New World. More than 180,000 Jews fled Spain and as many as 150,000 of them entered Portugal, thus raising the Jewish numbers to 15 percent of the total population.[85] These Spanish Jewish refugees encountered a litany of abuses, many accepting a forced conversion to Christianity as a means to escape death; they would eventually escape Iberia to become explorers, mathematicians, cartographers, and merchants aboard Portuguese and Spanish vessels en route to New World ports—Manila being one.

When Christianized Crypto-Jews, also known as "Marranos," reached the Philippines, they no doubt engaged in the Spanish galleon trade between Manila and Acapulco.[86] The brothers Jorge and Domingo Rodriguez are the first recorded Crypto-Jews to arrive in the Spanish Philippines, reaching Manila in the 1590s. By 1593 both had been tried and convicted at an auto-da-fé in Mexico City because the Inquisition did not have an independent tribunal in the Philippines. The Inquisition imprisoned the Rodriguez brothers and subsequently tried and convicted at least eight other so-called Christianized Jews from the Philippine Islands.[87] A Jewish presence in these islands during the subsequent centuries of Spanish colonization remained small and unorganized. John Griese writes that "Spanish law would not have permitted an organized Jewish religious life," so that Philippine Jews would have had to practice Judaism in secret as other conversos did throughout the world.[88] The Philippines had the rare distinction of being colonized by the Spanish, thus becoming the only Roman Catholic enclave in the Far East. Although there was a Portuguese presence in Asia, the small Iberian country did not have the population to secure its holdings through colonization, so its ports remained barely manned outposts. Castilian Catholic prejudices against Judaic adherents would have discouraged the settlement of openly Jewish practitioners, although as conversos, they blended into the Catholic Spanish society of the elite and continued to fulfill their utilitarian mercantilist roles through the end of the nineteenth century.

As the Spanish galleon trade between Manila and Acapulco closed down in 1815 due to the Mexican War of Independence, contact between the Crypto-Jews of the Philippines and other merchant Jews of New and Old World ports ultimately ceased, resulting in a loss of cultural ties with other Jewish communities. The first permanent settlement of openly practicing Jews in the Philippines in the nearly four hundred years of Spanish colonial rule began with the arrival of three Levy brothers from Alsace-Lorraine who fled the aftermath of the Franco-Prussian War in 1870. As entrepreneurs, their business ventures over the years began with a merchandising business importing watches, La Estrella del Norte, and eventually branched out into perfumes, pharmaceuticals, and automobiles.[89]

The opening of the Suez Canal in March 1869 provided a more direct trading route between Europe and the Philippines, which allowed all passenger and cargo ships to follow "along warm-weather sea lanes of the

Mediterranean through the canal along the Red Sea, and finally into the Indian Ocean."[90] Thus, as businesses grew, the number of Jews in Manila grew as well. The Levy brothers were soon joined by Turkish, Syrian, and Egyptian Jews, creating a multiethnic community of about fifty individuals by the end of the Spanish period.[91] It was not until the Spanish-American War at the end of the nineteenth century—when the United States purchased control of the islands from Spain—that the Jewish community started to grow in the "first and only official American colony" in Asia.[92]

When the Philippines became an American concern, it created opportunities for American Jewish citizens to take advantage of this new frontier, creating a wave of Jewish migration to East Asia that was neither Middle Eastern nor European. The arrival of American military forces to the Philippines brought a few Jewish servicemen who decided to remain in the islands after their military discharge and become permanent residents. Jewish teachers from the United States also arrived with a contingent of "Thomasites," a delegation of volunteer teachers, who gave public instruction to Filipino children. In 1901, five hundred American teachers and some of their families boarded the US Army Transport *Thomas* at San Francisco Pier, bound for the Philippines.[93] Trained by prestigious institutions in the United States, these young men and women were selected by the American Civil Service Commission to establish a modern public-school system in the newly acquired territory of the Philippines and to conduct all instruction in English. By 1902, the number of American teachers, labeled Thomasites, had swelled to more than a thousand.

In addition to education, new markets for import-export businesses drew young American Jewish businessmen, many of whom set up shop in the islands as well. In this regard, the attraction of the Philippines for Jewish American merchants in setting up outposts for their larger home companies back in the United States seems consistent with the "Port Jew" identity of the Sephardic Jews of the Atlantic seaports and the merchant Jews of other port cities in Asia.

Three important names appear in the Jewish community of Manila shortly after the turn of the century: Emil Bachrach, Morton I. Netzorg, and Israel Königsberg. Annette Eberly, a freelance author and Philippine resident, recorded that Emil Bachrach arrived in Manila in 1901 and soon "built a commercial empire of fairly substantial proportions."[94] Because he is regarded as the first American Jew to permanently settle in the Philippines, the synagogue and cultural hall, which the Bachrach family financed in subsequent decades, bore his name: Temple Emil and Bachrach Hall.

Bachrach encouraged his extended family to resettle in the Philippines and experience the good life provided by this beautiful archipelago. Eberly, quoting Mina Gaberman, Bachrach's niece, stated that living in Manila "was distinctly colonial and elegant in those days. It had a special air of a sumptuous, civilized world."[95] Bachrach's economic successes allowed him to be a generous philanthropist, who supported both Jewish and Christian causes.

By 1918, twenty years after the Americans appropriated the Philippines from the Spanish, the Manila Jewish community totaled about 150 families, including a small number of White Russian Jews who had sought asylum following the Bolshevik Revolution.[96] Aside from these few Russian Jews who became a part of the multiethnic Jewish community in Manila, Russian Jewish immigration to Asia had little effect on the Philippines. Although institutionally trained rabbis, cantors, and *shochetim* (kosher butchers) did not appear on the scene permanently until well after World War II, lay members of the Jewish community in Manila and Jewish refugees filled these roles at various times in the first few decades of the American period in the Philippines.[97]

We must remember that peace did not prevail in the Philippines following the 1898 Spanish-American War until 1902, after the three-year-long Philippine War of Independence. No religiously practicing Jewish community existed at that time, and one would not be officially formed until 1917. It took about ten years of American rule in the Philippines for the influx of international Jewish businessmen, teachers, and ex-soldiers to gather themselves into an official community. Frank Ephraim, a Jewish refugee survivor of the Philippines, recounts that by 1919, the 150 Jewish families who lived in Manila were of various nationalities and denominations, and that religious services at the time were held in family homes. Ephraim recalled that "in 1919, Yom Kippur services took place in the Eagles Hall, where Mottel Goldstein, a Russian Jew, officiated. That year the Jewish community was formally organized."[98] These events demonstrated a growing Jewish identity in Manila, led by the merchant Jewish families, who sought the establishment of a form of Jewish worship that could be sustainable within their unique community.

In 1911, the expanding Jewish community in the Philippines gained one of its most important families. Morton "Israel" Netzorg and his wife, Katherine, came from the United States and joined the Philippine public-school teacher corps of Thomasites. Their son, Morton "Jock" Netzorg, was born on February 4, 1912, in the town of Nueva Caceres. His memoir, written in 1987, relates the family's many business ventures and the educational influence they had on the lives of the children of Manila's most prestigious families.[99] Some of those students included "the daughters of Paul McNutt, General Sutherland, Ambassador MacMurray, [and] General Casey."[100] Israel Netzorg became the representative of the Jewish Welfare Board (JWB) in the Philippines, with the responsibility of overseeing matters involving Jewish sailors and soldiers. He was also the representative of the American Jewish Joint Distribution Committee (JDC), a US-based Jewish charity that raised funds to assist Jewish communities throughout the world.[101] Jewish merchants in the Philippines filled multiple roles within their own Jewish community as well as the larger Philippine community, as they joined in and frequently led civic organizations.

According to Netzorg, businesses from the American mainland began to arrive in increasing volume in 1920. Manila Jewry included the founder of the Makati Stock Exchange, the conductor of the Manila Symphony Orchestra, and other professionals such as physicians, dentists and architects.[102] The Frieder Brothers, a family instrumental in saving German Jewish refugees in the late 1930s, arrived in 1921 and expanded their family's stateside cigar business, known as the Helena Cigar Factory, into a lucrative venture in Manila. The Frieder Brothers' economic prosperity, along with their high level of societal interaction, provided them with the safety and status that allowed them to be leaders of the newly formed Jewish community. Eberly described this emerging Jewish society as a "little Jewish flavor in this nineteenth-century lifestyle of the very rich. The Jewish families did go to the Temple for special occasions, and the existence of the adjacent social hall [did] serve to centralize and focus Jewish interrelationships and concerns, but it was all very low-key."[103] This emerging Jewish Philippine community was organized more for social fellowship and ethnic continuity, adapting their ideal of Jewishness to their circumstances.

Once Temple Emil was built in 1923, primarily through the generous contributions of the Bachrachs, Netzorgs, and Frieders, the Jewish community in Manila commissioned Mottel Goldstein, the Russian Jew who had been serving as a lay rabbi, to hire an ordained rabbi from Shanghai. Israel Königsberg, who had settled in Shanghai immediately after World War I, had been a Jewish chaplain in the army of the Austro-Hungarian Empire. While in Shanghai, he had received cantorial training and, upon meeting up with Mottel Goldstein, was hired to officiate services in Temple Emil in Manila in 1924. Jock Netzorg was the first bar mitzvah held in the Philippine Jewish synagogue.[104] Netzorg, who later taught in the Jewish

Sunday school at Temple Emil, recounted how Emil Bachrach provided bus service by picking up Jewish children from all over town, driving them to Temple for Hebrew Sunday school and then driving them all back home again.[105] The Jewish community of Manila, which gradually increased in size in the 1920s and early 1930s as businessmen and merchants from the United States and the Middle East began filtering into East Asia, along with political refugees from Russia and other parts of Europe, remained a predominantly American-led Jewish community.[106]

By 1936, the Jewish community in the Philippines had a distinctly cosmopolitan makeup with a total population of about five hundred. Even though there were no separations into ethnic or national communities as existed in Shanghai, one would not describe the Philippine Jewish community as uniform either. It wasn't until the Nazi danger to European Jewry arose in the 1930s that a united Jewish consciousness in the Philippines sprang into existence as the small, decentralized, and mostly secular Jewish community of Manila took heroic steps to save its fellow Jews from sure destruction. As Bachrach's niece, Gaberman told Eberly in 1975, "We only really became Jewish-conscious in a deep way when this terrible threat came out of Europe, and suddenly there were Jews in desperate need of help."[107] Netzorg maintained that his father considered his most important deed in the Philippines was "bringing refugees out of Hitler's Germany."[108] Indeed, Morton I. Netzorg played a vital role in saving the lives of hundreds of German refugee Jews, including Joseph's.

Open Hearts

JEWISH RESCUE IN THE PHILIPPINES

The "Manilaners" presence in the Philippines was just one in a long series of Jewish migrations to the Pacific archipelago.[1] Jews in the Philippines dates back to its colonization by the Spanish in the sixteenth century when Crypto-Jews, who found life difficult and dangerous in their Iberian homeland, sought safety abroad. Many would become the explorers and merchants that populated almost every port in the newly discovered territories during the Age of Exploration, including the Philippines. Its first openly Jewish community would not establish itself until the United States had taken over the islands after the Spanish-American War and created an East Asian outpost for its military as well as its businesses. Manila would be the new home for an eclectic gathering of Jews by the 1920s and the core for the rescue of European refugees in the 1930s.

In the first three decades of the twentieth century, persecuted Jews from eastern and western Europe sought respite in any nation willing to grant them safe haven. While the majority of Europe's fleeing Jews headed west, a relatively smaller number of them fled east in a significant wave of Jewish migration to southern and eastern Asia. Refugees found safe ports in existing Jewish diaspora locations in China, India, Singapore, Japan, Thailand, and the Philippines. Joseph was just one of thousands of refugees boarding passenger liners from Baltic and Mediterranean ports en route to Asian destinations. Refugees from encroaching Nazi expansion found asylum in every country in the greater Asian world, but it was in the Philippines that an American-led Jewish community was empowered by the Commonwealth officials to organize refugee rescue programs, which would be proposed as templates for organized rescue in other parts of the world.[2] Through a selection plan based on distinct professional and vocational needs of the greater Philippine community, nearly one thousand European refugee Jews immigrated as resident aliens primarily into Manila but also into outlying provinces as well. Joseph came to Manila through these efforts. Another two to three hundred refugee Jews came to the Philippines as temporary immigrants through a sponsorship program that had the potential to save hundreds, if not thousands, more, were it not for the bombing and occupation of the Philippines by the Japanese and the advent of World War II in the Pacific. At this point, rescue turned into incarceration again for some, such as Joseph, and attempts at survival for all.

EARLY RESCUE, 1937–38

The migration of Jews escaping Europe between 1933 and 1941, which included Joseph and his mother in 1939, was the last major immigration of Jews to the Philippines. Jews fleeing Nazi Germany came to the Philippines as early as 1933, but they were few in numbers and their escape almost entirely undocumented. Frank Ephraim, an Austrian emigrant and survivor of the selection rescue in the Philippines, related many stories of these immigrants in his 2003 treatise *Escape to Manila: From Nazi Tyranny to Japanese Terror*. The first significant influx of European refugee Jews to arrive in Manila, however, did not come directly from Europe but from the Jewish refugee community in Shanghai. With the renewal of hostilities between the Japanese and Chinese in 1937, the four million inhabitants of Shanghai faced the dangers of war in an occupied territory as various civilian communities sought escape from the city's battlegrounds.

Germany's shift of alliance from China to Japan at this time alarmed German Jews in Shanghai, who feared German pressure on Japan to adopt Nazi discriminatory policies against its German Jewish population. The Manila Jewish community feared for these refugees as well, and the Jewish Refugee Committee of Manila (JRC), composed of influential and affluent American members of the Philippine Jewish community, was formed with the intention of rescuing German members of the Shanghai Jewish community.[3] These Jews had already been deprived of their German citizenship, and the Gestapo presence that was taking root in Japanese occupied areas threatened their existence in Shanghai as well.

When the Sino-Japanese War broke out on July 7, 1937, the JRC received a telegram from Shanghai seeking assistance for their refugee Jews. The small Jewish community in Manila immediately raised a sum of $8,000, but before the money could be dispatched, the wealthier Sephardic Jews of Shanghai stepped up and cared for the needs of their refugees on their own. The JRC, under the leadership of Philip Frieder in Manila, decided to hold the funds in escrow to meet some future need. That need came almost immediately when, one month later, the German government sent a boat to Shanghai to remove all German nationals from the war zone. In so doing they also took aboard about thirty Jewish German refugee families. All of these German nationals, including the Jewish refugees, were deposited in Manila, where the German government signed an agreement with the Philippine government to the effect that those people removed from the war zone in China would not become public charges. The German Consul in the Philippines suggested to McNutt that it would be best for the Jewish community to take charge of the German Jewish refugees. This suggestion was adopted, and the refugees were placed in various Jewish homes and, eventually, jobs were found for all of them.[4] This rescue, observant of US immigration directives that enforced the exclusion clause regarding refugees not becoming public charges, set the precedent for the later immigration program in Manila that involved efforts to rescue victims from Europe's Jewish communities—the efforts that specifically saved Joseph and 1,300 other refugees.[5]

The experiences of the German refugee Jews who fled Shanghai in August 1937 is related in the memoirs of Max Berges.[6] He and his wife, Annie, fled Germany to Shanghai in 1935 and recounted the horrifying ordeal of living in a war zone in Shanghai, and then the twist of fate that brought them to Manila.

To our unbelievable surprise the German Consulate General called us, offering us evacuation with the passenger liner "Gneisenau" which was going to be diverted from Japan to Yang tze-kiang [Yangtse River]. We could not decide to accept the risk of setting foot on German soil again and a German ship was just that. We refused at first, but the Consulate called again assuring us that under the circumstances we would be absolutely safe and be regarded as *Auslands-deutsche* (Germans living abroad).[7]

Berges further recounted how the German consulate "offered us a free trip to Manila as guests of the German Reich." The irony of the event was not lost on Berges as he observed how Germans "at home killed and imprisoned the Jews" but in Shanghai "they saved them."[8] The event became even more surreal when Berges and the other refugee German Jews from Shanghai joined several hundred German nationals on the dock under protection of brown-shirted storm troopers wearing Nazi swastika armbands as the assembly prepared to board a launch that would take them all to the SS *Gneisenau*. Once the launch arrived at the ship, all abroad scaled up the side of the ship on a "Jacob's Ladder" with what Berges described as "a nightmarish determination."[9] But Manila was not their first destination.

After two days at sea, the German refugees from Shanghai—Jews and non-Jews alike—reached Kobe, Japan, where they stayed for three days. This experience turned even more bizarre for the refugee Jews: a welcoming committee of Germans from Kobe, Yokohama, and Tokyo met the ship in company of a German brass band playing rousing national tunes while shouts of "Heil Hitler" resounded throughout the welcoming throng. The German Embassy in Japan even presented the refugees, Jews included, with fruit baskets adorned with swastikas. When the voyage to Manila resumed, tensions on board cautioned the Jewish refugees to keep aloof from the other passengers. After enduring a horrifying typhoon at sea, described by Berges as "a super-chimerical orgy of total evil,"[10] which precipitated a collision with a rudderless freighter, the damaged SS *Gneisenau* eventually made port in Hong Kong, where all aboard remained for several days while the ship underwent repairs. Finally, the last leg of their journey to Manila transpired peacefully. Berges describes their arrival:

> I won't ever forget how deeply we breathed in relief as we walked down the gangplank and stepped on Pier Five in Manila. With the exception of the two of us all other non-American evacuees had only been granted temporary visas for the Philippine Islands by the American Consulate General in Shanghai.[11] They were all supposed and expected to return to Shanghai whenever conditions were normal again there. . . . Everything went all right at our arrival in Manila. We weren't retained on the Gneisenau and were welcomed by a Jewish Relief Committee. . . . There were reporters and press photographers on the pier because like in Kobe we were the first Shanghai evacuees. . . . However, unlike our arrival in Shanghai, there was a Jewish Reception Committee to greet us and take care of us because

none of us had any means to pay even for a single meal, leave alone lodging. . . . We certainly were received by high-fluting speeches and very
kind-sounding words and finally taken to Hellman's Boarding house for
temporary shelter.[12]

Max Berges and his wife, Annie, remained in Manila for the next sixteen
months, until December 1939, at which time they completed their paper-
work for the second time and immigrated to the United States, having received letters of recommendation from Albert Einstein that significantly
aided in their successful immigration.[13] The spontaneous rescue of German
refugee Jews from Shanghai became the impetus for the better-devised rescue plans that followed.

RESCUE BY SELECTION: ORIGINS, 1938

Refugee rescuers in the Philippines operated selection and sponsorship
programs unlike any Jewish rescue operations anywhere else in the world
during the years of Nazi-led persecutions in Europe. These plans involved
a collaboration of efforts from political dignitaries and businessmen in the
Philippines, relief organizations in both the United States and in Germany,
and even government officials in the US State Department. While some
programs proved successful, others were thwarted, and ultimately, even
those refugees who were saved underwent further depravations under the
invading Japanese. Joseph's story helps bring to light the efforts of the many
to rescue the few, or in Joseph's case, the one.

The Philippine rescue of the German Jews from Shanghai in 1937 came
to the attention of the Refugee Economic Corporation (REC), an affiliate
of the American Jewish Joint Distribution Committee (JDC) headquar-
tered in New York City.[14] Incorporated in 1934, the REC, originally called
the Refugee Rehabilitation Committee, specialized in funding Jewish settlements in countries that agreed to take in refugee Jews.[15] Exactly how the
plan was conceived to initiate further rescue in the Philippines has become
shrouded in legend over the past seventy years. Some credit President
Quezon for initiating the offer, others claim that High Commissioner
McNutt devised the plan, and still others place members of the Jewish
Refugee Committee (JRC) in Manila at a poker table with Eisenhower,
Quezon, McNutt, and Frieder, where these gambling buddies hashed
out the plan while indulging in fine cigars rolled by S. Frieder & Sons
Manufacturing.[16] According to the documentary record, however, once

information spread to the REC that the Philippines could be a safe haven for further Jewish immigration, the notable correspondence between the real initiators began: Charles Liebman and Bruno Schachner of the REC in New York; Paul V. McNutt, the US High Commissioner for the Philippine Islands; Philip Frieder and his brothers, of the successful Jewish merchant family in the Philippines and directors of the JRC in Manila; Manuel Quezon, president of the Commonwealth nation of the Philippines; and Joseph C. Hyman of the New York–based JDC.

Correspondence between Liebman and McNutt in May and June 1938 reveals that the REC initiated contact with McNutt through mutual acquaintances with two brothers, Julius and Jacob Weiss, the former an associate with the REC and the latter an Indiana state senator and personal friend of McNutt.[17] Paul McNutt's May 19, 1938, letter to Julius Weiss, the brother of his friend and colleague Jacob Weiss, is the earliest discovered official record discussing rescue in the Philippines:

> In performance of my promise made to your brother Jacob, as soon as I returned to the Islands, I discussed the possibility of absorbing a part of the Jewish political refugees from countries in Europe with the Commonwealth Officials and the responsible leaders of the Jewish community in Manila. Several conferences have been held and serious study given the entire problem.[18]

An obscure South Haven newspaper article printed sometime in 1940 found amog the papers of Paul V. McNutt housed in the Lilly Library at Indiana University sheds some light on how this "promise" to Jacob Weiss came about.[19] The article discusses McNutt's involvement with the refugees.

> Senator Weiss wrote a letter to High Commissioner McNutt, asking simply what McNutt thought of the possibilities of refuge in the Philippines. By return mail came a letter from McNutt. He said he'd talk to Weiss in a few weeks when he returned to the United States. . . . There was no opportunity for the two to talk in Indianapolis. In Washington there was a reception. The line looked a mile long. Thousands were grouped around and in front of McNutt. When Weiss came into view, McNutt stopped him. They talked there in full view of thousands for 10 minutes. . . . McNutt explained that he had to visit the President, the Secretary of State, and a dozen other important government officials. Would Weiss stay in Washington for breakfast two days hence? . . . "Jake," said McNutt, "it's all

arranged. The visas will be okayed by me and won't have to clear through the State Department. When I get back to Manila I'm going to arrange for the proper reception of these refugees."[20]

The article described how McNutt, upon his return to the Philippines, "organized the Jewish community in Manila" and sent details of a selection plan in a letter to Weiss.[21] This supports the correspondence from McNutt to Julius Weiss in May 1938 that discussed components of the plan. While this article may take some liberties in its summations, it helps situate a timeline of when the idea for rescue in the Philippines was first conceived.

McNutt arrived in Washington on February 23, 1938, and remained there for one month before returning to the Philippines, at which time meetings were convened with leaders of the Jewish community in Manila.[22] We learn from correspondence between Liebman and McNutt that Weiss had made the inquiry on behalf of the REC.[23] A memo of a conversation in Cincinnati on November 26, 1938, revealed that "a letter from the Refugee Economic Corporation . . . asked whether it would be possible to allow 100 German Jewish families to settle in the Philippines."[24] The undated newspaper article in McNutt's collection tells us that the initial letter from Jacob Weiss to McNutt inquiring about rescuing refugees in the Philippines must have been sent before McNutt traveled to Washington in February 1938, perhaps as early as December 1937. In the communiqué of May 19, 1938, from McNutt to Weiss, McNutt stated, "I find that the commonwealth officials are quite sympathetic to the idea of receiving those who can be absorbed. With the foregoing in mind I asked a representative committee of Jewish leaders to prepare a list of those who might be absorbed at the present time."[25] From this we know that meetings had already transpired prior to mid-May 1938 to devise a program of selection in bringing German refugee Jews to the Philippines.

The November 26 memo revealed that McNutt had shown the initial inquiry from Weiss on behalf of the REC to Philip Frieder and that Frieder responded affirmatively, "provided they could select the type of people who were to come and provided also that the Refugee Economic Corporation could supply these hundred families with enough money to maintain them for about ten weeks after their arrival in order that they might learn the language and become acclimatized."[26] This confirms that the REC agreed to advance funds in order to meet the stipulations voiced by the Jewish community of Manila and commissioner McNutt that the refugees not become public charges. The importance of McNutt's role in this selection program cannot be overstated. Without his initiation of the dialog between the Philippine Government, the US State Department, the Jewish community in Manila, and the American Jewish relief organizations, it is doubtful this plan would have germinated. McNutt's willingness to work with the many agencies involved in this rescue effort was key to the success of the program.

RESCUE AND THE US DEPARTMENT OF STATE, 1938–40

In the May 19, 1938, letter from McNutt to Weiss, we learn that McNutt understood that the Immigration Quota Act of 1924 did not apply to the Philippines when he requested that members of the JRC in Manila present him with "a list of those who might be absorbed" into the current Philippine economy.[27] At that time the Philippine government was engaged in a complete overhaul of its immigration practices and would not complete the ratification process of their new immigration laws until 1940. Therefore, during the first five years of the Commonwealth government, greater freedom existed for refugee immigration, but it was vital that immigrant aliens not become a drain on the host nation. Absorption of Jewish refugees into the Philippines thus became dependent on the economic ability of the existing community to support the increased population rather than an imposed quota limitation. The leaders of the Jewish community in Manila, led by Morton Netzorg, Samuel Schechter, and the Frieder brothers, composed and sent to McNutt a list of needed professionals who could be economically absorbed immediately into the community. McNutt included this list of various professions and skills, which required about "one hundred families," in his communiqué with Weiss.[28] His correspondence reflects how sincerely he supported the efforts to rescue German Jews: "I am deeply interested in the solution of the problem of caring for political refugees and I am anxious to have any experiment in the Philippine Islands succeed. . . . I should be very glad to do anything in my power to assist in handling these matters."[29]

In postwar correspondence between Charles Liebman of the REC and Dr. Isaiah Bowman, a geographer and consultant to the US State Department, Liebman recounted the history of the rescue of Jews in the Philippines and declared that "Mr. Paul McNutt was the prime mover."[30] He explained how "McNutt succeeded in persuading the Philippine Government and our State Department to grant visas for a considerable number of selected immigrants."[31] A communication between the REC and Stuart Crocker of New York's Red Cross War Fund on February 17, 1942, described McNutt as eager "to help the refugees whose plight he keenly felt."[32] His magnanimous position reflected a genuine altruistic attitude and, whether or not he felt it would serve some political or economic agenda, his involvement was crucial. But the success of the selection plan hung on other contingencies as well, such as the cooperation of the US State Department and support from various relief organizations around the world.

Julius Weiss immediately shared his May 19, 1938, communiqué from McNutt with Bruno Schachner, assistant secretary of the REC, who wrote a letter to the Hilfsverein der Juden in Deutschland (Relief Association for Jews in Germany; hereafter, Hilfsverein) in Berlin on June 1, 1938, recounting the initial provisions for a rescue plan for refugee immigration to the Philippines.[33]

> Gentlemen:
> We are informed by the United States High Commissioner for the Philippine Islands, who is turn bases his opinion on information furnished him by leaders of the local Jewish community, that there could be absorbed in the Philippine Islands, within a relatively short time, the following persons:
> 20 Physicians, among whom should be one eye, ear, nose and throat specialist, one skin specialist, and one or two surgeons.
> 10 Chemical Engineers
> 25 Registered Nurses
> 5 Dentists, who should have their own equipment
> 2 Ortho-Dentists
> 4 Oculists
> 10 Auto Mechanics
> 5 Cigar and Tobacco Experts
> 5 Women Dressmakers, stylists
> 5 Barbers — men and women
> 5 Accountants
> 5 Film and Photograph Experts
> 1 Rabbi, not over forty years of age, conservative, married and able to speak English.
> 20 Farmers
> We are trying to organize the immigration of these people, and we should be indebted to you if you could meanwhile prepare a preliminary

list of people meeting the requirements outlined above. As soon as we have completed arrangements, we will proceed with a final selection. Please let us know, meanwhile, whether all the various classes of persons could be found among the people registered with you, and if not, which ones are lacking. In view of the delicacy of the negotiations involved, we expect you to keep this matter entirely confidential, and under no circumstances to give it any publicity whatsoever. In addition, we would appreciate it if you would not approach the United States High Commissioner on your own behalf, in order not to confuse him by a variety of inquiries.[34]

The Hilfsverein began assembling applicant names immediately and in spite of the resolve "to keep this matter entirely confidential," word spread rapidly of a rescue opportunity in the Philippines.

An official correspondence from Charles Liebman, president of the REC, to McNutt on June 10, 1938, disclosed Julius Weiss's transmittal of McNutt's May 19 communiqué to the REC and how the REC had "taken the liberty of transmitting the list of desirable immigrants to a social-work agency in Germany, which will, in turn, select from among the applicants for emigration those who might be welcome in the Philippine Islands."[35] Liebman assured McNutt that no plans for sending the selected immigrants to the Philippines would be made until their total economic assimilation in the community could be guaranteed, thereby eliminating "any special problem[s]" that would be caused by their arrival. Liebman reminded McNutt of Germany's emigration policies restricting the amount of assets that Jews could take out of the country and how it would be necessary for "outside agencies . . . [to] care for them for an initial period" until they could become self-supporting.[36] Liebman asked McNutt for an estimate "as to how much money would be required to support a person or a family at a subsistence level, and how long the period of adjustment [was] likely to last." Liebman finished his letter to McNutt with a sincere appreciation for McNutt's generosity and interest in the "fate of refugees."[37] This challenges Ephraim's portrayal of McNutt's initial ambivalence to refugee rescue.

In a return communiqué dated June 24, 1938, McNutt informed Liebman that subsistence for a single person for a seventy-five-day period amounted to about fifty dollars, seventy-five dollars for a family of two, and about ninety dollars for a family of three.[38] McNutt revealed that he understood the Jewish Joint Distribution Committee "was prepared to supply single persons with 900 marks, and families with something over

2000 marks," advising further that single persons come with at least $125 and families with $235. He later related challenges surrounding the ongoing rescue of refugees arriving independent of the proposed selection plan:

> The local Jewish community is comparatively small, and few are in a posi-
> tion to support the local fund. The burden actually falls on about five
> families. Because of the fact that the local group furnished all of the funds
> to care for the forty refugee families which have arrived during the past
> few weeks and will be required to meet the needs of others who come on
> their own account, I do not feel that the local group should be asked to do
> more.[39]

McNutt assured Liebman that the JRC in Manila would receive the refugees when they arrived and arrange for their lodging. He further advised Liebman that all future contact regarding the rescue of refugees by this plan could be directed personally to Philip Frieder in Manila.[40]

As the various agencies worked to put the selection program into play, refugees arrived in Manila independently, most en route to Shanghai. They disembarked at Manila seeking asylum on American soil and hoping that residence in Manila would lead to quota status for eventual immigration to the United States. Ephraim maintains that immigration to the Philippines represented a back-door entrance into the United States, but such a proviso certainly did not exist, either in the US immigration laws at the time or in the Philippine laws being formulated.[41] The memorandum of the conversation held in New York on November 28, 1938, between Mr. Hyman of the JDC and Morris Frieder, brother of Philip Frieder of Manila, summarized the destitute circumstances of these refugees:

> Approximately 350 refugees have arrived in Manila independently. Most of
> these are totally without funds and are constituting a serious problem for
> the Jewish community there. There are, all told, about 60 Jewish families
> in Manila, (the American Jewish Yearbook lists the Jewish population of the
> Philippines as 500) of whom Mr. Frieder says there are only about 6 Jew-
> ish families who are in a position to contribute. It costs about .50 cents a
> day to maintain each of the 350 refugees there.[42]

Jock Netzorg's father, Morton Netzorg, but better known as "Israel," was also a member of the JRC in Manila; Jock told Michael Onorato, his interviewer, how the community practiced the principle of tithing to support the refugees who arrived before financial support was received from the REC.[43] By this means the Jewish community of Manila raised an average of $2,000–$2,500 monthly for the refugee rescue efforts. For McNutt and other Commonwealth officials, it was vital that entrance into the Philippines follow a controlled, organized process so that indiscriminate immigration would not overload the community and scuttle the plan. With financial support promised by the REC for the needs of selected immigrants to the Philippines, another situation needed to be dealt with, namely, how to obtain visas for the immigrants.

In a written communication from Schachner of the REC to Frieder dated July 29, 1938, Schachner revealed that applications from refugees in Germany had already arrived from the Hilfsverein in Berlin. After informing Frieder of their intention to transmit those lists to the JRC in Manila, Schachner asked if Frieder "anticipate[d] any difficulties in obtaining visas for those people" who would be approved by the JRC for immigration to the Philippines.[44] This begs the question of when the US State Department was informed about the plans to select Jewish refugees for immigration to the Philippines. Two weeks prior to this correspondence between Schachner and Frieder, McNutt received a radiogram from the Department of State through the office of the Secretary of War, dated July 13, 1938: "Have been informally advised emergency entry into the Philippines of several hundred Jewish refugees from Europe being arranged. Please radio all information available."[45] Apparently having heard through the grapevine of intended rescue in the Philippines, a more official statement was sought. In reply, McNutt stated:

> Approximately forty families of Jewish refugees, who came to Philippines on own initiative or because of connections here, have been absorbed. Through cooperation [of] leaders local Jewish community and Commonwealth officials, arrangements have been made to take one hundred additional families of approved professions and vocations in three groups at intervals [of] sixty days. If this experiment is successful it may be possible to absorb others. In order to prevent attempted entry of more refugees than can be cared for properly it is considered unwise to give any publicity to the movement.[46]

The significance of these radiograms lies in the fact that the dispatch agency for these encrypted messages was the Bureau of Insular Affairs within the Department of War, which transmitted copies of all communiqués to the

Department of State: "The Secretary of War presents his compliments to the Honorable Secretary of State and is pleased to enclose herewith a copy of a radiogram (No. 518, July 16) relative to the entry of Jewish refugees in the Philippines."[47] The reaction of the State Department can best be understood by examining an episode in early September 1938, which suggests that the State Department was not completely supportive of the Philippine immigration plans.

Cordell Hull, the US secretary of state, received a telegram dated September 6, 1938, from the American Consul in Milan inquiring about immigration for five hundred non-Italian refugee Jews to the Philippines. The Jewish Central Refugee Committee for Italy had inquired at the Milan consulate about obtaining visas for the refugees, stating that Jewish relief organizations in Paris and London would finance all necessary expenditures. The US Consul stated that "unless otherwise instructed visas will be granted here under the Immigration Laws of 1917. Please instruct."[48] Hull immediately responded that the matter was being broached with the Philippine authorities and "pending the Department's further instructions, visas should not repeat not be granted."[49] Similar telegrams were dispatched to American embassies and consuls in London, Zurich, and Rotterdam. Hull then sent a communiqué concerning the refugees to McNutt on September 12, 1938.

Please inform the Commonwealth Government in strict confidence that the Department of State has received a telegram from the American Consul General in Milan, Italy saying that the Jewish Central Refugee Committee for Italy proposes to have five hundred non-Italian Jews of whom one-half are merchants and one-quarter professional persons obtain visas and proceed to the Philippine Islands. It is stated that these applicants will be furnished with transportation and landing money by refugee organizations. Information from other sources indicates the possibility of a movement from Central Europe to the Philippine Islands. The Department of State has telegraphed the Consul General at Milan and certain other officers in Europe that the matter is being taken up with the appropriate authorities of the Philippine Islands and that no action in the cases of the persons in question should be taken pending the receipt of further instructions from the Department. The Department of State brings the foregoing to the attention of the Commonwealth authorities for their information and consideration and for a statement of their desires in the matter. The attention of the Commonwealth authorities should be called to the fact that

aside from the question of policy involved in the admission into the Philippine Islands of these and similar groups of persons from Central Europe,
there are also involved technical questions of admissibility under section 3
of the Immigration Act of 1917 which excluded among other classes of
aliens, persons whose passage is paid for by any corporation, association,
society, municipality, or foreign government either directly or indirectly
and persons likely to become a public charge.[50]

Several important observations can be made as a result of this radiogram
from Hull to McNutt regarding the issuance of visas for Jewish refugees
fleeing to the Philippines. It shows that the State Department had not
been officially notified earlier about rescue immigration to the Philippines.
It also reveals that the State Department viewed this rescue as a way for
undesirable "Central" Europeans to enter US territories. Another implica-
tion is that while the State Department could not cite quota restrictions on
immigration to the Philippines, it did focus on exclusionary clauses of the
1917 Immigration Laws in an effort to derail the rescue.

How should we view the process of organizing a selection plan for Jewish refugee rescue in the Philippines that ensued without disclosure to US
State Department officials? Obviously, McNutt had regarded such a disclosure as unnecessary and considered it an affair that fell totally within the
discretion of his office and that of President Quezon, who had already offered his support for the program. (McNutt's July 16 radiogram to Burnett
mentioned Commonwealth officials having approved of the plan.)[51] Because Cordell Hull requested clarification of the immigration procedures for
the Philippines from McNutt, it tells us that he too recognized McNutt's
authority over the issue since additional duties and functions delegated to
the office of the High Commissioner under the provisions of section 7 of
the Independence Act were forwarded to him on March 1, 1937, when he
accepted his appointment. These instructions granted the High Commissioner authority to waive passport and visa requirements for aliens in certain categories.[52] Recalling the contents of the undated newspaper article
from McNutt's manuscripts, the article quoted McNutt as saying: "it's all
arranged. The visas will be okayed by me and won't have to clear through
the State Department."[53] The manner of the issuance of the visas in the
execution of the plan confirms McNutt's official preeminence over the State
Department in approving applicants for visas. An examination of important events regarding immigration practices in the Philippines in 1937 and

1938 offers added contextualization for the procedures initiated in order to facilitate controlled immigration of refugee Jews into the archipelago.

According to McNutt's quarterly report of December 1937, "considerable confusion" occurred in 1937 when instructions from the State Department advised the consular officers overseas "that they had no authority to refuse to issue visas for aliens desiring to proceed to the Philippines, except for such aliens whose entry might be considered harmful to the public safety."[54] His report further stated that the State Department advised the consular officers that "admissibility of aliens is one to be determined by the immigration officers of the Philippine Islands upon arrival at Philippine Ports."[55] McNutt recounted how the observance of State Department directives by the consular officers abroad had allowed "large numbers of aliens from various disturbed regions of the world" unlimited influx into the Philippines, creating a serious problem that the Commonwealth government was ill equipped to handle.[56] According to him, Philippine immigration authorities "were disposed to admit without question an alien who presented a travel document bearing the visa of an American consul."[57] Neither consuls abroad nor immigration officers in the Philippines exercised appropriate restrictions when needed. When the administration of the immigration laws was transferred from the Commonwealth Department of Finance to the Department of Labor, officials unschooled in the Immigration Laws of 1917 failed miserably in their execution of those laws. That fact became evident in McNutt's report to Roosevelt the following year.

McNutt related in his quarterly report at the end of 1938 that multiple appeals from American and foreign consuls requested "copies of the regulations governing the administration of the applicable immigration law in the Philippines," so officials could advise immigrants properly as to what to expect under Philippine Law.[58] Earlier that year, McNutt's office wrote a memo on this growing problem, which documented serious infractions by Philippine officials. The brief depicted Philippine immigration as having "no regulations and the whole thing [being] handled on a purely hit-or-miss system."[59] McNutt's observation of the ineptitude of the Philippine immigration officials to execute laws and procedures effectively was written April 29, 1938, during the time when he and the JRC conferred together on procedures for refugee rescue in the Philippines.

McNutt's office advised President Quezon that he hire experts on immigration laws and practices in the United States to restructure immigration laws for the Philippines. McNutt reported that such advisors arrived in December 1938. But during the earlier months of 1938, Quezon opened a probe into allegations of misconduct within his immigration office and, as a result, he suspended twenty-three officers and employees from the immigration service and prosecuted four. During this time of upheaval and restructuring of immigration policies and offices, authority over refugee selection for the issuance of all visas into the Philippines was entrusted to the JRC in Manila, an official act that took the power of visa selection out of the hands of US State Department Officials and American consular officers abroad and put it directly into the hands of the JRC and Paul V. McNutt.

In response to Cordell Hull's inquiry regarding Philippine immigration policies for the five hundred non-Italian Jews seeking visas to the Philippines, McNutt advised Hull that the "commonwealth officials [Quezon and staff] and local committee [referring to the JRC] think it unwise to attempt absorption additional refugees at this time . . . visas should be given only to those selected from lists submitted in advance to Commonwealth officials and committee. Commonwealth officials concur in opinion that, with such safeguards, experiment will be successful and maximum number of refugees can be absorbed."[60] From this point forward, it was clear that immigration of refugee Jews into the Philippines would be under the auspices of Commonwealth officials, namely Quezon, McNutt, and members of the JRC. Several communiqués went back and forth between the offices of the State Department and McNutt that detailed the selection plan for State Department officials.

> Initial request and placement of refugee families in the Philippines came from the Refugee Economic Corporation . . . and was submitted to Commonwealth officials and to a Committee of Representatives Jewish Citizens headed by P. S. Frieder. . . . All concerned agreed to absorb 100 families of approved records in designated professions and vocations in three groups at intervals of sixty days. . . . Selections based on these records now being made by Commonwealth authorities and committee. Suggest that when lists are complete, they be forwarded to Department of State in order that appropriate consular officers be authorized to give visas. Commonwealth officials request that visas be given only to them on approved lists.[61]

A JDC memo reveals that this selection plan intended "to be increased to five hundred if initial efforts [were] successful."[62] There has been no evidence thus far of any other rescue of Jewish refugees where the power of the consular officers in selecting those so fortunate as to receive an immigration visa was taken from the consuls and put into the hands of a local committee of Jewish businessmen.

The State Department, however, did not accept its impotence in this matter quietly. More communiqués ensued as State Department officials felt the need to emphasize the authority of the Immigration Laws of 1917 over the influx of refugee Jews in the Philippines, drawing attention to certain clauses they felt excluded any sizable immigration of Jews from Europe.

> In view of the small sums which it is stated the selected refugees will have in their possession, and in the absence of information that plans have been made for placement of refugees and for their support in the meantime, you may wish to invite the attention of the authorities to the provisions in section 3 of the Immigration Act of 1917 relating to the exclusion of aliens likely to become public charges. This act is applicable to the Philippine Islands and as the Commonwealth authorities are responsible for the enforcement of the Act in the Philippine Islands, they will wish in giving tentative consideration to the cases of these refugees to go into the matter of their admissibility or inadmissibility under the provisions of the Act, including those relating to aliens likely to become public charges. . . . To avoid exclusion under the public charge clause, aliens must establish that they have sufficient means of support or such assurances of continuing support by persons able to support them.[63]

McNutt's short response on October 25, 1938, assuring State Department officials that "all refugees now in [the] Islands have been placed satisfactorily" while explaining how the "responsible local committee has undertaken placement and support of all others selected" accompanied the first official list of German refugee Jews selected for immigration into the Philippines.[64]

After the Hilfsverein in Berlin received the JRC profession-and-vocation preference list, they compiled applications from German Jewish candidates and forwarded them to the REC, which then sent them to the Philippines, where a three-man committee from the Jewish community, led by one of the Frieder brothers, evaluated them.[65] The committee checked their prerequisites for immigration, including current passports, applicant background information, former professional or other activities, available

funds to offer temporary sustenance, and the likelihood of eventual successful assimilation into the current community. When the committee
had the assurances it needed, it recommended the issuance of visas by
name and address of the applicants in the form of an affidavit, which was
presented to McNutt for his approval. Once approved by Quezon and
McNutt, both of whom looked for the necessary documentation that the
JRC had adequate funds on deposit for the candidates, the list was radioed
in code through the War Department via the Bureau of Insular Affairs to
the State Department. Through this communication process, McNutt directed that the State Department request "that appropriate consular officials be authorized to give visas" to the listed names of selected refugees.[66]
This first selection list, composed on October 25, 1938, authorized visas for
more than one hundred Germans Jews—men, women, and children—
along with six refugee Jews from Austria. This list was augmented one
month later by McNutt with another forty-six names from Germany and
two names from Italy, totaling one hundred families in all.

McNutt requested confirmation of official notification to the appropriate consular officers on three different communiqués until an official
reply confirming the transmissions came on November 30, 1938, from
George Messersmith, assistant secretary of state.

> The names of the refugees contained in telegrams no. 811 of October 25,
> and no. 883 of November 22, 1938, from the High Commissioner have
> been transmitted by mail to the consular officers in the respective districts
> of the aliens' residences. The consular officers have been requested to in-
> form the Department regarding the action taken in the cases of the refu-
> gees referred to and upon receipt of the reports the War Department will
> be informed. The procedure of having the names of the refugees for whom
> the Philippine authorities have granted authorization for entry into the
> Philippine Island communicated through the War Department to the
> Department of State for transmission to the appropriate consular officers
> is considered to be satisfactory.[67]

Evidence of State Department compliance with the provisions of the Jew-
ish refugee selection plan went even further as Messersmith also informed
McNutt that consular officers in Singapore, New Zealand, Australia,
Netherlands, East Indies, India, Egypt, and Shanghai had been notified
"that visas should not be issued to German refugees proceeding to the
Philippine Islands without notice of authorization for entry into the Islands

having been received from the Philippine authorities through the Department of State."[68] This widespread communication to consular officers abroad spurred inquiries regarding non-German and non-Jewish refugee immigration into the Philippines as well.

When instructions from the State Department reached the consular offices advising them not to issue immigration visas to the Philippines except to persons on a pre-approved selection list,[69] clarification for exceptions to the rule began to pour in. One such communiqué from Singapore stated that "strict interpretation of the Department's telegram dated November 22, [1938] 7 p.m., indicates that the procedure outlined may be applicable to all persons proceeding to the Philippines Islands. If not is it applicable to non-German refugees, to non-destitute German refugees, or only to German destitute refugees?"[70] Messersmith repeated this inquiry to McNutt "to obtain an expression of the views of the Philippine authorities regarding the cases of persons other than those of German refugees" seeking visas to the Philippines at US consular offices.[71] When a similar inquiry came in from the American Embassy in Paris, the response sent can only be categorized as astonishing: "Information has been received from the Philippine authorities indicating that the procedure outlined in the circular instruction of November 30, 1938, diplomatic serial no. 3008, should be followed in the case of all refugees desiring to proceed to the Philippine Islands."[72] This is significant in that it tells us the JRC in Manila had been empowered to review all applications for immigration to the Philippines, not just those of Jewish refugees. In light of the complete disarray of the immigration offices of the Commonwealth government at the time, assigning this immigration application oversight to the JRC made a great deal of sense. They already had an effectively organized system in place. Not only did the JRC select European Jews for immigration, they also selected non-Jewish and non-destitute immigrants as well. Visa records of the State Department testify that in addition to names of refugee Jews being granted visas through the JRC selection plan, names of other classifications of refugees also appeared: "Commonwealth authorities authorize issuance of visas to following persons: Miss Hertha Gottscheer, Vienna, Austria, Catholic refugee."[73] Names of Roman Catholic priests and nuns also show up in the visa records.

Queries about rescue opportunities in the Philippines started to come in from all directions. Joseph Hyman, executive director of the JDC, responded December 27, 1938, to Col. Julius Ochs Adler of the *New York Times*.

Dear Colonel Adler: Dr. Jonah Wise mentioned to me that you wished some information concerning the settling of a German immigrant in the Philippines . . . immigrants are admitted entirely on a selective individual basis in limited numbers, acceptability being dependent on background and former professional or other activities of the applicant. It virtually lies within the discretion of the High Commissioner to determine who should be admitted and who may not be . . . a gentleman by the name of Mr. Frieder, one of the outstanding Jewish leaders, is the chairman, and very largely on his recommendation to the Philippine Immigration Commissioner and Governor McNutt is [application] formally approved.[74]

Rabbi Wise had been head of the JDC and had worked extensively in the United States and Germany to facilitate aid to German refugee Jews. He also represented the JDC at the Evian Conference.[75] Dialogs concerning refugee rescue in the Philippines had now reached highly influential circles.

Inquiries from private parties, referred to the JDC and wishing to guarantee financial support for relatives in Europe so that they could obtain visas to the Philippines, came from many directions. This following reply from A. M. Warren, chief of the Visa Division, to Mr. Stephen Skodak of Lorain, Ohio, represents numerous letters to dozens of private parties seeking information on immigration to the Philippines:

> I have your letter of June 2, 1939, requesting to be advised of the procedure to be followed by two chemical engineers, subjects of Hungary, in affecting their immigration into the Philippine Islands. The Philippine authorities have requested that advance authorization for entry into the Islands be obtained from the Philippine authorities at Manila before visas may be issued. It is understood that the names of persons desiring to proceed to the Islands may be submitted to the Philippine authorities by the Jewish Refugee Committee, Post Office Box 2233, Manila, Philippine Islands.[76]

Not only do we have a selection rescue plan of Jews saving Jews; but we also have a selection plan of Jews saving non-Jews as well.

RESCUE AND JEWISH RELIEF ORGANIZATIONS, 1938–40

Various Jewish relief organizations share credit for the implementation of the JRC selection plan. The first Jewish relief organizations involved with rescue in the Philippines, other than the Jewish Refugee Committee in

Manila, were the Hilfsverein in Berlin, and the REC and the Jewish Joint Distribution Committee (JDC) in New York. The JDC, founded in 1914 to provide relief for Jews in Palestine and Eastern Europe, was the primary organization for the distribution of funds from the American Jewish community to Jews in Germany. It had a virtual monopoly on overseas aid. A general trend in American Jewry against unification of Jewish relief organizations existed during the years between the world wars. These agencies separated into the religious community versions of Reform, Conservative, and Orthodox, along with innumerable political, social, and cultural distinctions.[77] Sometimes these agencies got in each other's way in their quests for philanthropic resources (see the treatise on the Mindanao Resettlement Project in chap. 4). However, in the initial financing of the JRC selection plan, the REC held the reins.

The successful implementation of this rescue plan depended solely on its financial viability. From the very beginning, when McNutt sent the May 19, 1938, communiqué to Weiss listing needed professions and vocations of refugees, he stressed that the refugees "be provided with sufficient funds to care for their needs for seventy-five days."[78] As the selection plan progressed into fruition during those early months, the REC pledged "that the proper financial arrangements" would be made to insure its success. A REC memorandum dated October 1, 1938, revealed intentions to expand the plan. "Through intervention of the United States High Commissioner for the Philippine Islands, the Hon. Paul V. McNutt, the Jewish community of the Philippine Islands found employment possibilities for one hundred persons, divided into various occupational groups. This figure is later to be increased to five hundred if initial efforts are successful."[79] The memo stated that the JRC had requested four hundred dollars for the temporary support for each family until they could support themselves. "Since it is impossible to find the money any other way, it is suggested that the Émigré Charitable Fund provide these funds on a loan basis. There is asked, therefore, an initial appropriation of $10,000 for the support of 21 refugees in this manner."[80] The JRC in Manila kept exceptionally accurate records of the monies distributed to the rescued refugees and, in turn, collected monies from the employed refugees as payment against their loans. But there were always more refugees applying for immigration to the Philippines than there were monies to support them.

A communiqué from Frieder to the REC in New York on October 31, 1938, illustrated the precarious position of the community, as nonselected immigrants arrived almost daily.

Every steamer that is coming here from Europe is bringing refugees without visas to enter the Philippine Islands. We do everything possible so that they can stay here but all this requires money as none of them have any funds whatsoever. Last week one of the Italian steamers brought 150 en route to Shanghai. Fourteen of these remained. About fifteen did the same thing a few days before. We now have so many here that in a short time it will be impossible for us to take care of them. We are advised that another steamer, due this week, is bringing sixteen. We are placing them as fast as possible, but they cannot be absorbed so quickly. Therefore, we must support them, and our small community here cannot do this. For this reason, I telegraphed you last week asking for financial assistance. The Philippines are still open, but it won't be long if these refugees are not taken care of without government assistance.[81]

This situation limited the ability of the Manila Jews to offer financial support for the selected refugees that were soon to arrive from Europe.

Funds from other US Jewish refugee relief organizations became crucial. Frieder's earlier telegraph requested the REC to petition the JDC on their behalf for $10,000 "for 1939 to supplement our local contributions."[82] Two weeks later, when Morris Frieder, brother of Philip Frieder of the JRC, met with Joseph Hyman of the JDC in Cincinnati on November 28, 1938, he personally communicated the dire situation in Manila as "approximately 350 refugees [had] arrived in Manila independently" and the local Jewish community simply could not finance their support until they could all be absorbed into the economy. Morris Frieder further stated that "the Philippines might easily become an important resettlement center for German Jewish refugees if it were handled right and that it was dangerous to these future prospects to allow these 350 refugees to become public charges and thus alienate the sympathy of the native population."[83] Earlier that day, Morris Frieder had met with the REC and they placed $5,000 at the immediate disposal of the JRC—monies that had been allocated by the JDC. Frieder stressed their need for another $5,000, and Hyman informed him "that in view of the many demands being made upon the JDC it was difficult for [them] to consider a larger allotment." Since the JDC had not yet made its budget for 1939, Hyman assured Frieder that they would do their best to allocate another $5,000 in a few months' time, which they did in February 1939.[84]

Preceding the first wave of arriving immigrants selected by this JRC plan, a German rabbi and his wife arrived from Hildesheim in September

1938. Josef Schwarz, who had worked with Cysner in Hildesheim from 1933 to 1937, would soon play a critical role in bringing him to Manila. Schwarz's settlement in the Philippines marked a historic moment, for he was the first ordained rabbi to reside and serve in the Philippines.[85] He faced a significantly diverse community of ethnicities, languages, cultures, religious practices, and especially economic standings. Bringing religious unity to this conglomerate of differences required a form of worship that promoted uniformity. Rabbi Schwarz urged Temple Emil's board of directors to create a position for a cantor to officiate at religious services and who would also teach Sunday school, train choirs, and organize other musical programs.[86]

Having obtained permission from the JRC, Rabbi Schwarz cabled his friend Joseph Cysner on November 22, 1938, at his last-known place of employment, the Hamburg Temple. Amazingly, the telegram made its way to Poland and found Joseph in Zbaszyn. The English translation read: "Do you want to come? Modest Salary. Side jobs provided. Wire Manila today. Send response. Heartfelt greetings. Schwarz."[87] No doubt Joseph informed his friend of his detention at Zbaszyn and his urgent need to emigrate, for Joseph's name made it onto the third list of refugees selected and approved in December 1938 by the JRC for visas to the Philippines: "For the State Department: Local Jewish Refugee Committee and Commonwealth Government Officials have approved a third list of selected refugees. It is requested that instructions be given the appropriate Consular officials authorizing them to issue permanent visas for the Philippines to the following list: Joseph Cysner, 24 years; care American Joint Distribution Committee, Warsaw, Poland."[88] A dozen other names, mostly from Germany, appeared on that list as well. Joseph then proceeded to obtain the necessary Polish papers to secure his release.

With the telegram from Schwarz and references from leaders of the refugee community in Zbaszyn, Joseph traveled to Warsaw to obtain a Polish passport and his visa from the American Consul General in Warsaw, John K. Davis. A few weeks later another communiqué from the State Department arrived on Davis's desk, informing him that "the Commonwealth Government has granted authority to issue permanent visa to Joseph Cysner even though Polish Government will not permit him to return to Poland. Please issue instructions to American Consul in Warsaw authorizing him, to issue permanent visa for the Philippines to Cysner."[89]

Joseph needed to return to Germany to settle his affairs and since Poland would not allow him to return, obtaining the visa before he left

Poland was imperative. Unbeknownst to the State Department, as of their April 20 communiqué, Joseph had already obtained his visa and was preparing to sail for the Philippines. The Warsaw Consular General Davis confirmed to his bosses in Washington that "I have the honor to acknowledge the receipt of the Department's instruction of April 24, 1939 (file No. 811B.55 J/160) and, in compliance therewith, to report that a visa was issued to Joseph Cysner on March 13, 1939, for the purpose of enabling him to proceed to the Philippine Islands."[90] When Joseph eventually arrived in Manila on May 15, 1939, the Philippine Jewish community had already been expanded by several hundred refugees who had begun arriving in December 1938, bringing the total Jewish population, residents, and refugees to nearly one thousand, the largest number of Jews in Manila yet assembled.

A life in transition can be a difficult adjustment no matter how qualified one is in his profession; nevertheless, Joseph proved to be more than adaptable. His unique talents and abilities enhanced the religious life of the Jewish community in Manila in many ways, from conducting religious services at the temple to forming and training choirs, teaching religion classes, and training young men for their bar mitzvahs. As John Griese wrote, under the tutelage of Rabbi Schwarz and Joseph:

> Jewish life in Manila flourished . . . the Sunday school was revived, a *Chevra Kadisha* [funeral and grave committee] was founded, a Jewish debating club brought those interested in discussing Jewish art and science together, a Youth Club was founded, regular performances were given by a Musical Club and a Dramatic Club, and a Woman's Auxiliary was formed to assist in Jewish welfare work. In addition, a community home was founded in Marikina for the aged and indigent. Numerous social gatherings served to bring the Community together.[91]

But some refugees experienced difficulty adjusting to their new life in the Philippines, and adaptability attributes of the permanent "immigrant" colonizer versus the temporary "migrant" worker serves to explain some of these problems.

A detailed report from May 1940 by Alex Frieder revealed that a small minority of the refugees could not, or would not, adapt to their new lives in this new environment, failing to adjust to the need to change professions, or learn a new language, or just "to evince to even a small degree a spirit of co-operation and mutual helpfulness."[92] Those unwilling to adjust demonstrated a migrant mentality of temporary existence in an environment that would always be, to them, a foreign host. Alex Frieder had experienced the height of the influx of refugees into the Philippines and his reflections on the successes and failures of refugees adapting to life in the Philippines offer valuable insights:

> I am unable to account for the failure of some of the immigrants to make full use of the opportunity [to attend English classes offered by the JRC] which has been placed at their disposal. It is strange to note the large attention of aged persons, all beyond the period of employment, and the efforts which they put forth to learn the language. On the other hand, a number of the younger persons, who so badly require English instruction, absent themselves from classes. They have been advised and admonished in vain.[93]

This observation supports the idea that some of the younger refugees may have harbored the notion that they would return to their prior lives and professions, while the more jaded "older" refugees knew such a hope was futile.

Alex Frieder's extensive and detailed report for the JDC in New York about the life of the rescued Jewish refugees in Manila also reveals more details about the selection rescue procedures. He had been the Frieder brother in charge of the JRC from December 5, 1938, to May 8, 1940, as a result of the rotational residency that the Frieder Brothers practiced while supervising their cigar manufacturing company in Manila. Whereas Philip Frieder played an integral part in the origination and implementation of the selection rescue plan in 1937 and 1938 during his residence in the Philippines, Alex Frieder coordinated the reception for the refugees, including their maintenance and employment in 1939 and 1940. Another brother, Herbert Frieder, took the reins of the S. Frieder & Sons Cigar Manufacturing Company and the Jewish Refugee Committee for the remainder of 1940 and into 1941. Morris Frieder, yet another brother, remained stateside during those years.

Alex witnessed the population of the Jewish community in Manila multiply fivefold with the influx of 850 refugees within an eighteen-month period, stating, "It can be readily asserted that there are few, if any, places in the world that have undertaken [a] bigger refugee burden in proportion to its former Jewish population than has Manila."[94] He detailed the operation of the JRC and its empowerment for this work by the Philippine government.

> The work of our committee in selecting immigration . . . has been such
> facilitated by our cordial relations with the Office of the United States
> High Commissioner, as well as with many branches of the Philippine
> Government, not only with the Office of the President of the Common-
> wealth. These look to this committee as the sole source of information
> and advice, and recommendations for permitting any immigration of any
> refugee from any part of the world to this country. All such applications
> arriving in this office of the US High Commissioner or in any of the various
> branches of the Philippine Government are routed to our committee for
> service and action.[95]

Frieder further stated that the JRC held a "semi-official status" in this immigration review process for the entire archipelago, detailing factors the
committee utilized in rendering their visa selections in a "nonsectarian"
manner.

> We are duty bound to give conscientious consideration to all cases alike,
> thus our "approved lists" have contained names of non-Jews. The harsh
> laws of the Reich were leveled against Jews on the grounds of race and not
> religion, hence many professed Catholics and Protestants of Jewish origin
> have been cast forth and we count a large number of these in our commu-
> nity. In addition to this should be mentioned the numerous cases of inter-
> marriage, so that a really considerable percentage of our immigrants is
> non-Jewish. I feel positive that I speak the complete truth in stating that
> we have shown absolutely no discrimination when offering assistance,
> although it must be admitted that most non-Jews after arriving in this
> country, do not look to us for aid.[96]

The immigration department of the Philippine Commonwealth government had been riddled with corruption, which also contributed to setting
up the JRC as a quasi-official government body of the Philippine nation.
Here we have this unique situation where a committee of Jewish businessmen facilitated rescue not only for fellow religionists in Europe but also for
non-Jews and non-Germans as well.

The JRC in Manila had composed three different lists of approved immigrants before the end of 1938 when Alex arrived in the Philippines, always receiving more applications than could possibly be approved. The JRC
endorsed additional lists of immigrants in every month of the first half of
1939, which became progressively shorter as fewer funds were available

until rescue-by-selection faced suspension in June 1939. Herbert Katzki, secretary for the JDC Committee on Refugee Aid in Europe, expressed in a memorandum concerning a visit made by Philip Frieder to the JDC offices on June 23, 1939 (Philip returned stateside while Alex took up residence in Manila) that the JRC was "receiving hundreds of applications for visas from people who undoubtedly would be desirable persons for settlement in the Philippines, but it was unable to approve any of them in view of its present financial circumstances."[97] By this date, 750 refugee Jews had arrived in the Philippines and two-thirds of them had successfully been placed in jobs. The Jewish community of Manila continued to raise $2,000 a month to support the indigent refugees. With the intent of resuming the "approval of immigration applications," thereby increasing the population numbers of refugees admitted into the Philippines, Philip Frieder requested a grant of $30,000 from the JDC, stating that "200 to 300 families per month could come in if there were sufficient funds to provide for them."[98] The JDC made those funds available in August 1939. As 1939 wore on, the ability to procure employment for refugees declined, and the Frieder Brothers, along with others of the JRC, devised recommendations for a future immigration policy that they felt needed to be considered and eventually implemented if rescue in the Philippines were to continue.

RESCUE BY SPONSORSHIP, 1940–1941

The rescue of Jewish refugees to the Philippines is a rare incident where three methods of saving lives through immigration transpired. The JRC selection plan morphed into a sponsorship program while plans continued for the mass resettlement of refugees on the Island of Mindanao (see chap. 4). Alex Frieder had laid out a detailed recommendation in his May 1940 message to the JDC of a "future immigration policy" for further refugee settlement in the Philippines in response to the escalating economic trials in sustaining an increased émigré population. Alex noted that before he could lay out the full details for this new sponsorship program, three factors needed to be considered: securing "substantial affidavit[s]" guaranteeing ample support for the applicants; a cash deposit in the committee trust fund to sustain every applicant for a minimum one-year's support; and more careful scrutiny of applicants' qualifications ensuring their ability to become self-supporting.[99] With regard to applicants seeking temporary residence "while awaiting permission to proceed to some other country," Alex Frieder recommended a cash deposit for two-year's support, along

with funds sufficient to purchase their passage to the country of their ultimate destination. He also recommended "that the above conditions be
waived in cases of applicants, applying directly from Europe, who, in the
opinion of our Executive Committee, possess the training and experience
and are within the desirable age limits, which will permit them readily to
find opportunity for gainful employment."[100] In order to avoid such incidents where sponsors of affidavits had "resolutely refused to make good
their sworn promises," Alex Frieder recommended that affidavits of support be filed through the auspices of their local Jewish relief organizations,
which would assume liability for insuring that the sponsors fulfill their
obligations as outlined in their affidavits.[101] Alex Frieder closed his comments with sincere expression of gratitude to the JDC and the REC for
their continued financial support of their rescue operations.

Committee members of the JDC convened a meeting on June 21, 1940,
with both Philip and Alex Frieder to discuss the "refugee situation in the
Philippines." The Frieders recounted that the resident Jews of Manila,
numbering 100 persons, of which no more than 12 were "comfortably situated," could no longer "contribute funds to the Jewish Refugee Committee" for the support of the indigent refugees.[102] At that time, approximately
800 refugees had been received into the islands, two-thirds of whom had
gainful employment. Another 182 visa applicants were en route, and more
visas stood ready to be issued. The Frieders sought confirmation from the
JDC that funds for facilitating rescue well into 1941 could be reasonably
promised, as the JRC in Manila needed to show guarantees to the Philippine government that all necessary monies would be available before visa
affidavits could be issued: "It was suggested that if we undertook by letter
to show you that we would provide you with $10,000 toward the latter
part of this year for use beginning January 1, 1941, such a commitment
would give you the necessary security to continue your immigration and
maintenance program. Messrs. Philip and Alex Frieder found this suggestion acceptable."[103] This illustrates the constraints the JRC had to deal with
as it affected rescue in the Philippines: without proof of monies already on
deposit or promised by valid relief organizations, visa affidavits for further
immigration of refugees to the Philippines would have been denied.

By the beginning of July 1940, sponsorship became the accepted extension of the selection program. Maintenance for a family of three for one
year amounted to $1,800, plus an additional $100 per person also needed
to be deposited for the administrative expenses of their rescue.[104] By October 1940, sponsorship procedures were well established:

The Jewish Refugee Committee requires that a deposit of $1,300 be made on behalf of each [single] applicant. The persons making the deposit must guarantee that the applicant will not become a public charge. The applicant must be in good physical condition. The deposit covers the applicant's maintenance at the rate of $50 a month for a period of two years. The remaining $100 constitutes a contribution to the committee for its general program of aid and to cover incidental expenses in each case. If a particular applicant is likely, by reason of occupational training or vocational experience, to be able to secure employment in the Philippines, the amount required to be deposited may be reduced.[105]

With the necessary monies on deposit, along with effective affidavits, visas for applicants could be secured within about a one-month period. But everyone involved in the rescue of refugees in the Philippines knew "that possibilities existing today may be changed or non-existent tomorrow."[106]

Under the sponsorship program, more refugees found haven in the Philippines, as funds were continually made available for rescue by the JDC. A November 7, 1940, memo by Robert Pilpel, secretary of the JDC Subcommittee on Refugee Aid in Central and South America and the Philippines, revealed that "about 1,100 refugees" now resided in the Philippines, along with a total white population of "not more than 5,000 persons."[107] The JDC considered the rescue operation in the Philippines so successful that an inquiry from Pilpel to the REC in October 1941 sought more detailed information on the origins and operation of the programs in the Philippines "and the applicability of the method used to the establishment of temporary havens elsewhere."[108] An REC memo on "Refugee Immigration in the Philippines" forwarded to Moses Levitt, secretary of the JDC, in response to Pilpel's inquiry recorded that "there are now about 1,300" refugees in the Philippines, most having entered "as participants in a program of selective immigration" and the other "have been admitted under a recently established system of temporary immigration." After a thorough recitation of the processes involved in both the selection and sponsorship programs and a closing note rendered on the "invitation of the Philippine Government . . . on large-scale settlement possibilities on Mindanao," Emery Komlos's note advised that "the pattern of the Philippine selective and temporary immigration would be applicable to the establishment of similar activities in other countries."[109] Although the methods of selected and sponsored reprieve in the Philippines became a template for rescue elsewhere, the reception refugees received in the Philippines could not be duplicated.

REFUGEES ARRIVE IN THE PHILIPPINES

Over a period of several years, hundreds of stateless Jews made their way to the Philippines by boat, train, and plane. For most, the Philippines loomed ahead of them as an unknown entity, an Asian island on the other side of the world. Rabbi Schwarz described it as "one of the remotest islands of the world [where] a small number of Jews from every corner of the globe found a new home."[110] How did they get there? How were they received? What was life like for them? Answers to these questions and others like them fill the testimonies of survivors' memories.

Many Jewish families had come to the Philippines following World War I, as did the parents of Martin Meadows, now a resident of Washington, DC. Martin could actually claim dual citizenship, being born in Manila in December 1930. His father, Hyman Medvedowski, a naturalized citizen of the United States, descended from a long line of Russian rabbis. Hyman and his family made several migrations in the early 1900s to Nagasaki, Seattle, Portland, and finally to Jerusalem. Hyman served in the British Army during World War I and participated in the recapture of Jerusalem from the Turks in 1917. After that supposed "war to end all wars," Hyman returned to Portland, changed his name to Meadows, and joined the US Army in 1927, which stationed him in the Philippines. There he met and married Dacha Rebekah Ritter, a Polish Jew who had originally left Europe in the 1920s to live with her aunt in Shanghai. After falsifying her age to buy passage on a boat from Italy to China, Dacha continued on to Manila bypassing Shanghai, after learning that her aunt had set up an arranged marriage for her to an Asian national. Dacha hired out as a nanny to a prosperous Philippine family in 1928 and met Hyman at Temple Emil in Manila. Martin, their only child, was born ten months after their February 1930 wedding. This family's story is typical of other narratives of Jewish families that had come to the Philippines in the early years of the twentieth century.[111]

In recounting his childhood growing up in Manila, Martin recalled attending the American school and thought of himself as an American first and as a Jew second. Although raised in an observant Jewish household not far from the synagogue, the predominantly secular nature of their lives in Manila had a greater influence on Martin than did his parent's Jewish heritage. Martin's father ran his own business, importing assorted makes and models of Swiss business machines, calculators, and typewriters—a business his father revived in the Philippines after World War II. Before the arrival of the refugees, Martin remembered the Jewish community being small but friendly, visiting other families such as the Königsbergs and the Netzorgs. Once the refugees started arriving, Temple Emil was cleaned up and refurbished, and a fairly vibrant Jewish life unfolded. Martin remembers his mother sewing the new curtains for the ark that held the community's Torah scrolls. He also remembers Joseph Cysner as a gentle, pleasant man with an easy disposition, who came to their home to give Martin Hebrew and piano lessons. This idyllic life of the Meadows family was typical for many of Manila's residents, but it came to an abrupt end with the occupation of the Philippines by the Japanese.[112]

Hans Hoeflein, his two sisters, and his parents, originally from Cologne, arrived in the Philippines on the SS *Gneisenau* in August 1937, before the idea of rescue to the Philippines took hold. They initially fled Germany for Spain in 1933, only to abandon Spain for Portugal when the Spanish Civil War broke out in 1936. Hans's father, Justin Hoeflein, was a well-respected and valued export manager for a multinational company. Although a Jew, the reason for his flight from Germany had more to do with his Socialist Party affiliations than his Jewishness. While chairman of the Socialist Party in Cologne, Justin Hoeflein received a warning from a colleague that he was going to be arrested by the Gestapo, which compelled the Hoeflein family's immediate escape to Spain.[113] As impending war loomed over Europe, Hoeflein's employers in Portugal wanted to keep him safe so they sent him as far away from Europe as possible: the Philippines being that destination. Hans remembers spending their first two weeks in Manila in a boarding house before moving into their rented home.

> When we stayed at the boarding house, there were other people that lived there. And there were Filipinos there, there were mestizos there, there were Europeans there. But at the age of 7 and really almost my entire life in the Philippines, we never thought in terms of white and brown, it was a non-issue. I had friends that were Filipinos. I had friends that were mestizos. I had friends that were Caucasians and they were your friends. You didn't make any kind of distinction like that.[114]

The Hoefleins had the advantage of Justin's employment in what Hans named the KL Deutsche, a business affiliated in Manila with the Philippine Engineering Corporation. This employment allowed them to live a very comfortable lifestyle in Manila. Hans, his sisters, and his mother attended an interdenominational Protestant church within the well-established white Christian community, having never been affiliated with the Jewish community in Manila.[115]

The Goldhagens from Hannover were another refugee family who had also arrived independent of the selection plan organized by the JRC in Manila, when securing passage to distant lands could still be accomplished. Juergen Goldhagen arrived with his mother in Manila on December 8, 1937, aboard the Dutch freighter the *Gaasterke*.[116] Juergen, now nearly eight years old, had not seen his father in nearly three years as he has been employed by friends in the Philippines in 1935. Juergen recalls their arrival as follows:

> When the boat docked, a host of brown men came aboard. Who were all these brown men? No one had told me that the Filipinos were brown, and I was totally surprised and bewildered. . . . I started to learn English at a Jewish school and then went to the Philippine Normal School, which was a public school. I was very unhappy there because I was the only white kid in my class. A few of the Filipino kids were friendly, but some wanted to fight me because I was white. I didn't want to fight anyone. I just wanted to be with friends. At that time, I was so lonely that I wished I had black hair and brown skin like a Filipino, instead of being blond and white. Once, I wrapped a thread around my finger and the tip became purple from the poor circulation. The color was more like the Filipinos, so why couldn't the rest of me be that color? No, I did not try to wrap the rest of my body in thread.[117]

Juergen desperately wanted to belong in his new environs. Similar to Hans Hoeflein and his family, Juergen's father was Jewish but his mother was Christian. Juergen and his parents also lived within the long-established white Christian communities of Manila, never interacting with the Jewish refugees that came in later years. The Goldhagens' and the Hoefleins' lives in the Philippines within the privileged white Christian communities were not always conducive to social interactions with Filipinos. Once friendships were made with other white families in Manila, Juergen's parents transferred him out of the Philippine Normal School, rarely associating socially with Filipino children again. Juergen's and Hans's experiences in the Philippines were very different from those of Jewish refugee children who arrived with their families in 1938 and 1939, whose lives centered around the synagogue, thereby taking part in establishing a vibrant Jewish community with its interconnections to their Filipino neighbors.

Ralph Preiss, born in Breslau in Upper Silesia in 1930, was the only child of Margot and Dr. Harry Preiss. In early 1938, when Dr. Preiss could no longer treat non-Jewish patients in Germany, he began actively searching for an avenue of escape. The Preiss family is a perfect example of those targeted Jews rescued through the selection plan and mentored in their new Philippine lives by the Jewish Refugee Committee.[118]

> My parents saw an ad, I guess, in the Jewish newspaper and it said twelve doctors were needed in the Philippines. My father applied and he was one of the chosen ones. So he was chosen in July but then . . . we didn't get that visa until January 4, 1939. . . . We knew in July already we're going to the Philippines so then my father looked up, what is the Philippines? And in an old encyclopedia that we had from 1897 it said, it was under the Spanish crown, so we started learning Spanish. We all learned a thousand words of Spanish.[119]

In the intervening months before their departure, Dr. Preiss started preparing his family for their lifesaving move by selling properties and using the money to buy medical equipment that he would ship to the Philippines. After Kristallnacht and the violence this pogrom unleashed on the Jewish businesses in their hometown, Dr. Preiss "was in hiding essentially until [they] left."[120] The Preisses secured passage on the SS *Potsdam*, another one of the three new German passenger luxury liners built by Norddeutscher Lloyd in 1934 for express travel to Asia. The SS *Potsdam*'s sister ships were the SS *Gneisenau* that brought the Hoeflein family to Manila and the SS *Scharnhorst* that carried Joseph to the Philippines two months later. Ralph remembers their passage as follows:

> The voyage was three weeks and we went all over. It was a beautiful voyage through the Suez Canal. I saw camels on both sides of the canal, it was really wonderful . . . the *Potsdam* only went to Hong Kong and then we had to change ships. We went on the *Tjinegara* to Manila, which was a Dutch ship . . . when we arrived in Manila the committee was there to greet us. It was amazing. Mr. Frieder . . . greeted every new boat that arrived . . . and they immediately herded us into a boarding house.[121]

The Preiss family docked in Manila on March 23, 1939. Although one of the earliest families selected for rescue to the Philippines, dozens of German Jewish families had already arrived independent of the selection plan.

Lotte Cassel Hershfield was a seven-year-old girl when her family left Upper Silesia in 1938. After her father had been arrested in mid-April 1938 and then released for illegally employing a young German woman as a housekeeper, Lotte recalled that "my dad realized that we would have to leave Germany and now the search began." They had heard favorable reports about opportunities in the Philippines from their neighbor "who was an engineer and who had been in the Philippines," and "it appealed to my dad because he felt it was a way out of Hitler's reach." Lotte recounts how the family began investigating the country since "the Philippines was not exactly on the historical list of studies in Germany." They obtained their visas from Breslau's vice consul Stephen Vaughn, whom Lotte describes as "a fairly Philo-Semitic individual and granted visas fairly easily and that is basically how we started about planning on going to the Philippines."[122] They sold their belongings and visited family members in Poland and Czechoslovakia before leaving for France in July 1938. She never saw any of those family members again.

> From Paris we took a train to Marseille and my mother cried the whole time. I could not understand. To me, this was somewhat of an adventure. From Marseille we boarded the ship and we were on that ship for three weeks. . . . I knew I was going to a new country, but it was somewhat exciting because I had been told of where we would reach certain ports and the first one was, we went through the Suez Canal. . . . From the Suez Canal we went to Colombo, which is Sri Lanka today. . . . After Sri Lanka we went to Djibouti which is in French Indonesia and that was not too desirable . . . Djibouti had about five huts. It was very hot, and my dad and my mother went into the city . . . and my mother came back and cried all over again because she felt this was going to be Manila.[123]

They could not have known that the reception awaiting them would be so welcoming. Apprehensions turned to relief, and relief to joy when they finally reached their destination in October 1938.

> In Manila we landed at Pier 7. My parents were kind of befuddled, however there was a Mrs. Kellerman and Mrs. Kellerman said "I have a bed and breakfast and generally the immigrants come and stay with me for a while until they find their own housing." And I was very impressed because we rolled up Dewey Boulevard into Pasay and the lovely beach, lovely beaches of beautiful banana trees and there were the Polo grounds I

remember. And we got to Mrs. Kellerman's and it was a Friday . . . and at night she served chicken soup with matzoh balls and with chicken and rice because there were no potatoes . . . and we had some local fruit and my mother cried all over again because this was heavenly. She never expected to have roast chicken and matzoh ball soup in Manila.[124]

Lotte's beloved cousin, Margot Cassel, arrived in Manila with her family on the same ship as the Preiss family five months after Lotte's family arrived. Margot remembers her mother having the same trepidation about what life would be like in the Philippines after she had spent time ashore in Port Said, Egypt.

We got off the boat and walked through the streets and then as you walk the streets as in many Middle Eastern countries the merchants get in your way—come in, welcome . . . and so forth and trying to pull us in. When we got back on the ship, my mother broke down and said, is this what our future country is going to look like? Is this how we're going to feel in our future country, and she was devastated.[125]

Margot remembers her excitement at seeing Lotte when their ship docked, as the Cassel brothers, their wives, and children celebrated their reunion. "After our first embraces Lotte said 'you won't believe it! How exciting it is. We live where we could walk to the sea and there are shells. I think it's very, very wonderful.' That was her declaration to me when we arrived."[126]

The closer it got to the onset of war with the Nazi invasion of Poland, the harder it became for refugees to secure transport out of European ports. Once the war started, civilian travel by passenger ships and planes out of Europe would cease. On November 12, 1997, the Jewish Family and Children Services in San Francisco conducted an oral history interview with John Odenheimer who, as a young man of eighteen, made an adventurous journey to the Philippines via multiple methods of travels just days before the Nazi invasion of Poland. He boarded a Deutsche Lufthansa Junker, probably the JU-52, which made passenger flights out of Templehof Airport from Berlin to Bangkok.

I left in August 1939. How to get out in 1939 was not easy, and I don't know whose idea it was, maybe my mother who was to some degree a fairly inventive person. She found out that there was a plane going from Berlin to Bangkok in August 1939. They wanted to start a service to Bangkok, and she got me a ticket on that plane. Because by that time I knew I was gonna go to the Philippines because my uncle and my cousin were there, and I did get a visa to the Philippines. I had to go to the American Consulate because the Philippines were a territory at that time. I got this visa and the question was how to get there. I had to get visa for everywhere and I did this by myself—visas for everywhere and I did this myself.[127]

John's flight to Asia included multiple stops for lunch and overnight stays in places like Beirut, Baghdad, Karachi, Calcutta, and Rangoon before arriving in Bangkok. After a four-day layover in Bangkok, he boarded another plane for Hong Kong with a layover in Hanoi. He was in Hong Kong at a group home sponsored by a Jewish relief agency on September 1, 1939, when Germany invaded Poland and started the war.

The British police came around to this group home and I was arrested as an alien and taken to jail in Hong Kong at La Salle College.[128] . . . After two weeks in that camp which was my first experience with being interned, all of a sudden, a black Mariah appeared and took me down to the harbor and put me on a ship, an Italian ship called the *Giulio Cesare* and I went to Manila.[129] It took me to Manila because they saw that I had a passport that had a visa for the Philippines—they knew I was a Jew and let me go and I arrived in Manila on 18 September 1939.[130]

John's journey from Berlin to Manila took at least a month, maybe longer, in which he traveled by train to Berlin, by planes to Hong Kong, and by ship to Manila. Once the war started, refugee escape from Europe to Asian ports was limited to the use of trains heading east through Siberia.

Max Weissler, another native of Upper Silesia, was born on December 13, 1929, to an observant Jewish Orthodox family; they had been warned to flee their home on the eve of Kristallnacht by the village constable who had instructions to arrest his father. They found temporary respite in Copenhagen for several months until his father secured a visa from the American Consulate for the Philippines. "Within a month, my father boarded a freighter from Rotterdam called SS *Ningpo*, which went through the Suez Canal stopped at several ports including Colombo and arrived in Manila on 11 July 1939."[131] Months passed before visas to the Philippines for Max and his mother were secured. Since war had started in the meantime, they would have to travel on trains headed east.

I remember that one early morning when we departed by train for Berlin, my aunt accompanied us to the railroad station. In Berlin, we stayed with a Jewish family for several days. There I recall going with my mother to various consulates and embassies where she received transit visas through Russia, Manchuria, Japan, China etc. . . . Following a day or two in Berlin and one early morning while still dark and with a special police permit to be on the streets, we walked with our suitcases to the railroad station . . . and boarded a train for Kaliningrad [Königsberg]. We arrived in Kaliningrad on 30 December 1940 . . . and with our suitcases made it to the airport for boarding a Russian plane for Moscow.[132]

Eleven-year-old Max and his mother arrived in Moscow "on the last day of December 1940," where they stayed for several days before boarding the Trans-Siberian Railway that eventually took them to the Russian-Manchurian border. There they boarded a Manchurian train for Harbin, China, and again, another train transfer in Harbin for Kobe, Japan. In Kobe, they boarded the large passenger liner, the *Asama Maru*, and eventually arrived in Manila in February 1941. They had traveled for a harrowing eight months before reaching safety in the Philippines.[133]

Jacques Lipetz and his family's escape from Europe to the Philippines in 1941 was an exception to the rule of traveling overland to the East as they took an unusual route in a westward direction. Although his parents were Ostjuden, Jacques was born and raised in Antwerp, Belgium, in 1932. When Germany invaded the Netherlands, Luxembourg, and Belgium on May 10, 1940, the Lipetz family fled their home immediately: "And I remember packing up and getting on a train and we were going to France."[134] Joined by multiple extended family members, the expanded Lipetz families sheltered in France long enough to get to Lisbon to board an American ship bound for the US. "In January 1941 we embarked on the SS *Siboney*. We got on this leaky tub . . . we crossed the Atlantic in the worst January on record for that time. . . . And I remember we landed in New York . . . it became clear we were not going to stay there."[135] Jacques relates that they had not received their quota numbers for immigration to the US, so the family decided to leave for the Philippines, where Jacque's paternal uncle had a business.

Anyway, we left, and we booked passage, I guess it was at the end of March or beginning of April [1941], on a Norwegian steamer, the *Ivarant*. My parents, my two brothers, and I, and we sailed from New York through the Panama Canal . . . and then up to San Diego and Los Angeles . . . and then we set sail from San Francisco for the Philippines in a Norwegian flag ship. . . . Anyway, we had a Pacific crossing.[136]

The Lipetz family arrived in Manila in May 1941, only to enjoy a short six months before the war reached them again with the Japanese bombing of the Philippines in December 1941, which effectively ended all rescue efforts in the Philippines.

FRIENDSHIPS AND COMMUNITY—"MANILANERS" IN THE PHILIPPINES

Those saved through the selection and sponsorship rescue plans adopted a "new" name for their community—"Manilaners"—a name that set them apart but still reflected their sense of belonging in their new Asian home-land, enjoying a safe existence in the Philippines. Margot Cassel Pins Kesten-baum gives one of the more poignant descriptions of what life in the Phil-ippines meant for the Manilaners who had abandoned their old European home for their new Asian one.

> When we had no place to go, the one place that did open its doors were in the Philippines Islands. . . . What we didn't know was the degree to which the Filipinos would also open their hearts. By what I mean, we didn't know what kind of people we were coming to. OK, so when you're dealing with people who are friendly, who are helpful, who take you at eye level, that is a very, very important and meaningful experience when you've come from a place where you have been degraded and humiliated in so many ways that the contrast was that you came out not only to an open door but you came to open hearts.[137]

Like Margot, her cousin Lotte also holds fond memories of a beautiful island inhabited by a generous people. She remembers that "it was a very free existence. We loved it. We got bicycles and we were able to bicycle, and we had our Filipino friends and our parents basically made a very good wage. We had a lavandera, a laundry woman, my dad had a chauffeur. We had a maid who was with us at all times . . . it was a leisurely life."[138] Life for the refugees among the Filipinos took all forms, from being classmates or pupils for the children, to being coworkers or employees and employers for the adults, to being mentors or, above all, being rescuers when the Jews needed Filipino help.

Hanna Kaunitz Weinstein Entell was born and raised in Vienna and was twenty years old when Hitler annexed Austria in March 1938. She and her first husband, Kazimir Roth, left Austria with Czech passports and stayed in Brussels for eleven months, arriving in Manila just before the war started in September 1939. When asked by her interviewer for her impressions of the Philippines, Hanna answered:

> It was the most amazing thing, because I had no conception of Manila at all. I knew nothing. I knew it was a tropical country. We got there, and it was really a much more cosmopolitan place that I ever pictured. They had a wonderful symphony orchestra that was led by a Viennese. They had so many cultural things there. When I was in Atlanta—that was in 1946—it wasn't nearly as cultural as Manila was when I got there in 1939. . . . We all liked the Filipinos very much. They're a sweet and gentle people. . . . They were professionals. They were lawyers. They were doctors. . . . They had beautiful stores there. I was working in one of the stores. Just unbelievable. When I got there, I didn't know one word of English. I had an English teacher—my husband and I [had] a private teacher—every morning. Every afternoon, we went to the classes that . . . the Jewish organization put together. We took a lesson every afternoon.[139]

The refugees became part of two communities—their ever-growing Jewish community centered around the synagogue, and the greater Filipino community that surrounded them all. Most found immediate acceptance and built instant friendships. Helen Beck, a Manilaner interviewed by Filipino American filmmaker Noel Izon, described the Filipinos as "the most kindest people I ever met. You know, and for me, this was heaven! I right away loved the Philippines . . . my best friends were Filipino."[140]

Charlotte Holzer Bunim was only five years old when she left Germany with her parents, Heinrich and Hedwig Holzer, and older brother, Siegfried, arriving in the Philippines in June 1939. She remembers that they lived next door to a Filipino family, a physician, his wife, and five children, who were her friends and playmates. When the Holzer's house was destroyed by the Japanese and they had no place to go, their neighbor "gave us a little corner of the hospital for us to live in for the time being.

And that was my relationship with them." Although Charlotte found the Philippines to be hot and unpleasant, she also felt safe there: "Nobody incarcerated us, nobody really bothered us."[141]

Margie Rosenthal's testimony was recorded for the United States Holocaust Memorial Museum on October 24, 1996. Her given name is Margit Meli Miedzwinski and she was born in Gleiwitz, another town in Upper Silesia, on July 19, 1927. She left Germany en route to the Philippines with her parents and younger sister on board the same ocean liner, the SS *Potsdam*, with the families of Margot Cassel and Ralph Preiss. When asked by her interviewer, Nancy Alper, if "the Filipinos treated you any differently because you were Jewish," she responded:

> No, they treated us very well. I mean to them Judaism didn't mean anything different. We believed in God. They believed in God. The majority of the people there were, anyway, Catholics . . . and they were very strict Catholics. They would go to Mass and they really respected everybody. And therefore, they believed in the Ten Commandments. Honor they parents, love they neighbors. And they really believed in that.[142]

Unlike the families of Juergen Goldhagen and Hans Hoeflein, who were not part of the Jewish Manilaners and lived within the already well-established Christian communities of Manila, and "as was typical of most of the foreign families, did not have much to do with the Filipinos on a social level," the Jewish Manilaner families lived a Jewish life, enjoying a sense of community along with their Filipino neighbors.[143] When asked by her interviewer for her first impressions of the Filipino people, Margot replied:

> Well, the first impression of the Philippine people was one of friendliness and openness. . . . Classmates were by and large very, very welcoming. They taught us their games which we did not know—jumping rope was new, jackstones was new. These were the games that we were commonly playing. . . . There was a great deal of sharing. It is of the nature of the Philippines that if a girl wore something you liked more than likely she would offer to give it to you, which is very much a part of the Philippine culture.[144]

The Jewish refugee children went to school with Filipino children in their Catholic-run parochial schools; boys and girls going to separate schools. In the beginning, the girls attended Santa Scholastica and the boys went to

De La Salle College, where Cantor Cysner began teaching music classes. Margot recounts experiences she and Lotte enjoyed when they advanced to another place of instruction.

> Lotte and I entered the Philippine Women's University at grade three and the things that stand out in my mind were first of all the fact that the teacher taught folklore with math and reading and everything else and then she invited us to tell our folklore and I told Grimm stories. [It was a] way of making us feel part of the group but I don't recall ever feeling deprived . . . I want to reiterate I was never meant to feel less than anyone else . . . we were included in all kinds of cultural events whether it was learning the songs of the country, the dances. I think Lotte and I took to the dances like ducks to water, we loved them. . . . We loved the rhythm, we caught on to them . . . [the] Philippine Women's University had a weekly assembly hall on Friday mornings. We loved to perform, and they loved to see us perform.[145]

Alongside the new friendships formed with the Filipino people, the Jewish community in Manila also offered an anchor to the refugees' lives, assisting them in many ways to acclimate to their new surroundings, whether through classes to learn English, helping them find employment, or providing cultural and recreational pursuits. Hannah describes the diversity of the Jewish community that formed in the Philippines, and the challenges because of that diversity.

> When the refugees came—we were about eight hundred refugees—we also had a rabbi. He . . . had a very hard task because he was a Reform rabbi from Germany. They're not nearly as Reform as the ones in the States. He had many Jews, the Spanish Jews who were very Orthodox; he had the American Jews; he had the Viennese Jews; he had the German Jews; and he had the Reform Jews in the German congregation. It was very hard. Everything was under one roof. . . . It was a nice congregation. . . . They had the life centered around the synagogue.[146]

Many of the refugees lived near enough to Temple Emil and its adjoining Bachrach Hall to which they could easily walk for the afternoon English classes, or for evening socials, for Shabbat services, or for Jewish Sunday school classes. Lotte Cassel recounts memories of community activities among the refugee families.

It was in Malate and we live there for about a year and then a good many of the German immigrants moved to Pasay. And Pasay was a much more livable area. It was near Dewey Boulevard . . . and we bought a house on Progresso. . . . Living on Progresso was a lovely experience because it was sort of a routine. In the morning the bus at Santo Scholastica would pick us up and bring us back again at four o'clock. Then we would have dinner and every evening the whole family and a good many of the other immigrants would walk. This was a daily routine. We would cross Harrison and we would walk down Dewey Boulevard . . . with the Brouwers who were also from Breslau . . . and he opened up a restaurant and a dance plaza. . . . We would sit there, and we could watch the sunset. You could watch the glorious reflection on the water.[147]

Lotte went on to describe the American GIs jitterbugging with their girls, her father enjoying a beer while she and Margot snacked on peanuts and pretzels, calling it "a glorious thing."[148] Lotte also remembers the efforts that went into maintaining their Jewishness, when possible, within their new Philippine colonial lifestyle.

In order for the Jews to be able to eat meat, they imported a *shohet*, which was the ritual slaughterer from Shanghai, a Mr. Hahn who had done this kind of work in Germany. So the community brought him over from Shanghai. And then we were able to have chickens at least because he would slaughter them ritually.[149]

Keeping kosher food laws was only one of the difficulties that observant Jews experienced as they tried to adapt their Jewish culture into their new Asian home. Joseph Cysner became one of the most important elements in helping bring this eclectic collection of nationally and culturally diverse Jews together.

REMEMBERING JOSEPH

The active members of the Jewish community in Manila have very warm memories of Joseph. In December 2018 Margot shared her appreciation for the Jewish life Cantor Cysner helped her find.

My memories of Cantor Cysner are vivid. My cousin Lotte Hershfield and I met him in Temple Emil (our Synagogue before destruction) in

1938/9. He selected the two of us to sing with the choir he conducted for the high holydays. So it was that we were introduced to the liturgy and prayers. My love for this music has remained with me. He taught us the first Chanukah songs, Israeli melodies.[150] Because of his inspiration Lotte and I, aged 8, attended every Friday evening service. During the Japanese occupation, Lotte and I walked to his home twice a week for Hebrew and religious lessons. These were very important for us, they created part of our Jewish identity. He was always friendly even when we let our minds wander. No less was the influence of "Mamenyu," his mother. She gave us warm welcomes and was always interested in our progress. Cantor Cysner helped shape our relationship to the Jewish religion, intellectually and emotionally. Until the liberation of Manila in 1945, Cantor Cysner was a cornerstone of our Jewish lives.[151]

Frank Ephraim and his parents docked in Manila and disembarked from the *Victoria* on March 16, 1939. Frank's monograph, *Escape to Manila*, recounts not only the details of his family's rescue in the Philippines and life in their island refuge but also details the lives of dozens of other Manilaners who made the Philippines their home. Frank remembers the important role Joseph played in all their lives, describing the Cysner home as a haven where Joseph "taught the bar mitzvah students, gave piano lessons, and organized festivities on Jewish holidays." For Frank and for all of the Manilaners, "the Cysner home was more than a house; it was a center of Jewish culture, thought, and music, and above all it provided the refugee children with Jewish resources that their parents could not afford."[152]
One of those students, Jacques Lipetz, fondly remembers Joseph's love of Jewish learning.

> And then I also met several times a week, because he lived nearby, with the Cantor, Joseph Cysner, where I would study Hebrew and Chumash with him . . . and I'll never forget, we even did a little bit of Rashi, because I was getting bored with Chumash, and he said, "O.K. Let me show you what comes next." And I can even tell you what in Rashi we studied. I remember that distinctly.[153]

Ralph Preiss recalls meeting Joseph for the first time at school, "where he became our music teacher." Since the Jewish community could not pay him enough to support himself and his mother, Joseph took another job teaching young boys, Filipinos and Europeans, at De La Salle College.

He found out that I had a good voice, so he made me soprano soloist, even in both, in our temple as well as in the La Salle College, where we sang on certain occasions. . . . He was very pleasant. He knew how to get us to work for him very well. He was very patient also. Somethings I had trouble, and he talked with me well. He did also a one-on-one tutoring. I took piano lessons from him when I stayed in his house in 1943.

Lotte also remembers the very active religious school Joseph conducted, and the sense of community Joseph helped create.

The immigrant community in Manila, the Jewish immigrants, it was an amazingly active and cohesive group. There was Temple Emil, the synagogue and it had Sephardic Jews of Spanish origin. It had the immigrant Jews and it had the Anglo-American Jews. There was a religious school that was run by Rabbi Schwarz and his wife Anneliese Schwarz and Cantor Cysner. Cantor Cysner was a dynamic cantor with a wonderful voice. He was sort of a Pied Piper. The kids adored him.[154]

Cantor Cysner brought together the divergent members of the Jewish community in Manila, uniting them in a revival of Jewish life and learning in the Philippines that has stayed with them their entire lives.

Mindanao, a New Palestine

The new life enjoyed by Joseph and his fellow Manilaners in the Philippines set a precedent for pursuing the potential of a joint American–Filipino–led mass resettlement prospect in the island nation. This massive project was explored through the auspices of the Intergovernmental Committee on Refugees (IGCR), vested by the governing representatives of the Evian Conference. As we will see, after years of exploration and negotiations, the proposed rescue of ten thousand Jewish refugees on Mindanao, the second largest island in the Philippines, was the only nationally sanctioned Jewish rescue operation of its kind in the world.[1] We have already seen how Holocaust historians have reviewed, concurred, and challenged scholarship concerning America's response, or lack thereof, to the plight of Europe's refugee Jews during World War II, indicting politicians, presidents, the press, and even Jewish relief organizers as bystanders-cum-perpetrators complicit in the death of Europe's six million Jews. Historians agree that more could have and should have been done to save Jewish lives, and most have offered a variety of viewpoints as to why it was not done. This research shows that while selective and sponsored rescue in the Philippines operated successfully, plans for massive resettlement of refugees on Mindanao ultimately failed. The success of one and the failure of the other lay in the fact that for many involved, humanitarian rescue was subordinate to other economic and sociologic expediencies.

In addition to rescue by selection and sponsorship, Mindanao in the southern Philippines became one of the more viable sites for a scheme of mass resettlement of refugees to be considered throughout the world in 1939. Its implementation was cut short by the December 8, 1941, bombing of Manila by the Japanese and their subsequent invasion in January 1942. Obstructionism by both the National Assembly of the Philippines and the US State Department to the resettlement plans on Mindanao tragically delayed its implementation until it was too late. President Quezon's generous offer of vast ranches on the island as sites for potential relocation of as many as one million Jews had been greatly slashed by State Department officials and by certain Philippine politicians until a more tolerable number of ten thousand refugees was unanimously supported. The backers of Quezon's resettlement proposal on Mindanao, such as the JRC, McNutt, and assorted Jewish Relief agencies in the United States, heralded the plan as having greater immigration potential than Israel and labeled it a new "Palestine."[2]

REFUGEE RESCUE THROUGH MASS RESETTLEMENT

Various sites for mass resettlement projects throughout the world rose and sank in the years following the initial meeting of the Evian Conference, mostly because the ulterior motives for assisting refugee Jews were not sustainable. All other proposed places of refugee resettlement masked other dubious objectives in accepting a potentially substantial Jewish population. The plan for Jewish resettlement in Costa Rica suggested that it could offer added security at the Panama Canal. Economic advantages spurred suggestions for colonization in the Caribbean, Brazil, and Haiti as American businessmen such as Henry Ford, a self-proclaimed antisemite, and William Randolph Hearst measured rescue from a purely capitalistic standpoint.[3] A resettlement plan for Alaska saw a mass influx of labor as advantageous for that underpopulated and economically stagnated territory. These proposals, and others, ultimately sank into oblivion because rescue was not their primary aim, and economic or political implausibility won out over humanitarianism. One after another these ventures failed to reach fruition. Mindanao was no exception. No matter how altruistic President Quezon may have been in his generous offer, his rescue ambitions stalled disastrously due to political and economic debates among members of the Philippine government, as well as antialien attitudes of certain State Department officials. Ultimately, mass resettlement rescue on

Mindanao failed due to Japan's entrance into the war, which in turn led to war between the United States and Germany that brought all rescue efforts in the Philippines to a halt. Had the plan not been delayed, hundreds if not thousands more Jewish refugees could have found respite in the Philippines.

The JRC in Manila, authorized by McNutt and Quezon, organized a selection plan that listed professionals who could be easily and rapidly assimilated into the Philippine economy. The plan called for this list to be circulated through the Hilfsverein, which compiled applications from refugees for the various professions, then sent them from Germany to the Refugee Economic Corporation (REC) in New York. They procured the funding for the rescue effort from the American Jewish Joint Distribution Committee (JDC). The applications were then forwarded to the JRC in Manila, which was composed of members of the Jewish community. That committee reviewed the applications and all required prerequisites, made selections from the applications, and then gave a list of names, with addresses in Europe, to McNutt for his approval.

After receiving joint approval from Quezon, McNutt would then wire the list to the State Department through the Bureau of Insular Affairs in the US War Department. State Department officials forwarded the lists to the appropriate US consuls in Europe with instructions that the listed persons be contacted, and visas issued for their immigration to the Philippines. Here is where true obstructionism by the State Department could have been exercised but was not. Nor were there any overt objections in any State Department memorandum concerning this rescue effort, although a few State Department officials pressed the exclusionary clauses of the Immigration Laws of 1917, which denied visas to people likely to become a public charge. This level of objection was miniscule at best and never enforced by the consuls abroad. [4]

Another argument supported by some historians concerns the Jewish relief organizations in the United States. It is true with the rescue efforts in the Philippines that infighting did occur with various Jewish relief organizations whose funding was needed to sustain the immigrants until they were financially viable on their own. The JRC in Manila expressed several times to the REC and the JDC that they could take in hundreds more refugees on a faster basis if more money was provided for their initial support. Sadly, before many of those arrangements could be resolved at the funding level, the JRC selection plan and sponsorship program, as well as the Mindanao resettlement project, all came to abrupt ends with the

Japanese attack on Pearl Harbor and the subsequent Japanese bombing and invasion of the Philippines.

If these rescue plans in the Philippines were either to confirm or dispute previous historical scholarship concerning deliberate executive or State Department obstructionism in rescuing Jewish refugees, the history of the mass resettlement project on Mindanao can do both. When it became known that the Philippines was rescuing German refugee Jews, State Department officials approached McNutt to inquire how many more refugees could be admitted and if large numbers could be accommodated in a mass resettlement plan. This seems to go against Wyman's claim that the State Department never intended to save refugee Jews. The Mindanao resettlement project was the brainchild of Quezon, McNutt, and the JRC in Manila. Although many sites for resettlement were entertained by the Roosevelt administration, the Philippines was only one of two considered remotely viable.[5] Unlike nearly all the other mass immigration plans, it actually achieved a ready state for implementation and was the only American resettlement plan that had been accepted by the State Department and by FDR's International Commission on Refugees, having received a go-ahead by all political and funding organizations involved.

That is not to say that certain individuals in the State Department didn't try to impede the project, because they did. And that certainly supports Wyman's accusations concerning antisemitic sentiments in the State Department. Documents show that US officials contended with each other over the viability of Mindanao as a resettlement site. Those in opposition did succeed in altering Quezon's initial offer of giving safe haven to fifty thousand refugees—if not eventually a million—by limiting the number of potential immigrants to no more than ten thousand. But a resettlement plan, which had secured funding to purchase well-established ranch lands on Mindanao Island, came to the same abrupt end as the selection and sponsorship plans when the Japanese brought war to the Philippines.

Indeed, there are accusations by Wyman, Feingold, and others that hold true in the Philippine rescue stories, concerning the presence of antisemitism among some officials; but there is also evidence that others in the State Department had a genuine desire to save Jewish refugees and did all they could to facilitate a workable plan, albeit motivated perhaps by some ignoble intentions. But time ran out, and no one could imagine that Hitler's hate would evolve into the systematic extermination of Europe's Jews. Although Feingold was correct that more could always have been done, Wyman's harsh indictment against FDR'S administration and the various

Jewish relief organizations seems too simplistic and fails to look at the implications of the small stories, such as the actual rescue of refugee Jews in the Philippines, which offer exceptions to his sweeping generalizations.

EVIAN, THE IGCR, AND MINDANAO

Days after an impromptu press conference at the Little White House in Warm Springs, Georgia, on March 25, 1938, when FDR publicly revealed the formation of an international committee to address the Jewish refugee crisis, he remarked in a private conversation on April 4, 1938, that the plan "was my proposal . . . I worked that out myself."[6] At the president's directive, the first intergovernmental meeting on the political refugee crisis opened at Evian on July 6, 1938, to facilitate the emigration of refugees from Germany and Austria. Delegates from thirty-two western countries met at the French resort to establish an international organization to work for an overall solution to the growing refugee problem. Roosevelt chose Myron C. Taylor, a businessman and close friend, to represent the United States at the conference. FDR tasked the US committee of this international agency to do as much as possible through private organizations and groups for the refugees.[7] During the nine-day conference, delegates from all the nations present expressed sympathy for the refugees while offering plausible excuses for refusing to increase their immigration quotas. Thus, the Evian Conference provided little to no relief for the refugees. The failure of the conference to facilitate an increase in options for refugee rescue permeates Holocaust literature to this day.

The only real outcome of this international conference was the organization of the Intergovernmental Committee on Political Refugees (IGCR), which held its first meeting in London on August 31, 1938.[8] The IGCR's main purpose, as stipulated by the resolution adopted on July 14, 1938, was to "improve the present conditions of exodus and to replace them with conditions of orderly emigration," and to "approach the governments of the countries of refuge with a view to developing opportunities for permanent settlement."[9] Still, the committee's pleas to the international community to relax immigration restrictions in order to fulfill its resolution fell on deaf ears, and the IGCR declined into inactivity. Even the United States' immigration quotas remained immutable due to political pressures by congressional restrictionists. Because of the Great Depression, many American citizens also believed that refugees endangered job security and would overburden social assistance programs for the needy. With

the Polenaktion deportations from October 27 to 29, 1938, followed by
the massive destruction of Jewish life and property during the Kristallnacht pogrom on November 9–10, 1938, public opinion, sympathizing
with the refugee issue, prodded Roosevelt to press the IGCR for results.[10]
In his diaries of November 17 and 18, 1938, the Canadian prime minister
Mackenzie King noted conversations he participated in at the White
House with FDR and several dignitaries in which Jewish refugee resettlement was discussed.

> Mr. Myron Taylor, who had special mission regarding the refugees now
> intensified by the treatment of Jews, was brought into the room to discuss
> that matter. . . . There was some discussion on what could be done. . . .
> [The president] did not think he could enlarge the quota of admissions. . . .
> He discussed with Taylor and Lindsay [Sir Ronald Lindsay, British ambas-
> sador to the United States] possible places of settlement where numbers
> could be sent. Spoke of parts of South America. Other parts in other lands
> as yet unpopulated which held promise of development.[11]

With this renewed purpose, the attention of the IGCR focused on several
potential havens of massive resettlement rescue for the growing refugee
problem.[12]

A radio address on November 25, 1938, by Myron C. Taylor, vice chairman of the IGCR and leader of the US delegation to the Evian Conference,
reveals that the director of the IGCR, George Rublee, had been actively
conducting a worldwide search for possible places of settlement.[13] By December 1938, the committee proposed more than fifty different resettlement
projects for investigation.[14] The Philippines, along with Alaska, Mexico,
the Dominican Republic, and Palestine, appeared among the many global
resettlement locations slated for scrutiny.[15] The relocation schemes for
German Jews were contemplated at the same time Joseph and eight thousand other displaced Polish Jews from Germany languished in Zbaszyn
and thirty thousand others suffered in concentration camps in Germany,
all desperately needing to emigrate.

A timeline established by an examination of documents from several
different agencies reveals that the first official expression of the idea of
locating a mass resettlement program in the Philippines came from one of
the Frieder brothers near the end of November 1938. Just three days after
Taylor's November 25 radio address about the worldwide search for resettlement locations, Morris Frieder met with Joseph Hyman at the JDC

offices in New York. The Frieder brothers alternated their residences between Cincinnati and Manila so that one brother ran the Frieder business in the Philippines on site for up to two years while the other brothers remained stateside. During this meeting in New York, which focused on the financial needs for subsidizing the selection rescue plan, "Mr. Frieder stressed the fact that the Philippines might easily become an important resettlement center for German Jewish refugees if it were handled right."[16] In other words, the future rescue of thousands through a resettlement plan depended on the successful assimilation of a few hundred in a selection plan, whereby the Philippines could trust the rescuers in their commitment to protect Philippine national interests.

The Frieders approached President Quezon regarding a larger resettlement plan in the Philippines on December 1, 1938. On December 8, 1938, Herbert Frieder had sent a letter from Cincinnati to Bruno Schachner at the REC offices in New York at the request of his brother Philip Frieder, who had sent him a letter from Manila written on December 2. In quoting the letter from Philip, Herbert Frieder revealed that his brother and members of the Jewish Refugee Committee (JRC) had a luncheon with President Quezon on December 1, 1938. According to Philip's letter, Quezon said he "heartily approved our plan of resettling as many of the refugees as we cared to in Mindanao. He was willing to give them all the land that they wanted, build roads for them, and do everything in his power so that they could reestablish themselves. He intimated that Mindanao is big enough to support as many people as Luzon had, but he would be happy if we could settle a million refugees in Mindanao."[17] Philip Frieder's assessment of Quezon's offer for refugee resettlement on Mindanao described it as "a bigger project than Palestine. The land is more fertile than Palestine, there are more minerals, timber—as a matter of fact, it is the richest land in the Philippines—virgin soil. This is such an enormous proposition that one can hardly visualize the potentialities of same."[18] Philip Frieder further informed his brother that McNutt and Quezon would be meeting on December 3, 1938, to discuss it further on an official level. According to Philip, Quezon wanted to contact McNutt so that he could take it up with the US State Department. Quezon was confident that McNutt would be on board with the program, and he was right.

On December 2, 1938, the same day Philip wrote his letter to his brother Herbert about their luncheon with Quezon, Paul McNutt, having had a conversation with Quezon, radiogrammed a communiqué to Secretary Hull with his assessment of Quezon's intentions. The Bureau of Insular

Affairs transmitted it to the secretary of war in Washington, DC, who received it via translation on December 3, 1938. The cable was then forwarded to the State Department on December 5, 1938.

President Quezon has indicated willingness to set aside virgin lands in Mindanao for larger groups of Jewish refugees who wish to engage in agricultural enterprises of related activities in the development of community life in underdeveloped and practically uninhabited areas. Soil and climate conditions in Mindanao favorable to development of agricultural industries supplemental to Philippine agricultural economy. Philippine National Economic Council about to approve Mindanao colonization plan for Filipinos. It is believed that this program would be materially aided by colonization plan for Jewish refugees through development by organization directing refugee colonization of sources of supply, medical, and hospital and other services near areas. Local Jewish Committee, in cooperation with Refugee Economic Corporation of New York, will submit plan for colonizing refugees in Mindanao for approval of Commonwealth officials. The situation is now such that the larger program for the colonization of refugees in Mindanao can be successfully inaugurated if a message of approval is received from you. President Quezon is anxious that nothing be done which is not in accord with the policies of the United States. I urge your consideration of the suggestion and strongly recommend its approval if the proposal is in accord with established policies. McNutt.[19]

Two important observations about this message from McNutt to Secretary of State Hull should be noted. McNutt fully understood that refugee resettlement meant Jewish resettlement, and he was not afraid to state that. The message also demonstrated McNutt's personal interest in rescuing Jews by strongly urging Cordell Hull to approve the resettlement plan.

While McNutt was transmitting his message to Hull, Joseph E. Jacobs, chief of the Office of Philippine Affairs within the State Department and acting for Under Secretary of State Sumner Welles, composed a cable to McNutt also on December 2, 1938, inquiring about the number of refugees the Commonwealth government of the Philippines had already absorbed — since the State Department was now fully aware of the selection rescue plan in operation — and how many more it felt it could handle.[20] While the formal version of the confidential letter given to the secretary of war for transmittal to the Philippines bore the personal signature of Acting Secretary of State Sumner Wells, an "advance copy" of the letter attached to a handwritten note by Jacobs, dated December 2, 1938, went to a Col. Eager of the US War Department.[21] Apparently crossing communication corridors with McNutt's communiqué, the finalized State Department inquiry of December 5, 1938, reads:

> At the next meeting of the Intergovernmental Committee on Political Refugees, which is expected to be held in London in the near future, a further intensive effort will be made by the powers to find a solution of the German refuge problem. . . . It is believed that the question of how many such refugees the Commonwealth authorities believe could be absorbed annually in the Philippine Islands may arise. If, therefore, the Commonwealth authorities feel that they would care to participate in this effort, the Department of State would appreciate receiving at an early date an estimate of how many such refugees could, within the restrictions imposed by existing immigration laws applicable to the Philippine Islands, be absorbed annually over a period of years. The Department would also appreciate being informed as to the approximate number of German refugees who have come to the Philippines since January 1 of this year and have remained there.[22]

The State Department assured McNutt that Myron Taylor would convey "any statement which the Philippine Commonwealth may wish to make."[23] McNutt's communiqué of December 2–5, 1938, had already disclosed that 205 refugee Jews had arrived and that the local Jewish Committee had cared for their needs.[24] As McNutt had indicated, the Philippine National Economic Council stood ready to approve a colonization plan for Filipinos on Mindanao in an effort to relieve overpopulation on Luzon, and Quezon believed that program could be aided by a colonization plan for Jewish refugees on the island as well.[25] This local resettlement plan of Quezon's for Mindanao, involving both Filipinos and Jews, and offering already allocated redevelopment funds and an organizational structure, demonstrated another motive to humanitarian-inspired Jewish rescue—a plan to use the presence of Jewish refugees as cultural leverage against Muslim insurrection and Japanese exploitation on that Philippine island.

Back on June 6, 1936, Quezon had announced a plan to develop the southern region of Mindanao by systematically resettling Filipinos from the crowded areas of Luzon and Visayas onto tracts of land in the less-populated areas of that island.[26] The Commonwealth government declared huge tracts of lands as public domain and made them available for purchase by foreign and domestic investors. Quezon believed the presence of a white community with hospitals, clinics, and other service professions supplied by European immigrants would further economic and social development of the area, which would ultimately benefit his own people. While this can be technically seen as a prime example of Jewish rescue being facilitated for politically and economically convenient reasons, we should not discount Quezon's humanitarian intentions either. In an extemporaneous speech given in April 1940, Quezon stated: "On no better occasion could we have shown our hospitality than in welcoming to these lands people who have been forced out of their homes."[27] But while Quezon's chief concerns were either for the persecuted Jews of Europe or for the ultimate benefit of his own Filipino people, McNutt had no ulterior motive other than doing the right thing for the right reason.

McNutt relayed to the State Department that the local JRC in Manila and the REC in New York were prepared to submit a plan to Quezon and Commonwealth officials in the Philippines for the colonization of refugees on Mindanao. He believed the settlement of refugees there could be successfully inaugurated if approval came immediately from Cordell Hull. The ensuing message exchanges between the State Department, McNutt, and the REC of New York in the early days of December 1939 exposed an escalating conflict between humanitarian expediency and State Department reluctance.

With McNutt's December 5 radiogram now in hand, Jacobs drafted a reply on December 6, 1938, again over the signature of Acting Secretary of State Sumner Wells, which stated that "there is no objection on policy grounds to the Commonwealth authorities giving considerations to the matter of colonizing in Mindanao refugees from Germany or elsewhere in Europe."[28] However, Jacobs cautioned about avoiding any difficulties for the Commonwealth or for the United States, "which would result if a large number of refugees were hurriedly settled in Mindanao and the colonization plan were found to be unworkable." He stressed the provisions of the immigration laws of 1917 and suggested "it may not be possible . . . to permit a large group of immigrants, which the plan would necessarily envisage, to enter under the conditions peculiar to their situation."[29] Another communiqué to McNutt the very next day advised him to "confer with Messrs. Brandt and Wixon" once they arrived in Manila around December 12, 1938. These two State Department officials had been sent to the Philippines to assist the Commonwealth government in writing the island nation's new immigration laws.[30] Jacob's responses revealed his skepticism for the project. When he informed McNutt that Myron Taylor would convey Quezon's official reply, he was apparently not prepared for the enthusiastic offer rendered.

A few days later, on December 13, 1938, a telegram sent to George Rublee, director of the IGCR in London, signed by Sumner Welles, seemed genuinely more favorable to the plan. It appears that the message was composed by Theodore Achilles, acting chairman of the Departmental Committee on Political Refugees of the European Division, and not by Jacobs, which accounted for the supportive tone of the message. Achilles conveyed that immigration to the Philippines, while governed to a certain extent by the Act of 1917, was "not subject to numerical limitations."[31] Achilles informed Rublee that the Commonwealth government had been requested to consider how many refugees it could absorb annually, and Achilles assured Rublee that more specific information about mass immigration into the Philippines would be available in time for the upcoming IGCR meeting in January 1939. Achilles also stated that large sums of money were available for general development of Mindanao due to the plans of the Commonwealth government to colonize the island with its own Filipino citizens as well. He further explained that the island was sparsely populated and climatically favorable and capable "of supporting a very considerable population."[32] The telegram informed Rublee that the United States had approved of the project and that the State Department hoped to supply more specifics in time for the IGCR meeting. The content of this State Department communiqué composed by Achilles certainly gave an affirmative outlook on mass Jewish immigration to Mindanao.

Meanwhile, McNutt conferred with Quezon about refugee colonization on Mindanao; then he telephoned Welles at the State Department on December 16, 1938, and stated "that President Quezon and the Commonwealth authorities are prepared to admit during 1939 some 2,000 families of Jewish refugees into the Philippines for colonization on the Island of Mindanao, and about 5,000 families annually until a total of 30,000 families has been reached."[33] With this amazing support from the Commonwealth authorities of the Philippines, Mindanao quickly went to the top of the list as a potential haven for refugee resettlement.

MINDANAO AND US STATE DEPARTMENT OBSTRUCTIONISM

These immigration totals, however, alarmed a number of officials in the State Department, and certain men sought to discredit the plan. Apparently, officials within the Office of Philippine Affairs, Jacobs being one, believed that an opportunity existed to settle only a small number of doctors, engineers, assistants, and advisors in the Philippines in conjunction with "their plan for the colonization of Filipinos from Luzon (which is overpopulated) on the Island of Mindanao." These officials "had in mind that . . . a reasonable number, say one or, at the most, two thousand persons might be absorbed in the Philippines over a period of years."[34] The Office of Philippine Affairs, according to Jacobs, did not have in mind that such a large number of families in one year, or the thirty thousand families over a period of about five or six years, could be absorbed. These numbers could have translated easily into one hundred thousand "persons," something Jacobs obviously objected to. A contest of wills over these proposed immigration numbers for settlement on Mindanao was building.

Welles divulged his December 16 telephone conversation with McNutt to Francis B. Sayre, chairman of the Interdepartmental Commission on the Philippines. Sayre was the son-in-law of Woodrow Wilson and a career State Department diplomat who was appointed High Commissioner to the Philippines immediately after McNutt left in July 1939.[35] Sayre related in a responding memo to Welles that he "discussed the proposal with one or two others," Joseph Jacobs being one.[36] Jacobs in turn drafted the memorandum of the conversations between McNutt and Welles, and Welles and Sayre, wherein Jacobs related the opinion of the Office of Philippine Affairs that they "had in mind" far fewer immigrant numbers, as previously mentioned. Jacobs went on to declare that such a large colonization plan as offered by the Commonwealth Officials had a number of "elements of danger."[37] His list of eight reasons why such a venture would be ill-advised contained derogatory tones that denigrated the ability of Jewish refugees to adapt.

Jacobs's arguments stated that climate conditions were unsuitable to white settlers; that a current lack of roads prohibited the convenience of modern travel; that the ability to produce cash crops may not be sufficient enough to appease a European style of living; that there was a questionable ability of white labor to grow tropical products; that the ability to initially finance these settlers until they could maintain themselves by their own efforts was questionable; that the United States really didn't want to inject a "German and white element of this size" into a strictly racially Asian area; that there was a potential "refugee problem of grave proportions" should the resettlement plan fail; and the final objection was that such a "grandiose plan, which would . . . seem to take care of almost one-fourth of all the Jews in Germany" would lessen the interest of other countries of the world in assuming their proper share of the responsibility of rescue. Jacobs's anti-Jewish tendencies were truly revealed when he asserted that the 30,000 Jewish families on Mindanao would appeal "to their co-religionists in the United States to exert their efforts to have our historic policy [referring to Philippine independence] changed. Do we want to add another troublesome group to our stay-in-the-Philippines advocates?" Therefore the official recommendation by the Office of Philippine Affairs, according to Jacobs, was to wait on any stipulation of immigration numbers "pending further study."[38] Jacobs passed his memorandum onto Sayre immediately.

Sayre attached this memo by Jacobs to his personal note to Welles, wherein he had mentioned discussing the proposal "with one or two others." His personal note to Welles characterized Quezon's offer as a "scheme" that was "utterly impracticable" and, if a failure, would ultimately be laid on the State Department's doorstep. He went on to declare that "I am in favor of some such proposal as that contained in the draft telegram proposed by the Philippine Office and attached to its memorandum," referring to Jacobs's recommendation to wait before stating any specific immigration numbers to the Philippines.[39] Sayre then met with Welles and presented him with Jacobs's memo expounding on the inadvisability of white refugee settlement on Mindanao, with his own written opinion on the matter, and with a proposed reply to be cabled to McNutt in Manila. This radiogram to McNutt from the State Department, written by Jacobs, pronounced that "the mere suggestion of such a large number as 2,000 families in one year, and 30,000 families as an ultimate objective—almost one-fourth of all the Jews in Germany—might arouse hopes which later could not be fulfilled, and might deter the other powers, which could better absorb these refugees than the Philippines, from taking as large a quota as they otherwise would agree to take."[40] Jacobs's draft proposed a complete revision of Quezon's original offer, thus countermanding the previous State Department promise of issuing "any statement which the Philippine Commonwealth may wish to make."[41]

Jacobs's suggested proposal for the IGCR Conference reflected a newer, more restrictive representation of the Philippine Commonwealth's stand on the refugee resettlement issue. His proposition allowed for a possible five hundred "able-bodied" professionals in 1939 with an indeterminate number of refugees to follow in subsequent years, provided that the first wave of immigrants to Mindanao proved themselves adaptable to the lifestyle and had procured adequate support for themselves and their families. Jacobs had lowered resettlement numbers in Quezon's original generous offer. The draft further advised that "the Commonwealth government cannot estimate the number of settlers who could thus be absorbed," only that the number "may be large," another prevarication of Quezon's original proposal.[42] When Sayre presented Wells with this draft intended for McNutt and Quezon, along with Jacobs's memorandum detailing his objections, Sayre recounted in his memo of the day that "Mr. Welles read only the draft of the letter to [McNutt], which contained the moderate program which we [Sayre and Jacobs] had in mind. Mr. Welles said that this draft was not satisfactory to him and that he felt that something more positive would have to be done."[43] Jacobs marked the draft to McNutt "not to be used."[44] An obvious difference of opinion existed among these State Department officials regarding resettlement rescue on Mindanao.

Welles advised holding off on any decisions on the program for transmittal to the IGCR until conferences could be held with the REC in New York along with other relief organizations to ascertain what level of financial commitment they were prepared to make for resettling refugee Jews on Mindanao. The State Department in turn requested that McNutt "consult the private organizations concerned as the extent to which they would be prepared to finance the settlement and maintenance of the refugees in the Philippines."[45] Yet another December 17 communiqué from McNutt related the intent of President Quezon to send a representative to the IGCR meeting and that Quezon would, in a few days, send "a tentative plan covering number of refugees to be absorbed and conditions to be imposed."[46] Quezon's plan, revised in anticipation of future provisions in the new Philippine immigration laws being formulated by the National Assembly, offered a newly reduced number, which still exceeded Jacobs's and Sayre's expectations.

A few days passed and Quezon's plan had not yet arrived. On December 21, 1938, Jacobs inquired through the Bureau of Insular Affairs regarding the delay.[47] After being informed on December 22 by McNutt of Quezon's ill health, his much-awaited statement "setting forth the terms and conditions for colonization of Jewish refugees in the Philippines" arrived on December 23, 1938.[48] President Quezon cabled through McNutt that "the Commonwealth government is happy to be able to cooperate . . . in an effort to find a solution of the German refugee problem, which this Government realizes must be approached from broad Humanitarian grounds."[49] He affirmed that the Philippines felt prepared to let the selection rescue plan continue, which had been in operation since May 1938. He also revealed that the selection plan would need to eventually conform to the new Philippine Immigration Laws, which were "now being drafted with the assistance of experts from the State and Labor Departments of the United States Government." Quezon believed they would be able to accept "as many as 1,000 persons annually" under this selection plan.[50] Quezon then detailed proposed stipulations for "refugee settlement on Mindanao and other sparsely populated areas of the Philippines."[51]

1. that a responsible committee representing refugees or acting on their behalf shall submit a satisfactory plan to finance such settlement;
2. that the settlers will agree to engage in subsistence farming and not to grow money crops that now enjoy protection in the American market;[52]
3. that they shall take out naturalization papers as early as possible thereby expressing their intention to become Filipino citizens;
4. that until they become Filipino citizens, they shall reside in the land reserved for them;
5. that the number of refugees to be admitted as settlers shall be fixed for the time being by this Government acting upon the recommendation of the committee in charge of the settlement in course of preparation, having in view the committee's ability to take care of the settlers, provided that the total number shall not exceed 10,000 persons; and
6. that the plan contemplated, and its execution shall be subject to the immigration laws now in force or which may hereafter be passed by the National Assembly.[53]

Quezon's offer to settle a maximum of ten thousand "persons" was markedly smaller than his earlier official offer of thirty thousand "families." Quezon had judicially outlined cautionary conditions for resettlement that mimicked State Department concerns. The State Department conditionally accepted Quezon's proposal, but even with this lowered immigration total, certain State Department officials remained dissatisfied.

Nevertheless, plans were made to open a dialogue between the State Department and private relief organizations to determine how much capital the refugee agencies in the United States could raise to finance the rescue. Achilles related information to Welles on December 30, 1938, concerning a meeting of various national Jewish relief agencies being held in Baltimore on January 20, 1939. The Council of Jewish Federations and Welfare Funds, the agency heading up the meeting, intended to open a drive in

1939 to raise twenty million dollars for relief purposes throughout the world. Achilles suggested that the State Department inquire of the organizations just how much in the way of relief funds they could provide for Mindanao, knowing that a Philippine representative for the IGCR would soon set sail for the IGCR conference. It was imperative to relay that information to the Philippines before his departure.[54]

When word reached the State Department on January 3, 1939, that Quezon's representative would not be able to attend the IGCR meeting later that month, State Department officials grabbed the opportunity to amend Quezon's proposal yet again and cabled a version of an "official Philippine statement" to be delivered at the IGCR Conference, slated for January 26, 1939, on behalf of the Commonwealth government concerning its resettlement plan. The formal directive reflected nearly all of President Quezon's remarks made in his December 23 cable, along with his assessment that one thousand refugees could be admitted annually under the existing selection plan. However, one very telling omission was made—an altered version of Quezon's fifth provision regarding the resettlement plan for Mindanao: "that the number of refugees to be admitted as settlers shall be fixed for the time being by the Commonwealth Government acting upon the recommendation of the committee in charge of the settlement in course of preparation, having in view the committee's ability to take care of the settlers and the consequences of large-scale settlement upon the national economy of the Philippines."[55] The proposal explained the obvious omission of Quezon's offer for settlement of ten thousand refugees on Mindanao as an attempt to "avoid a commitment to a definite numerical figure which experience might prove to be either too high or too low. The American delegate might, however, confidentially mention the figure of ten thousand for illustrative purposes."[56] Therefore, contrary to Jacobs's prior assurance to McNutt that Myron Taylor would convey "any statement which the Philippine Commonwealth may wish to make" in regard to mass resettlement in the Philippines, Quezon's original offer of an eventual rescue of one million refugees had all but been reduced to an "illustrative" amount of possibly ten thousand.[57] Quezon accepted the variations and conveyed his approval of the address through the proper communication channels. His eager willingness to further the cause of the rescue of Europe's refugee Jews, demonstrated by his compliance to State Department alterations in time for the IGCR meeting, is better understood when scrutinized against the history of Mindanao Island itself.

RESCUE ON MINDANAO—PROS AND CONS

An official statement composed by the US State Department for the IGCR described the Island of Mindanao as the southernmost part of the Philippine Archipelago with an area of thirty-seven thousand square miles. It depicted Mindanao as sparsely inhabited, climatically favorable, and believed to be capable of supporting a considerable population—this description derived from McNutt's December 3, 1938, rendition of Quezon's characterization of the island. Quezon's redevelopment plans for Mindanao had been in the works for several years. Consequently, a conference of Philippine officials had convened on October 12, 1938, to discuss the plans by the Commonwealth to develop the island. The Institute of Pacific Relations printed the findings in an effort to illuminate some of the problems of development studied at that conference.

Fred Maxey, executive secretary of the Philippine Council with the Institute of Pacific Relations, described Mindanao as the second largest island of the archipelago but with a population in 1935 of only 1.5 million, 11 percent of the country's total population.[58] Eulogio A. Rodriguez Sr., secretary of the Commonwealth Department of Agriculture and Commerce, estimated that the island of Mindanao could feed 40 million inhabitants with "it's numerous rivers, virgin forests, vast land area, and mineral resources" combined with its "more than 5,000,000 hectares of [untouched] fertile agricultural lands."[59] Rodriguez also revealed that Mindanao's paradise-like qualities were both a blessing and a curse, as it became more imperative to colonize and civilize Mindanao in order to secure it from "invading hordes" seeking to exploit its abundant resources.[60] Understanding the ethnic history of Mindanao helps contextualize these comments as they pertain to Quezon's civic plans for the island.

Catherine Porter, a journalist for the Institute of Pacific Relations in the 1930s and 1940s, wrote dozens of articles covering political, social, and economic issues relating to the Philippines during these decades, drawing attention to Philippine concerns about Mindanao. She also described Mindanao Island as the "second largest in the archipelago, rich in agricultural and mineral resources, which have been barely tapped." But she also revealed that "it has a large Moro population, and in Davao is the largest group of Japanese in the Islands."[61] These two foreign communities in the Philippines, especially on Mindanao, created apprehensions among Commonwealth officials over Philippine rule and future economic viability in the region. In April 1937, Porter related that the Japanese had "entrenched themselves in the Philippines" through their control of hemp plantations on Mindanao. Japanese settlers accomplished this through "illegal leases" procured via various questionable practices that presented "a popular example of the Japanese menace in the Philippines."[62]

> Stories have been rife about land-grabbing in this province, about the illegal means employed by the Japanese to secure leases, and about the threat to the whole future of the country implied in the establishment of this little "Japao," or "Davaokuo," as it is sometimes called in the Philippine press . . . in some cases title has been secured by the marriages of Japanese to native women who are acting within their rights in filing homestead claims. . . . In other cases Japanese resort to the device not unknown to other races and countries, of having a Filipino lawyer or "dummy" secure leases for them.[63]

Japanese exploitation of Filipinos helped them secure controlling interests in the hemp-producing plantations, which provided the greater part of the Philippines' exports for this important cash crop. This presence of a growing population of Japanese settlers on Mindanao presented an alarming situation, which Philippine officials believed could be minimized by the presence of white immigrants to the area. The "invading hordes" mentioned by Rodriguez no doubt alluded to Japanese exploitation and eventual assimilation of Mindanao by Japan if the Commonwealth failed to populate the island with Philippine citizens.

Quezon and others of the Commonwealth government believed a program to settle large numbers of refugee Jews would further help their own plans to resettle Filipinos from the northern areas of Luzon and Visayas, believing that both groups could stimulate the economy in the south and protect the area from Japanese infiltration.[64] The *Los Angeles Times* published an AP article from Washington, DC, on June 4, 1939, that reported the "settlement of tens of thousands of German Jewish refugees in the Philippines to offset the influence of Japanese there."[65] The article explained how both the Philippine and US governments worried over the twenty thousand Japanese inhabitants on Mindanao, who owned "more than 50 percent of the arable land, [and] 70 percent of the abaca production."[66] The Japanese controlled "more than 50 percent of the lumber, copra, hemp, and fish exports, [and] 95 percent of Davao's exports to the United States." The Japanese on Mindanao controlled the only viable exports being exploited on the island at the time and, according to the *LA Times*, they regarded Mindanao "as a vast and potential field for immigration and settlement." The advantage of Jewish settlers on Mindanao appeared to be their anticipated ability "to compete on equal terms with the Japanese and not be utilized by them."[67] Quezon obviously saw the presence of a considerably sized Jewish community in his country as a social and economic asset to guard against further Japanese infiltration. But there was another ethnic population he sought containment of as well—the Moros.

Mindanao was one of three island groups in the country, with Luzon and Visayas being the other two. Luzon, in the north, was home to a vast urban population of Christian Filipinos and other nationalities in and around the capital of Manila. Mindanao, by contrast, was sparsely populated, primarily rural, and home to almost all of the country's Muslim, or Moros, population, which numbered 650,000.[68] Accumulated bitterness between the Moro inhabitants and the ever-increasing Christian Filipino population on Mindanao resulted in an acceleration of violence throughout the 1920s. The Moros rejected Filipino government officials as the United States appointed more and more Philippine nationals to civil service positions on Mindanao after the American takeover in 1898. The creation of the Philippine Commonwealth government in 1935 gave complete control of Mindanao over to Commonwealth officials, a political condition vehemently opposed by the Moros.[69]

Throughout the opening decades of the twentieth century, all western colonial powers with Muslim populations feared the impact of possible Islamic insurrections in their territories.[70] Moro leaders on Mindanao threatened secession from the Philippines if religious guarantees for their Islamic laws, customs, and traditions were disregarded. The Moros were enraged when the Commonwealth government shut down Moro religious tribunals that adjudicated legal matters under Islamic law.[71] As Christian Filipinos from the northern islands continued to settle in the thinly populated areas of Mindanao, tensions grew, and Quezon became anxious to find solutions to issues raised by Muslim predominance in the south. Quezon had made an extensive tour of Mindanao provinces in August 1938 and spoke at many rallies. While speaking in Lanao on the development of that predominantly Moro province on Mindanao, he stated:

> I want you to live peacefully. I want you to work and make this province rich; and I want you to be benefitted by the development of this province. . . . I want you to realize that I am interested in your welfare, that I

have no prejudice against you, that I am not going to favor a Christian Filipino simply because you are against him, that if you are right, I will stand by you, whoever your opponent may be, even if he is my friend. I want you to feel that the Government of the Philippines is your own government, the President of the Philippines your President, and that your President and your Government are anxious to serve you and to improve your conditions.[72]

Quezon's offer for Jewish settlement on Mindanao came just three months after his extensive trip to the area, and he may have hoped that the settlement of Jews on Mindanao would act as a buffer between Christians and Muslims. The possibility that the refugees would merely be going from one type of persecution into another certainly existed, but their usefulness to the overall future of the area, along with their immediate resettlement needs, seemed to outweigh these considerations. Whether Quezon saw the rescue of Jews in the Philippines strictly through glasses shaded with a utilitarian use for the Jewish refugees, it does not change the importance of his efforts to facilitate their rescue, which were not always strictly pragmatic.

In 1939, Quezon gifted his own personal property to the JRC in Manila as a resource for them to further the selection plan rescue of Jews by financing and constructing housing on the site. In an annual accounting sent on February 17, 1940, by Alex Frieder to Robert Pilpel, secretary of the JDC regarding the disposition of their funds in 1939 for the benefit of the refugees in Manila, he reported four rented community houses in operation with "the fifth one in the course of building . . . which is situated on a conveniently located farm owned by President Quezon." Alex further explained that the new communal building "will house forty to fifty persons" who "will work on the farm and so provide themselves with fruits, vegetables, poultry, etc., so that their living costs will be reduced."[73] The facility, Mariquina Hall, eventually accommodated forty refugee families in a farming co-op on a three-hectare (seven acre) farm in Quezon City: in essence, a Jewish kibbutz in the middle of the Philippines.[74] At the dedication of the site on April 24, 1940, Quezon's extemporaneous speech in the presence of several hundred refugee Jews and Filipino dignitaries, politicians, and businessmen declared:

> What a blessing to the Filipinos it should be if we learn from these few refugees who come to these Islands how to make even the rocky land of

Mariquina produce enough quantities to support 40 persons. What a magnificent lesson we can get from that! That would simply mean that the Filipinos have no reason to fear; that if 40 people can raise enough to support them on four hectares, we with a population of 200 million people will be well off, if we can learn to do just that. So I think the Filipinos are going to realize that in allowing these few refugees to come to these islands, we are not only performing a humanitarian act, but we are, in the end, going to profit from this humane act as is always the case. . . . It is my hope, and indeed my expectation, that the people of the Philippines will have in the future every reason to be glad that when the time of need came, their country was glad to extend to a persecuted people, a hand of welcome.[75]

Not only do Quezon's words here confirm his intent of benefitting socially and economically from rescuing Jews, but he alludes to objections and fears within Philippine society regarding the presence of Jews in their country.

Not everyone in the Commonwealth government rallied behind Quezon's policy on rescuing refugee Jews. Emilio Aguinaldo was one such opponent. Regarded as both a Philippine patriot and a dangerous dissident, Aguinaldo incited the Philippine Revolution as a patriot against its Spanish overlords in 1895 and led its armies in conjunction with US forces in the Spanish-American War of 1898. He then proclaimed Philippine independence and established himself its first "president" and commander-in-chief against US hegemony in a three-year Philippine-American War of Independence. On April 28, 1939, Aguinaldo told a reporter of the *Manila Bulletin* his reasons for opposing the plan to admit Jews to the Philippines. In the first place, Aguinaldo professed that millions of Filipinos wanted to settle on Mindanao, and he believed that they should have first preference to the choice areas. It was in his second objection that the age-old rhetoric of anti-semitism raised its ugly head.

Jews are dangerous people to have around in large numbers. By natural abilities, by their temperament, and by their training in business, they have succeeded in predominating and absorbing the people of places they settled. They are by nature ambitious and selfishly materialistic and are not anxious to help the country in which they live. . . . If the Germans, strong, well organized, and well trained as they are in all fields of human activities, find themselves unable to cope with the Jews to such an extent

as to cause Hitler to expel them from Germany, how can we Filipinos expect to compete with the Jews? If cultured highly industrialized, strongly
organized Germany could not stand the Jews, how can we expect primitive
Mindanao to do so?[76]

Aguinaldo's assessment of Jewish "abilities," which he felt endangered Filipinos, were nearly the same virtues that Quezon believed would bless
them.[77] On February 16, 1939, the *Manila Bulletin* published an official
statement authorized by Quezon concerning the admission of Jews to the
Philippines for settlement on Mindanao and reported that

> the policy on the matter declared that those to be admitted not only will
> be selected for their fitness for agricultural life and for their knowledge of
> farm technology but that they will be provided with funds in order that
> they could finance the development of the lands to be assigned them.
> With the knowledge these refugees of modern agriculture gained from ex-
> perience in various nations of Europe they should prove of distinct help to
> Philippine farmers because of the example they will set.[78]

Quezon's enthusiastic support of the resettlement of Jews on Mindanao,
for whatever his reasons, propelled it into the forefront of US intentions to
facilitate an American contribution in relieving the plight of the Jews in
Europe.

THE MINDANAO EXPLORATION COMMISSION

Plans therefore progressed for studying, locating, and purchasing suitable
lands on Mindanao Island for Jewish refugee habitation. At a January 18,
1939, meeting in Washington, Charles Liebman of the REC informed
Philip Frieder, who had just arrived from Manila, his brother Morris
Frieder, Jacobs, and Achilles of the Office of Philippine Affairs, that he
contemplated "sending a mission of experts to Mindanao composed of a
colonizer, a public health expert, an agronomist, an animal husbandry
specialist, and an hydraulic engineer."[79] When Liebman inquired of Jacobs
whether US government personnel could participate in this exploratory
mission, he was advised that "with missions now being formed to make
studies in British Guiana and the Dominican Republic, no assurance
could be given that the Departments concerned would be in a position to
furnish additional experts for a third mission."[80] Although Jacobs "strongly

emphasized" that the Department of State was truly interested in settling the "largest numbers of refugees" possible on Mindanao, but still be compatible with US State Department and Philippine interests, his excuses for noncompliance and "sound safeguards" resembled suppression rather than support.[81] However, prior to this meeting on January 18, 1939, the State Department enlisted the services of Dr. Isaiah Bowman to present his expert opinion on the viability of settlement on Mindanao.

Bowman, then the president of Johns Hopkins University and director of the US Geographical Society, prepared a preliminary report at the request of Theodore Achilles of the Office of Philippine Affairs, which was delivered to George Warren of the President's Advisory Committee on Political Refugees on January 21, 1939.[82] Bowman's conclusions stated that "Mindanao seems to offer sufficient possibilities to guarantee a successful future for selected groups of European settlers."[83] These initial findings determined that the southern island contained 31 percent of the land area of the Philippines but only 10 percent of the total population. The general consensus of Bowman's documentary sources maintained "that Mindanao possesses great agricultural possibilities because of its exceedingly fertile virgin soils." The report further explained that most of the island lies below the typhoon belt, so its climate favored new settlers better than any other location. Bowman claimed that the province of Bukidnon in the north could become "the principal livestock-raising province of the Philippines." The province of Lanao to the west offered plateaus of rich soil for extensive agriculture, and the province of Cotabato to the south, Bowman asserted, could support commercial crops such as coffee and tea.[84] Mindanao continued to get highly favorable reports as a viable site for mass resettlement.[85]

As a result of Bowman's initial report, a Philippine scientific mission formed, under the auspices of the Advisory Committee of Political Refugees, with Bowman as advisor. That scientific mission, the Mindanao Exploration Commission, consisted of five experts who started arriving in Manila during the first weeks of April 1939. On April 21, the commission chairman O. D. Hargis and the other members of the committee, Dr. Stanton Youngberg, Dr. Robert L. Pendleton, Dr. Howard F. Smith, and Captain Hugh J. Casey, began their evaluation of lands in the Philippines for mass refugee resettlement. Hargis, chairman of the group, worked in the agricultural division of the Goodyear Rubber Company and had twenty-five years of experience in the Panama Canal Zone, in Sumatra, Java, and on the island of Mindanao itself. He had specialized in large-scale plantation operations at all these sites. Stanton Youngberg served as director of the

Philippine Bureau of Agriculture from 1925 to 1932 and worked on the staff of the Philippine Governor-General in 1933 as an advisor on agricultural issues.[86] Robert Pendleton came to the commission directly from the US Department of Agriculture. Howard Smith represented the Public Health Service, and Hugh Casey, from the Army Engineer Corps, went as the hydroelectric specialist. This commission of experts spent several weeks investigating all aspects of massive refugee resettlement and its plausibility in the Philippines.

While commission members began arriving in the Philippines, Alex Frieder, now the Frieder brother on site in Manila, notified Liebman in New York of commission members arrivals. After informing Liebman of preliminary meetings he had had with Youngberg and Smith, Alex Frieder happily reported to Liebman in an April 6, 1939, communiqué that President Quezon had made yet another resettlement offer to the committee— "the whole island of Polillo which is due east of Manila." Frieder explained that the island "has an area of four hundred square miles, inhabited by only seven thousand Filipinos."[87] Several aspects of Polillo made it a very desirable site for resettlement consideration.

Emphasizing the fact that Quezon had personal jurisdiction over the island, Frieder quoted Quezon as stating that "he would take great pride in seeing Polillo inhabited by our refugees and if we accepted, he would authorize the appropriation of a sufficient sum of money from the National Treasury for an adequate road system through the island."[88] According to Frieder, Quezon mentioned creating an independent municipality on Polillo with one of the members of the JRC as governor or municipal president. Even more surprising, Quezon related to Frieder that the Filipino inhabitants of Polillo implored Quezon during a recent inspection trip to "divert the settlement of refugees from Mindanao to Polillo as they felt they [Jews] could be immensely beneficial to their [Filipinos'] progress."[89] Frieder further revealed that Quezon believed that "forty to fifty thousand refugees" could easily settle there. When asked if he intended settlement on Polillo instead of Mindanao, Quezon relied that they could consider "both Polillo and Mindanao." Frieder's communiqué to Liebman exclaimed that they now had the "wonderful prospects of settling both Mindanao and Polillo, which enlarges the quantity of refugees who can be settled."[90] While the rest of the world prevaricated over taking in Jewish refugees, Quezon came up with offer after offer to populate his country with Jewish immigrants.

Stanton Youngberg, as commission secretary, informed Bowman via post on April 15, 1939, of their scheduled "inspection trip to the Island of Polillo" the next week.[91] Although Polillo's tropical climate inspired discouraging early assessments from commission members, they wanted to appease Quezon's exuberance over Polillo and consented to a guided inspection tour as "a politic thing to do."[92] Copies of these communiqués concerning Polillo made it into the hand of Jacobs, who commented to Achilles his concern over Quezon's proposal for settling "between forty and fifty thousand refugees on the Island of Polillo . . . [what] white refugees would do there is a bit beyond my imagination. I would not, however, belittle its importance as a possible home for some refugees."[93] However, commission members all concurred, after a trip to the island on Quezon's presidential yacht, that "Polillo Island offers no possibility for the settlement of European refugees."[94] The commission turned its attention to Mindanao immediately following their April 19 excursion to Polillo. Even though Polillo offered no viable opportunity for mass resettlement, it remained open to any refugees wanting to settle there, as were all other potential places of habitation in the Philippine Islands to those who arrived through the selection plan.

The commission members arrived on Mindanao in the middle of May 1939, "making preliminary surveys" necessary in ascertaining "the areas that are neither available nor suitable" for mass resettlement so that they could concentrate their energies on viable locations. Youngberg remarked in a May 29, 1939, report to Bowman that the changes and improvements to living conditions on Mindanao since his last visit there six years prior were "really astounding," mentioning advancements in "road building" and "land settlement."[95] After visiting all the provinces of Mindanao available for settlement and assessing the island with aerial surveillance, a supplementary commission report (issued July 7, 1939) to Isaiah Bowman detailed certain private matters that commission members deemed inadmissible with their final, public report. One such item was the message by Jorge B. Vargas, Quezon's executive secretary, of the growing opposition in Philippine circles to refugee settlement in the Philippines. The report stated:

> Frequent opposition has been expressed toward this settlement in the press and still more often to members of your commission in private, and no doubt more often still by influential people to various members of the

President's cabinet and quite frankly to the President himself. At least we can infer the latter from the statement that Mr. Jorge Vargas, the President's secretary, made to Dr. Youngberg. The general sentiments expressed have been to the effect that the Philippines should be reserved for the Filipinos.[96]

Commission members' apprehensions concerning anti-Jewish opinions among certain members of the National Assembly tainted their expectations for achieving a successful resettlement program on Mindanao.

Alex Frieder, who joined the commission members at a parting luncheon with Quezon in July 1939, reported to his brother Morris in Ohio on the findings discussed at that luncheon and their apprehensions over the rising antisemitic attitudes they encountered. Alex detailed the old rhetoric that was all too familiar, ranging from Jews being "schemers" who are out to "own the Philippines," to the secret brotherhood of Jews who annually find a "Christian child to kidnap and drink its blood."[97] But Quezon's reactions to the several "influential persons" who had voiced these outrageous accusations to him reassured the commission of his resolve to facilitate a peaceful refugee rescue.

> He assured us that big or little, he raised hell with every one of those persons and made them ashamed of themselves for being a victim of propaganda intended to further victimize an already persecuted people; He immediately told us in unequivocal terms that we could have all the land we needed, not only for the 10,000 persons, but for 30 or 50,000 and that he would personally see to it that thousands of hectares more of private leased lands would be surrendered to us by transfer. . . . He again repeated that he could see in this development a distinct benefit to the country as well as a haven for the refugees . . . and he asked me not to be depressed by any subversive rumors.[98]

The commission felt confident that with Quezon's personal assurances for the success of the operation that it could, with "absolute certainty," present Washington with a highly favorable proposal for refugee resettlement on Mindanao. A radiogram from the commission members in Manila to Ernest Gruening, director of the US Department of the Interior, written immediately after their luncheon with Quezon, conveyed a brief summary of their initial findings. They maintained that "several hundred thousand acres" were available for "large scale European settlement" on the Bukidnon Plateau and they recommended "action be initiated looking towards acquirement by purchase of land leases."[99] Commission members left the Philippines the next week to finalize their report stateside prior to its official submittal to the State Department in October 1939.

In early August 1939, officials of the JDC, along with Morris and Philip Frieder, met to discuss the results of the commission's findings. Philip Frieder informed the committee that a 10,000-acre tract of land on Mindanao could be readied immediately for colonization. It contained nearly 3,000 head of cattle along with "large maintenance crops and citrus fruits. It could be leased from the government for 20 to 25 years" for $80,000.[100] Philip further informed them that "300 families now in Manila could be transferred as soon as the barracks are built," estimating that construction would cost another $45,000. Philip maintained that this site could "take care of 600 to 700 families, allowing about 40 acres per family."[101] While all agreed about the importance of the venture, they cautiously deferred any long-range decisions until the October 1939 meeting of the IGCR in Washington.

The official "Report of the Mindanao Exploration Commission," forwarded on October 2, 1939, to James G. McDonald, chairman of the President's Advisory Committee on Political Refugees, summarized the recommendation "that negotiations be undertaken at once" to purchase lands on Mindanao for the "establishment of a refugee colonization project."[102] With report in hand, the committee met on October 13, 1939, and discussed the viable settlement projects still pending. Topics included Mindanao, the Dominican Republic, and Guiana. However, memoranda of conversations between State Department officials prior to that meeting revealed some disturbing sentiments.

Robert Pell, from the European Division within the State Department, was advised by George Warren, the acting secretary for the committee, concerning the upcoming meeting on the thirteenth. Warren expressed to Pell how anxious Dr. Bowman was that the Philippine project be given very serious consideration because Bowman felt that Jacobs, from the Office of Philippine Affairs, "was not very favorably disposed toward the enterprise."[103] Pell then had a conversation with Jacobs just five days later on October 9, 1939, at which time Jacobs expressed his wish not to attend the October 13 meeting because he felt his involvement in the matter did not warrant his attendance. Jacobs's explanation offered recollections of events and conversations from December 1938 that contained some troubling misrepresentations.

PARADISE LOST

Jacobs related to Pell on October 9, 1939, that when the IGCR was hunting for locations for refugee settlement projects in 1938, he, Jacobs, had been directed by Welles to send inquiries to the Philippines per the IGCR's request. Jacobs then stated that the Commonwealth government had replied that there could be opportunity for the assimilation of about one thousand persons total and that Mr. Welles had considered the offer to be inadequate. Jacobs's misstatements did not stop there. Apparently Welles had discussed refugee rescue in the Philippines at a Washington, DC, state dinner party with the Philippine commissioner, where Welles explained "the interest President Roosevelt was taking in this matter and had urged him to inform President Quezon of the interest of the President and to express the hope that a better offer could be made than that of 1,000 persons."[104] Jacobs asserted to Pell that Quezon only inflated the immigration number to fifty thousand when Welles urged Quezon through the Philippine Commissioner to the United States to make a better offer.[105] This was a brazen misrepresentation of the chain of events. Quezon's offer to admit two thousand refugee families in 1939, and then five thousand families annually until thirty thousand or more families had been reached, was deliberately squelched in December 1938 by Jacobs and Sayre. Jacobs neglected to tell Pell that it was he, Jacobs, who had suggested the far more moderate number of five hundred refugees total over many years, to which Welles then responded that it was not enough.

According to Pell's memorandum of his October 9, 1939, conversation with Jacobs, Welles had called Jacobs into a meeting with Sayre to discuss the Mindanao resettlement project.

> Mr. Sayer took a very strong line against the settlement project. Mr. Welles argued back heatedly and there was no definite conclusion. Mr. Jacobs then remarked that in his opinion the settlement of a large number of refugees in the Philippines could not be justified on social, economic, or political grounds. The major question of policy was whether the United States wished to remain in or leave the Philippines. Jacobs said that he believed that the United States should get out, hook, line and sinker. The settlement of *these people*, who would be financed by a New York group, would mean a further call on the United States to stay in the Islands.[106]

Motivations for Jacobs's misrepresentations can be explained by his obvious objections to any kind of refugee rescue in the Philippines that, he believed, would encumber the United States. But his lack of basic human compassion for the fate of thousands of stateless Jews, displayed in his characterization of their rescue as neither socially, nor economically, nor politically expedient, speaks volumes. McNutt and Quezon had constantly urged higher immigration resettlement numbers than the State Department (namely Jacobs and Sayre) wanted to approve.

Pell noted the disavowal of the Mindanao resettlement project by these two State Department officials when he acknowledged to Adolf Berle, the assistant secretary of state, on October 10, 1939, that "Welles had been very much in favor of going forward with a big project while Mr. Sayre and he [Jacobs] had opposed it."[107] Sumner Welles, one of FDR's most trusted advisors and a longtime friend, advanced the project by giving State Department approval. The REC then proceeded with a plan to acquire the existing plantation on Mindanao. Replete with buildings, livestock, and fruit orchards, it was ideal for the initial settlement of about one hundred selected engineers, agriculturalists, and construction contractors who could begin the implementation of the Mindanao resettlement plan.[108]

A preliminary cost estimate, "premised on the purchase and colonization of approximately 100,000 hectares of privately owned or leased grazing lands to be settled ultimately by 10,000 refugees," detailed expenditures such as land and equipment purchases, shelter construction, agricultural costs, and forestry expenses to run a sawmill. The projected grand total for the settlement of those refugees over ten years came to just over six million dollars.[109] Charles Liebman of the REC actively sought co-sponsorship for the Mindanao resettlement project from the Agro-Joint branch of the JDC. The Agro-Joint was an arm of the JDC founded in 1924 to promote agricultural settlements for indigent Jewish farmers in various states of the Soviet Union. Agro-Joint played a significant advisory role during the push for mass resettlement sites for Jewish refugees during the pre–World War II years, as well as providing considerable operational funds and organizational manpower.[110] But Liebman maintained that the REC should be the sole agency managing the distribution of all funds for the "colonization and rehabilitation of refugees" on Mindanao.[111] This became a critical issue over the next two years in the Mindanao resettlement project saga.

After receiving the go-ahead from all quarters, Liebman immediately formulated a budget for the first year of colonization on Mindanao and forwarded the completed projection figures to Youngberg in Manila during the first week of November 1939. While Liebman and the REC actively pushed forward with plans for the eventual resettlement project on Mindanao, JDC officers conversed often in an effort to ascertain for themselves the viability of a successful resettlement in the Philippines. One message from Paul Baerwald, chairman of the JDC, intended for James N. Rosenberg, a board chairman for the JDC, hinted at potential problems over jurisdiction between the different organizations involved:

> Mr. Rosenberg said that no Philippine reports are in the possession of Agro-Joint. . . . It has been fully discussed by the Refugee Economic Corporation, President's Advisory Committee, the State Department, Dr. Bowman, former Governor McNutt, present Governor Sayre and the brothers Frieder. Messrs. Ittleson and Rosenwald are informed, as members of the Refugee Economic Corporation, the matter should have been brought up by me to the J.D.C., but somehow it was not, and one of the reasons was that I wanted Mr. Rosenberg's personal support in the first instance. . . . My hope and expectation is that a substantial sum will be made available to the Refugee Economic Corporation for the furtherance of the Philippine plan.[112]

Following weeks of official inquires and meetings by officials of the REC, the JDC and Agro-Joint, a sum of $100,000 "for the Philippine work" was appropriated by the Argo-Joint in early January 1940.[113]

The REC proceeded with its plans to acquire the plantation on Mindanao, with its buildings, livestock, and orchards, and quickly began the implementation of the resettlement plans on Mindanao.[114] Liebman, of the REC, informed Pell and the State Department on November 29, 1939, that a deposit for the purchase of two pieces of property—the Day and the Worcester Ranches—had been made. He also stated that the central committee of the REC had asked the various countries to gather dossiers on prospective colonists to the Philippines.[115] While waiting to obtain title on the Day and Worcester Ranches, some serious obstacles arose in the National Assembly of the Commonwealth government.

These two properties were owned by the surviving family members of Dean C. Worcester, one of the first Americans to settle on Mindanao and who worked there for the US government for many years. The Day Ranch covered 3,150 acres, of which 2,000 were arable. The purchase of this ranch included 1,400 head of high-grade Indian cattle, twenty-two horses, ranch houses, corrals, and fences. The Worcester Ranch encompassed 8,500 acres, half of which was arable, with a ranch house, 2,700 head of cattle, thirty-eight horses, fences, and various buildings. There was at the time a government lease on the Worcester Ranch, due to expire in 1959. The annual rental of these two properties was considered nominal.[116]

The commission had estimated that these two ranches could ultimately accommodate between six hundred and eight hundred refugees handling cattle ranching, fruits, corn, and vegetable farming. But the transfer of title of those properties became complicated due to certain policies of Philippine landholding laws, which prohibited individuals or corporations from acquiring holdings that exceeded 1,064 hectares (2,629 acres). The National Assembly had set up a holding firm earlier, designated the National Development Company (NDC), which circumvented the landholding laws by acquiring title to large tracts of land and then granting long-term leases to private parties. The REC fully intended to lease the ranches in this manner, with the intent that once the refugees obtained Philippine citizenship, they would purchase their farms as legal landowners.[117] Opponents to the resettlement of refugees within the National Development Company and the National Assembly attempted to scuttle the plan. Ultimately, this opposition would stall the Mindanao project until it was too late for successful implementation before the Japanese invasion.

On February 23, 1940, Youngberg, secretary of the Philippine Exploration Commission and engaged by the REC to be the general manager of the Mindanao resettlement plan, informed Liebman that he had obtained some "disquieting" information that accounted for the "slowness of action on our Mindanao project."[118] The National Assembly was in the process of drafting and passing a new immigration bill. There was "strong opposition to the annual national quota of 1000," which was the proposed number of Jewish refugees to be allowed entrance yearly into the Philippines for colonization purposes. The opposition parties also noted that if Quezon wanted the bill to pass, he had better compromise with a much lower quota number of five hundred based on national origins. When Youngberg inquired from an "old Filipino friend," who had been a member of the Philippine senate, if the opposition stemmed from anti-Jewish attitudes in the Assembly, the retired senator told him "that there is and that it is deep, quite extensive, silent but powerful."[119]

According to the senator, the opposition in the assembly believed that Quezon had acted impulsively when he offered Mindanao lands for a massive Jewish resettlement plan without consulting with the leaders of the National Assembly. Youngberg attached an article with his communiqué to Liebman from the *Manila Daily Bulletin* of February 18, 1940. The article claimed members of the assembly opposed high alien quotas, being "alarmed by prospect of a 'flood of foreigners.'"[120]

> The high-level quotas in the immigration bill now before the assembly's labor and immigration committee, bringing up pictures of a "flood of

aliens," is understood to have aroused opposition within the committee. Informal discussion of the present draft of the bill disclosed alarm at such a quota of 1,000 annually for nationalities affected by the measure. Some committee-men argued that it would nullify the nationalization program, add to the unemployment situation and, after five or ten years, flood the country with more foreigners than could be absorbed. . . . Several committeemen were reported yesterday in favor of either abolishing the quota system altogether or placing the quota at, say, 100 or 200 for each nation whose nationals would be subject to immigration rules. Another provision they propose is that if any quota is established, the immigration commissioner should be given ample power to suspend it if in his opinion further admission of the nationals of a particular country would endanger domestic security or create a problem, social or otherwise.[121]

In light of these views, Youngberg closed his letter to Liebman with his own misgivings about the future of the Mindanao resettlement project, recalling "one of the last admonitions you gave me the evening I left your office was to the effect that we must be sure that we will not create any nasty minority situation for the future. . . . I have begun to believe that the High Commissioner is very likely of the same opinion," who at that time was Francis B. Sayre, one of the original obstructionists to the resettlement strategies for rescue of Jews in the Philippines.[122] Due to unfavorable rhetoric in the National Assembly and among those who viewed refugee resettlement as a violation of Philippine landholding policies, progress on the Mindanao resettlement project temporarily stalled until the final draft of the Philippine Immigration Laws was passed and proponents of resettlement rescue could proceed under the new provisions.

Prior to June 1940, when the National Assembly passed a final proposal for the new Philippine Immigration Act, the island nation had never restricted immigration into the country through any kind of a quota system. This was due in part to the extension of US immigration laws of 1917 to the Philippines, which regulated immigrant selection qualitatively but not quantitatively. After years of "scandalous conditions" in the Philippine immigration offices, which resulted in a two-year investigation that yielded arrests, indictments, and department closures, the National Assembly passed the Philippine Immigration Act of 1940.[123] The act provided a flat quota for the entrance of all nationals in an effort "to make restrictions nondiscriminatory."[124] Originally set at one thousand immigrants per country annually, that quota number was later lowered to five hundred during subsequent assembly meetings. This quota system could have significantly restricted the refugee rescue measures operating in the Philippines were it not for the "humanitarian" clause of the act. This special provision, Section 47, stated that, "notwithstanding the provisions of the Act, the President is hereby authorized . . . (b) For humanitarian reasons, and when not opposed to the public interest, to admit aliens who are refugees for religious, political, or racial reasons, in such classes of cases and under such conditions as he may prescribe."[125] This exception to the quota restriction would therefore allow Jewish mass resettlement on Mindanao to operate as originally planned, rescuing one thousand immigrants or more annually. Few knew the role the Frieder Brothers played in the inclusion of that provision.

> The Commonwealth enacted a quota immigration bill which limits immigration to 500 persons per country annually. However, it empowers the President to permit extra-quota immigration for so-called social and humanitarian reasons. . . . The bill has been approved by the President of the United States and becomes effective January 1, 1941. The Frieder Brothers are satisfied that the refugees will be permitted to come in as extra-quota immigrants, they [Frieders] having been instrumental in securing the inclusion of the provision in the law.[126]

When the *New York Times* reported that Quezon had "signed a bill limiting immigration annually to 500 from any nation," it also noted that political observers believed the quota was meant to limit "unrestricted immigration from Japan."[127] Quezon no doubt hoped that quota numbers limiting further Japanese incursion into Mindanao, along with resettlement programs for Filipino and European colonists would help secure Philippine control of the island in the future.

With this one hurdle to Jewish colonization successfully cleared, all agencies involved in the implementation of the resettlement project on Mindanao resumed their plans. Alex Frieder reported to the board of directors of the JRC prior to his return to the United States in May 1940.

> Both the American and Philippine governments have agreed in principle to a resettlement project in Mindanao for 10,000 refugee immigrants. The Refugee Economic Corporation made possible a thorough and exhaustive survey by a highly competent committee of lands desirable for European colonization. The committee determined upon tracts located in the

Province of Bukidnon, Mindanao. Negotiations with government entities necessarily involve long delays. This has been the condition which we have gone through. But I am happy to state that at a conference this week, all differences were ironed out and that contracts for all land under option to us and contracts for the utilization of these lands will be terminated within a few days. This project, when in operation, should mark one of the great milestones in the history of the resettlement of our co-religionists, necessitated by the terrible Diaspora of the Twentieth Century.[128]

Days turned to weeks and weeks turned to months as endless delays and negotiations, along with the impending national elections in the Philippines, diverted attentions elsewhere.

An August 13, 1940, letter from Kenneth Day, co-owner of the ranches on Mindanao, to his friend Richard Ely in the Bureau of Insular Affairs attested to the problems arising in the acquisition of his properties. Day related how just after the papers had been signed and he was about to be paid, lawyers halted the transaction until "the question of transferring Philippine lands to foreign owners" could be settled. Important and powerful members of the National Development Company (NDC), the government corporation that served as "landlord" over large tracts of leased lands, "were not kindly disposed towards the project."[129] They managed to stall the transaction for the acquisition of the Day and Worcester Ranches by the REC for many months, until Quezon finally stepped in after his re-election in 1941, with enough new political clout to demand the NDC finalize the contracts.[130] But, as the saying goes, it was too little too late.

Everything had been ready to go. The combined monies of the REC and the Agro-Joint, which amounted now to $200,000, had been sitting in accounts, waiting to be dispensed. State Department officials no longer worked at trying to dissuade their superiors from enjoining the resettlement plans.[131] Names of the first one thousand colonists had been selected and approved, and the JRC stood ready to request their visas.[132] As late as November 10, 1941, plans for refugee resettlement in the Philippines continued:

Negotiations with the Philippine government have been going on for a long period due to the fact that the new immigration bill was pending in the Philippine Legislature.[133] With the passage of the bill, negotiations were resumed as to details, and recently President Quezon instructed the officials of the Immigration Department to follow through on the contract, and at the present time the various details are being discussed. It is expected that in a comparatively short time all outstanding questions will be resolved. However, the increasing gravity in the Far Eastern situation has naturally raised certain questions as to whether it would be desirable to undertake the settlement project at this time.[134]

No one knew that within a month the ability to bring Jewish refugees into Mindanao would be forever lost when the Philippines were occupied by Japanese forces.

Mindanao was the last hope for a mass resettlement strategy aimed at aiding the tens of thousands of Jewish refugees victimized by Nazi Germany. Hitler's plan for massive Jewish deportation mutated into one of extermination, implemented from late 1941 until the end of the war. With the failure of the West to provide a successful mass rescue operation for Europe's Jewish population, "thousands of Jews entered the cattle cars bound for Auschwitz, under the impression that they were being resettled in the East."[135] An irony of the "Final Solution" lies in its reflection of the western world's failed attempts at rescue through resettlement. "The decision to murder followed directly from the failure to resettle."[136] Indeed, Hitler mentions this failure of the West to take in Jewish emigrants as rationale for Nazi policies against Jews in his infamous January 30, 1939, Reichstag speech.

It is a shameful spectacle to see how the whole democratic world is oozing sympathy for the poor tormented Jewish people but remains hard-hearted and obdurate when it comes to helping them—which is surely, in view of its attitude, an obvious duty. The arguments that are brought up as an excuse for not helping them actually speak for us Germans and Italians.[137]

Mindanao joined the long "shameful" list of resettlement plans considered at one time by the international community that had failed to materialize. But its failure does not diminish the intentions of President Quezon to provide a haven for thousands of persecuted Jews in dire need of sanctuary. On March 14, 1939, Jorge Bocobo, president of the University of the Philippines and soon to be secretary of public instruction, addressed an audience of Manilaners at a gathering of the Jewish Junior League.

It is a most striking fact that the Philippines is probably the first country to make an offer for a planned, large-scale settlement of Jewish refugees from Germany. While other democratic nations have been willing to help the persecuted Jews of Germany, nevertheless their established national policies as expressed in their immigration laws do not permit them, for the present at least, to admit Jewish immigrants in large numbers. . . . But the situation calls for immediate action in order that the Jews in Germany may at once be delivered from the clutches of oppression. So, the Philippines has come forward to give an example to other democratic countries for a liberalization of immigration laws.[138]

The Philippines was the first country to offer a safe sanctuary for Europe's refugee Jews, and even though the resettlement rescue plan was never fully implemented, the Filipino people can be proud of their nation and their president for stepping up to do what other nations of the world would not.

First page of Cantor Cysner's memoir written in German while in Zbaszyn, Poland, recounting his deportation experiences in the Polenaktion of October 27–29, 1938. Cantor Joseph Cysner Collection. Courtesy of the Jewish Historical Society of San Diego.

A rare photograph taken during the internment of refugee Jews in Zbaszyn, a Polish border camp, ca. 1939. The pictured wedding couple, Max and Rosi Schliesser, were from Bamberg, Germany, also Joseph's hometown. They sent this photo to their cousins the Naglers in Bamberg, with a message of "Comfort and Remembrance" noted on the back. Joseph, standing behind Max and Rosi, performed the marriage along with Rabbi Erwin Zimet (*left*) of Berlin. Rosi's uncle Richard is on the right. Cantor Joseph Cysner Collection. Courtesy of the Jewish Historical Society of San Diego.

This telegram from Manila, dated November 22, 1938, and sent to Hamburg, reached Cantor Cysner in Zbaszyn and requested his services as cantor for the Jewish Community of Manila in the Philippines. Telegram reads: "Do you want to come? Modest Salary. Side jobs provided. Wire Manila today. Send response. Heartfelt greetings. Schwarz." Cantor Joseph Cysner Collection. Courtesy of the Jewish Historical Society of San Diego.

This beautiful cover piece of the testimonial presented to Cantor Cysner when he left
the detainment camp at Zbaszyn was created by fellow refugees in watercolors and is a
rare piece of Holocaust art. The Hebrew in the center reads "Tzion" (Zion). Cantor
Joseph Cysner Collection. Courtesy of the Jewish Historical Society of San Diego.

The interior of this testimonial from Zbaszyn bears the signatures of the council members of the camp. They herald Cantor Cysner's contributions to the overall well-being of Zbaszyn prisoners, adults and children alike, who benefited from his talents and kind administrations. Cantor Joseph Cysner Collection. Courtesy of the Jewish Historical Society of San Diego.

Top right: The Jewish Temple Emil in Manila, April 1940. Next to it on the right side of the photograph is the community center, Bachrach Hall. Both the temple and the community center were demolished by the Japanese during their occupation of the Philippines in World War II, making it the only Jewish synagogue on American soil destroyed during the war. Cantor Joseph Cysner Collection. Courtesy of the Jewish Historical Society of San Diego.

Bottom right: The exterior portico of Temple Emil. The temple was located on the west side of Taft Avenue just north of San Andres Street, approximately where Marc 2000 Tower, 1973 San Andres Street, is today. Cantor Joseph Cysner Collection. Courtesy of the Jewish Historical Society of San Diego.

Interior of Temple Emil, ca. April 1940. Cantor Cysner is standing on the bimah, the raised platform, between the Torah Ark behind him and the Torah Lectern in front of him, officiating at the bar mitzvah of three young men from the congregation. Cantor Joseph Cysner Collection. Courtesy of the Jewish Historical Society of San Diego.

Cantor Cysner with Jewish refugee children in Manila dressed in their costumes for the celebration of their Purim festival, which commemorates the Jewish Queen Esther saving her people from the plot to kill all the Jews by Haman, the royal vizier of her husband, the Persian king Ahasuerus. Cantor Joseph Cysner Collection. Courtesy of the Jewish Historical Society of San Diego.

Cantor Cysner with his students from De La Salle College, a private Catholic school for boys. We know this was taken before the Japanese occupation because we see Filipino children in company with Jewish refugee children and others of different ethnic communities from Manila. Cantor Joseph Cysner Collection. Courtesy of the Jewish Historical Society of San Diego.

The Temple Emil congregation calendar of planned events for fiscal year 1941–42, which was interrupted by the Japanese invasion and occupation of the Philippines in January/February 1942. The members of the community who served on the board of directors are named. Cantor Joseph Cysner Collection. Courtesy of the Jewish Historical Society of San Diego.

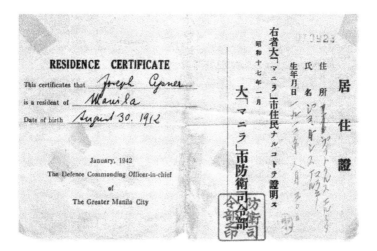

Cantor Cysner's Philippine residency card, issued by the Japanese and dated January 1942, showing his status as a civilian enemy alien in the occupied "Greater Manila City." Cantor Joseph Cysner Collection. Courtesy of the Jewish Historical Society of San Diego.

Cantor Cysner's STIC meal tickets from February and March 1942, which show that
he was living in the gymnasium of Santo Tomas Internment Camp (STIC) during the
first several months of the Japanese occupation of the Philippines and the internment
of civilian enemy aliens. Cantor Joseph Cysner Collection. Courtesy of the Jewish
Historical Society of San Diego.

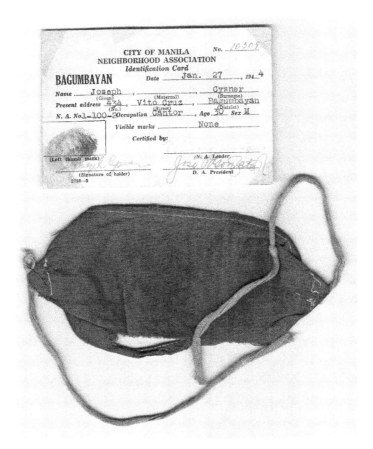

Cantor Cysner's red internee armband issued to him by the Japanese, signifying that he was on release from Santo Tomas Internment Camp (STIC) and was registered as a civilian enemy alien allowed to live outside camp and to resume his profession as cantor for the Jewish Community in Manila. Cantor Joseph Cysner Collection. Courtesy of the Jewish Historical Society of San Diego.

Cantor Cysner standing in the middle of American GIs who attended Sunday Services on July 29, 1945. Cantor Joseph Cysner Collection. Courtesy of the Jewish Historical Society of San Diego.

The High Holy Days, September 1945, were held in the damaged Rizal Stadium before an audience of several hundred military personnel. Cantor Joseph Cysner Collection. Courtesy of the Jewish Historical Society of San Diego.

Attendees at the High Holy Days held at Rizal Stadium in September 1945, taken on the evening of Kol Nidre, which is both the opening prayer and the name of the service that begins Yom Kippur. Cantor Joseph Cysner Collection. Courtesy of the Jewish Historical Society of San Diego.

Chaplain Levy (*left*) and Cantor Joseph Cysner conduct the first prayer at the memorial service for the reconstruction of Temple Emil, November 9, 1945. Cantor Joseph Cysner Collection. Courtesy of the Jewish Historical Society of San Diego.

American GIs in the ruins of Temple Emil on November 9, 1945, commemorating the anniversary of Kristallnacht by dedicating the site for the reconstruction of the synagogue. The US Armed Forces in the Philippines raised $15,000 for the project. Cantor Joseph Cysner Collection. Courtesy of the Jewish Historical Society of San Diego.

Left to right: Chaplain Levy, (unknown), Rabbi Schwarz, Chaplain Weinberg, (unknown), Cantor Cysner, and Chaplain Nussbaum, all of whom conducted the memorial service in the remains of Temple Emil on November 9, 1945. Cantor Joseph Cysner Collection. Courtesy of the Jewish Historical Society of San Diego.

GIs Chip In for Synagogue
Manila Temple to Be Rebuilt

By DARRELL BERRIGAN
N. Y. Post Far East Editor
(Copyright, 1945, New York Post)

Manila, Nov. 10—Gentiles and Jews gathered last night in what is left of the only synagogue in the Philippines to inaugurate a campaign to reconstruct the gutted temple.

American soldiers of all faiths crowded into the roofless building and overflowed into other rooms and onto the street. Donations for the synagogue, which will serve as a memorial to the Jews killed in the Philippine campaign, came from Negroes, Catholics and Chinese as well as Jews. All who donated, whatever their faith, became lifetime honorary members of the synagogue.

Jewish GIs chose Nov. 9 for the ceremony because on this date seven years ago Hitler burned Germany's synagogues.

Wanting to do something for the Jewish community here, which numbers about 1,100, the GIs de-

Exit 'Summer'

Indian Summer was staging what appeared to be its finale today as clouds hovered over New York and the Weather Bureau forecast a mercury drop to 40 degrees tonight.

cided on restoration of the synagogue as more important at present than food. Engineers swept the area for mines, electricians set up lights and a microphone, carpenters built the altar, and other servicemen cleared debris from the synagogue.

New York Post article from November 10, 1945, reports on the memorial held in the Philippines to rebuild the Manila synagogue and how US Army Engineers swept the area for mines and cleared the debris for the event. Cantor Joseph Cysner Collection. Courtesy of the Jewish Historical Society of San Diego.

Japan and Europe's Refugee Jews

The Japanese attack on Pearl Harbor propelled the reluctant United States into World War II and ended all refugee rescue operations in the Philippines, launching another era of terror and deprivation not only for the Jewish refugees from Europe but for their American Jewish benefactors as well. The invasion of the Philippines by the Japanese in January 1942 and the subsequent fate of the rescuers and those rescued under Japanese occupation begs contextualization within the unusual political relationship of Germany and Japan. The Jewish German refugees feared antisemitic reprisals from the conquering Japanese military, patterned after the Nazi-invoked violence against the Jews in Europe. What influence, if any, did Nazi anti-Jewish propaganda have on the Japanese? As unlikely allies as Japan and Germany appeared to be, understanding the diplomatic history of these two fascist states provides important perspective to the handling of the "Jewish question" during the war by Germany's Asiatic ally, which impacted Joseph and the hundreds of other Jewish refugees in the Philippines. Some Japanese journalists linked international economic Jewish hegemony to American capitalism, which then justified Japan's war with the United States as it attempted to save Asia from the so-called evil designs of American-led world Jewry. But another more utilitarian aspect of Japanese antisemitism lay in its once intended exploitation of world Jewry's perceived financial syndicate to Japan's advantage. This evolved into a variant antisemitism known as "philosemitism," a form that found fertile ground in certain circles of the Japanese hierarchy.[1] Marvin Tokayer and Mary Swartz, in their book *The Fugu Plan: The Untold Story of the Japanese and the Jews during World War II*, summarize the ambitions of an ultranationalist faction of Japanese militarists, industrialists, and politicians that conspired to manipulate an imagined world confederacy of Jewish financial houses into granting millions of dollars to Japan's development designs in Manchuria.[2] The accompanying proposed "Fugu Plan" would involve a mass relocation and resettlement scheme taking advantage of the already persecuted and stateless German Jews. The details of this conspiracy and its impact on the rescued Jewish refugees of the Japanese-occupied Philippines are outlined in subsequent sections in this chapter.

A complete reversal of fortune occurred in the Philippines, when the Japanese imprisoned all noncombatant civilians from countries at war with Germany and Japan, leaving all other civilians alone, namely, those Jewish refugees with German and Austrian passports. The irony, of course, is that the Nazis saw all Jews as Germany's greatest enemy, but the German and Austrian refugee Jews were ignored by the Japanese. They were considered allies, while the refugees' American and British benefactors were interned as enemy aliens. Joseph, who was born in Germany but carried a Polish passport, was also incarcerated by the Japanese. His experiences with the Japanese occupation, internment at Santo Tomas, and conditional release fall within the historical context of other civilian experiences under Japanese occupation in the Philippines. Incidents of torture, abuse, and systematic starvation abound during the three-year occupation by the Japanese. Attempts by Nazi party leadership in the Philippines to persuade their Asian allies of the necessity to intern the German Jews as enemy aliens as well fell on deaf ears. The Japanese could not be swayed by the Nazis to establish a Jewish ghetto in Manila. These two militaristic regimes shared little respect for each other, either politically or culturally, although that had not always been the case in the wider picture of their foreign relations.

JAPAN AND GERMANY: UNLIKELY ALLIES

Official diplomatic dealings between the two nations date back to January 24, 1861, as a result of the Prusso-Japanese treaty. When faced with Western imperial expansionism, Japan sought to make the most of its compulsory leap into modernity by seeking the services of Europe's finest and most advanced technicians. Using Germany as their "model of modernization," the Japanese employed more than three thousand foreign advisors, known as the *oyatoi gaikokujin* (hired foreigners). The Japan of the Meiji period hired German agriculturists, medical and natural scientists, administrators in law and economics, military advisors, mathematicians, engineers, and people versed in the liberal arts and humanities. Japan also fashioned its 1889 constitution after the Prussian model.[3] This brief apex of German-Japanese relations fell sharply with the advent of the first Sino-Japanese War of 1894–95, when Germany joined Russia and France to protest Japan's war of expansion in China. Called the "Triple Intervention," European interference in Asiatic affairs ended Japan's philo-Germanic tendencies.[4] Further insult was made by the kaiser's use of the discriminatory slogan, "Yellow Peril," which slandered Japan while he was seeking to facilitate a rapprochement with Russia, and thus Japanese acrimony toward Germany festered for years to come.[5]

Germany's own expansion plans in Asia added more fuel to Japan's already simmering resentment against its mentor. In 1897, Germany announced Weltpolitik, its new imperialistic foreign policy aims, which was formulated to promote Germany as a key player on the world stage of empires.[6] Seizing on an incident against Catholic missionaries in Shantung, the German Imperial Navy occupied Kiao-Chow Bay in November 1897. In an effort to defuse any kind of action that could be viewed as an invitation to war, the Western powers conceded Germany its newly acquired Chinese port, much to Japan's chagrin.[7] As tensions rose between Tokyo and St. Petersburg, Germany exploited the situation in February 1904 by encouraging a Japanese attack on the Russian naval base at Port Arthur (now Lushun, China). Hoping it would keep "Tsarist Russia busy in East Asia," Germany envisaged that this Russo-Japanese War would sufficiently weaken Russia for years to come, thus neutralizing any future military ambitions westward.[8] Tables turned as Japan's subsequent victory over Russia in Manchuria gave Japan new leverage in its own imperialistic ambitions in Asia.

Germany's international position declined when Britain and France ended their Asiatic colonial disputes with a détente that did not include Germany. When the World War I victors stripped the defeated Germany of its colonies abroad and its territories at home, postwar burdens of moral guilt and financial reparations crippled that country's ability to negotiate in the international arena for years to come. Japan, once considered by Germany an inferior power in international matters, now eclipsed its former exemplar. However, in its postwar years, Japan realized that it lagged behind in military technology and, once again, turned to its one-time tutor with secret negotiations for Germany's military expertise, thus setting the stage for renewed diplomatic relations between these unlikely allies.[9]

Germany's eventual acceptance into the League of Nations in 1926 improved relations once again between Berlin and Tokyo. But Japan's fascination for the culture of the Weimar Republic was not reciprocated as German society showed little interest in Japanese traditions, which soured diplomatic relations between them once again. As the Weimar's democracy came under internal attack from the political extremes of the right and the left, Japan's military capitalized on its own anarchy at home and instigated a surprise occupation of Manchuria for its natural resources. Both nations came under totalitarian regimes with imperialistic goals, which heightened diplomatic caution in each nation.[10]

Hitler's racist ideology that claimed white Aryan supremacy over the "culture-bearing" and "culture-destroying" races of the world was regarded by the Japanese as little different than the kaiser's "Yellow Peril" slurs hurled decades earlier.[11] Germany's foreign ambitions that favored trade relations with China as vital to its Asiatic strategy now aggravated Japanese and German tensions. Japan viewed Germany's swap of military supplies to Chiang Kai-shek in exchange for Chinese raw materials for armament manufacturing as Western interference in Asian concerns. It was acceptable for Japan to benefit from German military expertise but not for Germany to offer its capabilities to China, Japan's nemesis in the region. However, the overtures of German officials in seeking a bilateral anti-Soviet arrangement with Japan were infinitely more attractive.[12]

The German-Japanese Anti-Comintern Pact, signed in Berlin on November 25, 1936, was aimed directly against the Soviet Union. In March 1919, leading members of the Communist Party in Russia founded the Communist International (later known as Comintern). The organization's aim was the overthrow of the international bourgeoisie and the creation of an international Soviet republic. The Comintern gained strength during the 1920s, but its efforts to foment revolution, notably in Germany, were unsuccessful. Although the Anti-Comintern Pact ostensibly protected the world from the Communist International, Germany and Japan secretly agreed that if either power became involved in a war with the Soviet Union, the other must remain neutral. They also agreed not to enter into any kind of treaty with the Soviet Union that was not in accord with the Anti-Comintern Pact.[13] No sooner had the ink dried sealing the provisions of the pact, when Japan attempted to bring China into an anticommunist accord as well. Japan's pressures on China jeopardized Germany's highly favored trade relationship with that country and created a political conundrum for the Third Reich—Who would Germany support in the event of another Sino-Japanese War? Germany's worst fears in the matter came to the fore with the onset of the second Sino-Japanese war in July 1937.[14]

Japan's abrupt move against China jeopardized its German ally's own interests in the region, and it was remarkable that Germany still continued to favor an alliance with Japan—even seeking to expand certain provisions of their pact. The addition of Italy in November 1937 as a junior partner into the Anti-Comintern Pact with Japan and Germany encouraged both Mussolini and Hitler to see the possibility of redirecting the provisions of the pact into an anti-Western powers treaty rather than solely an anti-Russian directive. After repeated attempts to broker some kind of cessation of hostilities between the warring factions of China and Japan, Germany was left with no other option but to choose one over the other: trade with China that served its war industry at home, or the anti-Soviet alliance with Japan.[15] Kurt Bloch's 1938 article in the *Far Eastern Survey* of the Institute of Pacific Relations, "German-Japanese Partnership in Eastern Asia," implied that a win for Japan in the Sino-Japanese War ensured that "Germany [could] reenter the Chinese market as Japan's ally."[16] Thus Germany's choice of Japan over China could still allow Germany to continue its war-industry trade with China—or so Germany hoped. Hitler's new Asian policies, which openly recognized the Japanese puppet state in Manchukuo, occurred almost simultaneously with the Anschluss: Germany's 1938 annexation of Austria and its invasion of Czechoslovakia.[17]

Japan began to lose its advantage in the Sino-Japanese War and redirected its foreign policy in an anti-Western direction by aggressively turning toward southern China, bringing Japan into repeated conflicts with British, French, and American interests in that region. As Germany sought to expand its borders in Europe, Japan looked to do the same in East Asia, both butting up against the same Western powers. This resulted in German and Japanese government factions arguing over proposed changes to the Anti-Comintern Pact. Japan looked into certain conditions that would broaden future military actions against the West, which Germany declined to accept. The German-Russian Nonaggression Pact, also known as the Molotov-Ribbentrop Pact, signed in August 1939 on the eve of World War II was the kiss of death for the Anti-Comintern Pact, resulting in political and military upheavals in Japan.[18] Cabinet and consular resignations within the Japanese Empire, all resulting from the failed negotiations with Germany and that country's new alliance with Japan's archenemy Russia, crippled what little amiable accord may have existed between the two fascist regimes.[19] When the Japanese Army later sought a renewed German alliance with a specific aim against Britain and the United States, the new Japanese government, at odds with its army, worked to end hostilities in China through peaceful arrangements with the same Western powers. Efforts to pull Japan back into an anti-Western alliance with Germany met with staid resistance until relations with Japan and the West once again collided in China.[20]

In January 1940, when a British blockade cruiser boarded a Japanese ocean liner and forcibly removed German nationals (known as the *Asama Maru* incident), it triggered renewed negotiations between Germany and Japan, just as Japan had established a puppet government in Nanking over British and American objections. In order to advance its own imperialistic designs against the West, Germany stirred up anti-American sentiments in Japan, hoping to enlist a Japanese alliance against the Western powers it had so tenaciously sought.[21] Then Germany stunned the world with its victory over France and its march into Paris in June 1940. Sensing that the tables had turned, Japan now actively sought an alliance with Germany, recognizing that Germany now controlled French and Dutch colonial holdings in Asia. Dangling French Indochina in front of the covetous Japan, Germany set a high price on its Asian-market accessions. With the installation of a new cabinet sympathetic to Japan's militaristic agenda, Japan now moved closer to acquiescing to German interests.[22]

A July 1940 conference in Berlin between German and Japanese dignitaries revealed the full scope of Germany's intentions in binding Japan into a new alliance "to deter the United States from interfering in the last stage of the war in Europe and the expected postwar settlement."[23] Asking for Japan's military support in a war with Britain, Germany felt certain that this would keep the United States at bay. A Japanese counteroffer expressed these sentiments while proposing other concessions that tied up British interests in East Asia and afforded Germany its raw materials so vital to its war effort. Battling Japanese factions that pitted pro-German militarists against distrustful Japanese cabinet members resulted in another collapse of the Japanese government. The prevailing Japanese militarists moved Japan quickly toward the Axis coalition, which the pro-German faction heartily desired.[24]

Over the next several weeks of July and August 1940, Germany turned the tables on Japan and now waltzed around negotiations for the Tripartite Coalition, feeling secure in its expectation of a speedy win in the Battle of Britain without Japanese assistance. Japan interpreted Germany's stalling actions as indicative of a future postwar "new world order" that would leave Japan bereft of spoils. Feeling an urgent need to secure its own self-interests in East Asia, Japan pushed south into French Indochina, securing German acquiescence in a fait accompli. This, along with a waning British front and hints of Japanese treaties with Western powers, spurred Germany into quickening its steps toward a three-power treaty between Germany, Italy, and Japan.[25]

The Tripartite Pact of September 1940 tied Germany, Italy, and Japan into a coalition of totalitarian regimes, which felt itself fated to command a new global world order. It became immediately clear that the signers of the pact implied one overarching, silent intent with each articulated provision—nullification of American interference in their expansionist plans. At that time neither Germany nor Japan wanted to engage the United States in war; both felt that the formation of this alliance accomplished that aim. Cloaked in the public verbiage of world peace from orations emanating from Tokyo and Berlin lay both the anti-American enmity of the Japanese and the antisemitic hatred of the Nazis. Within a year, Germany launched its invasion of Russia, and Japan attacked American harbors and bases in Hawaii and the Philippines. So much for keeping the United States out of the war.[26]

NAZI ANTISEMITISM VERSUS JAPANESE "PHILOSEMITISM"

During those decades of convoluted negotiations between Germany and Japan leading up to the Tripartite Pact of 1940 and Japan's bombing of Pearl Harbor near the end of 1941, what role, if any, did the Jewish question play in it? As the occupying force in the Philippines for three years, did Japan adopt any of the antisemitic practices championed by Nazi party adherents in Manila, whom Japanese delegates and military personnel must have encountered? We have already seen that Japan and Germany had had an on-again/off-again diplomatic rapport for nearly a century preceding the 1941 invasion of the Philippines. A closer look at the heart of the "student-teacher" relationship that Japan favored with Germany in the last decades of the nineteenth century reveals that significant contributions to Japan by

German scholars, scientists, and technicians originated from *Jewish* German mentors.

The exact number of Jews in the *oyatoi gaikokujin* (hired foreigners) teams of alien advisors may never be known, but perhaps the greatest and most influential German-Jewish advisor to the modernization of Meiji Japan was (Isaac) Albert Mosse. A Prussian-born German judge and legal scholar, he advised Prime Minister Prince Ito Hirobumi in 1882 that the Prussian Constitution lent itself as a perfect model for the Japanese style of monarchy. Mosse served in Japan as a foreign advisor giving invaluable assistance to the drafting of the 1889 Meiji Constitution. So well loved was he in Japan that he lived there until 1890, fulfilling many government advisory positions and being awarded the prestigious Order of the Rising Sun by the emperor. Other Jewish-German advisors also left legacies of friendships and contributions that should not be underestimated in the overall scheme of Jewish-Japanese relations during World War II.[27]

That being the case, understanding the history of Japanese and Jewish interaction in the first decades of the twentieth century becomes even more important. In 1904, when Japan stood on the verge of losing its war with Russia, a chance dinner meeting in London between Takahashi Koreckiyo, Japan's financial commissioner, and Jacob Schiff, an American international banking mogul, significantly changed the balance of power between the warring nations of Imperial Russia and the underdog empire of Japan. Schiff, born into a prosperous Jewish family in Frankfurt, Germany, in 1847, immigrated to America as a young man of eighteen and became a partner in a brokerage firm in Manhattan before turning twenty. His illustrious investment banking career progressed rapidly, instating him as the head of the firm of Kuhn, Loeb & Co., one of the most influential private international banking houses in the West, at the very time of the fortuitous meeting with Prime Minister Takahashi. Schiff needed little encouragement from the US government to participate in its new economic plans for American and foreign investment in the Far East after their acquisition of the Philippines from Spain and its new Open-Door Policy. He recognized the potential for success by investing in Japan's war with Russia—investments that would change the outcome of that war for Japan and, Schiff hoped, for the Jews of Russia.[28]

Schiff objected vehemently to the antisemitic persecution of his fellow Jews in Russia, and this was no secret to Takahashi. In a memo written by him and included in the compilation of Schiff's letters edited by Cyrus

Adler, Takahashi's words tell the motives of the two hundred million dollars in loans made to Japan by Kuhn & Loeb's foremost executive.

> His sympathy was fully enlisted for Japan. At the same time, he had a grudge against Russia on account of his race. He was justly indignant at the unfair treatment of the Jewish population by the Russian Government, which had culminated in the notorious persecutions. . . . He felt sure that if defeated, Russia would be led in the path of betterment, whether it be revolution or reformation, and he decided to exercise whatever influence he had for placing the weight of American resources on the side of Japan.[29]

Takahashi further affirmed that he and Schiff had become good friends and that Schiff enjoyed private audiences with the emperor, from whom he and Albert Mosse had received the Order of the Rising Sun.[30] Without these monies lent to Japan, which purchased necessary munitions to fight Russia, Takahashi felt certain that Japan would have lost the war and its footing in Asia: "His achievements will remain in the state records of the country and in the hearts of his Japanese friends."[31]

Schiff's foresight in mounting this successful investment in Japan yielded a sizable profit for the company and not only advanced his international banking reputation but also furthered antisemitic rhetoric, which claimed Jews intended to take over the world's markets. His financial acumen during the Russo-Japanese War "earned him Japan's lasting gratitude and Russia's lasting anger."[32] In 1911, the journalist Herman Bernstein documented this accusation made by the Russian minister of finance: "Our government will never forgive or forget what that Jew, Schiff, did to us. . . . He alone made it possible for Japan to secure a loan in America. He was one of the most dangerous men we had against us abroad."[33] Schiff's actions that favored, impressed, and saved Japan, however, failed to bring any collateral benefits for the Jews suffering in Russia. Instead, it provided even more fodder for the effects stemming from the publication of the single most damaging piece of antisemitic propaganda: *The Protocols of the Elders of Zion*—a literary hoax claiming to be the secret plot of a clandestine council of Jewish Elders to take over the world. First published in Russian in 1903, translations soon proliferated and antisemites around the world used its faux tenets to indict successful Jewish businessmen, bankers, academics, lawyers, and scientists as members of an elitist Jewish plot. It is ironic that when Japanese soldiers, exposed to the doctrines of the *Protocols*, spread the stereotype of the powerful and influential image of the "rich Jew" back to Japan, leaders of that nation saw it as a virtue rather than a vice that Japan could eventually exploit to its advantage.[34]

The first Japanese translation of *The Protocol of the Elders of Zion* came nearly five years after the initial exposure of Japanese soldiers to its inflammatory text during their deployment in Russia as part of the Siberian Intervention of 1918–22. The Siberian Intervention was a temporary military coalition of Western forces from Britain, Canada, Czechoslovakia, France, and the United States, along with troops from Japan. These peacekeepers were all stationed in the coastal areas of Russia to secure the maritime ports and Western interests from hostile takeovers by the Bolshevik Red Army following the fall of the Romanov dynasty in the Russian Revolution of 1917. Most Western forces pulled out by 1920 while Japanese troops stayed on well into 1925. This brought them into close associations with antisemitic White Russians, who possessed copies of this provocative reading material. Many of the Japanese soldiers took the publication back home with them. One such individual was Higuchi Tsuyanosuke, a Japanese professor of Russian who spent more than three years in Siberia with the Japanese Army. Higuchi, a convert to the Russian Orthodox Church, lamented the demise of the Romanov dynasty. He wholeheartedly bought into the anti-semitic rhetoric that claimed Jewish complicity in Russia's collapse. Upon returning to Japan, he published antisemitic lectures in Japanese based on *The Protocols, Yudayaka—The Jewish Peril*, writing, "No matter how barbaric and bestial the Russians may be, if the Russian Revolution had been led by Russians, it would not have been as brutal as it was . . . when one learns that the leaders of the communist regime are all Jewish and then reads through the plans of the Jewish conspiracy, everything becomes clear."[35] The complete Japanese translation of *Protocols* was published in 1924, produced by Yasue Norihiro, one of the first Russian-language-trained Japanese soldiers assigned to Siberia during the Intervention. He went on to become a colonel in the Imperial Japanese Army and would be considered a foremost "authority" on Jewish affairs, along with navy captain Inuzuka Koreshige.[36] Gao Bei, East Asian international relations historian, in his book *Shanghai Sanctuary: Chinese and Japanese Policy toward European Jewish Refugees during World War II*, points out that these two men were eventually "either individually or jointly responsible for making Japan's Jewish policy."[37] According to Bei, both men devised plans "grounded in anti-Semitic ideas" to extort Jewish cooperation in advancing their military ambitions in China.[38]

As the writings of these and other Japanese antisemites appeared, usually disseminated by the ultranationalists, more rational "liberal" voices opposing the inflammatory rhetoric emerged as well. This is yet another example of the dichotomy of intellectual thought, which marked Japanese society in the late 1920s and early 1930s and resulted in the continuous turnovers in leadership. Even though anti-Jewish sentiment in Japan remained a minority opinion, by World War II it had spread like an infectious disease throughout the ultranationalist militarists of Japan, who felt obliged to strengthen their alliance with Germany by adopting their antisemitic doctrine as well. The more rational liberals of Japan resisted the racial ideology of the Third Reich, which, after all, categorized the Japanese themselves as racially impure. Ironically, as early as 1933, Japanese newspapers characterized Nazi anti-Jewish policies as "inhumane" treatment advancing the "extermination of the Jews"—an ideology often minimized in Western thought as hyperbole.[39] These early critical opposition voices to Nazi Party tactics, represented in nearly every newspaper in Japan, sounded alarms that few people heeded as Nazism began to establish its ideological hold in Japan.[40]

Societal views of Hitler and Nazism changed rapidly in Japan after 1935 as German antisemitic literature began to flood the country, due in part to the rapprochement of diplomatic relations binding the two countries in the Anti-Comintern Pact of 1936. Japanese intellectuals, in an effort to justify growing solidarity with their German ally, once again commended the virtues of German culture and principles, antisemitism included. Japanese publications legitimized German antisemitic propaganda while extolling the foresight of Hitler in waging a cultural war against its pervasive Jewish menace. The Nazi Regime also promoted its pseudoscientific racial agenda in Japan with "research" programs supported by reputable Japanese organizations. Couple these ideologies with the growing nationalism of the Japanese Empire, which increasingly moved toward a one-party political system patterned after the Nazi Party system, and the ability for any dissenting rational voices against the antisemitic agenda of Hitler to be heard in Japan was, in effect, silenced.[41] That being said, it is important to remember that Japan lacked the centuries-old tradition of Christian antisemitism. This distinction may explain the unusual idiosyncrasies of Japanese antisemitism of the 1930s and 1940s epitomized by the prejudices of Yasue and Inuzuka.[42]

The prevalence of Japanese antisemitism filled several sociopolitical purposes unique to Japan's own nationalistic fervor in its pre–World War II years. It helped build solidarity with Germany by showing its new fascist ally a willingness to adopt that country's ideological rhetoric against world Jewry in connection with its alliance against world Communism. Antisemitism in Japan also became a unifying agent against the growing presence of politically active forms of Christianity, which voiced opposition to antisemitic attitudes in—and criticism of—Japan's imperial aspirations. Japanese nationalism centered on its emperor and his deification, which was religiously offensive to both Christianity and Judaism. Politically, Japan's brand of antisemitism also rationalized the failure of the Japanese military in its Siberian campaign of the 1920s, claiming its defeat came about because of the capitalistic agenda of world Jewry perpetrated by the West. This aspect of Japan's antisemitism added credibility to its anti-American posturing preceding the bombing of Pearl Harbor and declaration of war on the United States. Various journalistic diatribes linked international Jewish economic hegemony to American capitalism, thus justifying Japan's war with the United States as it attempted to save Asia from the evil designs of American-led world Jewry. But perhaps the most utilitarian aspect of Japanese antisemitism lay in its once-intended exploitation of world Jewry's perceived financial syndicates for Japan's eventual advantage.[43]

THE FUGU PLAN

One version of Japanese antisemitism, or "philosemitism," began to emerge in the early 1930s, in conjunction with the rise of militarism in Japan and its rampantly growing nationalism. Jingoistic degrees of Japanese patriotism produced a group of ultranationalists who saw Japan's future in its territorial rule of the Chinese provinces of Manchuria. This "Manchurian Faction" operated in opposition to other parties in Japan, which favored southern expansion instead and would eventually instigate war with the Unites States. It was within the Manchurian Faction that a pseudo-pro-Jewish philosophy developed, which was "not interested in eliminating the allegedly powerful and wealthy Jews but rather in utilizing their great wealth and influence for Japan's 'Greater East Asia Co-Prosperity Policy.'"[44] The Fugu Plan was a secret alliance, which conspired to manipulate an imagined world confederacy of Jewish financial houses into granting millions of dollars to Japan for the development of Manchuria. Certain details of the Fugu Plan reveal yet another mass resettlement scheme that sought to take advantage of an already persecuted and stateless people: the German Jews.

The 1979 seminal work by Marvin Tokayer and Mary Swartz, *The Fugu Plan: The Untold Story of the Japanese and the Jews during World War II*, tells the amazing story of a secret scheme to create a semiautonomous Jewish state in Manchuria. The book illuminates the impact that Japanese philosemitism could have had on world events, possibly avoiding the Pacific War between the United States and Japan, therefore theoretically changing the outcome of the war in Europe. Tokayer and Swartz maintain that members of the Manchurian Faction who instigated the military assault on Manchuria in 1931 that gave birth to Manchukuo conceptualized the Fugu Plan to help advance this newly formed Japanese puppet state. They believed that if Jewish refugees fleeing Europe could be enticed to settle in Manchukuo, then Japan could harness their creative energies, industrial skills, and wealth to develop the area, making it productive and lucrative for Japan. Jewish settlements in Manchukuo would thereby naturally produce sympathies with the communities of wealthy Jews in Western nations, such as the United States and Britain, who would then obligingly donate vast sums of money to assist their co-religionists in settling and developing the territory.[45]

Pamela Rotner Sakamoto, historian and consultant on Japan-related projects for the United States Holocaust Memorial Museum in Washington, DC, documents in her book *Japanese Diplomats and Jewish Refugees: A World War II Dilemma* the first recorded mention of the idea to settle fifty thousand Jews in Manchukuo: "In 1933, N.E.B. Ezra advanced the idea of a settlement for as many as 50,000 [German Jews]. . . . He wrote Vice Minister Shigemitsu in September 1933 about a settlement for 1,000 families or 50,000 people in all escaping Hitler's anti-Semitic policies."[46] Although not immediately supported by minister Mamoru Shigemitsu, the idea was embraced and advanced by Japanese entrepreneur and politician Yoshisuke Aikawa, in a 1934 essay he authored titled "A Plan to Invite Fifty Thousand German Jews to Manchukuo."[47] According to Tokayer and Swartz, Aikawa's article that promoted the Jewish mass resettlement idea throughout Japanese society met little or no opposition. The positive reception of Aikawa's ideas for Jewish resettlement in Manchukuo is supported by an August 5, 1934, *New York Times* article out of Tokyo.

> Yotara Sugimura, a Japanese diplomat, told a press conference today that Japan would welcome 50,000 German Jewish refugees as settlers in the Japanese-protected Manchukuo Empire. Expressing sympathy for Jewish people, Mr. Sugimura suggested that the refugees would find excellent conditions for settling in Manchukuo. He pointed to the richness of the

soil which he said is worked only by primitive methods at present. Mr. Su-
gimura formerly was director of the political section of the League of
Nations Secretariat at Geneva.[48]

Aikawa, already a leading industrialist in Japan with ambitions to harness
the resources of Manchuria, had bought into the antisemitic rhetoric of
global Jewish power.

Tokayer and Swartz maintain that Aikawa aligned with Yasue and
Inuzuka in their plans to exploit Jewish wealth in furthering their aspirations in Manchukuo. The authors quote Inuzuka, who attended an informal meeting of the co-conspirators.

> This plan is very much like Fugu [the Japanese blowfish whose deadly
> poison must be removed before it can be eaten]. If we are indeed skillful in
> preparing this dish—if we can remain ever-alert to the sly nature of the
> Jews, if we can continue to devote our constant attention to this enterprise
> lest the Jews, in their inherently clever manner, manage to turn the tables
> on us and begin to use us for their own ends—if we succeed in our under-
> taking, we will create for our nation and our beloved emperor the tastiest
> and most nutritious dish imaginable. But if we make the slightest mistake,
> it will destroy us in the most horrible manner.[49]

In what the historian David Kranzler described as a "love/hate relationship," these ultranationalists, who were perceived as the most influential
antisemites in Japan, advanced a plan that had the potential of saving
thousands of Europe's refugee Jews.[50]

The actual policies of the Fugu Plan began to emerge in 1934 and
peaked by December 1938, just weeks following the internment of thousands of refugee Jews in Zbaszyn, Poland, the violence of Kristallnacht
throughout Greater Germany, and the negotiations for mass settlement
plans under the auspices of the IGCR, the humanitarian agency leftover
from the Evian Conference. While Western powers saw the onslaught of
tens of thousands of refugees as an impending economic disaster, the Japanese furtively sought to woo those same refugees for mass settlement in
Manchuria. One side, the West, looked cautiously, or not at all, for potential sites for Jewish relocation, while the other advanced resettlement sites
in the East, anticipating hefty monetary help from the Jewish communities
of the West for these refugee settlements. The irony of it is sublime, especially when one considers how many Jewish refugees found safety through

the auspices of the allies of the Nazis rather than from the enemies of the Nazis. The rationale behind the Japanese policies that proposed providing havens for thousands of Jews in the several different communities under Japanese jurisdiction can only be seen as deliberately self-serving. The Manchurian Faction "saw these Jewish communities as a potential weapon in their hand for utilizing the Jewish power."[51]

As the Japanese utopian vision of Manchukuo began to fade when Jewish residents actually fled from Harbin in the face of accelerated anti-semitic violence from the White Russians, efforts to bind Jewish interests to Japanese territories were accelerated. The Japanese granted communities of Jews in eight Asian territories under Japanese occupation to form the Far Eastern Jewish Council in 1937.[52] Completely oblivious to Japan's hidden agenda, the council conducted the first Far Eastern Jewish Conference in 1937 with more than seven hundred delegates and spectators. Japan's "Jewish experts" spoke at the proceedings, superficially encouraging the Jewish attendees to facilitate resettlement of their co-religionists in Japanese territories to protect them in a racially tolerant environment, while secretly hoping they would build business interests that would bring in Western money. The massive development plans for Manchukuo never materialized as Europe's Jews became more suspicious of Japanese intentions and the acceleration of Nazi violence against the Jews in tandem with progressing negotiations between the German and Japanese governments.

As the powers in Japan clashed over its alliance with Germany, a series of diplomatic standoffs in Japan resulted in threats to recall German-sympathizing officials. These conflicting opinions included Japan's intended policies regarding its resident Jews as well. Just as Japan's army generals clashed with its naval admirals on policy, so did pro-Nazi sympathizers wage ideological battle with Japan's Jewish supporters—the former believing in the elimination of the Jews and the latter in their control and exploitation. Eventually, both factions agreed that they needed to utilize world Jewry's political and economic powers to better Japan's interests; therefore an official statement of policy in December 1938 from the ministers of Japan openly detailed a new Jewish policy.

1. Jews living in Japan, Manchuria, and China are to be treated fairly and in the same manner as other foreign nationals. No special effort to expel them is to be made.
2. Jews entering Japan, Manchuria, and China are to be dealt with on the basis of existing immigration policies pertaining to other foreigners.

3. No special effort to attract Jews to Japan, Manchuria, or China is to be made. However, exceptions may be made for businessmen and technicians with utility for Japan.[53]

These policy directives initiated in Shanghai no doubt carried over to Japanese administrative styles in the Philippines.[54]

What started in early 1939 as a humble and tentative settlement proposition by a wealthy Manchurian Jew to open an industry in Manchukuo with European refugee Jews ballooned into a Japanese immigration scheme of mammoth proportions. By mid-July 1939, the backers of the Fugu Plan had produced a ninety-page proposal detailing measures to attract Jewish financiers both in Shanghai and in the West. The report called for the formation of Jewish refugee settlements in colonies ranging in population size from a few thousand to nearly one million. The proposal endorsed religious, cultural, and educational autonomy for Jewish settlers who would be ruled politically by the Japanese. Although the entire financing of the settlement plans would rest on the Jews themselves, the Japanese suggested an estimated figure of one hundred million dollars for the settlement of thirty thousand refugees.

The Fugu Plan proponents saw their strategy frustrated by an unanticipated foe—the Jewish community of Shanghai itself, which not only suffered from enormous overcrowding but also insisted on immigration restrictions. Having no practical insight into the Japanese idealistic vision of funds rolling in to support an even greater influx of refugees into Shanghai, the governing committee for the International Settlement officially restricted immigration into that location, allowing only those who had a contracted job or financial support in the sum of four hundred American dollars. Although the entry of refugees into Shanghai nearly ceased, the supporters of the Fugu Plan initially saw this as merely a delay to their dreams of future Jewish dollars. They proceeded with plans to contact the United States' most influential Jewish citizen, Rabbi Stephen Wise, in hopes of generating support from what they perceived was America's rich and powerful Jewish community.[55]

Rabbi Wise became the centerpiece of the Japanese plan to extort financial backing from US Jews for this massive resettlement scheme in Japanese territories. As a personal friend of President Roosevelt and a leading public figure among America's Jews, Rabbi Wise stood in a position of power next to the American president in the minds of the Fugu Plan promoters. When a meeting in New York in 1940 between Wise and a delegate of the Fugu Plan failed to sway Wise into supporting "a prearranged settlement area in either Manchukuo or China" in exchange for "trade arrangements with the United States," which would lift the embargos against Japan, the delegate of the Fugu Plan turned to the Joint Distribution Committee instead.[56] The JDC's investigation into the identity of the Japanese delegate revealed that he had no authority from the ruling Japanese military government to conduct any negotiations involving Japan. In just a matter of weeks, the new foreign minister of Japan led negotiations for the formulation of the Tripartite Pact with Germany and Italy that ended any hopes for the Fugu Plan, realistically or idealistically. These rapprochements between Germany and Japan in 1939 and 1940 yielded official and unofficial alliances whose goals involved either the nullification of US power or the exploitation of it. These carefully constructed coalitions failed, resulting in the bombing of Pearl Harbor, the invasion of the Philippines, and the declaration of war against the United States by the Axis powers.

The signing of the Tripartite Pact ended the aspirations of the Fugu Plan supporters and their hopes of acquiring some kind of diplomatic leverage that would end the embargos against Japan—embargos that greatly curbed its importation of raw materials to support its ambitions for war. Japan changed its focus from development of Manchuria to the acquisition of territories in China farther south in an effort to acquire the resources it badly needed. Such expansionist plans would precipitate engagements with British and American forces in Asia. Japan rationalized that a surprise attack on US military installations at Pearl Harbor and the Philippines would cripple an American response to Japanese aggression in southern Asia. Confident in its ability to create its Far Eastern Asian confederacy of nations, Japanese ministers expected a need to acquire funding for reconstruction purposes in the near future.

Japanese ministers, those convinced of Jewish control over the world's markets, vied with those elements of the Japanese Empire who fully swallowed the Nazi antisemitic rhetoric with its designs for eradication of the Jews. When considering the Japanese occupation of the Philippines and the fate of its Jewish residents during those years, knowledge of the details surrounding the Fugu Plan adds extra dimension to our understanding of the refugees' experiences at the hands of their captors.

JAPANESE STRATEGY IN THE PHILIPPINES

Japan did not see itself as a combatant in World War II. In its view, it engaged in Dai Toa Senso, the Greater East Asia War—a dispute that began in 1937 with China as its primary enemy. Therefore, Japan's attack on

American bases in the Pacific was but an extension of its efforts to win the Sino-Japanese conflict, which actually began with Japan's invasion of Manchuria in 1931. Japan entered the triple alliance with Germany and Italy in hopes that it would assist Japan in its expansionist ambitions against the colonial holdings of Western powers in China. When Britain and the United States retaliated by freezing Japanese assets abroad and boycotting its much-needed oil imports, Japan prepared to move against the Dutch East Indies in order to grab its oil fields and thereby acquire the resources needed to continue its Sino-Japanese conflict. Japan believed one thing stood in their way—the US Pacific Fleet at Pearl Harbor and American military installations in the Philippines and other Pacific Islands.

With visions of Asiatic imperial grandeur, Japan believed that if it took out the US installations in Hawai'i, the Philippine Islands, and other places in the Pacific, nothing would stop the formation of the Greater East Asia Co-Prosperity Sphere, with Japan as its destined leader. Therefore, the only obstacle in Japan's aspirations to control the entire arena of the Pacific Islands and China was a few planes and ships at Hawai'i and the Philippines.[57] The promoters of the Fugu Plan never achieved their vision of untold amounts of Jewish wealth pouring into Japanese territories by providing havens to refugee Jews before the outbreak of the war. A question does arise as to what influence Japanese philosemitism for Jewish exploitation had on Japan's treatment of the Jewish residents of the Philippines when they invaded that US territory during the opening days of 1942. Jurisdiction over issues of religion and the churches in the Philippines during the occupation came under the purview of the Religious Section of the Propaganda Corps of the Japanese Military Administration (JMA).[58]

Just hours after the Japanese entered Manila, the commander in chief of the Japanese Armed Forces advised the Commonwealth authorities that Japan wished only the best for its fellow Asians, the Filipinos, and valued their alliance in the Greater East Asia Co-Prosperity Sphere. With a history of Christianity in the Philippines going back three hundred years, Japan no doubt realized that most Filipinos belonged to the Roman Catholic Church or some other Christian denomination. The 1939 census reported that of the sixteen million inhabitants of the Philippine Islands, 78.8 percent belonged to the Catholic Church, and a total of 91 percent of the population itself identified themselves as Christians.[59] The Philippines were islands of Christian Asians in a mixed sea of Buddhists and Muslims, the predominant religions of Asia. The Japanese military knew that it must curry the favor of the Christian churches in order to secure peaceful

Philippine cooperation to Japanese occupation; therefore, the Japanese High Command announced a policy intending "secured religious freedom for all" that would be administered by a special "Religious Appeasement Operations Section" organized by the Japanese Army General Staff.[60] The editor of the *Manila Times* and the *Philippine Magazine*, A. V. H. Hartendorp, kept a clandestine diary of events for President Quezon during the Japanese occupation. This diary related how "the Japanese from the first made a big play for the cooperation of the churches in the Philippines."[61] The Religious Section within the Propaganda Corps of the JMA operated tirelessly in the first year of occupation in an effort to promote Japan's "spirit of universal brotherhood."[62]

The Religious Section's personnel included clergy, seminarians, and laity from both Catholic and Protestant communities in Japan; thirteen members of the task force were Catholics and twelve were Protestant. They were hired as civilian employees of the army for one year, having been sought out and employed as early as August 1941, showing well the intentions of the Japanese Army in occupying the Philippines months before the December bombings.[63] The commander of the Religious Section, Lt. Col. Narusawa Tomoji, had more than a passing familiarity with Christianity because his wife was a practicing Catholic, while he himself was Buddhist.[64] The members of the Religious Section arrived in Manila on the heels of the military invasion. According to Hartendorp, Narusawa immediately distributed a leaflet that declared:

> It is the desire of the Imperial Japanese Army to foster freedom of religious worship and it seeks to do everything possible for the protection of the Christian Churches and therefore does not anticipate activities harmful to the progress of its task. The Imperial Japanese Army addresses all Christians and asks the full cooperation of spiritual leaders and laymen worshippers in the establishment of that mutually prosperous sphere in Greater East Asia and of a just peace throughout the civilized world.[65]

Narusawa and his staff then made personal visits to the clergy of the Catholic and Protestant churches. Although the Religious Section treated the predominant Catholic community of leaders with delicate diplomacy, they were much less conciliatory with the minority Protestant denominations and hardly knew how to handle the community of Jews. At a conference of Protestant leaders in the Philippines held in late January 1942, Narusawa pressured the various Protestant denominations into signing a declaration of alliance to the Greater East Asia Co-Prosperity Sphere. American and Filipino Protestant leaders who declined to comply found themselves summarily interned in civilian detention camps.[66]

Narusawa had categorized Japan's East Asian quest as "Japan's holy war," one that stood on a spiritual plain similar to that of Christianity's war against evil, with Japan's eternal enemies being communism and capitalism.[67] Even though such stereotypes went hand in hand with the widespread antisemitic rhetoric of Europe, most of Japanese society knew little or nothing about modern Jews, and Narusawa appears to have come with a preconception of old stereotypical ideas about Jews, which were quickly dispelled. With residency records in hand, along with an old picture depicting an Orthodox rabbi, Narusawa officially visited the home of Rabbi Schwarz. Momentarily nonplussed by Rabbi Schwarz's modern attire, Narusawa informed him that the supervision of the Jewish synagogue now came under complete jurisdiction of the Religious Section of the JMA. Narusawa demonstrated his naiveté regarding the true nature of Judaism in this meeting with Rabbi Schwarz and, to his credit, responded favorably to Schwarz's illuminating discourse on the history of the plight of the Jews in Germany.[68] Narusawa also garnered Philippine esteem when he expelled Japanese soldiers from local churches on several occasions. In light of the Japanese policy of religious tolerance meant to earn the favor and cooperation of the Christian churches, it would have been dishonorable to discriminate against refugee Jews—a violation of their own policy of religious tolerance. However, this policy only secured "free worship of religion" as long as it was compatible with Japanese rule.

The Religious Section, which operated throughout 1942 as a mouthpiece for the interests of the religious communities in the Philippines, was disbanded in December 1942. In 1943, when anti-Japanese guerilla movements rose up in the Philippines and the war in the Pacific turned against Japan, jurisdiction over religious affairs defaulted to the JMA itself.[69] Nazi sympathizers within the Japanese military command tried to enact antisemitic actions against the Jewish community of Manila at different times during the occupation, but for the most part they suffered relatively little harm at the hands of the Japanese during the occupation, at least in comparison to the plight of their fellow Jews in Europe.

JAPANESE INVASION AND CIVILIAN INTERNMENT

By the time the Japanese entered Manila in January 1942, the Jewish community of Manila had swelled with European refugees beyond all expectations, reaching its maximum population of about 2,500 members. Samuel Schechter, president of Temple Emil, noted on September 1, 1940, in a board of directors' communiqué that "our community has increased about eightfold since the advent of Jewish persecution in many countries of Europe."[70] During the height of its prewar immigration years, the Philippines benefited from the arrival of such renowned Jewish refugees as Dr. Herbert Zipper, who became conductor of the Manila Symphony Orchestra, and his wife, Trudl, who taught modern dance to many well-known Filipino performers.[71] Dr. Eugene Stransky, a specialist in blood disorders, and Ernest Kornfeld, a respected architect, also contributed to Philippine professional and cultural life with their expertise.

Joseph Cysner secured an additional position as a music instructor at the Catholic De La Salle College in Manila and developed a reputation for his classical vocal training, performing for President Quezon on numerous occasions.[72] Annette Eberly recorded the testimony of Paula Brings, who arrived from Austria in March 1939 with her husband, Dr. Theodor Brings, who became a professor of physics at the University of the Philippines. According to Brings, "you could never find as generous and solid a group of people anywhere else in the world. They gave . . . unstintingly in times of crisis; they have never neglected the needs of the destitute and the sick."[73] This once American-dominated Jewish community that had saved Joseph and those 1,300 European Jews from potential extermination now faced an unexpected persecution of their own. An amazing turn of events put the fate of the American and British Jews into the hands of the German and Austrian Jews when the Japanese, after entering Manila in January 1942, summarily interned all "enemy alien" civilians in Santo Tomas University.

The Japanese entered Manila without encountering any resistance when General Douglas MacArthur retreated with the American forces and declared Manila an "open city" on December 26, 1941.[74] Three weeks prior, on the "date which will live in infamy," Japanese forces devastated the American fleet at Pearl Harbor and prompted the United States to enter the war with Japan and its allies in Europe. Few people realize that the naval base at Honolulu was not the only American military base destroyed that day; bombings also took place on December 8, 1941, on the other side of the international dateline. On that day numerous US installations in the Philippines were attacked from the air by the Japanese: Davao City in Mindanao, Camp John Hay at Baguio, Clark Field in Pampanga, the airfields at Iba, Zambales, and Nichols Field near Manila. Unlike Pearl Harbor, Japanese forces made shore landings on all four sides of Luzon, the island home of Manila. With forces outnumbered and military installations destroyed, MacArthur had little choice but to retreat, leaving Manila at the mercy of the approaching Japanese forces.[75]

On January 2, 1942, three battalions of Japanese soldiers entered Manila from the north while another battalion and a regiment entered from the south. The Japanese immediately set up points of registration and ordered all civilians to file their nationalities. Within a matter of days, the Japanese began busing American, British, British Commonwealth, Dutch, Polish, Belgian, and other citizens of any country at war with Japan or Germany, to Santo Tomas University for immediate internment at the Santo Tomas Internment Camp (STIC).[76] Established by Spanish Dominican Fathers in 1611, the university consisted of several sizable buildings with sixty large classrooms and many smaller offices set off from spacious foyers, all situated within a fenced compound of about fifty acres. Before the opening of Los Baños Camp, which later received several hundred internees from Santo Tomas, the university became the temporary residence of nearly five thousand civilians, held in ever-worsening conditions of disease, filth, starvation, and torture.[77]

The Japanese government's incarceration of thousands of American noncombatants at various locations in the Philippines during the war marked the first time in US history that American civilians were captured by an alien power, interned on American soil, and subjected to three years of systematic starvation.[78] Of the three main civilian internment camps in operation from 1941 to 1945, the largest numbers of internees (85 percent) were held at Santo Tomas University, designated by the Japanese as Internment Camp #1.[79] In 1943, one-third of those internees were transferred to the second largest internment camp, Los Baños, in the Laguna Province area, thirty-five miles south of Manila and designated as Internment Camp #2. Other smaller sites, collectively labeled as Internment Camp #3, were at Baguio on the island of Luzon, and various places on the islands of Cebu and Mindanao.[80]

When the US forces pulled out of Manila, declaring it an "open city," announcements over the radio directed all Americans in the outlying areas to relocate to the city proper. In previous months, concerned American businessmen in Manila had formed a committee, intent on preparing for the possibility of war and occupation by the Japanese. Plans had already been made that secured sites for possible internment of civilians in the event of an invasion. Santo Tomas University and other such sites were chosen by the committee and submitted to the High Commissioner's office at the US Embassy in Manila. When Japanese forces entered Manila, those locations, along with lists of all the names and addresses of civilian aliens in the Philippines, were voluntarily handed over to the occupying forces. The Japanese immediately designated the university as an internment camp for civilian nationals from countries at war with Japan, Italy, or Germany: the Axis nations of the Tripartite Pact. On January 4, 1942, approximately three hundred enemy alien civilian men arrived at the internment camp, bused in from their point of registration at Rizal Stadium in Manila. Martin Meadows, who was just eleven years old when he was interned, was the son of an American businessman in Manila and a member of the Jewish community in the Philippines. He vividly remembers that event:

> When the Japanese arrived, we listened to the announcements of what to do. The Americans pulled out declaring Manila an open city, so the Japanese would stop bombing. Anyway, as the Japanese approached, the radio announcement by local authorities came that Americans should move in from the outlying districts. . . . So we moved in with this German [Jewish] family, the Rechters. Until the Japanese came, we stayed with the Rechters in their apartment. . . . Then the announcement came early in January 1942 that all males, enemy alien males, should show up at Rizal Stadium with enough stuff for three days. So my father went to Rizal Stadium and they were then taken to Santo Tomas. My mother and I continued to stay with the Rechters and we used to take trips to Santo Tomas by horse driven *caretellas* and take him stuff through the line. We could see him on the other side of the fence—there were certain hours you could do that. Now that went on for three weeks. We stayed with the Rechters and then my mother and I went into the camp exactly three weeks to the day after my father.[81]

Hyman Meadows, Martin's father, was part of that first incarceration of enemy civilian males on January 4, 1942, along with Joseph Cysner, who held a Polish passport, and leaders of the Jewish community, Samuel Schechter and Morton Netzorg, and other American and British Jewish businessmen.

The Japanese did not perceive a difference between German nationals and German Jews, so the majority of the Jewish community at Manila, which had been enlarged by more than one thousand German-Austrian Jews, did not face internment at STIC. However, about 250 other members of the Jewish community were immediately interned.[82] Having spent five years freeing refugees from Nazi oppression, the American Jews of Manila now faced a serious threat of their own. Joseph's Polish passport accounted for his treatment as a civilian enemy alien. Already familiar with forced internment in Zbaszyn, Joseph was able to draw on past experiences to sustain himself and others in the civilian internment camp.

Life in the Philippines, both inside STIC and without, changed forever in those early days of January 1942. From the very first day of internment, the organization and care of the prisoners became the concern of a central committee of internees. Earl Carroll, initial chairman of that committee, tells of his appointment to the job in a 1945 newspaper article.[83]

> It was sheer chance that made me a leader at Santo Tomas . . . I had come back as production manager for my insurance company. . . . The day after my arrival in Manila I went to a luncheon where Francis Sayre, United States High Commissioner, was speaker. At that luncheon the Americans were making plans to evacuate their womenfolk and children to the country in event of war and bombings of Manila. I was appointed District leader for the Malate district, a section of Manila made up of apartment houses, residential hotels and fine homes. Then came Pearl Harbor, the Lingayen Gulf landing, MacArthur's evacuation of Manila and the entry of the Japs. On January 4, 1942, Jap soldiers rapped at every door in the Malate district and ordered Americans and British to assemble at once in Rizal Memorial Stadium with food for three days. We obeyed of course. There were three hundred of us. They took us to Santo Tomas University and informed us it was our place of internment for the moment. Late in the day I was standing at the end of a hallway in the main building of Santo Tomas looking down into a palm-fringed patio and wondering when if ever I would again hold my wife or tousle the cropped blond hair of my six-year-old Robert. Standing behind me was a small group of Americans, lost in the same gloomy thoughts that held me. Footsteps approached and, without turning, I recognized the voice of a Jap as he spoke in English to one of the American group. "Who is your leader?" he demanded. Someone, remembering I had been Malate district leader, pointed to me. The Jap stepped over and tapped me on the shoulder. I turned. "Well, you're it," he said. "What do you mean, by 'it'?" "We're making you the general chairman of the camp," he said. "You are going to take care of your own internal problems. The commandant will be in tomorrow afternoon. We are withdrawing. We'll have the gate open and no guards. If anybody leaves or anything happens, you are responsible."[84]

Committee organization developed with members coming from both the American constituency of captives as well as from the British. It is worth noting here that the different religious affiliations of camp internees came under the purview of this central committee from the very first day of internment.

> On the morning of the first full day in Santo Tomas I [Earl Carroll] called a meeting of fifteen of our Manila businessmen, mostly young executives like myself. . . . We sat down in the second-floor offices of a Santo Tomas college dean to establish some kind of organization. We knew we had to organize our own people. An executive committee was established, with me as general chairman. . . . Committees were created for sanitation, policing and all the other functions of a small city. . . . Those of us who were there that morning recall with pride that religion was one of the first matters we attended to, and we did it in the good old American manner. We were Protestant, Catholic, and Jew. We were determined to have no religious intolerances dividing us in the site of the enemy. And we did not have. Not ever.[85]

Several firsthand accounts about the details of camp life have been written, but few of them discuss specifics concerning the experiences of the Jews in camp. Morton Netzorg, representative of the JWB in the Philippines and a member of the JRC in Manila, immediately took a role in camp life by serving on the camp religious committee.[86] Samuel Schechter, president of the Jewish community in Manila, authored the chapter on Judaism in the larger work by Frederic Harper Stevens, who also wrote a firsthand account of life in STIC. Based on the testimony of these leaders, we can only assume what the general state of affairs at the camp was like for its Jewish internees. Observant Jews in camp prayed daily, wearing their tallitsim and tefillin, and held minyan on Shabbat.[87] For the general population of less observant Jews, there were occasions when minyan for Yahrzeits were held, as well as assemblies for the High Holy Days of Rosh Hashanah and Yom Kippur.[88] Schechter noted that Pesach Seders were held in 1942 and 1943, but the traditional observance of this day of deliverance had to be abandoned in 1944. Schechter poignantly observed that ritual fasting for Yom Kippur bore little difference to the daily state of starvation by 1944.[89]

As a member of the Department of Religion at STIC, Netzorg participated in formulating the policies the committee put together in the "Ten

Commandments for Santo Tomas." As Stevens recounts, they were posted throughout the camp.

I. Thou shalt have no other interest greater than the welfare of the Camp.

II. Thou shalt not adopt for thyself, or condone in others, any merely selfish rule of conduct, or indulge in any practice that injures the morale of the Camp. Thou shalt not violate the procedures agreed upon by the authorities or by the majority, for punishment can surely be visited upon all—innocent and guilty alike—because of the misdeeds of a few.

III. Thou shalt not betray the ideals and principles which thou wast taught, so that in the future thou wilt not be condemned for neglecting thy heritage.

IV. Remember the work of the Camp, to do thy share. Six days shalt thou labor and do all thy work assignment, and also, as on thy rest day, refresh thy mind and heart with worship. For thy work will be satisfying and effective only when it is done in the right spirit.

V. Honor thy forefathers by recalling vividly their struggle for better things, that thou mayest contribute now and in the days to come to the realization of their ideals.

VI. Thou shalt not hinder the best development of youth in the Camp.

VII. Thou shalt not break down family relationships.

VIII. Thou shalt not steal.

IX. Thou shalt not injure thy neighbor's reputation by malicious gossip.

X. Thou shalt not covet thy neighbor's shanty or his room space. Thou shalt not covet they neighbor's wife, nor his fiancée, nor his influential position, nor anything that is thy neighbor's.[90]

While appearing both practical and somewhat amusing, these camp rules reflected some of the greatest social challenges faced by the inmates at STIC.

Samuel Schechter recounted to Frank Ephraim a brief recollection of general events concerning the small Jewish population in STIC. Not all were Americans, but as Schechter recalled, there were strictly observant Orthodox Jews from Poland, along with students from the Mirrer Yeshiva who were later sent to the internment camp at Los Baños.[91] Norbert Propper was one of those unattached young people who were tasked to help "build this new camp from scratch." He describes how they had to stand for roll call every day: "It was always a fearful situation. Machine guns were trained on us so you did not know if one day they would decide to do away with us."[92]

Hartendorp's authoritative and definitive account of life under the Japanese occupation is generated from his personal experiences as an inmate at STIC. On December 31, 1941, he was advised by Quezon's executive secretary, Jorge B. Vargas, one day after Quezon had appointed Vargas as Head of the Civilian Emergency Administration and two days before Japanese forces entered Manila, that "President Quezon wants you to keep a record. Keep the best record you can."[93] Hartendorp kept a clandestine typewritten account daily for the three years that the camp was in operation, supported by the internee camp officials who "appointed him camp historian and extended to him all possible aid and protection."[94] He recorded that the most pressing problems of camp life addressed by the committee in the beginning months were sanitation and health, food, lodging, and discipline. The Japanese left the camp members to their own devices to solve these and other problems. The central committee of the camp organized work details out of basic necessity to provide for the immediate needs of the incarcerated, placing everyone in some kind of job, without bias of gender, age, or income. Everybody worked: from detail in the kitchen, either cooking or washing dishes, to sanitation and pest extermination, to gardening and laundry duties. School was set up for the children and teenagers who were interned with their parents; they were locked inside a university with a library, so there was no shortage of books, however challenging the level of difficulty may have been. Norbert Propper characterizes his time spent in STIC as the most intellectually stimulating months of his life. Inmates could study languages, business skills, literature, art, and music, attend concerts, and take high school and college-level courses from highly trained professionals in their fields—all inmates themselves.[95]

When the Japanese began bringing entire families into STIC for internment, women and men were assigned to different rooms on different floors, disrupting the basic bonding of families. Men had already been assigned classrooms on one floor, and women and children were assigned to different floors and sometimes different buildings. Martin remembered his mother was assigned to a classroom on the first floor of the main building, close to the main entrance doors. Martin joined his father in a classroom on the third floor of the same building, already overcrowded with about forty or fifty men. A camp infirmary was set up with trained doctors and medical personnel who were also internees in the camp. Martin recalls that the medical care in the camp's infirmary eventually surpassed the hospital care outside the camp. Life inside the camp immediately turned dreadful for Martin just after he and his mother joined his father in STIC. He contracted dysentery and spent three weeks in the camp infirmary. Martin's overall memory of life in Santo Tomas was one of constant hunger and overcrowding. The inmates at Santo Tomas vied for floor space on which to sleep, cramming forty or fifty people in a classroom and sleeping across desktops.[96]

In the 2006 documentary *Victims of Circumstance—Santo Tomas Internment Camp* produced by Lou Gopal, internees described the annex, a separate structure behind the main building where women with small children were housed, as "a crying, sick, vomiting mess for two months at least."[97] Others told how all their cots were crammed together with no space between them. "We had only twenty-eight inches of space and that space was like gold, because if your neighbor next door moved an inch too much, she was right at your back."[98] Joseph was billeted in the gymnasium, another structure separated from the main building, where single men were kept. Internees tell sometimes humiliating but amusing stories about the total breakdown of privacy in the overcrowded conditions that housed some five thousand people when internees were brought in from outlying camps in Bacolod, Cebu, and Davao.[99]

All the firsthand accounts from prisoners of STIC describe the distinct differences of Japanese administration over the camp in the first two years as compared to the final year.[100] The civilian camps in the Philippines, at the other sites as well as at Santo Tomas, were not like the POW camps, which were set up for captured military personnel: POWs were usually young men in good health who underwent horrible abuse and mistreatment at the hands of their captors. Civilian internees, on the other hand, came in all shapes, sizes, ages, and genders. From the outset, the Japanese camp administrators of Santo Tomas were more humane than were the administrators of the POW camps, at least in the beginning, perhaps because the first Japanese camp overseers at Santo Tomas were appointees of a civilian administration and were not members of the Japanese military.[101] The first camp commandant, Hitoshi Tomoyasu, a retired Japanese military policeman, left STIC in the second month to become chief of Manila's regular police force. He was succeeded by an English-speaking Japanese diplomat named Ryozo Tsurumi.[102] While these first camp overseers were certainly not as sadistic as those who came later under the command of the Japanese military, life in Santo Tomas under the watch of these administrators was anything but easy. Earl Carroll, selected by Tomoyasu to organize the civilian camp, recalled the first execution of STIC internees in February 1942. Three young British nationals who had escaped from STIC on February 11, 1942, were arrested and executed in Carroll's presence.

> Tomoyasu sent for Stanley [fluent in Japanese] and me and the room monitors shortly before noon. They piled us into cars and put a squad of soldiers into a bus. Then off we drove while the camp watched silently. We went to the San Marcelino jail in Manila and the three prisoners were brought out. When they saw us, they began smiling. They thought they were to go free. When we drove to the Chinese cemetery north of Manila, and stopped near a large, freshly dug grave, they knew. "Why, we haven't even been tried!" exclaimed Laycock. And that was that. The stuff we had been given about a court martial was a Jap lie. Tomoyasu asked me if I had anything to say to the men. I do not recall all that I told them. But I remember saying this: "Your names will not be forgotten at Santo Tomas. You are dying as martyrs to freedom." Takahashi [second in command] seated the three on the mound of earth beside the grave with their feet dangling in. . . . Then the Jap detail took up positions fifteen feet in front of the men and took out their side arms. Takahashi was grinning when he gave the order to fire. Those pistols were small bore, and would kill a man only if the bullet struck a vital spot. . . . They fired and fired. I counted thirteen shots. Week's body fell in last. Then the Japs stood over them, firing down into the grave. Groans still were coming from that grave when the Japs began to shovel dirt into it. The Japs were still shooting when Tomoyasu turned away, mumbling to himself. He went behind a clump of bushes and looked the other way. Stanley told me Tomoyasu was saying, "Its butchery. They should have the proper instruments." Maybe he meant swords. Before the Japs were driven from Manila, they killed nearly four thousand people at the cemetery. And most of the dead were beheaded. The next day the executive committee read this into the minutes: "All three men faced their end bravely and heroically without faltering. And the committee wishes to record its admiration for their superb courage."[103]

No doubt performed in such a manner as to impress upon the civilian committee members the seriousness of their internment at STIC, Carroll and the other members of the organizing committee met every morning and worked hard at representing the interests of all camp internees to the Japanese administrators.

Within the first ten days of internment at STIC, more than three thousand prisoners had been dumped on the site: "some 2,000 people were lodged in the main building, 400 in the annex, and 700 in the gymnasium, the third building to be occupied," where Joseph eventually stayed.[104] Inevitably, the initial three days' worth of supplies that internees had brought in with them ran out; thereafter the imprisoned depended primarily on the local Red Cross for supplies and food. The package deliveries started up on January 15, 1942, and became the camp umbilical cord for the captives. Families, friends, and former employees of the interned lined up outside the front gates from 8:00 to 8:20 a.m. and from 3:00 to 3:20 p.m. every day to pass food and other necessities to waiting hands. Those who had no benefactors on the outside were provided meals in camp by the Red Cross, which had been granted privileges to establish a kitchen inside STIC. Hans Hoeflein remembers how he and his mother would go often to the internment camp "to take food and things. We would get notes from our interned friends as to what they wanted, and we would try to bring it to them. There was a big shed where the outside people could meet the internees and give them what they had asked for."[105] The Japanese would watch the exchanges closely, inspecting the packages for contraband. But food was usually the main item brought through the package lines.

Civilian internment was especially hard for Jews who would not compromise the requirements of their dietary laws of kashrut (kosher). Refusing all cooked food prepared in the kitchens at Santo Tomas, they prepared their own rice and vegetables passed to them by members of the Jewish community through the package line. Norbert Propper remembers that "Joseph Cysner did a lot for me. Especially when I was in the internment camp."[106] Norbert relates how Joseph's mother, who was not interned because of her German passport, would stew chickens for them and bring it to the camp, which enabled them to maintain their kosher dietary laws. Without the assistance of the non-interned Jewish refugees in Manila, the interned Orthodox Polish Jews, including Joseph, would not have had the ability to maintain their religious dietary observances. Rabbi Schwarz and others gathered, prepared, and passed along kosher food items to their fellow observant Jews and the Mirrer Yeshiva students. By March 1943, an estimated one thousand internees were receiving supplies through the package lines daily.[107] These continued with intermittent closures at the whim of the Japanese until early 1944, when the Japanese military "locked us in, took over the feeding themselves, and placed us on a starvation diet."[108] This kind of desperation led to the formation of resistance movements.

Two Viennese Manilaners, Hanna Kaunitz Entell and her brother Fred, joined three different clandestine groups, all part of the resistance movement in the Philippines: "We were able to send food and medicine in to the prison camp. . . . I had three runners, three people who would go back and forth, who would take things in for me . . . during the war, the three heads of the underground were beheaded—every one of them that I knew."[109] Hannah tells how her brother's illegal activities were discovered and that he was then imprisoned, beaten, and tortured by his Japanese jailers. "We were able to really do a lot. My brother Fred—somehow they found out things about him. He was imprisoned . . . in the dungeons. It was the worst kind of prison that you can imagine. People there were tortured and killed by the Japanese. Somehow, thank God he was able to get out."[110] He was one of the fortunate few who survived his imprisonment.

Earl Carroll's memoir of the first six months of his internment reveals more about the little-known operation of the underground black-market trafficking that he and others like the Kaunitzes organized in an effort to stave off the systematic starvation of both the STIC internees and the POWs at Cabanatuan. Apparently, the Japanese invaders presumed that all the assets of the rich American businesses were still securely held in the vaults of the Philippine banks. The Japanese did not know that all paper currency had been burned in anticipation of the Japanese occupation and "daring American subs had shipped out with the securities and bullion."[111] Anticipating that the Americans and British could pay for their own food and supplies while interned, the Japanese captors "gave us not one grain of rice, not one peso of money, not one ounce of medicine" during those early months of confinement. With the instruction to "buy your own food," Carroll conducted purchasing forays with what money was carried into the camp by the internees, as it had been pooled to benefit all interned. The money, however, soon ran out, and once the Japanese learned that the retreating American forces had left the Philippines penniless, the Japanese Foreign Office, in charge of the civilian internment, had no other recourse but to grant a spending allotment of twenty-five cents per person per day for food and other necessities. In a highly inflated war-torn market, this amounted to next to nothing. Thus, Carroll felt that he had no other choice but to enter the underground world of black-market racketeering. Carroll explained how the black market operated.

We could starve slowly, or we could go into the money black market and trade IOUs—American promises to pay if and when—for Jap occupation pesos. The Jap money was called "Mickey Mouse" by the Filipinos. . . . So I became a trafficker in Mickey Mouse currency. The penalty if caught was confinement at infamous Fort Santiago, where many were tortured and few emerged alive. This Mickey Mouse currency provided just enough margin to keep us on a plain but sufficient diet. We simply added the black-market money to the Jap allotment and went on buying in the open market.[112]

Carroll wore a red armband labeling him an internee of STIC while on special leave from the camp, an item Carroll described as a "priceless possession" that acted as a "passport at the gate" enabling him to "roam Manila in pursuit of [his] secret life" as a black-marketeer.[113] This clandestine operation brought him into contact with Israel Königsberg, "a scholarly Russian Jew who opened his heart and pocketbook to those among us who were destitute."[114]

Israel Königsberg and his wife came to Manila from Shanghai in 1924, eventually establishing a successful bookstore in the Philippines. Königsberg had been a prominent member of the Jewish community and the Philippine business world for many years, so he lost no time in giving any help he could to the imprisoned. Earl Carroll described the clandestine encounters they shared.

> A Russian Jew with Filipino citizenship, [Königsberg] ran a bookstore and felt he owed his prosperity to Americans. When I walked into his shop he smiled and said, "Let's see now. You came in today to buy ledgers for your camp records, didn't you?" And I nodded. That gave us a story to stick to if caught. . . . We went to a back room and he handed me sheaves of Mickey Mouse for my IOUs. I had IOUs signed by our poorest people, and I told him frankly his chances of recovering on them were slight. But he took them. When we finished our transaction, he handed me an extra sheaf of pesos. "Get this through to the men of Cabanatuan," he said. . . . I don't know what hands it passed through to reach our starving troops at Cabanatuan, but I know it got there.[115]

Eventually Königsberg's black-market activities, which provided both money and medicine to American POWs, were discovered by the Japanese when a missionary and fellow conspirator's papers were found after her arrest and torture. Königsberg spent the remainder of the occupation imprisoned at Muntinlupa Prison east of Manila, "barely surviving on starvation rations."[116] He was not reunited with his wife and daughter until after escaping his own execution shortly before the liberation of Manila.

Life in Santo Tomas moved forward with increasing difficulty as the internees' health and stamina gradually declined. With the fall of Corregidor—the only surrender of US Armed Forces in American military history—came the notorious Bataan Death March, which gave the Jewish community in the Philippines its first casualty of the occupation—David Netzorg, son of Morton Netzorg. David had joined the army shortly after the bombing of Pearl Harbor. After surviving the Death March that killed thousands along the way, the maimed and tortured POWs were brought to Camps O'Donnell and Cabanatuan. David died shortly after his arrival at Cabanatuan in April 1942.[117]

Both Schechter and Netzorg remained locked up with the other Jewish internees for the full three years of their incarceration, but Joseph Cysner obtained an early release after eight months, always wearing the mandatory red armband that signaled to all Japanese that he was furloughed from the camp. Rabbi Schwarz, who took over the leadership of the Jewish community in Manila after the occupation by the Japanese, convinced Narusawa of the Japanese Religious Section that Joseph's elderly mother, who was not held captive, required her son's support, and the religious services at the synagogue could not continue without their cantor.[118] Joseph's release was obtained, and he resumed his life of service to both the Jewish and non-Jewish communities of Manila, while assisting Rabbi Schwarz and the other German and Austrian Jews in their efforts to aid the imprisoned Jews at STIC with food and approved provisions. While such releases were rare, they were not unheard of.

Frank Ephraim's monograph, *Escape to Manila*, is the first published account based on stories from the survivors of the Jewish community in the Philippines. Frank remembers an incident at the synagogue shortly after Joseph's return to the community. The Ephraim family was one of the rescued refugee households with Austrian passports not confined in Santo Tomas. Frank recounts how services continued at the synagogue after the occupation with only forty or fifty people in attendance, due to travel and curfew restrictions imposed by the Japanese.[119] Following his release in September 1942, Joseph organized a male choir to prepare music for the High Holy Days. Temple Emil celebrated Yom Kippur on September 22, 1942, nine months into the Japanese occupation of the islands. Frank recounts that afternoon as follows:

> About 1 p.m. there was a flurry of whispered voices and subdued commotion inside the sanctuary as Joseph, facing the Ark of the Covenant, which stood at the head of the temple, was chanting the early afternoon prayers. Suddenly the double door of the sanctuary began to slowly open, and there appeared Morton Netzorg, the former secretary of the Manila Jewish Refugee Committee. He was followed by more than fifty of the internees, including Samuel Schechter, former president of the congregation. They had been allowed to leave the internment camp to attend Yom Kippur services. The atmosphere was electric. The choir could see what was happening because they faced the congregation, but Joseph, fully absorbed in his liturgical passages, turned his head. . . . He immediately saw what was happening, and with a nod here and a hand signal there, the most holy services were interrupted to an emotional welcome for the interned brethren.[120]

Martin Meadows recalls this occasion when his father and mother left camp in the company of armed Japanese guards for the High Holy Days celebration. Their stay was all too short, only a few hours, before they returned to their imprisonment. For those observant Jews who would not violate their travel restrictions on a holiday, services were held in a room on the fourth floor of the main building in STIC. This scenario was repeated for the High Holy Days of 1943 as well.[121] Frank remembers the Jewish internees being "fewer and much thinner" in 1943 than the year before.[122]

On February 9, 1943, Joseph petitioned the "Commandant of the Japanese Imperial Forces" at STIC for permission to conduct education classes out of his home.

> Sirs, I am a Polish citizen (born August 30, 2912, in Bamberg, Germany) and was permanently released from the Internment Camp due to my religious activities with the Temple Emil Congregation. I have to support my 72 years old Mother, who due to her age needs quite often medical treatments and special care. To maintain our livelihood and give proper care and attention to my old Mother, I hereby appeal to your kindness to permit me to give private elementary lessons to children and also singing lessons.

I believe that if your answer is in the affirmative, I will be able to support my Mother and myself providing her with the needed care. Thanking you for your kind consideration and hoping that you will grant my request, I am very respectfully yours, Joseph Cysner.[123]

Permission was given, which allowed Joseph to conduct classes for refugee school children in his home, along with piano and Hebrew lessons for children and adults. He also resumed his teaching at the Catholic De La Salle College, where he was appointed choirmaster. As Frank describes it, Joseph's house was a "beehive of activity," as he labored to maintain some kind of normalcy in the lives of his congregants despite the harsh conditions of the occupation.[124]

In December 1943, Martin turned thirteen while interned at STIC, the age when young Jewish boys participate in bar mitzvah, the coming-of-age ceremony marking their passage into adulthood. The Meadows family, as longtime members of the Jewish community in Manila, petitioned the Japanese camp commandant for a special release, which was granted only to father and son. Martin and his father left his mother behind and ventured into the city; it was the first time Martin had left STIC in nearly two years of imprisonment. They both wore the required red armbands designating them as STIC internees. Joseph called together a minyan and performed the ceremony for his former student, who had to return immediately to his confinement with his father. This would be the last reunion of Jewish internees with any of their fellow religionists in the city until the liberation of Manila in 1945. As the calendar advanced to 1944, the harshest year of internment at Santo Tomas began.

Carroll describes early 1944 as the moment when the Japanese Army "marched back into Santo Tomas and set about deliberately starving us to death."[125] Nearly every account written by survivors of STIC call it the "Year of Starvation."[126] By January 10, 1944, the Japanese War Prisoners Department of the JMA had complete supervision of STIC, initiating "drastic changes" in camp life, including closing the package lines, forbidding vendors on site, and taking over complete control of the prisoners' food rations.[127] Through ingenious and potentially deadly deceptions, Earl Carroll, still operating as head of the finance and supplies committee, was able to maintain lifelines with the outside world, which barely managed to stave off complete starvation in the entire camp.[128] Survivors recount stories of inedible rotten food being provided by the Japanese, which was served to the malnourished and systematically starved internees. Diseases

associated with diet deficiencies raged through the camp. According to
Martin, as many as six people died daily toward the end of their imprisonment. Martin, an adolescent boy, lost forty pounds during his incarceration,
and his mother weighed just eighty pounds when liberated. The average
weight loss among the men was fifty pounds, and some lost nearly half
their body weight. Death statistics show that of the 435 deaths recorded
in the thirty-seven months of STIC's operation, 95 died in the first three
months of 1945 alone.[129]

It is evident in the various testimonies of Jewish survivors of Santo
Tomas that an organized Jewish group did not exist in STIC. When asked
specifically about that, Martin could not recall any special organization of
Jews in camp. The autobiography of Esther Robbins Hutton, a young Jewish girl caught up in the invasion of Manila with her mother and brother
as they were in transit from Shanghai to the United States, never once
mentions knowing other Jews in camp or of being aware that there was a
Jewish community in Manila. Esther shared the story of how their camp
family, augmented by the presence of their protector, Edgar Bruce Green,
a Jewish businessman from China also caught in the war while passing
through the region, had improvised a bar mitzvah for Esther's brother
while in camp in January 1945.[130] Had they known about Rabbi Schwarz,
Cantor Cysner, or Temple Emil and petitioned for a temporary release
for the event, as did Martin's family, the new Japanese military camp
commander would never have allowed it. We may assume that the family
was unaware of other Jews in Manila, either in camp or without, or that
conditions in camp in 1945 prevented or discouraged such awareness.

MANILANERS UNDER JAPANESE OCCUPATION

While camp inmates battled malnutrition, disease, and exposure (many
built shanties on the campus grounds in order to have some kind of family
residence), the citizens of Manila tried to adapt to life under Japanese occupation. In addition to trying to assist their friends and families who had
been interned, residents of Manila also struggled to find work and to pay
for basic staples of life. American and British companies, the largest employers on the islands, went out of business when their owners and execu-
tives joined the food lines in camp. Houses and businesses were searched
and seized without warning, thus providing lodging for the Japanese forces
while making their owners homeless as well as jobless. Japanese soldiers
looted stores, homes, and farms, wantonly destroying property and any

possessions that they did not steal. The pillaging Japanese targeted American and British holdings specifically, without thought to religion or social distinction.

According to the testimonies of the Manilaners, they themselves suffered relatively little at the hands of the Japanese because their status as "Germans" identified them as allies. For the most part, the Japanese did not care if they were Jewish. Lotte Cassel relates how Japanese soldiers came to their home and asked to see their passports: "He wanted to see passports and, in the passport, of course was the big 'J' in our passport for 'Jew' as we left Germany . . . and he wanted to know what this 'J' stood for. [My father] said it stands for my wife's name Jenny, which wasn't even so. And so, the guy said, you're not really German. Oh yes, my father said, absolutely, we're German. After all they kicked you out. So my Dad said, look, your mother also spanks you once in a while but you still love her, so he finally left."[131] Charlotte Holzer also notes the unusual but not unexpected way her father dealt with the passport issue: "My father's passport was a German passport with a big red 'J' on it, which means Jew, and when the Japanese would stop him and ask for his papers, his passport, he would put his thumb on the 'J' so that all they would see is German — so they didn't really bother us."[132] One of the biggest intrusions Manilaner children experienced under the Japanese were the changes in their school courses.

Charlotte recounts returning to school to find the curriculum altered by the Japanese. Not only did they have to learn to read and write Japanese, but to this day she still remembers the words to the Japanese national anthem.[133] Ralph Preiss, another Manilaner, remembers pages of their textbooks being glued together, the Japanese version of censorship of all historical materials pertaining to the British and the Americans.[134] The Christian-German youth Hans Hoeflein relates how they had lots of visits in school "from Japanese Propaganda people" who would "talk to the students about how much better the Japanese system was than the US system and how lucky the Filipinos were to be part of the Greater East Asia Co-Prosperity Sphere."[135] Margot Cassel recalls the bravery of one of her teachers at the Philippine Women's University: "During the Japanese occupation, we were not allowed many subjects . . . but every once in a while, Miss Manzo would close the door and she would teach us Philippine history. . . . She could have been killed, she could have lost her job, she could have gotten the school in trouble, but she was fantastic. You just felt the excitement of that history."[136]

Manilaners also tell of living through deprivation and fear, recalling everyday displays of Japanese brutality. Hans is just one of many to share recollections of abuses Japanese would inflict for the smallest of offenses. Ralph can still speak the Japanese phrase "I'm your friend," which they repeated over and over as they bowed to the soldiers. He remembered how important bowing became and the penalties inflicted indiscriminately when *gaijin* (foreigners) disrespected the Japanese by failing to bow. All civilians were required to bow to the Japanese when you passed by them. Failing to bow, or not bowing quickly enough, or not bowing deep enough would result in any manner of punishment from face slapping, to beatings, and even to being bayoneted.[137] Charlotte remembered the Japanese Army as a mass of poor, ragtag, hungry soldiers who stole food and hid to eat it. She recounts, "The Nazis were intelligent, cultured people and they killed our people while the most beautiful classical music was playing. The Japanese were very barbaric, because if they caught someone stealing food, like the Filipinos stealing, they would hang them right there on a tree, but they did the same thing to their own. . . . I remember them as being cruel people but cruel to their own and not just the enemy."[138]

In spite of the poverty and the pernicious acts of random violence by the Japanese, Jewish life and culture for the Manilaners, especially for the youth like Ralph and Charlotte, continued undisturbed, in large part because of Cantor Cysner. Joseph continued to prepare the Jewish boys, like Ralph Preiss, for their bar mitzvahs—just as he had for Martin Meadows—and participated in their ceremonies. Hebrew classes resumed, and Joseph returned to the Catholic Boys School of De La Salle College, where he taught music classes and organized boys choirs. Jewish families continued to observe Shabbat and the High Holy Days. However, attendance at synagogue declined significantly under the Japanese occupation with restrictions on travel, enforcements of curfews, and the posting of sentries at strategic locations.[139]

The Japanese censored all media and press, rationed basic commodities, and swiftly punished all infractions of their multitude of directives. Therefore, non-interned refugee Jews suffered the same indiscriminate Japanese brutality along with the non-Jewish residents of Manila. Suspicion and fear became a part of everyday life as informant organizations, under firm Japanese orders, reported violations of their regulations. Punishable offenses included use of typewriters, listening to overseas radio broadcasts, stealing, and teaching concepts other than the "propagandized" Japanese versions of academic subjects. Penalties were administered through beatings, imprisonment, starvation, torture, and executions.[140] Within two weeks after their initial invasion, the commander in chief of the Japanese Expeditionary Forces identified seventeen acts deemed punishable by death, ranging from espionage, rebellion, murder, and stealing to disturbing the peace and spreading rumors.[141]

President Quezon was evacuated from Manila by submarine on February 20, 1945, at the urging of General MacArthur, leaving Jorge Vargas as mayor of Greater Manila in charge of negotiations with the Japanese.[142] Urged to cooperate with the occupying forces, Filipino leaders under Vargas presented a proposal to organize the Philippine Executive Commission according to Japanese demands for a central government compatible with the forthcoming New World Order. With political reorganization completed, officials of the commission "had to give speeches to their countrymen to explain the side of the government and urge cooperation."[143] Support among commission members for the JMA ranged from full collaboration to passive resistance. Since the Japanese held absolute power, all actions by commission members had to pass their approval. Conditions of life in Manila proper, dictated directly by the occupying Japanese forces, varied significantly from life in the provinces.

Firsthand accounts from refugee survivors outside Manila reveal the many dangers life posed at that time and the tactics Jewish families implemented in order to survive. Otto Emmerich, his wife, Lisa, and their three sons, Ernest, Helmuth, and Alfred, survived for three years "living in the forests and fields" of Mindanao, using their wits to outsmart their Japanese invaders. Recorded testimony of the youngest son, Alfred, reveals that the family worked at times as civilian informants of Japanese troop movements on the southern island. Alfred recorded the words of his father.

> Everyone will remember the Jap invasion of Davao . . . so do I. To make it short, after nine hours of fighting we had to run into the mountains. I had no idea of the whereabouts of my family but after 17 days we assembled one by one in the Davao hospital. My wife and youngest son were hurt by bombs; the others were sick on account of starvation in the mountains. I don't even remember how many ailments I had. In the hospital the Jap didn't bother us at all. They had never seen a Jew and accepted us as "Nazis."[144]

Alfred recounted their fears that someone in town would reveal that they were Jews and disclose their "work" on the island of Mindanao with a consequence that Alfred described as *"corta civisa* (beheading)."[145]

After an adequate time of recuperation, the Emmerich family returned to their abandoned farm in Licanan on Mindanao, where they began cultivating and eating papaya and trading with other farmers for vegetables and other staples. According to Alfred, the Japanese "invented" a new business practice unique to the invaders called "party-party," meaning fifty-fifty. Japanese officials came to the Emmerich farm and demanded that half the planted and cultivated farmland be given to them, and it was. Everyone who passed by the Japanese squatters on the trails and roadways near the farm was required to hand over half of what they were carrying, no matter what it was. The Japanese "tenants" who lived in a storehouse on the Emmerich farm began to accumulate a nice brood of chickens from their "party-party" business. As Alfred recounts, necessity being the mother of invention, the Emmerich family, being hungry for something other than papaya three meals a day, built a clandestine chicken hutch in their attic and sprayed a path of corn kernels leading up to the loft. There the chickens would roost, lay contraband eggs for the Emmerich family, and then return on their own to the yard of their Japanese overlords.[146]

Stories such as these reveal the ingenuity borne from desperation. But the fate of the imprisoned was never far from their minds as Alfred tells how they would give what produce from their harvests they could spare to "trustful Filipinos to deliver to the civilian camp where captured Americans were starving."[147] It wasn't long before the Japanese fifty-fifty practice became one hundred to nothing, and the Emmerich family had to leave their farm and turn it over to the Japanese. They decided not to return to their house in the city of Davao, which had been ransacked earlier by the Japanese, and took to the neighboring farmlands. There, they were evicted two more times by the Japanese and lived a hand-to-mouth existence in the junglelike region for the next three years, until their eventual liberation by the Americans.

GERMANS AND NAZIS IN THE PHILIPPINES

January 1943 brought a new threat to the Jewish refugees in the Philippines as antisemitic rhetoric targeted the non-interned German and Austrian Jews. This Nazi-inspired diatribe can be seen as a momentary aberration in the history of Jews and Germans in the Philippines. Ironically, the first Germans to set foot on these islands came with the same wave of Spanish explorers that brought the Philippines its first Jewish inhabitants in the sixteenth century. Even though Spain isolated the Philippines from foreign settlement from 1593 to 1815, German Jesuits accompanied other non-Castilian Jesuits to evangelize the Philippine natives. German pharmacists, physicians, and scientists were also granted a presence in the islands during the centuries of Spanish rule. But the formation of a settled German community did not take place until Spain opened Manila to world commerce in 1834. In 1849, after trade with German companies had been well established, German consulates began to appear. Over the next several decades, German scientists, educators, scholars, and historians sought new horizons and exciting opportunities in the Spanish colony.[148]

With the onset of the Spanish-American War in 1898, European countries vied for commercial and colonial footholds in East Asia—and the Philippines topped the list for most favored colonial possession. German Foreign Office documents reveal that German intentions for imperial hegemony in the Philippines inspired a naval standoff in Manila Bay between the US and German Navies at the end of the Spanish Colonial Era.[149] Germany's plans for its own colonization of the Philippines failed with the annexation by the United States of all the islands. Under the Americans, international commerce continued to flow into Manila, along with more foreign managers, workers, missionaries, military personnel, and politicians. By 1903, 368 Germans resided in the Philippines, with more than two-thirds of that number living in Manila. World War I brought an era of uncertainty to diplomatic relationships in the Philippines, as it did in the rest of the world, but Manila was "the only safe neutral port for German merchant vessels trading along the China coast."[150] The US Governor General in the Philippines, Francis B. Harrison, granted the German Consul safe passage on an American transport when recalled from his post. Harrison reflected that "the Philippines was singularly free from incidents of warlike import" during the war—though it was certainly not the case during World War II.[151]

In the years between the wars, numerous German companies opened offices in Manila, contributing to the Philippine economy and supporting a sophisticated, cosmopolitan ideal of colonial life. With the rise of Nazism in Europe, there came difficult years for the German community in the Philippines. The social organization of the Philippine German community, the German Club, reported significant resignations of club membership in the early years of Hitler's chancellorship.[152] The German Club had always adopted a policy of nonpolitical involvement, and this annoyed Nazi Party members in the Philippines. With the outbreak of the war in Europe in 1939 and the alliance of Germany with Japan, another wave of

German Club resignations ensued, cresting in 1940 and 1941 as the clouds of an impending Pacific War caused many to flee the islands, especially when "on July 9, 1941, the German Consulate in Manila was ordered closed by the U.S. Government" followed by Paul McNutt "suspending the movement of all bank account funds of German nationals."[153] The bombing of Pearl Harbor and the Philippines, along with Hitler's declaration of war on the United States, precipitated the arrest of civilian German nationals and their incarceration at the National Penitentiary at Muntinlupa. When the Japanese invaded Luzon and advanced into Manila unchallenged, the tide turned for the alien civilians as the Japanese freed the Germans and interned American civilians instead, along with others from Allied nations now at war with Germany and Japan.[154]

The history of the German community in the Philippines during the 1930s and 1940s does not necessarily equate with the history of the Philippine Nazi Party, which had organized a local branch: the Ortsgruppe Manila. The History Committee of the German Club in Manila maintains that membership in the Nazi Party was completely voluntary with "no compulsion or intimidation employed to persuade German residents of Manila to become members." However, the 1938 arrival of the German Consul, Gustav Sakowsky, a Nazi Party member adamant in recruiting new party members from within the community, caused severe tension between the German Club and the German Consular Office: Sakowsky had declared the German Club to be an "enemy of the Third Reich" and demanded that all party members sever their association with it. Edgar Krohn, a member of the History Committee in 1996, maintains that those few who did join the party "conducted themselves at all times in a very correct manner, were never vindictive or overbearing, and never committed any unlawful acts." This tension deflated significantly when Sakowsky returned to Germany in 1939; he had been replaced as the German Consul in the Philippines by Dr. H. Lautenschlager, who never once tried to promote Nazi practices of compulsion, discrimination, or persecution.[155]

Attempts at racially motivated persuasion finally appeared in the Philippines in 1943 with the arrival of Franz Josef Spahn, the new leader for the Philippine Nazi Party, Ortsgruppe Manila. Spahn carried an arrest warrant for the president of the German Club, seeking his execution by the Japanese military police. But the warrant's rejection by the local members of the Ortsgruppe Manila seemed to indicate their unwillingness to conform to their party's expectations.[156] Thus the first episode of a dangerous antisemitic presence in the Philippines came not from the German community but from the Japanese Military Administration itself.

In January 1943, the JMA suddenly began running notices in the local papers, warning that Jews in the Philippines would "be dealt with drastically."[157] The Manila *Tribune*'s headline for January 26, 1943, read: "Jews Given Stern Warning." The age-old rhetoric described the Jews as "people without a motherland . . . a wandering race . . . parasites of the countries in which they live."[158] It went on to itemize trumped-up charges of hoarding commodities to raise prices, exploiting native women, and even acts of espionage. It is unclear whether any members of the Nazi Party incubated the diatribes or if the JMA acted on its own volition. One year later, in January 1944, rumors about forcing the German Jews into a ghetto began to circulate. Spahn called for the immediate internment of aliens guilty of "acts inimical to the peace, security, and interest of the Republic of the Philippines."[159] By falsifying the facts concerning the abandonment of the Mindanao resettlement project and claiming that the Jews sabotaged the plan with the intension of dominating the Philippine urban economy, the Nazi Party leader in the Philippines deliberately targeted the Jewish refugee community in the Philippines.[160]

John Griese maintained that this imminent danger to the German Jews was averted by the more influential leaders of the Jewish community, including Rabbi Schwarz and Joseph Cysner, who negotiated with the JMA.[161] While the Japanese could not be bothered with Nazi plans to establish a Jewish ghetto in the Philippines, they did not object to episodes of abuse randomly waged against members of the Jewish community by Japanese soldiers. Frank Ephraim recounts the torture and death of a German Jew who was arrested for violating wartime rules by "aiding the enemy" when he gave an American prisoner a pack of cigarettes.[162] This and another dozen incidents of German Jewish suffering at the hands of the Japanese illustrated the horror of the time. The number of such incidents shows that these clashes, moreover, had more to do with the brutality of the Japanese occupation that any specific targeting of Jews.

Then, in June 1944, the news that American forces had landed on Saipan, 1,500 miles west of Manila, gave renewed hope to all.

Peletah—Deliverance

From June 15, 1944, when the American forces first landed on Saipan, it would be another nine months before the Philippines were finally released from Japanese control on March 3, 1945. Eyewitness accounts record the return of the US military to the Philippines and the trauma of that liberation for Joseph and all the civilians there, including the Manilaners. During those most destructive months of the war, the exiled Philippine President Quezon died, having never seen the fulfillment of his efforts to advance colonization on Mindanao for Jewish refugees. In October 1944, American forces began their bombing raids on strategic Japanese locations in and around Manila. Japanese troops expelled the Jewish community from their synagogue, their social hall, and even their homes, converting buildings into ammunition dumps, barricades, and command centers, eventually dynamiting them and setting them afire. A fear of mass executions by the Japanese seized all as the US armed forces retook Manila district by district and block by block, and as one Manilaner describes it, "brick by brick."[1] A number of synagogue members throughout the city rescued the holy artifacts, the sacred lamp, prayer books, pulpit coverings, and the Torah scrolls. But even during this time, Joseph never faltered as a beacon of Jewish faith in the storm. Jacques Lipetz fondly remembers "during, or rather between air raids . . . taking two street cars to learn Chumash, hear music, and talk to Mr. Cysner."[2] Joseph never stopped administering to his flock.

When the freed inmates of the civilian internment camps returned to Manila, the sight of the destruction was overwhelming. Nearly everyone was homeless: Jews, non-Jews, Filipinos, Americans—no one was exempt from the carnage and destruction left in the aftermath of the war. The Battle of Manila was a violent end to three years of Japanese occupation. Newly secured lodgings for Joseph and his mother, and for Rabbi Schwarz and his wife, Anneliese, became the new religious centers for the community in the weeks immediately following liberation.[3] The Passover season of March 1945, which came on the heels of their deliverance, was infused with new meanings for the Philippine survivors. On March 23, 1945, a posting on the US Army bulletin board announced a Passover Seder for the surviving members of the Jewish community in Manila. Rare photographs of that event, along with others taken by the US Signal Corps at the High Holidays in September 1945, offer extraordinary documentation of these historic events. For most of the devastated refugees who had lost their homes and their livelihoods, their island paradise could offer them a secure harbor no longer, and most will abandon their beloved Asian sanctuary in search of yet another safe haven.

MANILANERS REMEMBER
SCENES OF WAR

As war in the Philippines persisted, the situation in Manila deteriorated rapidly. Lotte Cassel Hershfield shares a distinct memory of December 1, 1944, when her father and brother were taken from their home at gunpoint by Japanese soldiers. Now alone, Lotte rode her bicycle to the hospital to see her mother, who was recuperating from an operation. After reassuring her mother that everything "was perfect" at home, not wanting to alarm her of the unknown fate of her father and brother, Lotte relates:

> I reached home very late that night because I was interrupted on the way by an air-raid. The Yanks were bombing us again. When at last I did reach the house, there to my greatest surprise were father and brother. My Dad had altered [aged] at least ten years, almost beyond recognition. The brutal Japs had made them kneel down on the campus grounds of a school, letting them stare into the blazing sun, with guns and tanks facing them every minute, ready to let off a shot. Screams of men who were being tortured inside of the building could be heard. What they had suffered those eight hours, is impossible to describe.[4]

Cruelties perpetrated by the Japanese, similar to what the Cassel family had experienced, took place daily throughout the islands to countless peoples as the American forces advanced. These atrocities and other hardships suffered by the people of Manila at the hands of the Japanese had a universal application in that they were all victims of a war motivated by racial hatred—perpetrated upon Jew and Gentile alike. The devastation of war brought the diversity of the island populations together in joint efforts of survival. Margie Rosenthal, née Margit Miedzwinsky, remembers that during these months of battle,

> there were many times when we did not think that we would see the sun again. Whenever we started a new day, all of us got together, Catholics, Jews, Protestants, Mohammedans, and Chinese to pray to God. It was the same thing for each group—to get us through all the hardships safely and that we should be liberated by the Americans.[5]

The Japanese now viewed all civilians as subversive guerillas, and many fled the city into the mountains to escape their summary justice.[6] Jenny Hanna, born in Manila in January 1931, and her family, Jewish citizens of the Philippines, remembers how they "evacuated to Baguio on November 24, 1944, and stayed there until February 18, 1945. Then we went to the mountains with the natives (five kilometers away from Baguio), because the American planes were beginning to carpet bomb Baguio. . . . In the mountains we were safe from the bombing, but not so well off. Potatoes were about the only food we could eat."[7] Ralph Preiss and his family had been living in the Laguna Province nearly their entire residency in the Philippines since Ralph's father, Harry Preiss, worked for a soft drink bottling company in Lilio. During the years of the Japanese occupation, Preiss was given part of the equipment as payment for back wages owed him by the company; he moved the family to San Pablo, still in the Laguna Province, and set up his own business. During the war years, Preiss's Filipino business partner was also a member of the guerilla movement. Ralph remembers when this partner and other Filipino guerillas saved their lives during the liberation of the Philippines by American forces:

> Guerillas came and took us into the mountains because they overheard the Japanese were going to kill all white people. . . . Filipinos brought horses at two in the morning, just like that, and said you have to evacuate, take what you can. . . . This was in 1944 or maybe early 1945. We stayed in

the mountains for about three months and we had to move from camp to camp because the Japanese were after us and the guerillas.[8]

When the men returned from their mountain hideouts after the Battle of Manila, their town and their homes were completely destroyed.

As Americans forces advanced, the Japanese strengthened their positions in Manila in preparation for a last stand once the Americans reached the city. Frank Ephraim describes the entire city as a "giant fortress": the Japanese mined the bridges spanning the river, expelled people from concrete structures that they turned into fortified shelters, and set up machine-gun nests, barbed-wire barricades, and wire fences.[9] Anticipating Japanese actions against internees at the civilian internment camps, a daring rescue ensued at Santo Tomas. Abraham Van Heyningen Hartendorp, also known as A. V. H. Hartendorp or A. V. Hartendorp, an American editor at the *Philippine Magazine* in Manila before the war, kept a secret journal during his internment at STIC. He recounts the acceleration of allied military activity near the camp during those first days of February 1945, with American reconnaissance planes flying low over the camp, dropping messages that read, "Roll out the barrel." Hartendorp tells how camp inmates readied themselves for dearly anticipated freedom.[10]

> At nine o'clock, Saturday night, February 3rd, what started as a whisper turned into a great shout—"They're here! The boys are here!" People rushed to the windows and doors. Hundreds of internees were coming down the stairs, jamming the lobby of the main building. . . . The rumble was loud and very near. There was brief machine-gun and rifle fire at the gate, a few hand-grenade explosions; something vast and black burst through the flimsy sawali [bamboo] inner gate, then stopped as search-lights flashed across the campus and rockets went up which lighted the camp from end to end. The tank lumbered toward the main building, followed after an interval by others. As four of the tanks were coming to a halt, a fifth continued to move slowly around the back of the building to cover the rear entrance. Two officers walked in front of the first tank. "Hello, folks!" an American voice rang out.[11]

While liberation had come to the internees of Santo Tomas, another month of fighting still raged ahead before Manila could finally be repatriated. The Battle of Manila officially began on the day STIC was liberated on February 3, 1945, and lasted until March 3, leaving the city in total ruin.

As the Americans continued their advance on Manila, the Japanese feverishly fought a war of attrition against the civilian population. Frank Ephraim relates the devastation that battle caused.

> The northern part of the city up to the Pasig River was liberated very quickly. But the Japs still had time to burn the downtown district completely. The fighting for the river was very bloody for both the US forces and the Japs. Artillery on both sides was very strong. We never even knew where the Americans were, though they were so near to us. On February 7, violent shelling from mortars and 75mm hit the city everywhere, houses were destroyed, and people killed. That was a terrible day—nobody could go outside, because the defending Japs shot at everybody thinking he was a guerilla. Patrols of Jap house-burners walked around in the streets twenty-four hours a day.[12]

Retreating Japanese forces destroyed everything in their wake, purposely burning whatever they could rather than leaving anything behind for the Americans. Manfred Hecht, a Jewish youth who had fled Germany in 1939 with his parents, Kurt and Felice Hecht, remembers the evening of February 9, 1945.

> We were eating our supper when we heard a big commotion in the street. We all rushed out systematically to see what was going on. There we saw people rushing about in all directions. In the direction from which most people came from, we saw a huge mass of fire. It was quite far away from where we were. As we watched the fire, we saw new houses, as well as old, starting to burn, and always coming nearer and closer. The nearest fire was still ten houses away, when suddenly out of the crowd came about twelve Japs. They just kicked the door open and we were unable to run out. We stood there with fear and didn't dare to move. They looked around and started to talk and shout to each other. Then one of them, who had four bottles, smashed one of them on the table. It was gasoline. Another one lit a match and in less than a second the table caught fire. They laughed and went out again. We just stood there, and we were glad that they did not molest us at all. Well, then we immediately rushed out too, for the house was burning. We hardly reached the street before the whole house was totally afire.[13]

Armed with gasoline and matches, the Japanese indiscriminately burned businesses, homes, hospitals, and other places where residents were hiding, including Temple Emil and Bachrach Hall, as well as the residence of Joseph and his mother, making him once again a homeless refugee. Rabbi Schwarz records that "during the [B]attle of Manila, during the night of February 12, 1945, the old Temple Emil was set afire by retreating Japanese soldiers and burned down to its fire walls."[14] Temple Emil was "the only synagogue destroyed in battle on American territory during WWII."[15]

A pattern of Japanese massacres ensued, in which they machine-gunned citizens who were trying to save homes and buildings from the fires. The historian William Craig describes the scene: "For nearly one month, into late February, Manila was a slaughterhouse, the scene of multiple atrocities, as Japanese marines fought insanely to defend the strategically unimportant city."[16] Random shootings by the Japanese killed without discrimination of age or gender, and many children were brutalized and murdered. Rabbi Schwarz recounts how the Jewish community fared: "the Battle of Manila hit us hard. Almost seventy of our members lost their lives, hundreds were wounded, about 90 percent of our members were burned out completely, since the majority of our members lived south of the Pasig River. Hundreds suffered from malnutrition and complete exhaustion."[17] On February 10, 1945, Japanese soldiers murdered Jewish refugees and many other inhabitants of Manila in the Philippine National Red Cross building, mistakenly leaving one wounded Jewish survivor as a witness to the atrocity. There were nine Jews and a maid who took refuge in the lady's washroom. They were all killed except for John Lewy and the maid. The maid was unharmed, but Lewy took two bayonet thrusts, thus becoming a surviving witness to massacre.[18]

Carnage continued unchecked as the Americans advanced closer and closer to the heart of the city. Annette Eberly recalls a "fear of mass execution by the Japanese as the liberating armies approached Manila."[19] Margot Cassel Kestenbaum recalls when the Americans arrived.

> Huddled together in our air raid shelter, we anxiously waited the night to come. I now took my mother's place at the entrance and fought off the flying sparks with a wet diaper. Earlier that afternoon we had heard sporadic machine gun fire. Could my father be right, that it meant the arrival of the Americans? . . . A numbness now possessed me, and nothing seemed to matter. I had no interest in food. To eat, die or live, were all the same to me. As we were watching each other the tense silence continued. Suddenly a neighbor came running with the news that the Americans were at a small market near our neighborhood, and that we should make haste to get there. . . . A decision had to be made at once. Everyone took his

knapsack—but how to get out? Wouldn't the Japs surely shoot if they saw us? Risky as it was, we scrambled out of the shelter slowly, crawling southward toward the small market. Tearing our clothing and scratching ourselves at barbed wire entanglements, we managed to proceed. . . . Ahead I could see figures in uniforms. . . . The Americans were here and all looking splendid. I could not believe it. When we reached our goal amidst the soldiers, I sank down exhausted but serenely happy, knowing that the three years of suffering and pestilence were over.[20]

Countless testimonies of survivors of the Philippine campaign recount similar scenes of excitement and relief at seeing American soldiers once again in Manila. Charlotte Holzer Bunim remembers the day of their liberation as well.

What happened was when the Americans came back and they were fighting, the civilians were in the middle, so we were getting it from two sides, from the Japanese and from the Americans. We were in a bomb shelter . . . and we knew the Japanese were told to kill all white people, whoever is white, just get rid of them. We were in an air raid shelter for two or three people and we ended up with six or seven people and it was stifling. . . . I remember a soldier putting his foot down on one step, coming down into the air raid shelter and my father started saying the prayers you say when you are about to be killed. But as he was saying it, he started looking up to see who was coming down—we thought it was the Japanese ready to kill us all—and it was the first American we saw coming back, and [Dad] looked up and said, "blue eyes, blond hair" and he yelled out "God Bless America" and we started to cry.[21]

Nests of Japanese snipers still fired upon the liberating American soldiers and the rescued civilians as they fled to evade the bullets, and many died in the process. Charlotte recounted that "it was hell—we ran and got shot at but we survived."[22]

When the inmates of STIC and the prisoners of other camps, such as Los Baños, which were heroically liberated by US paratroopers on February 23, 1945, had rejoined their community, they returned to a landscape of devastation. Ninety percent of Manila's Jews were homeless, along with most of the city's population.[23] William Manchester, the biographer of General Douglas MacArthur, states that "the devastation of Manila was one of the great tragedies of World War II. Of Allied cities in those war years, only Warsaw suffered more."[24] Ephraim records the testimony of a Jewish army chaplain, Dudley Weinberg, in a letter written to the Frieders: "I have never seen such sadness, such destruction and such desolation. Pick up your bible and read the Book of Lamentations and you will have the story."[25]

RESTORATION AND NEW BEGINNINGS

The Japanese occupation ended violently with the liberation of the islands by the Americans and their allies. The returning internees of the civilian concentration camps, Jews and non-Jews alike, joined with the remaining population to try to rebuild their devastated communities. Everyone had been terrorized by the retreating Japanese forces. Since the end of the fighting, three more members of the Jewish community had died, bringing the total dead from the battle to seventy.[26] The upcoming Passover season of March 1945 carried a new meaning for Manilaners. The American military took extraordinary steps to assist the Jewish community in its recovery. American soldiers provided food, water, supplies, and medicine for the victims, and Joseph restored cultural activities, religious services, and youth group meetings. The US Army announced on March 23, 1945, that a Passover Seder would be held in conjunction with the surviving members of the Jewish community in Manila. Jacques Lipetz remembers that "on that Passover, they had a Seder, on the race track in Manila. . . . It was the largest auditorium. It wasn't covered, but it was, you know, open for the American army and all the Jewish civilians that they could muster." He relates how army jeeps provided "bumpy and dangerous" transportation back and forth from the Seder for the Jewish civilians, "and gave us matzoh, and [weeping] had a Seder."[27] On March 28, 1945, the racetrack bleachers, capable of seating thousands, were filled with US military personnel and all the Jewish civilians who were able to attend. In his memoirs, Ephraim describes that night as follows:

> To the liberated Jewish refugees, the event was truly staggering. Mingling and talking to the thousands of Jewish soldiers, sailors, and airmen was a thrilling experience—something we had never dreamed of. The servicemen and women were equally surprised to find Jews in this part of the world. They gave us all their C-rations and K-rations, their cigarettes, and the ubiquitous small bars of Hershey "tropics proof" chocolate. . . . Down on the racetrack, Joseph sang into a microphone over the din of thousands of conversations, his rich voice penetrating above the noise.[28]

Jacques Lipetz also remembers Joseph "the wonderful chazzan," and that memorable Seder service: "I doubt however that anyone since the Exodus had so sweet a Pesach."[29]

Months later, on September 12, 1945, a young American soldier of the 547th Signal Corps arrived in Manila on board the USS *Sea Flyer*, which had left Marseilles after the end of the war in Europe on a voyage of some sixteen thousand nautical miles before reaching the Philippines. That soldier, Norman Schanin, arrived during the High Holy Days, just in time, as he says, "to attend Yom Kippur services which were conducted in an open-air stadium in Manila proper. It was a moving experience to see this large stadium filled with thousands of Jewish army and navy personnel, officers and enlisted men and women praying together on Yom Kippur."[30] Joseph officiated as the cantor at those services, which were held in the battered Rizal Stadium. Schanin, a religiously observant soldier, sought out Jewish community members after the High Holidays and immediately participated in any and all services conducted in the Philippines. He observes that in the aftermath of the debilitating Battle of the Philippines, "the existing local Jewish leadership had neither the means nor the strength to maintain community life and activities." This was not due to a lack of desire but to a lack of means as many methods of transportation were gone, jobs were scarce, and everyone was just trying to survive. The clubhouse of the JWB, for which Morton Netzorg served as its representative in the Philippines, became a USO meeting place for Jewish military personnel and for those of the local Jewish community who lived close enough to participate in their events. Schanin discloses that he and fellow Jewish servicemen assisted the Jewish community "with appropriate army food" to assist them in keeping their *kashrut* laws.[31] By October 1945, Schanin received a change of orders and became the assistant to Chaplain Coleman A. Zwitman, a Reform rabbi from Florida, for the entire Manila area. Schanin was particularly instrumental in coordinating activities among the local servicemen "to help the local Manila Jewish community rebuild and reorganize itself."[32]

> The Jewish community, together with the rest of the civilian population, was still suffering from the experiences of war under Japanese occupation and the aftermath of the fierce fighting, as well as the burning of parts of Manila that accompanied the enemy retreat. We thus outlined our immediate priorities for helping the local Jewish community, such as the

rebuilding of the local synagogue and the provision of Jewish education for the children and youth. During the Japanese occupation, the local Cantor, Joseph Cysner, gathered children in his home and taught some Hebrew and the meaning of the holidays. Sometime after the war ended, he resumed teaching children to read the Hebrew prayer book.[33]

Because of Schanin and the Jewish chaplains, hundreds of American Jewish military personnel embraced Manila's recovering Jewish community and organized a fund-raising campaign to donate funds for rebuilding Temple Emil.

Edmund Rosenblum, an Austrian Jew who immigrated to America in 1939 and was drafted into the US Army in September 1942, also arrived in Manila in September 1945. He recounts:

> In Manila on our bulletin board appears a notice there's a meeting of all the Jewish soldiers on a Sunday afternoon to rededicate the Synagogue in Manila and also to commemorate all the Jewish soldiers who lost their lives in the Pacific—meeting Sunday afternoon—transportation will be supplied. It was in Manila proper . . . in the bombed-out shell. So, the Chaplain made a beautiful speech that they're gonna rebuild the synagogue which was destroyed by the Japanese—it was bombed and badly destroyed by the shelling of Manila. So we're gonna rededicate it and rebuild it. So, we ask you to be generous and we made a bundle of money.[34]

Schanin recalls that this bulletin was posted on October 24, 1945. He also relates in his memoir that "it was then decided to organize a campaign of raising funds to rebuild the Manila Synagogue and Community Center and to designate the project as a permanent memorial to those who gave their lives in the fighting for the Philippine Islands."[35] On November 9, 1945, on the anniversary of Kristallnacht, Joseph officiated at this memorial service in the bombed-out ruins of the old synagogue to inaugurate the planned reconstruction.[36] Schanin remembers that evening:

> The Memorial Service conducted in the ruins of the Manila Synagogue was a very moving experience. The synagogue overflowed with the hundreds of servicemen and women who stood shoulder to shoulder in the open area between the only remaining walls. The service was led by Rabbi Schwarz and Cantor Joseph Cysner from the local community, with the

participation of the leaders from the Servicemen's Committee. . . . The sum of $12,500 had been raised by the Servicemen's Committee when the campaign formally terminated.[37]

Additional contributions continued to pour in even after the campaign ended, until $15,000 was reached. According to Schanin, service personnel in the Philippines solicited contributions from family members and other groups back home; articles even appeared in New York newspapers championing the efforts of the "GIs" in assisting the destitute community.

The devastation in Manila was so severe that many who could no longer earn a living in the ravaged city immigrated to the United States. After the destruction of the synagogue and the Catholic De La Salle College where he taught, Joseph had no other choice but to join the ranks of the hundreds of Jews who again sought a new life in a new land. With his departure and that of the American Jews, who wanted only to return to their home country, and the European refugees, who had counted on the American-held businesses for much of their livelihood, the Jewish community membership decreased 30 percent by the end of 1946. Fewer than 250 European Jewish refugees could be counted among the estimated 600 Jews who remained in the Philippines at the end of 1948.[38] By 1954, the Jewish community of Manila counted a total of 302 members. While this ends the story of the rescue of European refugee Jews in Manila, it begins a new era in the story of Jews in the Philippines in the post–World War II decades with the emergence of a new cultural and religious community of Filipino Jews, descendants of blended marriages between American and European Jews and Filipinos.

Hundreds of Filipino Jews today, descended from forefathers of various Jewish diasporas, seek identification and validation of their Jewish heritage. A new memorial, dedicated June 21, 2009, now stands on the outskirts of Tel Aviv in the suburb of Rishon le Zion. Titled "Open Doors," the monument commemorates the rescue of refugee Jews in the Philippines and provides a site of pilgrimage for all Jews having connections to the Philippines, both genetically and socially.[39] New scholarship on the personal stories of Filipino Jews, their culture, their genealogies, and how they came to embrace their Jewish heritage waits to be written.

Joseph's odyssey that highlights the remarkable story of how one small community in East Asia managed to do what so many more capable nations of the world were reluctant to do—save Jewish lives—did not end in Manila. Over the next decade nearly every surviving refugee Jew from Europe who found a safe haven in the Philippines eventually made it to the United States. The State Department, which had once stalled the mass migration of Jews to the Philippines in fear that it would constitute a back-door entrance into the United States, wisely allowed all Manilaners a safe shelter on American shores, some refugees even passing through on their way to Israel. The 1,300 souls that were saved would multiply into thousands over the next half century, testifying to the incredible circumstances of their existence. It is remarkable that their Philippine and American benefactors managed to circumvent the State Department's propensity to obstruct Jewish rescue and more than quadruple the population of the islands' small, once inconsequential Jewish community. This tiny Asian Commonwealth saved them from the fate of the six million Jews who were murdered in the Holocaust. While those refugees, when compared to twelve million victims of Nazi atrocities, are not so many, to those who found sanctuary in the Philippines, it meant that each life saved was a nation redeemed.[40] Joseph's deliverance and immigration to the United States brought a blessed reunion with his childhood friend and soon to be wife, Sylvia Nagler.

SYLVIA'S AND JOSEPH'S STORY

Sylvia Nagler had known Joseph Cysner her entire life, as they were raised together by neighboring families in Bamberg, although he was ten years her senior. She was a young schoolgirl when Joseph began his career in 1933 as a cantor in Germany, the same year Hitler was appointed chancellor. As Joseph worked in the Jewish communities of Hannover and Hildesheim between 1933 and 1937, witnessing the rising storm of Nazi antisemitism, Sylvia and her family endured the growing persecutions in Bamberg. When Joseph was expelled from Germany to Poland and held with nearly eight thousand other Polish Jewish nationals at the border town of Zbaszyn, Sylvia and her family watched similar expulsions of their Polish Jewish neighbors and, along with the other Jewish residents of Bamberg, shielded Joseph's widowed Polish mother from expulsion.

While Joseph languished at the detention site of Zbaszyn, his mother and friends in Bamberg suffered the violence and fear of the Kristallnacht pogroms of November 9 and 10, 1938. They watched their homes, businesses, and synagogues being ravaged and destroyed with the tacit cooperation of the Nazis. When news of the event reached Joseph in Zbaszyn, he not only feared for his mother; he also knew he would never again live in

Germany. As Joseph aided in the organization of the refugees at Zbaszyn, Sylvia and her family orchestrated her own escape to England. Once there, she petitioned for the extraction of her two younger brothers via the Kindertransport and was able to place both of them in homes in Scotland at about the same time Joseph obtained his visa to immigrate to the Philippines. Each had reached a haven from the impending Holocaust—Sylvia in London and Joseph in Manila—and each had labored to save family members, who were still living in Bamberg, from the ever-worsening plight of the Jews in Germany. Chaja Cysner joined her son in the Philippines while Sylvia had obtained visas for her parents to immigrate to Trinidad through the auspices of a wealthy Jewish businessman in London. It was merely a few days after the Naglers set sail for Trinidad and were in port outside London that Hitler invaded Poland on September 1, 1939, sealing in the remaining refugee Jews of Europe and impairing their escape. Sylvia called herself the "luckiest girl alive" when her parents disembarked in London.[41]

By combining the details of several interviews conducted with Sylvia into one narrative and contextualizing her experiences with the known history of Germany, the Nazis and the Jews of that period, we are able to see the layout of a synchronized history of both their escapes from Hitler's Germany. Interviews with Sylvia were conducted several times from January 2004 through January 2007; her last interview, on January 25, 2007, would be one month before she passed away. It was a humbling honor to have enjoyed her company and to be able to record her testimony of these events.

JOSEPH AND SYLVIA REUNITE

For more than seven years Joseph shared his "golden voice, personal warmth, and infectious spirit" with the members of the Temple Emil congregation in Manila, touching the lives of its members through his unique abilities as a teacher, director, and mentor.[42] The irony of Joseph's rescue in Manila came in January 1942, when the Japanese Army occupied the Philippines. The invading army arrested all civilian aliens who held a passport from a country at war with Japan or Germany and interned them for three years at Santo Tomas University, turning one of the world's oldest universities into a civilian prison camp overnight. Here, many of the American Jews, who had been the benefactors of the European refugee Jews, were now imprisoned, while the majority of the refugee Jews who were

German and Austrian were not.[43] Joseph, however, held a Polish passport after his German one was seized by the Nazis; thus, he was also arrested and incarcerated in Santo Tomas. He survived Nazi arrest, expulsion, imprisonment, and escape only to encounter it all over again at the hands of the Japanese.

Joseph was allowed a special pardon from incarceration at Santo Tomas to care for his mother, who held a German passport and was not imprisoned by the Japanese. He was able to lead services for the refugees, conduct lessons again in his home, and teach at the colleges during the last two and a half years of Japanese occupation. During his imprisonment in Santo Tomas, he had maintained correspondence with his siblings in New York, London, and Palestine. Letters soon came to him from his sister in London via a mutual friend, Sylvia Nagler, who then lived in London after her escape from Germany. Sylvia recalls,

> We had been corresponding, while I was in England, first with Red Cross messages when he was a prisoner in Santo Tomas. How this came about was because his sister Henrietta, the young one, had come from Berlin to London. She was walking across Oxford Circus and she saw my father whom she recognized. So we made contact. She begged me to write to him on her behalf. Why I don't know, maybe she thought her English wasn't good enough. I started to write Joseph first on her behalf, and he sort of fell for my letters. Eventually, we began writing to each other.[44]

Their correspondence continued until it became impossible to maintain during the last nine months of the war in the Philippines.

Joseph survived under the repressive administration of the Japanese during their occupation, but both his synagogue and his home were destroyed by the Japanese and nearly one hundred of his fellow Jews lost their lives during the Battle of Manila. When the US military forces arrived, they were astonished to find European refugee Jews in the Philippines, and the refugee Jews were surprised to see Jewish servicemen as their liberators. Joseph officiated over a special Seder of deliverance that Passover season of 1945, when thousands of servicemen and women from all over the Pacific Theater attended the service in the bleachers of the racetrack. Eventually, Joseph and most of the other European refugee Jews immigrated to America, as the destroyed Manila held no promise of any kind of prosperity. In spring 1946, Joseph and his mother left Manila for the United States, where he had accepted a position with Congregation Sherith Israel in San Francisco. Sylvia recounts that after Joseph arrived in San Francisco, he wrote to her in England, begging her to join him in America.

> And then he wrote to me that he was going to San Francisco and he wanted me to come. I said no way would I go to America. And this correspondence went on for, I think, it was almost a year, and then he began to phone saying come for a visit. And I went, going to New York first, and that is what happened.[45]

She came on a three-month visitor's visa in 1948, and they married soon after she arrived.

Having survived Zbaszyn confinement, Santo Tomas imprisonment, and the Japanese destruction of his home and synagogue, Joseph's story of deliverance merged with Sylvia's, his childhood friend from Bamberg. Their reunion and marriage in San Francisco in August 1948 was held in the company of family, friends, and fellow Manilaners who had traveled thousands of miles from London and the Philippines to attend. Sylvia recalls that dozens of families of Manilaners lived in the San Francisco area immediately after the war: "the people from the Manila community that had settled in San Francisco, were totally in love with my husband. They were just very wonderful. . . . I would imagine thirty or forty families that had settled in San Francisco, because it was the closest port to the States when they were able to leave Manila."[46]

When Joseph immigrated to America and married Sylvia, he divorced himself emotionally and physically from his German past. He was ashamed to have been a part of an age, part of a people who had inflicted such atrocities on the world; even though he himself had been a victim, he never considered himself a Holocaust survivor. Survivors were the wounded and broken who still retained scars on their bodies and on their psyches. And if Joseph could have taken their wounds on himself to relieve any of their suffering, he would have. Joseph and Sylvia never taught German to their children; nor did they share with them the horrors they had seen and experienced, hoping to shield them from the lingering effects of that war, just as Joseph had tried to shield children in Europe and the Philippines while they had been living it. Joseph embraced American life fully and proudly and became an American citizen a few years before his untimely death. At his sudden passing, communities from Bamberg, Hildesheim, Hannover, Hamburg, Manila, San Francisco, and San Diego mourned him. Rabbi

Schwarz had delivered these words to the congregation at Manila when Joseph first arrived in 1939, and they are fitting words still: "Blessed shalt thou be, when thou comest in. May your prayers edify our Congregation, may they inspire our people, may they heal the wounds inflicted by these times."[47] The greatest legacy of both Joseph and the Holocaust Havens he helped create in Zbaszyn and Manila will always be this: they healed wounds inflicted by the worst of times.

Conclusion

THE WILL TO SAVE

The years of research in finding Joseph, as well as finding out how his story impacts the field of Holocaust studies, have been the intertwining of two journeys—his journey as a refugee and my own as a Holocaust historian. The task of searching out his life's experiences unveiled not only the remarkable man that he was at the heart of the research but also the extraordinary history of incomparable refugee rescue plans that his life's journey helped illuminate. The uniquely devised selection and sponsorship programs in the Philippines, which is the bigger story that envelopes Joseph's odyssey, allowed European refugee Jews to flee their persecutions by any means possible and accomplished what most other nations of the world avoided: that of saving Jewish lives. The significance of Jewish immigration to the Philippines prior to the United States entering World War II goes beyond Joseph and the 1,300 refugee lives saved with him; it demonstrates that industrious persons can devise rescue in the face of both natural and contrived obstacles when there is a will to do so.

The sequence of rescue in the Philippines verifies that observation, beginning with the rescue of German Jews from Shanghai, whom fate delivered into the hands of the Jewish community of Manila via the strangely generous protection of the German Consul in the Philippines. And while American immigration laws restricted rescue into the United States both qualitatively and quantitatively, quota limitations on immigration into the

Philippines would not be enforceable until the Commonwealth government enacted its own immigration laws in 1941. By this time, the selection plan and sponsorship program had already successfully rescued well over one thousand refugees.[1]

The empowerment of the Jewish Refugee Committee (JRC) by the Philippine government over immigration applications prior to 1940 came during one of those favorable swings of fate when corruption had crippled the immigration offices of the Philippine government and a complete revamping of the immigration laws were in process. The JRC's impartial, nonpartisan approach to selection between 1937 and 1940 guaranteed its ability to continue to offer refuge to Jews through the newly constituted immigration laws of the Philippine government.

Different Jewish relief organizations share credit for the success of Jewish rescue in the Philippines as well. But the unique system of residential rotation that the Frieder brothers practiced between their homes in Ohio and Manila always placed one brother in charge of the rescue relief operations in the Philippines while the other brothers stateside continually visited offices of the REC and the JDC in New York to effectively cut through bureaucratic red tape that often tied up philanthropic purse strings. The presence of the Frieder brothers in the Philippines, along with their business affluence and humanitarian proclivity, assured a continual leadership over the rescue operations in the Philippines that had to adjust as conditions changed over the years.

Another important "fateful" sequence of events brought Paul V. McNutt to the Philippines as US High Commissioner from 1937 to 1939—the most important years for the organization and implementation of the selection rescue program. The importance of McNutt's role in the rescue of Jews in the Philippines cannot be overstated. His mediation between the JRC in Manila, the Jewish relief organizations in New York, President Quezon, and the US State Department committees and agencies was absolutely essential to the success of refugee rescue. It is doubtful if rescue could have been implemented without McNutt's intercession. By contrast, with regard to the failed resettlement plan on Mindanao Island, Francis Sayre—the High Commissioner of the Philippines after McNutt—showed absolutely no interest in rescuing Jews in the Philippines and never voiced any encouragement, official or otherwise, to Quezon or any other Commonwealth government official to help facilitate the implementation of the resettlement program.[2] Sayre had indeed been complicit in the manipulation of immigration figures and other impediments put in front of the Mindanao project that delayed its employment. By the time Sayre arrived in Manila, rescue through selection and sponsorship was so well established that it operated successfully in spite of his ambivalence.

The history behind the Philippine rescue of refugee Jews from Europe and McNutt's role in it also sheds new light on the still ongoing debate between scholarly communities on opposite sides of an argument with Franklin D. Roosevelt at its center. What were FDR's motivations behind his seemingly magnanimous actions in empaneling the Evian Conference as a tool to address the international refugee crisis? Did FDR truly seek a solution to it, or was he merely putting on a good show to improve his public image at a time when his rival's image was on the climb?[3] Those arguments and others detailed in this work may never be resolved, but unless historians include the facts behind refugee rescue in the Philippines, as well as FDR's attitudes toward Paul McNutt, which have been absent so far from the historiography, their arguments lack significant dimensions that this study brings to their claims.

The rescue of refugees in Manila could not have happened had Manuel Quezon not been the president of the Philippines at that time. Even though McNutt had jurisdiction over Philippine foreign affairs as FDR's proxy, Quezon could have yielded opposition to the rescue if he had had the mind to. But as we see, Quezon had many reasons to welcome Jewish refugees into his island nation, not least of all his own humanitarian instincts. Even though US State Department dealings, which exhibited anti-immigrant prejudices, effectively stalled Quezon's mass resettlement plans on Mindanao, it cannot extinguish the truth of his actions as the only head of state in the world at that time who openly welcomed refugee Jews to his country's shores for humanitarian reasons—an act that FDR rarely acknowledged, even when he was fully aware of it.[4]

Joseph's story of the Philippine sanctuary he helped build offers another testimony of the resilience of the Jewish culture as its people forged new lives in another diaspora to a faraway land. Manilaners all affirm that Joseph played an integral role in their ability to live their Jewish culture in their new Asian home. Joseph and Sylvia's happy ending after the war lasted for only twelve years; Joseph died of a massive heart attack in 1961 at the age of forty-nine, leaving Sylvia to raise three small daughters alone. She had lost the love of her life but kept his memory alive for their children and grandchildren by preserving his office intact and untouched for more than forty years, until she had to move closer to her children in Los Angeles. Sylvia's donation of his papers to the Jewish Historical Society of San Diego, where

I worked as an archivist, has forever changed my life. This is how I found Joseph's story and was friends with his wonderful widow, until she passed away in 2007. I miss her. I would like to have met him. With this unique story of a Holocaust survivor in my hands, I embarked on the quest of a lifetime—to be the historian this story deserved so that I could contextualize Joseph's odyssey within the larger narrative of Holocaust scholarship. Writing Joseph's story and that of Philippine rescue of refugee Jews from the Holocaust became my life's purpose to bear witness and to help the world to never forget.

Afterword

NEW LIVES, NEW LIFE

Now, the story of Joseph comes back to when I first met Sylvia Cysner in the summer of 2001. It was during the time I was working at the Jewish Historical Society of San Diego (JHSSD), housed at San Diego State University (SDSU), where Sylvia was a volunteer. We immediately became fast friends as she took me into her confidence and shared with me many intimate details about her children, grandchildren, friends, and acquaintances. However, she was shyly hesitant in discussing her own life and that of her long-deceased husband, Joseph Cysner. She resolved every year, to my amazement, to visit his extended family in Israel, regardless of the violence riddling the land she loved so much. As her health declined, we spent fewer afternoons together at the archives. In 2003, when her health prevented her from living alone in her San Diego home, Sylvia moved up to Los Angeles to be closer to her children. She had often told me that she would one day have to give up her house and wondered about her husband's books and music, which she kept in his preserved office. During her move, I was relieved to learn that the managers of the JHSSD had persuaded her to donate her husband's documents to the archive and that I would soon be given access to these new holdings.

I had no idea when I spent all those afternoons in the company of this energetic woman that I had been in the company of a true hero who had also been married to one. As I began processing Joseph Cysner's papers in the summer of 2003, I discovered that I was holding a remarkable story of a Holocaust survivor. Immediately, I made plans to further my proxy relationship with Cantor Cysner by scheduling interviews with Sylvia at her new residence in Santa Monica. In the course of our conversations, it became obvious that Sylvia had extraordinary life experiences of her own also worth documenting, starting with her dramatic escape from Germany in 1938. The life stories of this remarkable couple involved nearly every aspect of Jewish persecution and survival in the prewar years.

We have already read about Joseph's odyssey from oppression in Nazi Germany to refuge in the Philippines. Sylvia went via another path to freedom before she met up with Joseph in San Francisco. When she came to the United States to visit Joseph in California, they were both taking giant leaps forward into new lives. Could their long-distance "postal" relationship be enough of a foundation for a new life together? Joseph's Holocaust odyssey took him from a persecuted life in Germany to destitution on the border with Poland, then to a safe harbor in the Philippines that war had tragically transformed into a site of mass destruction. But he was alive. The remarkable feat of Jewish refugee rescue in the Philippines accomplished its goal: it saved his life and the lives of hundreds more—hundreds that over the decades have turned into thousands. Now he looked to his new future with Sylvia. His remarkable story could never have been shared with the world had it not been for Sylvia quietly preserving his legacy for their children.

Therefore, Sylvia's story is included here in her own words: her own brave and miraculous escape from Germany, along with her recollections of their life together, as short as it was. This is what Joseph was saved for—to live a life with the woman he loved, to father children whom he adored, and to continue his mission of serving his congregations with love and compassion. Here is her story in her own words.[1]

SYLVIA TELLS HER STORY

I was born in Bamberg in 1922. My father's name was David Max Nagler. My mother's name was Cecilia. My older brother was named Leopold and my little brother was Ferdinand, Freddy. And I myself just was a schoolgirl who went to school in Bamberg. From there I went to Jewish High

School in Munich. From Munich I was apprenticed after I graduated from the high school to a dentist in Nuremberg until the time when I had an opportunity to immigrate to England.

When the Nazis had won their elections in 1933, I remember I was very close then with a girl whose father was the commanding general of the regiment that was stationed in Bamberg, which was a famous regiment. I was very close friends with her in elementary school; going to school in her horse-drawn carriage kind of stuff. The moment it was 1934 to '35, this was finished! She wouldn't even look at me! So when you say persecution, but then you realize that it was all the Nazis who had won everything—it was everything theirs against the Jews, you realize that she really had no choice. We understood that there was the shouting on the radio, "They are Jews and they are the evil . . . the Jews." That's what you heard, that's what you understood. And then you realized that you know that that wasn't true, but they were the majority and we were the minority. The same as we are now. I've heard people say it couldn't happen here; of course it can happen here because of the lynching of the black people in the South and these kind of things. I mean people live in the illusion, unless you can wipe out the hatred of something unknown, you can never succeed. It's as simple as that or as difficult as that.

So, I was in school during this time when the Nazis were really pushing their anti-Jewish agenda. Eventually, we were thrown out of the public-school system. I was already in secondary school because in Germany, or in Europe, you go after fourth grade to secondary school. And of course, we were thrown out eventually. At first, they had these little things if your father was a war veteran in the First World War or if he had earned a medal for injuries and stuff like that, then they let you stay longer. I mean, I stayed longer because my father was a veteran and had a stiff finger from shrapnel. So there were then Jewish members of our community that were being taken and others were being left behind. And the other thing that happened was that the young men were taken already to concentration camps . . . like several Jewish young men who were in concentration camp being politically active in socialism and so on. They were taken to Dachau, which was the first concentration camp. Already, in the beginning, between '33 and '34, there were always riots where Jews were beaten up in the street. You were lucky if you weren't. Joseph didn't have to worry about himself, being he was in Würzburg, finishing college about that time in 1933. He was at a Jewish school, and they were somewhat protected but then after graduation he had to fend for himself. And so, after graduation, he had almost two years in Hildesheim and then just got to Hamburg when the deportation happened.

I went to Jewish boarding school in 1935 and 1936 in Munich because of the business of what was happening—being thrown out of secondary school. And then after that I went to the Jewish boarding school, and after the Jewish boarding school I went to a kind of junior college in Nuremberg until I was apprenticed to a dentist to become a dental technician, a Jewish dentist. And then after him some other offices.

In 1938, the week before Kristallnacht my father had been taken to prison for a week. But, you see, those were circumstances, they were very individual. He was in the First World War even with the mayor of our hometown, who had become an SS Stormtrooper. But he, in essence, still had remembered serving with my father, who protected my father and, instead of sending him to the concentration camp in Dachau, he kept him in the local jail with a couple of others of his buddies. So this thing had blown over, this riot, and so my father was quietly released home. Meanwhile, I think he had told my father; I don't know if he had told my father. Anyway, to make a long story short, I was sent to his office in the evening, one evening, and he told me that one of us has to get out, if we want to save our parents or something like that. I had two younger brothers. And I had to get out because he could no longer protect us.

Whether he sent for me to come see him or if my father sent me to go see him, I don't remember. Maybe it was my father who sent me after he was released from prison, from jail. That particular incident with the mayor was before Kristallnacht, but Kristallnacht followed before I could get away. But he had told me, he evidently knew something, but he said, "one of you has to leave because I can no longer protect your parents."

And anyway, so, that then started the ball rolling about who would go. I was the most urgent to go; one, I was the oldest, two, I was a girl, three, I looked very, you know, grown up, I had long blondish hair, braided like a nice German girl, at that time. And so they did; we decided as a family that I would go.

But before I could leave, Kristallnacht happened, not very long after I met with the mayor. He must have known something was going to happen. I was in Bamberg, cowering in the cellar with my family while we heard everything smashing around us. You know, my family's store, and we heard all of the glass, but we didn't know what it was exactly. I mean, we knew things were going on in the street and, of course, we had no idea whether we would come out of it alive or not. And the weirdest thing was, as horrible

as the whole night was, in the morning it was like, other than all of the destruction, as if nothing had happened. It was as quiet in the street as it could
be. People went about their business. It was the most unreal experience.
But we knew then. It was hard times, and still you couldn't persuade my
mother to leave because her mother was in Berlin. That was unbelievable.

And, of course, then, that morning we saw the fire glow, and from the
direction we realized it was the synagogue; it was burning in the city. Because from where we lived, you know, cities were such that you could see
the glow in the sky. Then, eventually, my father, who was also pretty gutsy,
made his way there in the evening to see what had happened. But they had
taken then our cantor, he and his wife and their younger daughter were
taken to a concentration camp. They had taken him, the cantor of Bamberg, and, who was also our Hebrew teacher.

They arrested a lot of the men, thousands of them, but they didn't take
my father and it was through the protection of this mayor. And the other
thing I would have to say, as you know, there was a hat factory in the back
of our place and the man who had leased the factory, also didn't squeal on
my dad. I mean, there were some good people. I know that not all Germans were bad, no such thing. I remember now the wife was daring and
the daughter of this hat manufacturer would go and buy milk and cheese
and stuff and bring it to my mother.

Those days after Kristallnacht were the scariest days of my life. I mean,
all of us, we wouldn't go anywhere out of the house for days after, and we
tried to get everything together for me to go. Kristallnacht was November
9, I won't forget. I left in December for Köln, where I had friends. So to
get away, I left for Köln in—it must have been right around December 1
because I arrived in England on January 1 or 2—something like that.

The plan was for me to appear as a German girl on holiday going to see
her friends. That was the plan. And then, how—I don't remember—it
seems we had a message that I was to send after I had crossed the border.
There was a telegraph office, I remember now, something that I had met
someone that—Yeah OK! Liesel Lotte! Yes. She was one of my friends
who lived in Köln and I was telling them we had agreed to say that I met
Liesel Lotte so that my parents would know that I had made it to the border.
As a code—"Ich habe Liesel Lotte getroffen."

My parents put me on the train when I was fifteen and a half years old,
never to know if they would ever see me again. I came with no papers in
the suitcase. You see there were all these laws in Germany. It's too detailed

to go into; you could not take anything out from Germany that had not been permitted and no more than ten marks. And I had obeyed none of those laws. I just left, my clothes were all new, which we were not supposed to do. And nothing, I had no permission slips, and I had money on me, and just the chance I would be able to make it through. I remember wondering how far I will go before someone stops me and that is the end of me.

I left my home in Bamberg in December 1939, and had no visa, no nothing. I did not know where I was going just by train across the Belgium border. I left with a suitcase full of pretty girl clothes and I went into the train without proper papers or proper permit to leave Germany. I remember when the Germans opened the luggage and the suitcase I carried, on top in the suitcase was a navy-blue taffeta dress. It was a party dress; it was the first thing they saw as if I were going to a party someplace. Everybody's, even non-Jews luggage was searched when you came close to the German border.

Not only that, but they said "Juden raus" = "Jews out [of the train]." I didn't even move. I just continued to sit there. They took a lot of Jews who had exit permits off the train. I do not know what happened to them. I remember myself standing in the window of the train as it went past from Bamberg to Nuremberg and I thought to myself, how far will I go or be able to go until someone catches me, because I had no passport. But on that train, I had told myself I wouldn't go into a compartment if there were Jews because the Nazis would take them off. And so I ended up with a German SS Stormtrooper in the front compartment. And he had no idea; I was very blond-looking with braids, like a German schoolgirl. The funny things that happened. This first encounter I had with this Stormtrooper on the train was the first time in my life I ate non-kosher food. This guy, this SS guy, had bought me a hot dog, this long German hot dog. I nearly choked but I ate it. He asked me where I was going and I told him I was visiting friends and he said that he was going also somewhere— Brussels, or something. And so I had a very nice conversation with this Nazi and then I vanished as fast as I could near the border!

I went from Bamberg, overnight I think, it was six or seven hours to get to Köln and it was from Köln to Brussels. I think we traveled through the night, because I remember boarding the train in Köln at night, so as not to have too many questions to answer and stuff like that. Next day was about noon or one o'clock that I got to Brussels. I sent that telegram to Liesel

Lotte. So you know, we didn't know what was going to happen. I remember that to this day. Friends of mine met me in Brussels and I went to the British consulate in Brussels, who helped me, and I got to England.

I went to the British Consulate and I told them to call these friends of mine in London. I had a telephone number to call them and they were to verify who I am, that they are expecting me. And they gave me a visitor's visa for three months. First, I went to the Jewry shop—what was it called— Immigrant Office with people, immigrants such as I, and you talked to the lady who was the director, and I told her my whole tale of woe. And she said, "You're not the only one—there are thousands like you." And so she said after our interview, what do you do? And I told her what I can do, and I was able to stay with friends and then I managed to get a job at a dentist office where I studied dental mechanics.

After that I was able to bring my two brothers because they came on the Kinder [children's] transports and then my parents came later. She helped me with my two brothers who came separately on what was this famous children's transport: first my older brother, who was fourteen, and then, my little brother, who was eight or nine. He had scarlet fever— [*chuckles*] oh God, on the ship—they wouldn't let him off the ship and I couldn't [*chuckling*] leave the ship for a day or so because they had a quarantine. And that was June or July of 1939.

I had then met this old English rich gentleman at the synagogue, and he took a shine to me and invited me home to lunch. So, I told him about my parents, and he had a cocoa plantation in Trinidad—Port of Spain, Trinidad. And he signed some papers, so it appeared to the whole world as though he were an employer. It said on there that my mother and father were to be hired as housekeepers, or something or other, on his plantation. This enabled my parents to get visas for Trinidad because Trinidad was an English colony. They got a visa in Munich to come and they left near the first of September.

I was the luckiest girl alive. We didn't know when or how but we felt, in London, we were sure it was going to be war. I think my father said they got his visa in Munich the twenty-third or something of August. On that Friday, I am on the train and I heard [Neville] Chamberlain say, "We are at war with Germany." And I was hoping they were arriving. I was hoping because they had left, and they were going via Amsterdam. I cabled my cousin in Amsterdam, who was there, that this was no time to make small business. My father is an Orthodox Jew [*chuckle*] and it's Friday afternoon, you see, before the Sabbath and there are three ferries coming. Don't you think they are on the last ferry! I waited at the ferries all day, from early morning, from when they first started. My parents didn't see my brothers until maybe two weeks later, or whatever. Because they were with me in London, and they put the children in with families in England. And when war was broken out, they had evacuated the children out of London. It was something else.

You should have been in our place. We took the mattresses off the beds and put them on the floor, and I don't know how many people would sleep there at times. My mother cooked for the whole lot. The other thing which was amazing was this—Friday war broke out and by Sunday morning you couldn't buy anything in the market. They locked up all of the stores in town because they were afraid, they were running out of food. My parents and my brothers never left England after that. England became our home. I had a wonderful life in London, I had friends. In the wonderful business, I was a dental technician, I had a dental lab. I worked for seven dentists and I was the only female dental technician in London at the time, because the men had all been called into the army. So they had to trust me once in a while. I really wished I had stayed in England.

I came to America nine years later. Let's see, the war was over in 1945, I think Joseph came to San Francisco either at the end of '46 or '47, because we had been corresponding, while I was in England, first with Red Cross messages when he was a prisoner in Santo Tomas. How this came about was because his sister Henrietta, the young one, had come from Berlin to London. She was walking across Oxford Circus and she saw my father whom she recognized. So we made contact. She begged me to write to him on her behalf. Why I don't know, maybe she thought her English wasn't good enough. I started to write Joseph first on her behalf, and he sort of fell for my letters. Eventually, we began writing to each other.

After Manila was liberated, he wrote to me that he was going to San Francisco and he wanted me to come. I said no way would I go to America. And this correspondence went on for, I think, it was almost a year, and then he began to phone saying come for a visit. And I went, going to New York first, and that is what happened. I had not seen him since his father's funeral in 1937. He brought me to San Francisco. I came as a visitor for three months and got married instead.

My best memories of San Francisco were the kindness of the congregation, the rabbi and his wife, who were very gracious and generous. Because the president of the congregation was not so gracious. He had, since my husband was a bachelor, he tried to match him up with a lot of young, wealthy girls. And when our engagement and forthcoming wedding was announced this president said to me: "And what is it that you have got"? Because I was no raving beauty, "and what is it that you've got that all these young wealthy girls do not have"? So I said, "You would be surprised." That was my answer. But the memories, and of course her birth, my daughter Charlotte, my mother-in-law's eightieth birthday. And there were many beautiful things that happened because the people from the Manila community that had settled in San Francisco, were totally in love with my husband. They were just very wonderful. Because my mother-in-law was such an old lady and had lived with him in the Philippines, they granted her visa to come with him. They came together to San Francisco. And I wish I could remember some of the names.

San Francisco was good, other than I did not know I was homesick for England. We had a number of offers and wanted to go east but we couldn't because of the climate, and his mother. So we came to San Diego. When the offer came, we moved to San Diego. My husband also had almost an obsession; he would only live in cities with a harbor. He was passionately in love with the sea. So you see, you can pick out Hamburg, Manila, San Francisco, San Diego; it always had the sea. Actually he had a very good offer to go to Sioux City, and the congregation there. It was a lot more money because they were very wealthy cattle dealers. And he said there is nothing to see but cattle yards. Pittsburgh was cold, and his mother wouldn't go there.

We had really ten absolutely wonderful years with the Tifereth Israel Congregation in San Diego. San Diego was a small Jewish community, and most people, because of parents and former affiliations, belonged to Rabbi Cohn's temple, the reformed synagogue at Temple Beth Israel. But when my husband came, he taught the young people, and the children just adored him. And so many of the families moved over to Tifereth Israel. So it grew a lot while we were there. Not only did he have the children's choir, but he wrote plays, and was loved of others, and so forth. We had ten wonderful years at Tifereth Israel.

It was a glorious time. From all the families, whose weddings and bar mitzvahs that we participated in and were invited to—people were very gracious in the congregation. I really loved that congregation. There were a lot of wonderful people there. And, of course, it all fell apart after my husband died. He was in the synagogue in the morning, it was the Purim festival, you know, with the chanting, the scroll of Esther and everything. He came home, had dinner. It was a Thursday evening; his mother's birthday was the following Saturday and we had a big dinner. My mother and father were visiting from England and he was teaching a music class at San Diego State. He said, sort of jokingly, that he didn't feel like teaching; he would like to have taken me out. So I said, "Well, why don't you play for me once." Then he went to class and he never came back. He finished teaching the class, gave back the tape recorder, joked with the dean, and that was it. They found him under the car: no sound, no horn; he was dead. And he was alone.

He was the warmest, kindest, most gracious human being that you can imagine. When he was in Santo Tomas, interned there, they used to call him the Angel of Santo Tomas, the other prisoners, because he went to them and sang to them and tried to cheer everybody up. He was a very gracious human being.

How fitting it seems now, in Sylvia's last recollections of Joseph in our visits together, that she should reminisce about his time in the Philippines. From these memories of her life, it was obvious to me that she had saved her family nearly singlehandedly, first by getting herself out of Germany through a clandestine escape; then she secured passages to England for her younger brothers on the Kindertransports, and she obtained visas for her parents to Trinidad that enabled them to leave Germany just in the nick of time. In the face of all this, she still counted herself "lucky" because war had begun on the day her parents had arrived in England, preventing their further passage to Trinidad, and leaving them "stranded" in London. Her parents and her brothers owed Sylvia their lives.

When you link her story to the remarkable survival odyssey of her husband, Joseph Cysner, you get a true tale of epic, heroic proportions, which did not embody the ageless epitaph of "they lived happily ever after." Maybe they did for a few years, but Sylvia lost the love of her life in the spring of 1961, when, after surviving both German and Japanese internments in the same war, Joseph died suddenly of a massive heart attack at the age of forty-nine on the eve of Purim, which, ironically enough, celebrates the deliverance of the Israelites from death by the hand of an anti-semitic despot. It seems somehow fitting that he should die on one of his favorite dates, a beloved Jewish Holy Day, as he anticipated spending the joyous occasion with his family.

And yet, this is not the end of Joseph's story. Everything that he did, all the memories of who he was still lives on in the hearts and minds of those who knew him. In hundreds, if not thousands, of lives, from Bamberg to Hildesheim, Hannover, Hamburg, Zbaszyn, Manila, San Francisco, and San Diego, Joseph instilled a love of Hebrew prayers, Jewish music, readings from the Torah, and teachings from Jewish philosophers, all given from a heart full of unmitigated compassion for all people. His unheralded life of kindness and unconditional love continues to live on in them all.

NOTES

Introduction

1. Frank Ephraim, *Escape to Manila: From Nazi Tyranny to Japanese Terror* (Urbana: University of Illinois Press, 2003).

2. See Dean J. Kotlowski, *Paul V. McNutt and the Age of FDR* (Bloomington: Indiana University Press, 2015), 233–58. I differ from Kotlowski concerning McNutt's motivations for organizing rescue in the Philippines, as Kotlowski (239) proposes that it was possibly based on McNutt's political ambitions to succeed FDR in the White House. See also Ephraim, *Escape to Manila*, 23. Ephraim gives McNutt his due as being the government official in place at the time but portrays him more as following the lead of the Frieders rather than the other way around, even characterizing him starting off as "lukewarm" over refugee issues.

3. Verne W. Newton, *FDR and the Holocaust* (New York: St. Martin's, 1996), 4.

4. Richard Polenberg, *The Era of Franklin D. Roosevelt, 1933–1945* (New York: Palgrave Macmillan, 2000), 16.

5. Bat-Ami Zucker, *In Search of Refuge: Jews and US Consuls in Nazi Germany, 1933–1941* (London: Vallentine Mitchell, 2001).

6. Joseph Cysner, "Zbaszyn, Oct. 30, 1938," pp. 1–3, Jewish Historical Society of San Diego (JHSSD) Archives, Cantor Joseph Cysner Collection, CJC02.01.

7. Sylvia's survivor story can be found in the afterword of this book.

Chapter 1. Joseph Cysner

1. David Sorkin, *The Transformation of German Jewry, 1780–1840* (Detroit: Wayne State University Press, 1999), 3–80. See also Andrei S. Markovits, Beth Simone Noveck, and Carolyn Hoefig, "Jews in German Society," in *The Cambridge*

Companion to Modern German Culture, ed. Eva Kolinsky and Wilfried van de Will (Cambridge: Cambridge University Press, 1998), 86–109.

2. Jacob Katz, *From Prejudice to Destruction: Anti-Semitism, 1700–1933* (Cambridge, MA: Harvard University Press, 1980), 107–46.

3. The synagogue where Joseph practiced was the Hamburg Temple, founded by the New Israelite Temple Society (Neuer Israelitischer Tempelverein) in 1818 as the first permanent Reform Jewish community. When statutory laws were relaxed in the German states, the Reform movement set up its own civic association (*verband*) when the state and the two Jewish religious congregations refused to recognize them as a legitimate religious community. (Reform Jews call their synagogues temples.) This struggle made setting up a permanent building difficult until the Hamburg Senate overruled the Ashkenazi chief rabbi's objections in 1841. The Hamburg Temple's first site was in the Poolstrasse and was registered in the name of the New Israelite Temple Society. In 1865, Jews were allowed to establish new congregations outside the two established ones (Ashkenazi and Sephardi). The Reform movement created their own worship association or Kultusverband while maintaining relations with the at-large Ashkenazi community organizations. The temple where Joseph served was in its third location on Oberstrasse 120, consecrated in 1931 under Rabbi Bruno Italiener. It was shut down within weeks of Joseph's deportation in November 1938. After being vandalized, it survived as a repurposed building both during and after the Nazi regime. Information obtained from Ina Lorenz, "Die Jüdische Gemeinde Hamburg 1860–1943: Kaiserreich—Weimarer Republik—NS Staat," in *Die Juden in Hamburg: 1590 bis 1990*, ed. Arno Herzig, Geschichte der Juden in Hamburg 2 (Hamburg: Dölling und Galitz, 1991), 78. See also Saskia Rohde, "Synagogen in Hamburger Raum 1680–1943," in *Die Juden in Hamburg: 1590 bis 1990*, ed. Arno Herzig, Geschichte der Juden in Hamburg 2 (Hamburg: Dölling und Galitz, 1991), 151, 157, 161–63.

4. Herbert Loebl, *Juden in Bamberg: Die Jahrzehnte vor dem Holocaust* (Bamberg: Verlag Fränkischer Tag, 1999), 223; Sylvia Cysner, interview by Bonnie M. Harris, Jan. 24, 2004, Los Angeles, CA, video recording.

5. Ostjuden was the generic term for Yiddish-speaking Jews from eastern European countries who immigrated to Germany and Austria, many due to the violent pogroms waged against them by the Russians.

6. Haskalah (Hebrew for "wisdom," "erudition") was an eighteenth- to nineteenth-century Jewish intellectual movement from central and eastern Europe. The movement had two goals: the integration of Jews into modern society while retaining Hebrew as a living literary language and establishing the local vernacular into liturgical life. It borrowed much from the Age of Enlightenment by its endeavor to combine religious tradition with secularism, focusing on education and

cultural reformation. This creation of secular Jewish culture emphasizing history and identity without relying on religious strictures contributed to the founding of the Reform movement, which gained popularity in central Europe. The movement helped break the hold of rigid orthodoxy on Jewish life, allowing for secular studies and giving more flexibility and modernity to the practice of Judaism in the West.

7. A Jewish cantor is called a chazzan (חזן) in Hebrew. According to Jewish custom, prayers were led by a *sh'liach tzibor* (emissary of the congregation), a position that can be filled by any adult Jewish male. Since almost all Jewish prayer is sung or chanted, the chazzan addresses his prayers directly to the Almighty on behalf of all those assembled for the worship service. Though the title can be applied in a general way to anyone who leads the service, it is more commonly an assigned position within the community and is filled by someone who has completed professional musical training and been ordained as cantor.

8. Ronnie S. Landau, *The Nazi Holocaust* (Chicago: Ivan R. Dee, 2006), 87.

9. Bryan Mark Rigg, *Hitler's Jewish Soldiers: The Untold Story of Nazi Racial Laws and Men of Jewish Descent in the German Military* (Lawrence: University Press of Kansas, 2004), 72.

10. Peter Pulzer, *Jews and the German State: The Political History of a Minority, 1848–1933* (Detroit: Wayne State University Press, 1992), 200.

11. Michael Brenner, *The Renaissance of Jewish Culture in Weimar Germany* (New Haven, CT: Yale University Press, 1996), 186–211.

12. Anthony Read and David Fisher, *Kristallnacht: The Unleashing of the Holocaust* (New York: Peter Bedrick Books, 1989), 58. See also William L. Shirer, *The Rise and Fall of the Third Reich: A History of Nazi Germany*, 3rd ed. (New York: Simon & Schuster, 1990), 30–33; and Doris L. Bergen, *War & Genocide: A Concise History of the Holocaust* (Lanham, MD: Rowman & Littlefield, 2003), 47–48.

13. Deborah Dwork and Robert Jan van Pelt, *Flight from the Reich: Refugee Jews, 1933–1946* (New York: W. W. Norton, 2009), 5–6.

14. *The Protocols* is a plagiarized publication composed between 1899 and 1902 professing a fictitious meeting of the 1897 World Zionist Congress in which Jewish leaders conspired to destroy the Gentile world through wars, corruption, and lasciviousness. Translations of the original Russian text circulated in dozens of languages all over the world and fueled growing antisemitic sentiments globally. See Bonnie Harris, "Anti-Semitism," in *Encyclopedia of Race and Racism*, vol. 1, A–C (New York: Gale, Cengage Learning, 2013), 137.

15. Brenner, *The Renaissance of Jewish Culture in Weimar Germany*, 32–33.

16. Saul Friedländer, *Nazi Germany and the Jews*, vol. 1, *The Years of Persecution, 1933–1939* (New York: HarperCollins, 1997), 1–4.

17. Shlomo Aronson, *Hitler, the Allies, and the Jews* (New York: Cambridge University Press, 2004), 3–9. See also Joseph Walk, *Das Sonderrecht für die Juden im NS-Staat: Eine Sammlung der gesetzlichen Massnahmen und Richtlinien, Inhalt und Bedeutung* (Heidelberg: Müller Juristischer Verlag, 1981).

18. Herbert A. Strauss, "Jewish Emigration from Germany—Nazi Policies and Jewish Responses (II)," in *Leo Baeck Institute Year Book XXVI* (London: Martin Secker & Warburg, 1981), 346–48.

19. For a more detailed examination of US immigration laws and policies, see chap. 2; Michael Lemay and Elliot Robert Barkan, *US Immigration and Naturalization Laws and Issues* (Westport, CT: Greenwood, 1999).

20. Robert D. Schulzinger, *The U.S. Diplomacy Since 1900* (New York: Oxford University Press, 1998), 164.

21. Michael R. Marrus, *The Unwanted: European Refugees from the First World War through the Cold War* (Philadelphia: Temple University Press, 2002), 148–58.

22. Yehuda Bauer, *A History of the Holocaust* (New York: Franklin Watts, 1982), 126–31. See also Marion A. Kaplan, *Between Dignity and Despair: Jewish Life in Nazi Germany* (New York: Oxford University Press, 1999), 18–49.

23. For more on the Madagascar Plan and Operation Barbarossa, see Christopher R. Browning, *The Origins of the Final Solution: The Evolution of Nazi Jewish Policy, September 1939—March 1942* (Lincoln: University of Nebraska Press; Jerusalem: Yad Vashem, 2004), 81–88, 103–7, respectively. See also Richard L. Rubenstein and John K. Roth, *Approaches to Auschwitz: The Holocaust and Its Legacy* (Louisville: Westminster John Knox Press, 2003), 163.

24. While the British limited the number of immigration certificates to Palestine due to unrest and violence from 1936 to 1938, the Zionists had set rigid standards for prospective immigrants, seeking only young and healthy agriculturalists fit for heavy manual labor. In response to these restrictions, the Gestapo promoted illegal immigration to Palestine in 1938 and 1939. See Francis R. Nicosia, *The Third Reich and the Palestine Question* (London: I. B. Tauris, 1985), 158–60. See also Gerald Ziedenberg, *Blockade: The Story of Jewish Immigration to Palestine* (Bloomington, IN: Author House, 2011).

25. Marrus, *The Unwanted*, 135–39. For extensive figures on Jewish immigration from Europe during these years, see Herbert A. Strauss, "Jewish Emigration from Germany," 346–47.

26. Trude Maurer, "Die Ausweisung der Polnischen Juden und der Vorwand für die Kristallnacht," in *Der Judenpogrom 1938: Von der Reichkristallnacht zum Völkermord*, ed. Walter H. Pehle (Frankfurt am Main: Fischer Taschenbuch Verlag, 1988), 54–56.

27. Read and Fisher, *Kristallnacht*, 41–44.

28. Ibid., 47.

29. H. H. Ben-Sasson, *A History of the Jewish People* (Cambridge, MA: Harvard University Press, 1976), 1022.

30. "Telefonische Weisung nach Warschau," Doc. No. 062, 26 Oct. 1938, Berlin, Politisches Auswärtiges Amt Archives, Berlin, Film 27–125, Band R 49013. See also Sybil Milton, "The Expulsion of Polish Jews from Germany, October 1938 to July 1939," in *Leo Baeck Institute Year Book XXIX* (London: Martin Secker & Warburg, 1984), 170–71; and Maurer, "Die Ausweisung der Polnischen Juden," 54–60.

31. Milton, "The Expulsion of Polish Jews from Germany," 172–74.

32. Ibid.

33. Beate Meyer, "Das Schicksaljahr 1938 und die Folgen," in *Die Verfolgung und Ermordung der Hamburger Juden 1933–1945*, ed. Beate Meyer (Freie und Hansestadt Hamburg: Landeszentrale für Politische Bildung, 2006), 25.

34. Expulsion testimonies of Rosa and Koppel Friedfertig from Hamburg relate how the Gestapo came to their door at 5:00 a.m. on the morning of October 29, 1938, and called their names and their three daughters' names from a prepared list. See Meyer, "Das Schicksaljahr 1938 und die Folgen," 115.

35. Maurer, "Die Ausweisung der Polnischen Juden," 64–65.

36. See Bonnie M. Harris, "Die Memoiren des Kantors Joseph Cysner: Ein seltenes Zeugnis der 'Polenaktion,'" trans. Insa Kummer, in Hamburger Schlüsseldokumente zur deutsch-jüdischen Geschichte, 25.10.2017, Institut für die Geschichte der Deutschen Juden, https://dx.doi.org/10.23691/jgo:article-94.de.v1. Here the reader can see images of actual pages from the German memoir.

37. A copy of the letter is in the possession of Lotte Cassel Hershfield and appears to be an authentic duplication. The provenance of the original is unknown. In February 2005, Lotte Cassel Hershfield sent a copy to me with other memorabilia she has saved over the years.

38. Joseph Cysner, "Zbaszyn, Oct. 30, 1938," pp. 1–3, English version of memoir in Jewish Historical Society of San Diego (JHSSD) Archives, Cantor Joseph Cysner Collection, CJCo2.01. The original text is reproduced as it appears and there was no attempt to make any corrections except to standardize the ellipses.

39. Joseph Cysner, letter titled "Zbaszyn, den 6. November 1938." See n. 37. Not to be confused with Cysner's journal of the same name.

40. Maurer, "Die Ausweisung der Polnischen Juden," 66.

41. "Germany Deports Jews to Poland," *New York Times*, Oct. 29, 1938, Ghetto Fighter's Museum Archives, Akko, Israel, Zbaszyn Clippings Collection.

42. "Germany Ceases Deporting Jews Pending Parlays," *New York Times*, Oct. 30, 1938, Ghetto Fighter's Museum Archives, Akko, Israel, Zbaszyn Clippings Collection.

43. The Union of Merchant Associations was an organization of Polish merchants from Greater Poland and Eastern Pomerania that began holding trade fairs
in 1917. The first Poznań Trade Fair convened from May 28 to June 5, 1921. Beginning in 1925, companies were invited from Czechoslovakia, France, Yugoslavia,
Latvia, Germany, Romania, Switzerland, and Sweden, creating the first international fair. The General National Exhibition of 1929 was visited by 4.5 million
people, with a significant number of attendees traveling through the Zbaszyn
station.

44. Wojciech Olejniczak, ed., *See You Next Year in Jerusalem: Deportation of
Polish Jews from Germany to Zbaszyn in 1938* (Zbaszyn-Poznań: Fundacja TRES,
2012), 21.

45. "Germany Deports Jews to Poland," *New York Times*, Oct. 29, 1938,
Ghetto Fighter's Museum Archives, Akko, Israel, Zbaszyn Clippings Collection.

46. Jerzy Szapiro, "Nazi Guns Force Jews into Poland," *New York Times*,
Nov. 1, 1938, Ghetto Fighter's Museum Archives, Akko, Israel, Zbaszyn Clippings
Collection.

47. The Shema, from the sixth chapter of Deuteronomy, is the final prayer of
Yom Kippur, the Day of Atonement and the holiest day of the year. It is also tra-
ditionally the last words spoken before death. "Hear O' Israel, the Lord is our
God, the Lord is One."

48. Joseph Cysner, "Zbaszyn, Oct. 30, 1938," 4–5. Further into his memoir
Joseph recalls Chanukah (1938) at the hospital and other places of assembly of the
refugees in Zbaszyn and the virtuoso violinist Dr. Broches playing on "whose precious instrument I saved." Dr. Broches was expelled from Hamburg to Zbaszyn at
the same time as Joseph and obviously they knew each other. Raphael Broches was
born in Warsaw on February 8, 1906, but lived most of his life in Hamburg after
World War I. An online biography of Raphael Broches tells of his offer to join the
orchestra in Palestine, but because he was working on his PhD in Hamburg, he returned to Germany to defend his dissertation and was caught up in the Polenaktion.
He stayed in Zbaszyn until August 1938, when the camp was dissolved. We know
he was in the Warsaw Ghetto in 1940 and played his violin that was saved by Joseph
in the Warsaw Ghetto Orchestra into 1941. Researchers believe he was transported
to the Treblinka death camp when the orchestra was disbanded, and there he
was murdered. See Barbara Müller-Wesemann and Sophie Fetthauer, "Raphael
Broches," in *Encyclopedia of Persecuted Musicians of the Nazi Era*, ed. Claudia
Maurer Zenck and Peter Petersen (Hamburg: University of Hamburg, 2007),
https://www.lexm.uni-hamburg.de/object/lexm_lexmperson_00002396.

49. Read and Fisher, *Kristallnacht*, 50. On January 27, 1939, the *Jewish Chronicle*
reported Endeks attacking the Jews in Zbaszyn and beating them in the streets. It

also noted that "it has been necessary to place a special police guard over the old mill where several hundred of the deportees are housed. All Jews have been forbidden to appear in the streets after 10 p.m." See "Endeks Attack Zbonszyn Jews," *Jewish Chronicle*, Jan. 27, 1939, 17, Ghetto Fighter's Museum Archives, Akko, Israel. Endeks were members of the Polish National Right-Wing Democrats and many members within the party were virulent antisemites. The posting of these guards to abate violence also served as a means of containing the Jews. Anyone violating the curfews could have been shot, Endek or Jew.

50. Joseph Cysner, "Zbaszyn, Oct. 30, 1938," 5–6.

51. "Germany Ceases Deporting Jews Pending Parlays," *New York Times*, Oct. 30, 1938, Ghetto Fighter's Museum Archives, Akko, Israel, Zbaszyn Clippings Collection.

52. Joseph Cysner, "Zbaszyn, Oct. 30, 1938," 6.

53. "Nazi's Inhuman Hounding of Polish Jews," *Jewish Chronicle*, Nov. 4, 1938, 26, Ghetto Fighter's Museum Archives, Akko, Israel, Zbaszyn Clippings Collection.

54. Ibid., 25.

55. Herschel's parents and sister were deported on Thursday evening, October 27, 1938, from Hannover. Herschel's sister, Berta, sent him a postcard from Zbaszyn dated October 31, 1938, which he had in his pocket when he shot vom Rath. See Read and Fisher, *Kristallnacht: The Unleashing of the Holocaust*, 39–40.

56. Joseph Cysner, "Zbaszyn, Oct. 30, 1938," 6.

57. For a full recounting of the expulsion of the Grynszpan family, see Gerald Schwab, *The Day the Holocaust Began: The Odyssey of Herschel Grynszpan* (New York: Praeger, 1990), 59–69.

58. Leni Yahil, *The Holocaust: The Fate of European Jewry, 1932–1945* (New York: Oxford University Press, 1991), 110.

59. Yad Vashem, "Kristallnacht," https://www.yadvashem.org/odot_pdf /Microsoft%20Word%20-%206461.pdf.

60. Joseph Cysner, "Zbaszyn, Oct. 30, 1938," 7.

61. Olejniczak, *See You Next Year in Jerusalem*, 35.

62. Jerzy Tomaszewski, *Auftakt zur Vernichtung*, trans. Victoria Pollmann (Osnabrück: Fibre Verlag, 2002), 261–62.

63. Gerd Korman, *Nightmare's Fairy Tale: A Young Refugee's Home Fronts, 1938–1948* (Madison: University of Wisconsin Press, 2005), 40.

64. Joseph Cysner, "Zbaszyn, Oct. 30, 1938," 7.

65. Emanuel Melzer, "Relations between Poland and Germany and Their Impact on the Jewish Problem in Poland, 1935–1938," *Yad Vashem Studies* 12 (1977): 223–25.

66. Emanuel Ringelblum (1900–1944) was a Jewish historian who later became director of the secret Oneg Shabbat Archive in the Warsaw Ghetto. For an extensive biography, see Yad Vashem, "Ringelblum, Emanuel," http://www1.yad vashem.org/odot_pdf/Microsoft%20Word%20-%205830.pdf.

67. Tomaszewski, *Auftakt zur Vernichtung*, 269.

68. Yad Vashem, "Emanuel Ringelblum's Notes of the Refugees in Zbaszyn," in "But the Story Didn't End that Way," http://www1.yadvashem.org/download /education/units/crystal_7.pdf.

69. Chazanim, probably what Cysner is referring to, is the plural for chazzan, or cantors. See n. 7.

70. Joseph Cysner, "Zbaszyn, Oct. 30, 1938," 8.

71. *Oneg Shabbat*, "joy of the Sabbath," is an informal gathering of Jews in a synagogue or private home on Friday evenings to express their happiness inherent in their Sabbath holiday. They entertain themselves with music, drama, community discussions, lectures, or the singing of religious melodies—all in keeping with the biblical injunction "and call the Sabbath a delight" (Isa 58.13).

72. Joseph Cysner, "Zbaszyn, Oct. 30, 1938," 9.

73. Jerzy Tomaszewski records that the gymnasium near the football stadium provided accommodations for many of the destitute children. See Jerzy Tomaszewski, "The Zbaszyn Stop," in *See You Next Year in Jerusalem: Deportation of Polish Jews from Germany to Zbaszyn in 1938*, ed. Wojciech Olejniczak (Zbaszyn-Poznań: Fundacja TRES, 2012), 80–81.

74. Tomaszewski, *Auftakt zur Vernichtung*, 278.

75. "Typhus Outbreak in Zbonszyn," *Jewish Chronicle*, Nov. 11, 1938, 29, Ghetto Fighter's Museum Archives, Akko, Israel, Zbaszyn Clippings Collection.

76. "Endeks Attack Zbonszyn Jews," *Jewish Chronicle*, Jan. 27, 1939, 17, Ghetto Fighter's Museum Archives, Akko, Israel, Zbaszyn Clippings Collection. Trefniak, a Yiddish word, comes from "tref," which is ritually unclean food. The word is more commonly spelled "treyf" or "treif." Trefniak is a non-Jew and also someone with malicious intent. On January 27, 1939, the *Jewish Chronicle* in London reported "Endeks" attacking the Jews in Zbaszyn and beating them in the streets. Joseph was probably referring to these episodes when drunken Endeks, National Democrat party members, conducted raids in Zbaszyn. For more on Endeks, see n. 49.

77. Joseph Cysner, "Zbaszyn, Oct. 30, 1938," 8.

78. Milton, "The Expulsion of Polish Jews from Germany," 191.

79. "Deaths in Concentration Camps," *Jewish Chronicle*, Dec. 23, 1938, 29, Ghetto Fighter's Museum Archives, Akko, Israel, Zbaszyn Clippings Collection.

80. Yad Vashem, "Emanuel Ringelblum's Notes of the Refugees in Zbaszyn."

81. "Starvation Conditions of Deportees in Poland," *Jewish Chronicle*, May 26, 1939, 20, Ghetto Fighter's Museum Archives, Akko, Israel, Zbaszyn Clippings Collection.

82. Maurer, "Die Ausweisung der Polnischen Juden," 67.

83. Melzer, "The Jewish Problem in Poland, 1935–1938," 222.

84. Milton, "The Expulsion of Polish Jews from Germany," 172–73.

85. Melzer, "The Jewish Problem in Poland, 1935–1938," 226. See also Maurer, "Die Ausweisung der Polnischen Juden," 68.

86. Jerzy Tomaszewski, "The Zbaszyn Stop," 79.

87. Melzer, "The Jewish Problem in Poland, 1935–1938," 228.

88. Norbert Propper, interview by Noel Izon, July 7, 2016, Menton, France, transcription by Michael Iannelli.

89. Shaliach in the singular means "messenger" or "emissary" in Hebrew. Shelichim is the Yiddish for its plural Shlichim, which denotes agents or emissaries acting for an agency facilitating Zionist movements in Palestine.

90. Joseph Cysner, "Zbaszyn, Oct. 30, 1938," 10.

91. The originals of these handwritten musically notated transcriptions can be found in the Cantor Joseph Cysner Collection in the JHSSD Archives.

92. Joseph Cysner, "Zbaszyn, Oct. 30, 1938," 10.

93. Ibid.

94. Chaja Cysner arrived in the Philippines on board the *Conte Verde* on June 2, 1940, along with ten other Jewish refugees. Joseph and his mother shared a small house on Vito Cruz Street, which also served as a Hebrew school and his music studio. See Ephraim, *Escape to Manila*, 70.

95. "Passenger Arrivals," *Manila Bulletin*, May 16, 1939, photocopy from personal papers of Sylvia Cysner.

96. The *Scharnhorst* was subsequently converted into an escort carrier, which was sunk by a US submarine in 1944. See Ben Stille, *Imperial Japanese Aircraft Carriers, 1921–1945* (Oxford: Osprey, 2006), 42.

97. "6 Days Quicker to Far East," *Straits Times*, Mar. 18, 1935, 4, Newspapers SG, National Library Board, Singapore Government, http://eresources.nlb.gov.sg/newspapers/Digitised/Article/straitstimes19350318.2.9.aspx.

98. Peter Nash, "My German Third Reich Passport Found in Shanghai," Dec. 8, 2012, https://www.passport-collector.com/my-german-third-reich-passport-found-in-shanghai/.

99. According to "Tourists & Refugees in Same Liner," *Singapore Free Press and Mercantile Advertiser*, Feb. 17, 1939, 9: "The North German Lloyd liner, Scharnhorst, which arrived at Singapore yesterday, carried 70 Germans on a cruise to Colombo. Another 80 Jewish refugees bound for Shanghai were also aboard the

liner." Newspapers SG, National Library Board, Singapore Government, http://eresources.nlb.gov.sg/newspapers/Digitised/Article/singfreepressb19390217-1.2.93.

100. Ephraim, *Escape to Manila*, 55–56.

Chapter 2. FDR, Evian, and the Refugee Crisis

1. David S. Wyman, *The Abandonment of the Jews: America and the Holocaust, 1941–1945* (New York: Pantheon Books, 1984), x.

2. David S. Wyman, *Paper Walls: America and the Refuge Crisis 1938–1941* (Amherst: University of Massachusetts Press, 1968), 155–83.

3. Arthur D. Morse, *While Six Million Died: A Chronology of American Apathy* (New York: Random House, 1968), 29–37.

4. Henry L. Feingold, *The Politics of Rescue: The Roosevelt Administration and the Holocaust 1938–1945* (New York: Holocaust Library, 1970), ix–xiii.

5. Saul S. Friedman, *No Haven for the Oppressed: United States Policy toward Jewish Refugees, 1938–1945* (Detroit: Wayne State University Press, 1973), 9–15.

6. Martin Gilbert, *Auschwitz and the Allies* (New York: Holt, Rinehart & Winston, 1981), 299–323.

7. Monty Noam Penkower, *The Jews Were Expendable: Free World Diplomacy and the Holocaust* (Urbana: University of Illinois Press, 1983), viii–x, 114–15, 174, 211.

8. Wyman, *Abandonment*, ix–xii. See also David S. Wyman Institute for Holocaust Studies, "Wyman Institute's Third National Conference Called 'a Huge Success from Start to Finish,'" 2005, http://new.wymaninstitute.org/2005/10/wyman-institute-update-october-11-2005/.

9. Verne Newton, ed., *FDR and the Holocaust* (New York: St. Martin's, 1996), 3.

10. Wyman, *Abandonment*, vii.

11. Ibid.

12. Ibid., ix.

13. Henry L. Feingold, "Review of David Wyman's *The Abandonment of the Jews: America and the Holocaust, 1941–1945*," in Newton, *FDR and the Holocaust*, 145.

14. Henry L. Feingold, *Bearing Witness: How America and Its Jews Responded to the Holocaust* (New York: Syracuse University Press, 1995), 11.

15. Ibid., 2.

16. William D. Rubinstein, *The Myth of Rescue: Why the Democracies Could Not Have Saved More Jews from the Nazis* (New York: Routledge, 1997), 1–4.

17. Ibid., 14.

18. David Cesarani, "Book Review: *The Myth of Rescue: Why the Democracies Could Not Have Saved More Jews from the Nazis*," *English Historical Review* 113, no. 454 (Nov. 1, 1998): 1258. See also Bob Moore, "Book Review: *The Myth of Rescue: Why the Democracies Could Not Have Saved More Jews from the Nazis*," *German History* 17, no. 2 (Apr. 1, 1999): 310.

19. Robert L. Beir, *Roosevelt and the Holocaust: A Rooseveltian Examines the Policies and Remembers the Times* (Fort Lee, NJ: Barricade Books, 2006), 71–74.

20. Robert N. Rosen, *Saving the Jews: Franklin D. Roosevelt and the Holocaust* (New York: Thunder's Mouth, 2006), xxiii.

21. Ibid., xxv.

22. Richard Breitman and Allan J. Lichtman, *FDR and the Jews* (Cambridge, MA: Belknap Press of Harvard University Press, 2013), 2–3.

23. Morse, *While Six Million Died*, 210–16.

24. Rosen, *Saving the Jews*, 62.

25. The FDR Presidential Library in Hyde Park, NY, records that McNutt met with FDR four times during his visit to Washington, DC, in 1938: February 24, 26, 28, and March 15. See n. 37.

26. Kotlowski, *Paul V. McNutt and the Age of FDR*, 38.

27. Linda C. Gugin and James E. St. Clair, *The Governors of Indiana* (Indianapolis: Indiana Historical Society Press, 2006), 289–90.

28. Kotlowski is referring to words used by McNutt in his characterization of McNutt's egalitarianism. See Paul V. McNutt, "Speech Delivered at the Twelfth International Convention of Lion's Club, Des Moines, Iowa," July 12, 1928, Indiana University Bloomington, Lilly Library Manuscript Collections, McNutt Mss., Box 14.

29. Dean J. Kotlowski, "Breaching the Paper Walls: Paul V. McNutt and Jewish Refugees to the Philippines, 1938–1939," *Diplomatic History: The Journal of the Society for Historians of American Foreign Relations* 33, no. 5 (Nov. 2009): 870.

30. For more on McNutt's years as governor, see Kotlowski, *Paul V. McNutt and the Age of FDR*, 127–201.

31. I. George Blake, *Paul V. McNutt: Portrait of a Hoosier Statesman* (Indianapolis: Central, 1966), 107.

32. Paul V. McNutt as quoted in "McNutt Protests Attacks on Jews," *Indianapolis Star*, Mar. 28, 1933, 1.

33. "McNutt Participates in Protest against German Treatment of Jews," *Indianapolis News*, Mar. 28, 1933, 12.

34. Kotlowski, *Paul V. McNutt and the Age of FDR*, 114.

35. Robert R. Neff, "The Early Career and Governorship of Paul V. McNutt" (PhD diss., Indiana University at Bloomington, 1963), 291.

36. James Farley, *The Jim Farley Story: The Roosevelt Years* (New York: McGraw-Hill, 1948), 71–72.

37. William Baehr, archives specialist, Franklin D. Roosevelt Presidential Library, email message to author, June 20, 2016. In that email, Baehr responded to my "recent request to the Franklin D. Roosevelt Presidential Library regarding the visit of Paul V. McNutt to the White House in late winter of 1938. Our database of presidential appointments (available online as FDR: Day by Day, link: http://www.fdrlibrary.marist.edu/daybyday/) [is] compiled from the Ushers' Logs, and Secretaries' Diaries."

38. "How Paul V. McNutt Aided the Refugees," Indiana University Bloomington, Lilly Library Manuscript Collections, McNutt Mss., Box 10.

39. Ibid. See also "Hoosiers Toss Paul McNutt at the Nation," *Hutchison (KS) News*, Feb. 23, 1938, 1, 8. See also chap. 3 for further details.

40. Breitman and Lichtman, *FDR and the Jews*, 102.

41. Stanley Karnow, *In Our Image: America's Empire in the Philippines* (New York: Ballantine Books, 1989), 323–25.

42. Department of State, *Press Releases*, XVIII, Mar. 26, 1938, cited in Dennis Ross Laffer, "The Jewish Trail of Tears: The Evian Conference of July 1938" (master's thesis, University of South Florida, 2011), https://scholarcommons.usf.edu/etd /3195.

43. Donald Winch and Patricia K. O'Brien, eds., *The Political Economy of British Historical Experience, 1688–1914* (New York: Oxford University Press, 2002), 165.

44. S. N. D. North, director, Department of Commerce and Labor, Bureau of the Census, *A Century of Population Growth—from the First Census of the United States to the Twelfth, 1790–1900* (Washington, DC: GPO, 1909), 9.

45. George Wheeler Hinman Jr., "National Origins: Our Immigration Formula," *US Review of Reviews* 70, no. 3 (Sep. 1924), in *Readings in U.S. Government*, by Finla Goff Crawford (New York: A. A. Knopf, 1927), 304–15.

46. L. Edward Purcell, *Immigration*, Social Issues in US History Series (Phoenix, AZ: Oryx Press, 1995), 43.

47. Edward Rhymes, *When Racism Is Law and Prejudice Is Policy: Prejudicial and Discriminatory Laws, Decisions and Policies in U.S. History* (Bloomington, IN: Author House, 2007), 190.

48. Purcell, *Immigration*, 59.

49. Oriana Bandiera, Imran Rasul, and Martina Viarengo, "The Making of Modern America: Estimating Migration Flows Using Administrative Records from Ellis Island 1892–1924" (University College London, May 2010), 13, https://

editorialexpress.com/cgi-bin/conference/download.cgi?db_name=res2011&paper_id=800.

50. US Citizenship and Immigration Services, *Policy Manual*, vol. 7, "Adjustment of Status, Part A—Adjustment of Status Policies and Procedures," Chapter 1—Purpose and Background, Early Immigration Laws, https://www.uscis.gov/policymanual/HTML/PolicyManual-Volume7-PartA-Chapter1.html.

51. Campbell J. Gibson and Emily Lennon, "Historical Census Statistics on the Foreign-Born Population of the United States: 1850–1990" (Washington, DC: US Census Bureau, Population Division, Feb. 1999), Working Paper No. 29, https://www.census.gov/population/www/documentation/twps0029/twps0029.html.

52. Robert DeCourcy Ward, "Our New Immigration Policy," *Foreign Affairs* 3, no. 1 (Sep. 15, 1924): 99–110.

53. US Citizenship and Immigration Services, *Policy Manual*, vol. 7.

54. Hinman, "National Origins: Our Immigration Formula," 304–15.

55. *Statistical Abstract of the United States* (Washington, DC: GPO, 1929), 100.

56. John B. Trevor, "An Analysis of the American Immigration Act of 1924," *International Conciliation*, no. 202 (New York: Carnegie Endowment for International Peace, Sep. 1924), 38.

57. Ibid., 58–59.

58. Bat-Ami Zucker, *In Search of Refuge: Jews and US Consuls in Nazi Germany, 1933–1941* (Portland, OR: Vallentine Mitchell, 2001), 35.

59. "Immigration Act of 1917," Feb. 5, 1917, H.R. 10384, Pub. L. 301, 39 Stat. 874, 64th Congress, US Immigration Legislation Online, University of Washington Bothell Library, 2009, http://library.uwb.edu/Static/USimmigration/39%20stat%20874.pdf.

60. Bill Ong Hing, *Defining America Through Immigration Policy* (Philadelphia: Temple University Press, 2004), 70.

61. "Immigration Act of 1917," Feb. 5, 1917.

62. Wyman, *Abandonment of the Jews*, 5–15.

63. Michael R. Marrus, *The Unwanted: European Refugees from the First World War through the Cold War* (Philadelphia: Temple University Press, 2002), 170–72.

64. Beir, *Roosevelt and the Holocaust*, 115–16.

65. Kenneth Munden, compiler, "Records of the Bureau of Insular Affairs Relating to the Philippine Islands 1898–1935, A List of Selected Files," NARA I, Oct. 1942, vii–viii.

66. George A. Malcolm (Philippine Supreme Court Justice), "Opinion for the United States High Commissioner," Jan. 9, 1939, NARA II, Record Group

126, Office of Territories, Classified Files 1907–1951, "High Commissioner—Administrative General," Entry 1, Box #752, folders 9-7-17.

67. Donald M. Seekins, "The First Phase of United States Rule, 1898–1935," in *Philippines, A Country Study*, ed. Ronald E. Dolan (Washington, DC: Federal Research Division of the Library of Congress, Country Studies DS655. P598 1993) 27, https://cdn.loc.gov/master/frd/frdcstdy/ph/philippinescountoodola_o/philippinescountoodola_o.pdf.

68. Ibid., 28.

69. Ibid., 29.

70. Ibid., 32.

71. Daniel Young, "American Colony and Philippine Commonwealth 1901–1941," *Welcome to the History of the Philippines, Pearl of the Orient Seas*, University of Alberta, Edmonton, http://www.ualberta.ca/~vmitchel/fw5.html.

72. Seekins, "The First Phase of United States Rule, 1898–1935," 39.

73. "The Philippine Independence Act (Tydings-McDuffie Act)," *Chan Robles Virtual Law Library*, Chan Robles Group, http://www.chanrobles.com/tydings mcduffieact.htm#XGNGKLyahA.

74. Seekins, "The First Phase of United States Rule, 1898–1935," 39.

75. Malcolm, "Opinion for the United States High Commissioner," Jan. 9, 1939.

76. Ibid.

77. Ibid.

78. Franklin D. Roosevelt to Francis B. Sayre, Sep. 7, 1939, "High Commissioner—Authority to the Philippines," NARA II, Record Group 126, Records of the Office of Territories, Entry 1, Box #752, folders 9-7-17.

79. David Kranzler, *Japanese, Nazis, and Jews: The Jewish Refugee Community of Shanghai, 1938–1945* (Hoboken, NJ: KTAV Publishing House, 1988), 86–88.

80. Susan Bachrach and Anita Kassof, *Flight and Rescue* (Washington, DC: United States Memorial Museum, 2001), xviii.

81. Ibid., 145–47.

82. Yaacov Liberman, *My China: Jewish Life in the Orient 1900–1950* (New York: Gefen, 1998), 116–23.

83. Bachrach and Kassof, *Flight and Rescue*, 147.

84. Liberman, *My China*, 118.

85. Rebecca Weiner, "Portugal Virtual Jewish History Tour," Jewish Virtual Library, American-Israeli Cooperative Enterprise, https://www.jewishvirtual library.org/portugal-virtual-jewish-history-tour.

86. John W. Griese, "The Jewish Community in Manila" (master's thesis, University of the Philippines, 1954), 21. Due to the violent pogroms against Jews

in fourteenth- and fifteenth-century Spain, hundreds of thousands were forced to convert to Catholicism or be banished from the Iberian Peninsula. Officially, these Jews were known as Cristianos Nuevos (New Christians), but they were commonly called conversos. Although publicly portraying themselves as Christians, many conversos continued to practice their Judaism in secret, earning them the names of Crypto-Jews ("hidden," from the Greek *kryptos*) or Marranos, which has three possible origins for the word. One comes from the Portuguese *marrar*, meaning "to force," and *marrano*, meaning "forced one"; another comes from the Spanish verb *marrar*, meaning to "deviate" or "err"; and the last is derived from the Arabic *muharram*, meaning "forbidden," referring to the ritual prohibition of eating pork. "Marranos" was used by "true" Catholics as a derogatory label for Crypto-Jews, denoting them as pigs who had deviated from the true worship of Christ. Conversos who referred to themselves as Marranos no doubt saw themselves as people who had been forced into Christianity.

87. *Encyclopedia Judaica*, vol. 13 (Jerusalem: Keter Publishing House, 1972), 396.

88. Griese, "The Jewish Community in Manila," 19.

89. "Philippines Jewish Community," *JTA: Jewish Times Asia*, May 2006, http://www.jewishtimesasia.org/manila/269-manila-communities/576-philip pines-jewish-community?tmpl=component&print=1&layout=default&page=. "La Estrella del Norte" is Spanish for "The North Star."

90. William H. Miller, *Picture History of British Ocean Liners, 1900 to the Present* (New York: Courier Dover, 2001), 17.

91. Jonathan Goldstein, "Singapore, Manila and Harbin as Reference Points for Asian 'Port Jewish' Identity," *Jewish Culture and History* 7, nos. 1–2 (2004): 276, https://doi.org/10.1080/1462169X.2004.10512023.

92. Annette Eberly, "Manila? Where? Us?," *Present Tense* 2, no. 3 (Spring 1975): 60.

93. Karnow, *In Our Image*, 196.

94. Eberly, "Manila? Where? Us?," 61.

95. Ibid.

96. Goldstein, "Singapore, Manila and Harbin," 276.

97. Jonathan Goldstein erroneously stated in several publications he authored that Cysner followed Schwarz as rabbi in the Philippines. Schwarz and Cysner had worked together in Hildesheim in the early 1930s, and Schwarz was instrumental in convincing the leaders of the Jewish community in Manila that they needed a cantor to help unite the rapidly growing congregation of refugees. Schwarz arrived in the Philippines in 1938, and Cysner in 1939. Cysner left the Philippines after World War II, about two years earlier than Schwarz. See Bonnie M. Harris, "From Zbaszyn to Manila: The Holocaust Odyssey of Joseph Cysner

and the Philippine Rescue of Refugee Jews" (PhD diss., University of California, Santa Barbara, 2009).

98. Ephraim, *Escape to Manila*, 14.

99. Jock Netzorg, interview by Michael P. Onorato, in *Jock Netzorg: Manila Memories* (Laguna Beach, CA: Pacific Rim Books, 1987).

100. Morton I. Netzorg to Jewish Welfare Board, NY, Apr. 15, 1945, American Jewish Historical Society Archives, National Jewish Welfare Board Collection, "Philippine Islands, 1945," 1–180, Box 198, Fld. 1.

101. Netzorg, interview by Onorato, 29.

102. Goldstein, "Singapore, Manila and Harbin," 279.

103. Eberly, "Manila? Where? Us?," 61.

104. Ephraim, *Escape to Manila*, 14–15.

105. Netzorg, interview by Onorato, 29–30.

106. Griese, "The Jewish Community in Manila," 23–24.

107. Eberly, "Manila? Where? Us?," 61.

108. Netzorg, interview by Onorato, 3.

Chapter 3. Open Hearts

1. "Manilaners" was the name adopted by the Jewish refugee community in the Philippines.

2. Emery Komlos to Robert Pilpel, Oct. 17, 1941, attachment: "Refugee Immigration in the Philippines," American Jewish Joint Distribution Committee (hereafter JDC) Archives, JDC Collection 33/44, File #784.

3. Frank Ephraim listed the members of the JRC in his manuscript "Escape to Manila: Finding Refuge from Nazi Persecution," dated April 23, 2001. I obtained Ephraim's original manuscript in October 2008 from Rabbi Marvin Tokayer, author of *The Fugu Plan*. He stated to me in an email dated October 2, 2008, "I knew Frank Ephraim, and was saddened by his premature passing—his published book, as all books, suffer from the scissors of the editor and/or publisher. . . . I think that I have his original manuscript which could certainly provide new and interesting information for your thesis." We exchanged addresses and Rabbi Tokayer sent me his copy of the original manuscript given to him by Frank Ephraim before his death. I copied it and mailed it back to Rabbi Tokayer. According to Ephraim's manuscript, members of the JRC were Philip Frieder, Julius Reese (formerly Reis), Samuel Schechter, Peter J. Wallowit, Mottel Goldstein, Dr. Kurt Eulau, and Morton I. Netzorg.

4. "Memorandum of Conversation Between Mr. Hyman and Morris Frieder

of Cincinnati, Ohio, on Nov. 28th [1938] at 3:30 p.m." JDC Archives, New York, JDC Collection 33/44, File #784.

5. Ephraim, *Escape to Manila*, 22. Frank Ephraim, a survivor of the Jewish refugee Community in Manila, presented a complete database of all the Jewish refugees who came to the Philippines to the JewishGen Family Genealogy website, in which he identified 1,301 names.

6. Max Berges, "Please, don't worry! Nothing came of it," Center for Jewish History, New York, Leo Beck Institute Archives, Max Berges Memoir Project, call no. MM8.334. Berges stated that thirty to forty Jewish couples left Shanghai on the SS *Gneisenau*.

7. Ibid., 271.

8. Ibid.

9. Ibid., 272–88.

10. Ibid., 330.

11. Ibid., 338. Just prior to the Japanese invasion of Shanghai, the Bergeses had been advised to see the American Consul in Shanghai to receive a visa to immigrate to the United States. That letter allowed them to receive a permanent visa to the Philippines rather than a temporary one.

12. Ibid., 330.

13. Albert Einstein Archives, Berges File-Correspondence M. L. Berges, 52/524–52/547, Hebrew University of Jerusalem, pp. 52–54.

14. Bauer, *My Brother's Keeper*, 157.

15. Ibid., 145; Richard Breitman, Barbara McDonald Stewart, and Severin Hochberg, eds., *Advocate for the Doomed: The Diaries and Papers of James G. McDonald, 1932–1935* (Bloomington: Indiana University Press, 2007), 798–99.

16. Sharon Delmendo documents that Dwight D. Eisenhower, while in the Philippines on Douglas MacArthur's staff, was not involved in Jewish refugee rescue in her work in progress: "Ike and the Jews: Was Dwight D. Eisenhower Involved in Jewish Refugee Rescue in the Philippines during the Holocaust?" (unpublished manuscript in author's possession).

17. For details about the background of the Weiss brothers, see Ephraim, *Escape to Manila*, 27–28.

18. Paul V. McNutt to Julius Weiss, May 19, 1938, JDC Archives, JDC Collection 33/44, File #784.

19. For more analysis on this subject, refer to the section titled "Evian, FDR, and Paul V. McNutt" in chap. 2.

20. "How Paul V. McNutt Aided the Refugees," n.d., Indiana University Bloomington, Lilly Library Manuscript Collections, McNutt Mss., Box 10.

21. Ibid.

22. "McNutt on Way Home with Data on China," *New York Times*, Feb. 11, 1938, 12.

23. Charles Liebman to Paul V. McNutt, June 10, 1938, JDC Archives, JDC Collection 33/44, File #784.

24. "Memorandum of Conversation Between Mr. Hyman and Morris Frieder of Cincinnati, Ohio on Nov. 28th [1938] at 3:30 P.M," JDC Archives, JDC Collection 33/44, File #784.

25. Paul V. McNutt to Julius Weiss, May 19, 1938, JDC Archives, JDC Collection 33/44, File #784.

26. "Memorandum . . . November 28th [1938] at 3:30 p.m."

27. Ibid.

28. McNutt to Weiss, May 19, 1938. Samuel Schechter was president of the Temple Emil congregation during these years.

29. Ibid.

30. Charles Liebman to Isaiah Bowman, Sep. 25, 1947, JDC Archives, JDC Collection 33/44, File #784: 1/13/41–9/25/47.

31. Ibid.

32. REC to Mr. Stuart M. Crocker, Feb. 17, 1942, JDC Archives, JDC Collection 33/44, File #784: 1/13/41–9/25/47.

33. Hilfsverein der Deutschen Juden was the original name of the Relief Organization of German Jews when it was founded in 1901. The Hilfsverein concentrated mainly on helping improve social and political conditions of Jews in Eastern Europe and the Orient. Just before World War I, it had thousands of members in Germany, America, Russia, and Palestine. It was also a distributor of American relief funds to Eastern Europe during the war. Between 1921 and 1936 it limited its activity to Jewish emigration from Germany. After the advent of the Third Reich, it had to change its name to Hilfsverein der Juden in Deutschland in 1935 as it could no longer continue its Jewish relief work abroad. It was officially dissolved in 1939 but continued to exist until 1941 as an emigration section of the Reichvertretung der Juden in Deutschland. See Ze'ev Wilhelm Falk, "Hilfsverein der Deutschen Juden," *Encyclopaedia Judaica*, accessed July 10, 2019, https://www.encyclopedia.com/religion/encyclopedias-almanacs-transcripts-and-maps/hilfsverein-der-deutschen-juden.

34. Bruno Schachner (REC) to Hilfsverein der Juden in Deutschland, June 1, 1938, JDC Archives, JDC Collection 33/44, File #784.

35. Charles Liebman to Paul V. McNutt, June 10, 1938, JDC Archives, JDC Collection 33/44, File #784.

36. Ibid.

37. Ibid.

38. Paul V. McNutt to Charles Liebman, June 24, 1938, JDC Archives, JDC Collection 33/44, File #784.

39. Ibid.

40. Ibid.

41. Frank Ephraim, "The Mindanao Plan: Political Obstacles to Jewish Refugee Settlement," *Holocaust and Genocide Studies* 20, no. 3 (Winter 2006): 410–36.

42. "Memorandum . . . November 28th [1938] at 3:30 P.M."

43. Jock Netzorg, interview by Onorato, 3.

44. Schachner to Frieder, July 29, 1938, JDC Archives, JDC Collection 33/44, File #784.

45. Burnett to McNutt, July 13, 1938, NARA II, Record Group 350, Records of the Bureau of Insular Affairs, General Classified Files 1898–1945, Box 1338, Entry 5, File 28943-1.

46. McNutt to Burnett, July 16, 1938, NARA II, Record Group 350, Records of the Bureau of Insular Affairs, General Classified Files 1898–19445, Box 1338, Entry 5, File 28943-1.

47. "Confidential," July 16, 1938, NARA II, Record Group 350, Records of the Bureau of Insular Affairs, General Classified Files 1898–1945, Box 1338, Entry 5, File 28943-1.

48. Gray, Milan to Secretary of State Hull, Sep. 6, 1938, NARA I, Record Group 59, General Records Department of State, Visa Division 1914-1940, Entry 704, Box 245, 811B.55, J/1.

49. Hull to American Consul, Naples, Sep. 7, 1938, NARA I, Record Group 59, General Records Department of State, Visa Division 1914-1940, Entry 704, Box 245, 811B.55, J/1.

50. Hull to McNutt, Sep. 12, 1938, NARA II, Record Group 350, Records of the Bureau of Insular Affairs, General Classified Files 1898–1945, Box 1338, Entry 5, File #28943-2.

51. McNutt to Burnett, July 16, 1938, NARA II, Record Group 350, Records of the Bureau of Insular Affairs, General Classified Files 1898–1945, Box 1338, Entry 5, File #28943-1.

52. Woodring to McNutt, Mar. 1, 1937, NARA II, Record Group 350, Records of the Bureau of Insular Affairs, General Classified Files, Office of the U.S. High Commissioner, Entry 5, Box 472, Folder 3038-B, 118.

53. "How Paul V. McNutt Aided the Refugees," Indiana University Bloomington, Lilly Library Manuscript Collections, McNutt Mss., Box 10.

54. Paul V. McNutt, "Quarterly Report of the United States High Commissioner to the Philippine Islands to the President of the United States Quarter

Ending Dec. 31, 1937," Indiana University Bloomington, Lilly Library Manuscript Collections, McNutt Mss., Box 9, p. 18.

55. Ibid.

56. Ibid., 19.

57. Paul V. McNutt, "Quarterly Report of the United States High Commissioner to the Philippine Islands to the President of the United States Quarter Ending December 31, 1938," Indiana University Bloomington, Lilly Library Manuscript Collections, McNutt Mss., Box 9, p. 66.

58. Ibid., 69–70.

59. Paul V. McNutt, Memorandum, April 29, 1938, Indiana University Bloomington, Lilly Library Manuscript Collections, McNutt Mss., Box 9.

60. McNutt, translation of coded radiogram received Sep. 15, 1939. NARA II, Record Group 350, Records of the Bureau of Insular Affairs, General Classified Files 1898–1945, Entry 5, Box 1338, Folder #28943-2.

61. McNutt, translation of coded radiogram received Sep. 30, 1939, NARA II, Record Group 350, Records of the Bureau of Insular Affairs, General Classified Files 1898–1945, Entry 5, Box 1338, Folder #28943-5.

62. "Memorandum re: Philippine Islands," Oct.1, 1938, JDC Archives, JDC Collection 33/44, File #784.

63. Messersmith to McNutt, Oct. 8, 1938, NARA II, Record Group 350, Records of the Bureau of Insular Affairs, General Classified Files 1898–1945, Entry 5, Box 1338, Folder #28943-6.

64. McNutt to State Department, Oct. 25, 1938, NARA II, Record Group 350, Records of the Bureau of Insular Affairs, General Classified Files 1898–1945, Entry 5, Box 1338, Folder #28943-8.

65. Herbert Katzki, JDC Office meeting, June 23, 1939, JDC Archives, JDC Collection 33/44, File #784.

66. Ibid.

67. Messersmith to McNutt, Nov. 30, 1938, NARA II, Record Group 350, Records of the Bureau of Insular Affairs, General Classified Files 1898–1945, Entry 5, Box 1338, Folder #28943-16.

68. Ibid.

69. The Department of State issued an official "Visa Instruction" regarding "German Refugees Proceeding to the Philippine Islands" for transmission to all U.S. Consuls and Embassies. Messersmith, Visa Instruction, Nov. 30, 1938. NARA I, Record Group 59, General Records Department of State, Visa Division 1914–1940, Entry 704, Box 245, 811B.55, J/19a.

70. Telegram from Singapore to Secretary of State, Nov. 25, 1938, NARA I, Record Group 59, General Records Department of State, Entry 704, Visa Division 1914–1940, Box 245, 811B.55, J/16.

71. Messersmith to Woodring, Nov. 30, 1938. NARA I, Record Group 59, General Records Department of State, Visa Division 1914–1940, Entry 704, Box 245, 811B.55, J/16.

72. "To the American Chargé d'Affaires ad interim," Paris, 12/14/38. NARA I, Record Group 59, General Records Department of State, Visa Division 1914–1940, Entry 704, Box 245, 811B.55, J/17.

73. War Department, Washington, May 19, 1939, NARA I, Record Group 59, General Records Department of State, Visa Division 1914–1940, Entry 704, Box 246, 811B.55, J/192.

74. J. C. Hyman to Julius Ochs Adler, Dec. 27, 1938, JDC Archives, JDC Collection 33/44, File #784.

75. Bauer, *My Brother's Keeper*, 131–32, 235.

76. Warren to Skodak, June 10, 1939, NARA I, Record Group 59, General Records of the Department of State, Visa Division, Entry 704, Box 246, 811B.55, J/210.

77. Yehuda Bauer, *American Jewry and the Holocaust: The American Jewish Joint Distribution Committee, 1939–1945* (Detroit: Wayne State University Press, 1981), 24.

78. Paul V. McNutt to Julius Weiss, May 19, 1938, JDC Archives, JDC Archives, JDC Collection 33/44, File #784.

79. Memorandum re: Philippine Islands, 10/1/38, JDC Archives, JDC Archives, JDC Collection 33/44, File #784.

80. Ibid.

81. Philip Frieder to REC, Oct. 31, 1938, JDC Archives, JDC Collection 33/44, File #784.

82. Philip Frieder to REC, Nov. 9, 1938, JDC Archives, JDC Collection 33/44, File #784.

83. Memorandum of Conversation Between Mr. Hyman and Morris Frieder on Nov. 28 at 3:30 pm, JDC Archives, JDC Collection 33/44, File #784.

84. Morrissey to Chase National Bank, Feb. 8, 1939, re: transfer of funds, JDC Archives, JDC Collection 33/44, File #784.

85. Ephraim, *Escape to Manila*, 31.

86. Ibid., 37.

87. Telegram, Schwarz to Cysner, Nov. 22, 1938, JHSSD Archives, Cantor Joseph Cysner Collection, CJC02.01.

88. McNutt to SECWAR, Dec. 8, 1938, NARA I, Record Group 59, General Records of the Department of State, Visa Division, Entry 704, Box 245, 811B.55, J/24.

89. State Department to American Consular Officer in Charge, Warsaw, Poland, Apr. 20, 1939, NARA I, Record Group 59, General Records of the Department of State, Visa Division, Entry 704, Box 246, 811B.55, J/160.

90. John K. Davis to the Hull, May 9, 1939, "Subject: Visa case of Joseph Cysner," NARA I, Record Group 59, General Records of the Department of State, Visa Division, Entry 704, Box 246, 811B.55, J/198.

91. Griese, "The Jewish Community in Manila," 27.

92. Alex Frieder, "Jewish Refugee Committee," May 7, 1940, p. 10, JDC Archives, JDC Collection 33/44, File #784.

93. Ibid., 12.

94. Ibid., 2.

95. Ibid., 3.

96. Ibid., 5.

97. Katzki, "Confidential," June 23, 1939, JDC Archives, JDC Collection 33/44, File #784.

98. Ibid.

99. Alex Frieder, "Jewish Refugee Committee," May 7, 1940, p. 19.

100. Ibid., 20.

101. Ibid.

102. Robert Pilpel, "File Memorandum," June 21, 1940, JDC Archives, JDC Collection 33/44, File #784.

103. Robert Pilpel to Jewish Refugee Committee, June 26, 1940, JDC Archives, JDC Collection 33/44, File #784.

104. Emery Komlos, REC to James Becker, Chicago, July 3, 1940, JDC Archives, JDC Collection 33/44, File #784.

105. Robert Pilpel to Lazaro Zelwer, Colombia, Oct. 8, 1940, JDC Archives, JDC Collection 33/44, File #784.

106. Ibid.

107. Robert Pilpel, to Edwin Goldwasser, "Memorandum re: Philippines," Nov. 7, 1940, JDC Archives, JDC Collection 33/44, File #784.

108. Emery Komlos to Robert Pilpel, Oct. 17, 1941, attachment: "Refugee Immigration in the Philippines," JDC Archives, JDC Collection 33/44, File #784.

109. Ibid. Komlos was assistant secretary of the REC.

110. Rabbi Josef Schwarz, "History of the Jewish Community Manila," Sep. 1947, copy sent to author by Lotte Cassel Hershfield, Feb. 15, 2005.

111. Martin Meadows, interview by Bonnie M. Harris, Sep. 17, 2007, Washington, DC, video recording.

112. Ibid.

113. Hans Hoeflein, interview by Noel Izon, Nov. 16, 2011, Easton, PA, transcription.

114. Ibid.

115. Hans Hoeflein, as detailed in Juergen R. Goldhagen, ed., *Manila*

Memories: Four Boys Remember Their Lives before, during, and after the Japanese Occupation (Exeter, UK: Shearsman Books, 2008), 16–26.

116. Goldhagen, *Manila Memories*, 14.

117. Ibid., 19.

118. The US retained a consulate in Breslau (Wroclaw, Poland, today), a Prussian city in Silesia, from 1919 until 1939, when it was relocated to Königsberg (Gdańsk today). The US vice consul there was Stephen Bernard Vaughn, who served in the various East Prussian consulates until 1939, when he was transferred to Berlin. Prior to that, Vaughn was instrumental in granting the precious few visas allowed by the State Department to fleeing Jews in 1938–39, before the issuance of all visas to the Philippines came under the jurisdiction of the JRC in Manila in October 1939. Abraham Ascher (who was ten years old in 1938), in his book *A Community under Siege: The Jews of Breslau under Nazism* (Stanford: Stanford University Press, 2007), researched accusations that Vaughn accepted bribes from desperate Jews fleeing the Nazis (his father among them) and instead found evidence that Vaughn had clearly "showed an interest in helping Jews." Ascher, *Community under Siege*, 138. Vaughn would be honored among those diplomats who had altruistically aided Jews on the Institute for the Study of Rescue and Altruism in the Holocaust website. In that short period between 1938 and 1939, Vaughn issued visas to Jewish families escaping Germany, ostensibly as "agricultural experts." Several Manilaner families were beneficiaries of Vaughn's efforts.

119. Ralph Preiss, interview by Bonnie M. Harris, June 17, 2008, New York City, video recording.

120. Ibid.

121. Ibid.

122. Lotte Cassel Hershfield, interview by Noel Izon, Nov. 17, 2011, Hartford, CT, video recording. See also note 118 regarding vice consul Stephen Vaughn.

123. Ibid.

124. Ibid.

125. Margot Cassel Pins Kestenbaum, interview by Noel Izon, June 3, 2016, Jerusalem, Israel, transcription.

126. Ibid.

127. John Odenheimer, interview by Peter Ryan, Nov. 12, 1997, San Mateo, CA, JFCS San Francisco Holocaust Center, 2 Tapes in Collections, USHMM, Accession # 1999.A0122.0346, RG-50.477.0346, https://collections.ushmm.org /search/catalog/irn509589.

128. La Salle College in Hong Kong was founded on September 5, 1917, by the Institute of the Brothers of the Christian Schools, a Roman Catholic religious teaching order founded by St. John Baptist de La Salle. When the British declared

war on Germany on September 3, 1939, the British War Department in Hong Kong set up La Salle College as an internment camp for German nationals arrested in Hong Kong.

129. A Mariah was a police wagon used to transport prisoners.

130. Odenheimer, interview by Ryan.

131. Max H. Weissler, "Life Story in the Philippines," Dec. 13, 2005, Hod-Hasharon, Israel, 5.

132. Ibid., 6.

133. Ibid.

134. Jacques Lipetz, interview by Nora Levin, July 21, 1988, from the Collection of the Gratz College Holocaust Oral History Archive, Transcription, USHMM, Accession # 1997.A0441.115, RG-50.462.0115.

135. Ibid.

136. Ibid.

137. Kestenbaum, interview by Izon.

138. Hershfield, interview by Izon.

139. Hanna Kaunitz Weinstein Entell, interview by Ray Ann Kremer, June 18 and Oct. 8, 1986, Atlanta, GA, OHC 10184, p. 18, Herbert and Esther Taylor Oral History Collection, Cuba family archives for Southern Jewish History at the Breman Museum, Atlanta, GA.

140. Helen Beck, interview by Noel Izon, Feb. 26, 2014, Santa Rosa, CA, video recording.

141. Charlotte Holzer Bunim, interview by Bonnie M. Harris, June 26, 2006, Lawrence, NY, video recording.

142. Margie Rosenthal, interview by Nancy Alper, Oct. 24, 1996, Washington, DC, USHMM Transcript, RG-50.106.0052. (Alper neglected to ask for the names of Margie's immediate family.)

143. Hoeflein, in Goldhagen, *Manila Memories*, 26.

144. Kestenbaum, interview by Izon.

145. Ibid.

146. Entell, interview by Kramer.

147. Hershfield, interview by Izon.

148. Ibid.

149. Ibid.

150. Most likely Margot is referring to either traditional Jewish liturgical music or pro-Zionist songs circulating during the time, since the state of Israel and "Israeli" songs did not exist prior to 1948.

151. Margot Cassel Pins Kestenbaum, email to Bonnie M. Harris, Dec. 26, 2018.

152. Ephraim, *Escape to Manila*, 71–72.

153. Lipetz, interview by Levin.

154. Hershfield, interview by Izon.

Chapter 4. Mindanao, a New Palestine

1. The Dominican Republic also received favorable attention but only a modicum of success was realized with the establishment of a Jewish refugee settlement in Sosua that ultimately sheltered just over seven hundred refugees. See Marion A. Kaplan, *Dominican Haven: The Jewish Refugee Settlement in Sosua, 1940–1945* (New York: Museum of Jewish Heritage, 2008). While it is true that the Trujillo regime made an official proposal welcoming Jewish refugees to its shores, Saul Friedman described it as an offer that "was little more than an empty gesture by a self-seeking despot" that brought him "a good deal of favorable publicity . . . but it never intended to really succor the desperate Jews of Germany." Friedman, *No Haven for the Oppressed*, 62–63.

2. Herbert Frieder to Bruno Schachner, Dec. 8, 1938, JDC Archives, JDC Collection 33/44, File #787a.

3. Feingold, *The Politics of Rescue*, 93.

4. See chap. 3 for the full details of this selection plan.

5. At a reception held at the White House on October 17, 1939, FDR addressed about a dozen officers and representatives of the IGCR. FDR stated: "I take great pleasure in announcing today that active steps have been taken to begin work on the settlement projects which have been made possible by the generous attitude of the Dominican Government and the Government of the Philippine Commonwealth." FDR, "Statement of the President on Opening the Meeting of the Officers of the Intergovernmental Committee," October 17, 1939, Franklin D. Roosevelt Presidential Library & Museum, Master Speech File 1898–1945, Series 1: Master Speech File, Box 48, "Address to Officers of the Intergovernmental Committee" (speech file 1248).

6. Breitman and Lichtman, *FDR and the Jews*, 102–4. The authors were quoting the detailed reconstructed notes made by the senior American in the League of Nations, Arthur Sweetser, of a private meeting with FDR held in the White House on April 4, 1938, in which Sweetser endeavored to persuade FDR to engage the US in the League of Nations.

7. Feingold, *The Politics of Rescue*, 22–28.

8. Ibid., 37.

9. Department of State press release, "Text of Resolution Adopted July 14, 1938, By Intergovernmental Committee on Political Refugees at Evian, France,"

NARA II, Record Group 59, IGCR, Country Files, "Philippines," Lot 52D408, Box 6.

10. Feingold, *The Politics of Rescue*, 42–44.

11. William Lyon Mackenzie King, "The Diaries of William Lyon Mackenzie King," Nov. 17, 1938, pp. 6–7, Library and Archives Canada, ID# 19578 and 19579, https://www.bac-lac.gc.ca/eng/discover/politics-government/prime-ministers /william-lyon-mackenzie-king/Pages/item.aspx?IdNumber=19573.

12. Richard Breitman and Allan Lichtman (*FDR and the Jews*, 98–160) wrote an exhaustive treatise on Roosevelt's actions concerning the Evian Conference, the IGCR, and the agenda of advancing mass resettlement sites for Jewish migration. They report no mention of the Philippines from FDR at any time as a viable site for resettlement, and yet it was one of the foremost sites on the IGCR list.

13. Radio address by Myron C. Taylor, "Confidential press release," Nov. 25, 1938, NARA II, Record Group 59, IGCR, Country Files, "Philippines," Lot 52D408, Box 10. The content of the address was released to the press for publication on Nov. 26, 1938.

14. Herbert Druks, *The Failure to Rescue* (New York: Robert Speller & Sons, 1977), 10.

15. Ibid.

16. "Memorandum of Conversation on November 28," JDC Archives, JDC Collection 33/44, File #784.

17. Herbert Frieder to Bruno Schachner, Dec. 8, 1938, JDC Archives, JDC Collection 33/44, File #787a.

18. Ibid.

19. Paul McNutt to Cordell Hull, "Translation of Radiogram in Code Received December 3, 1938," NARA II, Record Group 350, Records of the Bureau of Insular Affairs, General Classified Files 1898–1945, Entry 5, Box 1338, 1914–1945, File #28943-17.

20. Jacobs to McNutt, "Confidential," Dec. 2, 1938, NARA II, Record Group 59, IGCR, Country Files, "Philippines," Lot 52D408, Box 6. This draft copy bears an administrative code in the lower left-hand corner of the last page that identifies "JEJ" (Joseph E. Jacobs) as the author on "12/2."

21. A copy of the message in the above note was also found in NARA II, Record Group 350, Records of the Bureau of Insular Affairs, General Classified Files 1898–1945, Box 1338, 1914–1945, Entry 5, File #28943-18, with a handwritten note attached to it, signed by J. E. Jacobs and dated December 2, 1938, informing Col. Eager, of the War Department, responsible for all dispatches to the Philippines, that the enclosed "advanced copy of a letter" would be received by the Bureau "sometime tomorrow."

22. Sumner Wells to McNutt, "Confidential," Dec. 5, 1938, NARA II, Record Group 350, Records of the Bureau of Insular Affairs, General Classified Files 1898–1945, Box 1338, 1914–1945, Entry 5, File #28943-18.

23. Ibid.

24. Herbert Frieder to Bruno Schachner, Dec. 8, 1938, JDC Archives, JDC Collection 33/44, File #787a.

25. One of the economic results from the implementation of the Commonwealth status of the Philippines was the windfall revenues collected in the form of excise taxes on the export of coconut oil and sugar to the United States from the Philippines that was slated to be returned to the new Commonwealth nation. The return of the coconut excise taxes collected since August 1934 and transferred to the Philippines in one lump sum on July 1, 1937, was 114 million pesos, just over fifty million US dollars. Quezon planned on using portions of the funds to purchase large landed estates on the provinces and reselling them in smaller parcels to the tenant farmers working on those estates by financing loans to them. Quezon also planned on using the windfall to build roads and execute other forms of development on Mindanao to encourage resettlement of Filipinos from Luzon. See Satoshi Nakano, "The 'Windfall' Revenue Controversy, 1937–1941: A Perspective of Philippine Commonwealth History," Apr. 5, 2008, http://www.quezon .ph/wp-content/uploads/2008/04/commonwealth-funds-windfall-debate.pdf.

26. "Speech of His Excellency Manuel L. Quezon, President of the Philippines on the Development of Mindanao," June 6, 1936, Jorge B. Vargas Museum and Filipiniana Research Center, Quezon City, PI, Jorge B. Vargas Archives, *Messages of the President*, vol. 2. part 1, 1935–1936, 111. Philippine geography is divided into three island groups: Luzon, Mindanao, and Visayas. Visayas is in the central part of the country between the larger Luzon island group to the north and the southern Mindanao island group. It is named after the ethnolinguistic group, the Visayan (Bisaya), a sea-based culture that is predominant there and on most parts of Mindanao. Their uniqueness inspired some of its people to participate and provide leadership in the Philippine Revolution in the last years of Spanish colonialism, going so far as to establish their own confederation. The Visayas were eventually absorbed into the Philippine republic, and three Philippine presidents have been of Visayan descent.

27. Manuel Quezon, "Jews to Come in Gradually, Says Quezon," *Manila Daily Bulletin*, Wednesday, Apr. 24, 1940.

28. "From the Acting Secretary of State," Dec. 6, 1938, NARA I, Record Group 59, General Records Department of State, Visa Division, Box 245, 811B.55, J/21.

29. Ibid.

30. "Confidential for the High Commissioner," Dec. 9, 1938, NARA II, Record Group 350, Records of the Bureau of Insular Affairs, General Classified Files 1898–1945, Entry 5, 1914–1945, Box 1338, File #28943.

31. Welles to Rublee, IGCR headquarters, London, Dec. 13, 1938, NARA II, Record Group 59, IGCR, Country Files, "Philippines," Lot 52D408, Box 6.

32. Ibid.

33. Jacobs, "The Colonization of Jewish Refugees in Mindanao," Dec. 17, 1938, NARA I, Record Group 59, General Records Department of State, Visa Division, Box 245, 811B.55, J/21.

34. Ibid.

35. According to the Philippine historian Lewis E. Gleeck Jr., Sayre's personality was "ill-suited to the Philippine political scene." Although Sayre was selected for his knowledge and experience with the economic issues that dominated Philippine–United States relations at the time, "Sayre's austere and didactic personality was anathema to the mercurial and earthy Quezon." Gleeck further maintained that Sayre was almost a total failure as an effective High Commissioner in the Philippines because of his constant battle of wills with Quezon, especially with regard to the expenditures planned for the coconut excise tax refund. Sayre favored using the refund for military purposes in the defense of the Philippines, and Quezon objected wholeheartedly to the proposal, feeling that the United States was "less concerned with Philippine than American defense" interests. Quezon had marked these funds for Filipino needs, and the development of Mindanao was big on his list. Quezon believed expenditures for defense should fall squarely on the United States as they still held the military reins over Philippine independence. It is to Sayre's credit that he did not scuttle the selective refugee plan already in operation when he came to the Philippines in 1939. Sayre served as High Commissioner until 1941, escaping before the advent of the war. See Lewis E. Gleeck, *The American Governors-General and High Commissioners in the Philippines* (Quezon City: New Day Publishers, 1986), 341–59.

36. Sayre to Welles, "Dear Sumner," Dec. 17, 1938, NARA I, Record Group 59, General Records Department of State, Visa Division, Box 245, 811B.55, J/21.

37. Jacobs, "The Colonization of Jewish Refugees in Mindanao," Dec. 17, 1938.

38. Ibid.

39. Sayre to Welles, "Dear Sumner," Dec. 17, 1938.

40. Jacobs, "Confidential from the Acting Secretary of State to the High Commissioner," Dec. 17, 1938, NARA II, RG 59, IGCR, Country Files, "Philippines," Lot 52D408, Box 6.

41. Sumner Wells to McNutt, "Confidential," Dec. 5, 1938, NARA II, Record

Group 350, Records of the Bureau of Insular Affairs, General Classified Files 1898–1945, Box 1338, 1914–1945, Entry 5, File #28943-18.

42. Jacobs, "Confidential to High Commissioner," Dec. 17, 1938. NARA I, Record Group 59, General Records Department of State, Visa Division, Box 245, 811B.55, J/21.

43. Sayre, "Colonization of Jewish Refugees in Mindanao," Dec. 17, 1938, NARA I, Record Group 59, General Records Department of State, Visa Division, Box 245, 811B.55, J/21.

44. Jacobs, "Confidential to High Commissioner," Dec. 17, 1938.

45. "To: Mr. Welles, Re: Mr. Warren of the Advisory Committee," Dec. 17, 1938, NARA II, Record Group 59, IGCR, Country Files, "Philippines," Lot 52D408, Box 6.

46. McNutt, "Colonization of German Refugees in the Philippines," Dec. 17, 1938, NARA II, Record Group 59, IGCR, Country Files, "Philippines," Lot 52D408, Box 6.

47. Jacobs, "Subject: Colonization of Jewish Refugees in the Philippines," Dec. 21, 1938, NARA I, Record Group 59, General Records Department of State, Visa Division, Box 245, 811B.55, J/21.

48. Jacobs to Welles, "Note," Dec. 23, 1938. NARA I, Record Group 59, General Records Department of State, Visa Division, Box 245, 811B.55, J/21.

49. McNutt, "Message from President Quezon," Dec. 23, 1938, NARA II, Record Group 59, IGCR, Country Files, "Philippines," Lot 52D408, Box 6.

50. Ibid.

51. Ibid.

52. Clarification was sought for the phrase "money crops"; that is, did it refer to all exports? Reply: "'not to grow money crops' should be clarified as follows: 'not to grow crops competing with Philippine products now sold in the American market.'" McNutt, radiogram, Jan. 7, 1939, NARA I, Record Group 59, General Records Department of State, Visa Division, Box 245, 811B.55, J/35.

53. McNutt, "Message from President Quezon," Dec. 23, 1938. NARA I, Record Group 59, General Records Department of State, Visa Division, Box 245, 811B.55, J/35.

54. Achilles to Welles, Dec. 30, 1938, NARA II, Record Group 59, Country Files, "Philippines," Lot 52D408, Box 6.

55. To High Commissioner, Jan. 7, 1939, NARA I, Record Group 59, General Records Department of State, Visa Division, Box 245, 811B.55, J/36.

56. Ibid.

57. Jacobs to McNutt, "Confidential," Dec. 2, 1938.

58. Fred Maxey, "Mindanao—Island of Hope," in *The Development of*

Mindanao and the Future of the Non-Christians (Manila: Institute of Pacific Relations, Oct. 1938), p. 10, Jorge B. Vargas Museum and Filipiniana Research Center Archives, Jorge B. Vargas Collection, Office of the President Series, vol. 24, Oct.–Dec. 1938.

59. Eulogio Rodriguez, "The Economic Development of Mindanao," *Commonwealth Advocate* 4, nos. 10–11 (Nov.–Dec. 1938): 13–14.

60. Ibid.

61. Catherine Porter, "Ambitious Plans for Mindanao Announced," *Far Eastern Survey* 7, no. 23 (Nov. 23, 1938): 273.

62. Catherine Porter, "An Independent Philippines and Japan," *Far Eastern Survey* 6, no. 8 (Apr. 14, 1937): 86.

63. Ibid., 87.

64. For more information on Visayas, see n. 26.

65. "Jewish Philippines Refuge Studied to Curb Japanese," *Los Angeles Times*, June 4, 1939, NARA II, Record Group 350, Records of the Bureau of Insular Affairs, General Classified Files, File #28943, Box 1338, Entry 5.

66. Abaca is a banana species native to the Philippines and is primarily harvested for the fiber extracted from its leaf stems, also called Manila hemp.

67. "Jewish Philippines Refuge Studied to Curb Japanese," *Los Angeles Times*, June 4, 1939.

68. Sidney Glazer, "The Moros as a Political Factor in Philippine Independence," *Pacific Affairs* 14, no. 1 (Mar. 1941): 78.

69. Moshe Yegar, *Between Integration and Secession: The Muslim Communities of the Southern Philippines, Southern Thailand, and Western Burma/Myanmar* (New York: Lexington Books, 2002), 213–22.

70. Vincent J. H. Houben, "Southeast Asia and Islam," *Annals of the American Academy of Political and Social Science* 588 (July 2003): 150. See also Yegar, *Between Integration and Secession*, 222.

71. Yegar, *Between Integration and Secession*, 225–30.

72. Manuel L. Quezon, "Speech on Development of Lanao," Jorge B. Vargas Museum and Filipiniana Research Center Archives, Jorge B. Vargas Collection, *Messages of the President*, vol. 4 pt. 1, 1938, p. 194.

73. Alex Frieder to Robert Pilpel, Feb. 17, 1940, JDC Archives, JDC Collection 33/44, File #784.

74. "Quezon's Policy on Jews," *Philippines Herald*, Apr. 24, 1940, NARA II, Record Group 350, Records of the Bureau of Insular Affairs, General Classified Files, Box 1338, Entry 5, File #28943-23.

75. Ibid.

76. "General Aguinaldo Opposes Jews as Colonists," *Manila Bulletin*, Apr. 28,

1939, NARA II, Record Group 350, Records of the Bureau of Insular Affairs, General Classified Files, Box 1338, Entry 5, File #28943-23.

77. Similar attitudes existed among Japanese leaders and is explored in greater detail in chapter 5, where I discuss the tenets of the Fugu Plan.

78. "Benefits to P.I. of Admission of Few Jews Shown," *Bulletin*, Feb. 16, 1939, Jorge B. Vargas Museum and Filipiniana Research Center Archives, Jorge B. Vargas Collection, Office of the President Series, vol. 27, Jan.–Mar. 1939, p. 57.

79. Achilles, "Memorandum of Conversation," Jan. 18, 1939, NARA I, Record Group 59, General Records Department of State, Visa Division, Box 245, 811B.55, J/49.

80. Ibid.

81. Ibid.

82. Bowman to Achilles, Jan. 18, 1939, NARA I, Record Group 59, General Records Department of State, Visa Division, Box 245, 811B.55, J/46.

83. Isaiah Bowman, "Preliminary Draft of Memorandum on Settlement Possibilities on the Island of Mindanao," Jan. 21, 1939, NARA II, Record Group 59, IGCR, Country Files, "Philippines," Lot 52D408, Box 6.

84. Ibid.

85. Breitman and Lichtman adopt the characterization of Isaiah Bowman detailed in Neil Smith's book, *American Empire: Roosevelt's Geographer and the Prelude to Globalization*, in which Smith portrays Bowman as an antisemite determined to thwart Jewish resettlement ventures. Breitman and Lichtman further Smith's characterization of Bowman as a "lifelong eugenicist" who believed that "Jews lacked the skills and fortitude required of pioneers" (Breitman and Lichtman, *FDR and the Jews*, 127). In the massive study of Bowman offered by Smith, there is no mention of Bowman's work on the Mindanao resettlement proposal and the favorable recommendations he gave for the venture. If Bowman was indeed the antisemite these authors claim him to be, the communications and studies Bowman conducted in his evaluations for Jewish resettlement on Mindanao can neither support nor dispute those claims. No antisemitic intentions or language from Bowman were found in the documentary record.

86. Bowman to Achilles, Mar. 16, 1939, NARA II, Record Group 59, IGCR, Country Files, "Philippines," Lot 52D408, Box 6.

87. Alex Frieder to Liebman, Apr. 6, 1939, JDC Archives, JDC Collection 33/44, File #787a.

88. Ibid.

89. Alex Frieder to Liebman, Apr. 6, 1939, JDC Archives, JDC Collection 33/44, File #787a.

90. Ibid. Polillo Island lies about eighteen miles off the eastern coast of Luzon.

91. Stanton Youngberg to Isaiah Bowman, Apr. 15, 1939, JDC Archives, JDC Collection 33/44, File #787a.

92. Ibid.

93. Jacobs to Achilles, "Settlement of German Refugees in the Philippine Islands," Apr. 25, 1939, JDC Archives, JDC Collection 33/44, File #787a.

94. Mindanao Exploration Commission Report, "Settlement Possibilities on Polillo Island," May 14, 1939, p. 20, JDC Archives, JDC Collection 33/44, File #784.

95. Youngberg to Bowman, May 29, 1939, JDC Archives, JDC Collection 33/44, File #784.

96. Hargis, Youngberg, Pendleton to Bowman, "Confidential," July 7, 1939, JDC Archives, JDC Collection 33/44, File #784.

97. Morris Frieder to Morrissey, JDC, attachment "Mindanao Commission," Aug. 18, 1939, JDC Archives, JDC Collection 33/44, File #787a.

98. Ibid.

99. Jones to Gruening, Interior Dept. Washington, July 14, 1939 (NPM 1498 Manila OI CK 320), NARA II, Record Group 59, IGCR, Country Files, "Philippines," Lot 52D408, Box 6.

100. Evelyn M. Morrissey, "Memorandum of Meeting at Office of JDC, Tuesday, Aug. 8, at 10 am," JDC Archives, JDC Collection 33/44, file #787a.

101. Ibid.

102. "Report of the Mindanao Exploration Commission," Oct. 2, 1939, NARA I, Record Group 59, General Records of the Department of State, Visa Division, Box 246, 811.B55, J/333.

103. Robert Pell, "Memorandum of Conversation with George Warren," Oct. 4, 1939, NARA II, Record Group 59, IGCR, Country Files, "Philippines," Lot 52D408, Box 6.

104. Robert Pell, "Memorandum of Conversation with Joseph E. Jacobs," Oct. 9, 1939, NARA II, Record Group 59, IGCR, Country Files, "Philippines," Lot 52D408, Box 6.

105. Ibid.

106. Ibid., emphasis added.

107. Robert Pell, memo of conversation, Oct. 10, 1939, NARA II, Record Group 59, IGCR, Country Files, "Philippines," Lot 52D408, Box 6.

108. "Appendix, Composition of Initial Refugee Group For Mindanao Settlement" from office of the president, John Hopkins University, to Charles Liebman, Aug. 29, 1939, JDC Archives, JDC Collection 33/44, file #787a.

109. Ibid.

110. Yehuda Bauer, *My Brother's Keeper*, 57–104.

111. Charles Liebman to Paul Baerwald, Sep. 29, 1939, JDC Archives, JDC, Collection 33/44, file #787a.

112. "Message from Mr. Baerwald to be conveyed to Mr. Rosenberg," Nov. 8, 1939, JDC Archives, JDC, Collection 33/44, file #787a.

113. "Memorandum from Baerwald to Rosenberg, Jan. 5, 1940," JDC Archives, JDC Collection 33/44, file #787a.

114. Appendix, "Composition of Initial Refugee Group for Mindanao Settlement from office of President, John Hopkins University, to Charles Liebman," Aug. 29, 1939, JDC Archives, JDC Collection 33/44, file #787a.

115. Liebman to Pell, Nov. 29, 1939, NARA II, Record Group 59, IGCR, Country Files, "Philippines," Lot 52D408, Box 6.

116. Liebman to Pell, "attachment general description properties on Mindanao," Nov. 30, 1939, NARA II, Record Group 59, IGCR, Country Files, "Philippines," Lot 52D408, Box 6.

117. Ibid.

118. Youngberg to Liebman, Feb. 23, 1940, NARA II, Record Group 59, IGCR, Country Files, "Philippines," Lot 52D408, Box 6.

119. Ibid.

120. Ibid.

121. "Some Solons Alarmed by Prospect of Flood of Foreigners Oppose High Alien Quotas," *Manila Daily Bulletin*, Feb. 18, 1940, NARA II, Record Group 59, IGCR, Country Files, "Philippines," Lot 52D408, Box 6.

122. Youngberg to Liebman, Feb. 23, 1940.

123. Catherine Porter, "Philippine Immigration Restrictions Arouse Protest," *Far Eastern Survey* 9, no. 10 (May 8, 1940): 120–21.

124. Ibid.

125. "General Information concerning Philippine Immigration Laws," JDC Archives, JDC Collection 33/44, File-Philippine Immigration Laws 1940.

126. Robert Pilpel to Dr. Bernard Kahn, "Memorandum," Nov. 8, 1940, JDC Archives, JDC Collection 33/44, File #787a.

127. "Philippines Curb Immigration," *New York Times*, May 29, 1940, JDC Archives, JDC Collection 33/44, File #784.

128. Alex Frieder, "Jewish Refugee Committee," May 7, 1940, pp. 23–24.

129. Philip Hoffman to James N. Rosenberg, "Memorandum re: Telephone Conversation with Mr. Komlos Regarding REC—Philippine Project," Nov. 13, 1941, JDC Archives, JDC Collection 33/44, File #787a.

130. The first presidential election of the Commonwealth Nation of the Philippines elected Manuel L. Quezon in 1935 to a six-year term, with no provision for re-election. However, in 1940 the Constitution was amended to allow re-election

but shortened the term to four years. Quezon was then re-elected to an unprecedented second term in 1941. The Japanese installed the Second Philippine Republic
in 1943 with Jose P. Laurel as puppet president, while Quezon went into exile in
the United States, where he died in 1944. The Japanese-installed Second Republic
was dissolved after Japan surrendered to the Allies in 1945; the Commonwealth
was restored in the Philippines in the same year with Sergio Osmena, Quezon's
vice president, serving as president.

131. Robert Pilpel to Edwin Goldwasser, "Memorandum re: Philippines,"
Nov. 7, 1940, JDC Archives, JDC Collection 33/44, File #784.

132. "File Memorandum, Notes on Meeting Today at 10:00 am Concerning
the Refugee Situation in the Philippines," June 21, 1940, JDC Archives, JDC Collection 33/44, File #787a.

133. The Philippine Legislature was the legislative governing body of the Philippines from 1907 to 1935, during the American colonial period, and predecessor
of the current Congress of the Philippines. It was bicameral and the legislative
branch of the Insular Government. In 1935, the Commonwealth of the Philippines was established, and the National Assembly of the Philippines replaced the
Philippine Legislature.

134. Miss Morrissey to James N. Rosenberg, Status of the Philippine Project,
Nov. 10, 1941, JDC Archives, JDC Collection 33/44, File #787a.

135. Feingold, *The Politics of Rescue*, 90.

136. Ibid.

137. "Extract from the Speech by Hitler, Jan. 30, 1939," in *Documents on the
Holocaust*, 8th ed., ed. Yitzhak Arad, Israel Gutman, and Abraham Margaliot
(Lincoln: University of Nebraska Press and Yad Vashem, 1999), 132.

138. Jorge Bocobo, "Jewish Settlement in Mindanao—Address by President
Jorge Bocobo to the Jewish Junior League, Mar. 14, 1939," Bocobo Papers, University of the Philippines Main Library, Box 1, folder 20.

Chapter 5. Japan and Europe's Refugee Jews

1. Some historians see philosemitism or Judeophilia, defined generically as an
interest in, respect for, and appreciation of Jews, as merely the flip side of the same
coin of antisemitism; both are based on the same stereotypes, but one sees those
typecasts as negative traits while the other sees them as positive.

2. Marvin Tokayer and Mary Swartz, *The Fugu Plan: The Untold Story of the
Japanese and the Jews during World War II* (New York: Paddington Press, 1979).

3. Iikura Akira, "The 'Yellow Peril' and Its Influence on Japanese-German
Relations," in *Japanese-German Relations, 1895–1945: War, Diplomacy and Public*

Opinion, ed. Christian W. Spang and Rolf-Harald Wippich (New York: Routledge, 2006), 80.

4. Spang and Wippich, *Japanese-German Relations, 1895–1945*, 2.

5. Akira, "The Yellow Peril," 80–94.

6. David E. Kaiser, "Germany and the Origins of the First World War," *Journal of Modern History* 55, no. 3 (Sep. 1983): 445.

7. T. G. Otte, "Great Britain, Germany, and the Far Eastern Crisis of 1897–8," *English Historical Review* 110, no. 439 (Nov. 1995): 1159–60.

8. Spang and Wippich, *Japanese-German Relations, 1895–1945*, 3–6. See also Barbara J. Brooks, *Japan's Imperial Diplomacy: Consuls, Treaty Ports, and War in China* (Honolulu: University of Hawai'i Press, 2000), 118–20.

9. Michio Muramatsu and Frieder Maschold, eds., *State and Administration in Japan and Germany* (Berlin: Walter de Gruyter, 1996), 1–12.

10. Spang and Wippich, *Japanese-German Relations, 1895–1945*, 8–9. See also Kurt Bloch, "German-Japanese Partnership in Eastern Asia" *Far Eastern Survey* 7, no. 21 (Oct. 26, 1938): 242.

11. Spang and Wippich, *Japanese-German Relations, 1895–1945*, 10–11.

12. Gerhard L. Weinberg, *Hitler's Foreign Policy, 1933–1939* (New York: Enigma Books, 2005), 325–35. For more on Germany's trade arrangements with China, see Bloch, "German-Japanese Partnership in Eastern Asia," 241.

13. Weinberg, *Hitler's Foreign Policy*, 339. The pact was renewed in 1941 with eleven other countries as signatories. In order to dispel the misgivings of its allies in World War II, the Soviet Union dissolved the Comintern in 1943. See Ikle, *German-Japanese Relations*, 15–23. See also "Anti-Comintern Pact," Yale Law School, Lillian Goldman Law Library, The Avalon Project (2008), http://avalon .law.yale.edu/wwii/tri1.asp.

14. Weinberg, *Hitler's Foreign Policy*, 509.

15. Ikle, *German-Japanese Relations*, 70–73. See also Weinberg, *Hitler's Foreign Policy*, 517.

16. Bloch, "German-Japanese Partnership in Eastern Asia," 241.

17. Weinberg, *Hitler's Foreign Policy*, 518–22. See also Marius B. Jansen, *The Making of Modern Japan* (Cambridge, MA: Belknap Press of Harvard University Press, 2000), 616–24.

18. Ikle, *German-Japanese Relations*, 87–131. See also Jansen, *The Making of Modern Japan*, 625–30.

19. James B. Crowley, "A New Asian Order: Some Notes on Prewar Japanese Nationalism," in *Showa Japan: Political, Economic, and Social History, 1925–1989*, vol. 1, ed. Stephen S. Large (New York: Routledge, 1998), 186–207.

20. Ikle, *German-Japanese Relations*, 137–55. See also Robert L. Worden, "The

Rise of the Militarists," in *Japan: A Country Study*, ed. Ronald E. Dolan and Robert L. Worden (Washington, DC: Federal Research Division, Library of Congress, 1992), 55–60.

21. Ikle, *German-Japanese Relations*, 149–50. See also Francis Clifford Jones, *Japan's New Order in East Asia: Its Rise and Fall, 1937–45* (New York: Oxford University Press, 1954).

22. Ikle, *German-Japanese Relations*, 155–59. See also Christopher Szpilman, "Fascist and Quasi-Fascist Ideas in Interwar Japan, 1918–1941," in *Japan in the Fascist Era*, ed. E. Bruce Reynolds (New York: Palgrave Macmillan, 2004), 73–106.

23. Ikle, *German-Japanese Relations*, 159.

24. Ibid., 160–63. See also Joseph P. Sottile, "Imperial Japan and the Axis Alliance in Historical Perspective," in *Japan in the Fascist Era*, ed. E. Bruce Reynolds (New York: Palgrave Macmillan, 2004), 1–48.

25. Bernd Martin, *Japan and Germany in the Modern World* (New York: Berghahn Books, 1995), 265–85.

26. Ikle, *German-Japanese Relations*, 171–90. See also Fugiwara Akira, "The Road to Pearl Harbor," in *Showa Japan: Political, Economic, and Social History, 1925–1989*, vol.1, ed. Stephen S. Large (New York: Routledge, 1998), 230–38.

27. Werner E. Mosse, "Albert Mosse: A Jewish Judge in Imperial Germany," in *Leo Baeck Institute Yearbook XXVIII* (London: Martin Secker & Warburg, 1983), 169–84.

28. Naomi W. Cohen, *Jacob H. Schiff: A Study in American Jewish Leadership* (Hanover, NH: Brandeis University Press, 1999), 1–12.

29. Cyrus Adler, *Jacob H. Schiff: His Life and Letters*, vol. 1 (New York: Doubleday, Doran, 1928), 217–18.

30. The Order of the Rising Sun, established on April 10, 1875, is a Japanese national decoration awarded by the emperor to an individual for long meritorious civil or military service.

31. Adler, *Jacob H. Schiff: His Life and Letters*, 230.

32. Cohen, *Jacob H. Schiff*, 134.

33. Ibid.

34. David G. Goodman and Masanori Miyazawa, *Jews in the Japanese Mind: The History and Uses of a Cultural Stereotype* (New York: Free Press, 1995), 76–105.

35. Ibid., 81.

36. Inuzuka was a naval officer from Tokyo who was stationed on a battleship during the Siberian Expedition in the 1920s. After coming in contact with the anti-semitic literature of the White Russians, Inuzuka became one of Japan's leading "Jewish experts" and a self-proclaimed antisemite who lectured and published prolifically on the so-called Jewish menace.

37. Gao Bei, *Shanghai Sanctuary: Chinese and Japanese Policy toward European Jewish Refugees during World War II* (New York: Oxford University Press, 2013), 59.

38. Ibid.

39. Goodman and Miyazawa, *Jews in the Japanese Mind*, 89.

40. Ibid., 92.

41. "Although a small number of Jews suffered maltreatment at the hands of individual Japanese officials, few were imprisoned or restricted because of their identity. In these latter cases, the Jews were singled out because they were stateless persons, having been stripped of their Polish or German citizenship by Nazi policy, and not necessarily because they were Jews. Overall, Japanese policy and actions towards Jews as a group could be characterized as studied even-handedness. The Japanese did not single out the Jews for special attention or restrictions because of their "ethnic" or religious uniqueness. On the other hand, the Jews shared equally in the suspicion that the Japanese held for all neutral and non-Japanese nationals living within the Greater East Asian Co-Prosperity Sphere. The Japanese view of the Jews probably grew out of the complicated mixture of racism, nationalism, and fear of foreign conspiracy and secret control of international events that dominated Japanese national attitudes towards all foreigners, especially those living in western countries." Robert J. Hanyok, *Eavesdropping on Hell: Historical Guide to Western Communications Intelligence and the Holocaust, 1939–1945*, United States Cryptologic History, series 4, vol. 9 (Fort George G. Meade, MD: Center for Cryptologic History, National Security Agency, 2005), 99–100.

42. David Kranzler, "The Japanese Ideology of Anti-Semitism and the Holocaust," in *Contemporary Views on the Holocaust*, ed. Randolph L. Braham (Dordrecht: Springer Netherlands, 1983), 79–108.

43. Goodman and Miyazawa, *Jews in the Japanese Mind*, 106–34.

44. Kranzler, *Japanese, Nazis, and Jews*, 174.

45. Tokayer and Swartz, *The Fugu Plan*, 52.

46. Pamela Rotner Sakamoto, *Japanese Diplomats and Jewish Refugees: A World War II Dilemma* (Westport, CT: Praeger, 1998), 83. Nissim Elias Benjamin Ezra (1883–1936), aka N.E.B. Ezra, was a Baghdadi Jew born in Lahore, Pakistan, known to have founded the Shanghai Zionist Association (SZA) in 1903, becoming editor and publisher of its Zionist newspaper, *Israel's Messenger*, from 1904 to 1936.

47. Aikawa, who founded Nissan industries, served the Manchurian Faction as a consultant for the future of industrial and mining ventures in Manchukuo.

48. "Invites German Jews: Japan Willing to Have 50,000 Settle in Manchukuo," *New York Times*, Aug. 5, 1934, 4.

49. Tokayer and Swartz, *The Fugu Plan*, 52–53.

50. David Kranzler, interview by the filmmaker Diane Estelle Vicari, Nov. 8, 1998, for the making of *Sugihara* for PBS, http://www.pbs.org/wgbh/sugihara /readings/kranzler.html.

51. Ibid.

52. Xu Xin, "Jewish Diaspora in China," in *Encyclopedia of Diasporas: Immigrant and Refugee Cultures Around the World*, ed. Carol R. Ember, Mervin Ember, and Ian A. Skoggard (New York: Springer, 2004), 159.

53. Goodman and Miyazawa, *Jews in the Japanese Mind*, 111.

54. Tokayer and Swartz, *The Fugu Plan*, 65–67.

55. Ibid., 68–74.

56. Ibid., 75.

57. Nigel Cawthorne, *Reaping the Whirlwind: The German and Japanese Experience of World War II* (Cincinnati, Ohio: David & Charles, 2007), 146.

58. Terada Takefumi, "The Religious Propaganda Program for Christian Churches" in *The Philippines Under Japan: Occupation Policy and Reaction*, ed. Ikehata Setsuho and Ricardo Trota Jose (Quezon City: Ateneo de Manila University Press, 1999), 215–17.

59. Ibid., 215.

60. "Calendar of the War," *Tribune Supplement* (Manila), May 27, 1942, Jorge B. Vargas Museum and Filipiniana Research Center, Quezon City, PI, Jorge B. Vargas Archives, *Executive Commission Records Series*, EC1. See also Takefumi, "The Religious Propaganda Program for Christian Churches," 216–18.

61. A. V. H. Hartendorp, *The Japanese Occupation of the Philippines*, vol. 1 (Manila: Bookmark, 1967), 226.

62. Ibid., 227.

63. Takefumi, "The Religious Propaganda Program for Christian Churches," 216–18.

64. Frank Ephraim erroneously characterizes him as a Christian. See Hartendorp, *The Japanese Occupation of the Philippines*, 1: 227, and Takefumi, "The Religious Propaganda Program for Christian Churches," 218.

65. Hartendorp, *The Japanese Occupation of the Philippines*, 1:229.

66. Ibid., 230–33.

67. Elise Tipton, *Modern Japan: A Social and Political History* (New York: Routledge, 2002), 133. See also Walter A. Skya, *Japan's Holy War: The Political Ideology of Radical Shinto Ultranationalism* (Durham, NC: Duke University Press, 2009).

68. Ephraim, *Escape to Manila*, 93. Frank Ephraim relates this story in his book *Escape to Manila* as he heard it personally from Rabbi Schwarz.

69. Takefumi, "The Religious Propaganda Program for Christian Churches," 239.

70. Samuel Schechter, "Temple Emil Congregation Calendar," Sep. 1, 1940, JHSSD Archives, Cantor Joseph Cysner Collection, CJC01.03. See also Eberly, "Manila? Where? Us?," 61.

71. For the story of their rescue and survival, see Paul F. Cummins, *Dachau Song* (New York: Peter Lang, 1992).

72. For assorted performance programs, see JHSSD Archives, Cantor Joseph Cysner Collection, CJC01.06.

73. Eberly, "Manila? Where? Us?," 61.

74. Bernard C. Nalty, ed., *War in the Pacific: Pearl Harbor to Tokyo Bay* (London: Salamander Books, 1991) 58.

75. Ibid., 63–70.

76. Frederic H. Stevens, *Santo Tomas Internment Camp: 1942–1945* (New York: Stratford House, 1946), 8.

77. Several firsthand accounts by survivors of Santo Tomas support this statement. In addition to Hartendorp's and Stevens's works, see Emily Van Sickle, *The Iron Gates of Santo Tomas: The Firsthand Account of an American Couple Interned by the Japanese in Manila, 1942–1945* (Chicago: Academy Chicago Publishers, 1992); Bruce E. Johansen, *So Far From Home: Manila's Santo Tomas Internment Camp, 1942–1945* (Omaha: PBI Press, 1996); Celia Lucas, *Prisoners of Santo Tomas* (London: Leo Cooper, 1975); Frances B. Cogan, *Captured: The Japanese Internment of American Civilians in the Philippines, 1941–1945* (Athens: University of Georgia Press, 2000).

78. Emmet F. Pearson, Lt. Col. M.C., "Morbidity and Mortality in Santo Tomas Internment Camp," reprinted from *Annals of Internal Medicine* 24, no. 6 (June 1946): 990, American Historical Collection, Rizal Library, Ateneo de Manila University.

79. Ibid., 988.

80. Ibid. See also Henry Sioux Johnson, PhD, interview by Michael P. Onorato, "Living with Dignity: An Analysis of a Questionnaire Survey of Former American Civilian Internees" in *Henry Sioux Johnson: A Stranger in a Strange Land*, Michael P. Onorato, editor, Oral History Program, California State University, Fullerton, 1985, Appendix.

81. Martin Meadows, interview by Bonnie M. Harris, June 28, 2006, Washington, DC, video recording.

82. Stevens, *Santo Tomas Internment Camp*, 172.

83. Earl Carroll served in this appointed position until July 1942, when he convinced the Japanese commandant of STIC at that time, Ryozo Tsurumi, that camp elections for new leadership would help appease American internees' democratic sensibilities. Carroll headed up the important Finance and Supplies

Committee for the duration of his internment. Although elections were held and seven men, five Americans and two British nationals, were chosen from among the internees for the newly named Executive Committee, Tsurumi appointed Carroll C. Grimmell as the Chairman, who had ranked low in the election but could speak some Japanese. Grimmell served as the internal leader over the STIC internees amid complaints from disgruntled inmates who accused him of a variety of charges, from abuses of power to collaboration with the enemy. New elections in January 1943 resulted in a landslide win for Earl Carroll, but the new Japanese camp commandant team of Akida Kodaki and S. Kuroda nullified the election results and retained Grimmell as chairman. When the Japanese Military Administration (JMA) took over supervision of all camps in early 1944, they dismissed the Executive Committee and replaced it with a trio of men, now designated as the Internee Committee, with Grimmell still as the leader and Earl Carroll and British national Samuel Lloyd as the other members. Grimmell and three other inmates of STIC were arrested in December 1944 and executed in January 1945 for clandestine contact with guerillas and POW camps, supplying them with contraband supplies and money. See James Mace Ward, "Legitimate Collaboration: The Administration of Santo Tomas Internment Camp and Its Histories, 1942–2003," *Pacific Historical Review* 77, no. 2 (May 2008): 161–80). See also Rupert Wilkinson, *Surviving a Japanese Internment Camp: Life and Liberation at Santo Tomas, Manila, in World War II* (Jefferson, NC: McFarland, 2013), 94–103.

84. Earl Carroll, "The Secret War of Santo Tomas, Chapter 1," *Los Angeles Examiner*, Aug. 19, 1945, sec. 1, p. 14. (All further citations of Earl Carroll's articles will omit *Los Angeles Examiner* in the listings, as they all were published in this same newspaper.)

85. Carroll, "The Secret War, Chapter 2," Aug. 20, 1945, sec. 1, p. 8.

86. Hartendorp, *The Japanese Occupation of the Philippines*, 1:36.

87. Tefillin are ritual boxes made of leather with scrolls of selected scripture from the Torah inside, which are affixed to the arm and forehead during morning prayer. Their use is stipulated in Exodus 13:9 "And it shall be for a sign upon your hand and for a memorial between your eyes" and in Deuteronomy 11:18. The tallit (or talis in Yiddish) is the prayer shawl Jews wear that has fringes (tzitzit) on each corner as specified in Num. 15:38 and in Deut. 22:12, that people of Israel should "make them fringes in the borders of their garments throughout their generations, and that they put upon the fringe of the borders a thread of blue." The plural in Yiddish is talesim; in Hebrew talliot. In traditional Judaism, a minyan is the quorum of ten Jewish adult men over the age of thirteen required to conduct any public Jewish ritual, including Shabbat.

88. Yahrzeit is a Yiddish term meaning anniversary of a death. Jews observe

yahrzeit by lighting a special twenty-four-hour-long burning candle in memory of the deceased.

89. Stevens, *Santo Tomas Internment Camp*, 172–73.

90. Ibid., 169–70.

91. Ephraim, *Escape to Manila*, 167. The Mirrer Yeshiva was originally established in Mir, Belarus, in 1815, moving back and forth between Belarus, Lithuania, and the Ukraine because of the vicissitudes of war until the entire yeshiva fled to the Far East via Siberia, relocating to Kobe, Japan, in 1941 and then Shanghai, China, later in the war. There were smaller yeshovos who fell under Mirrer jurisdiction when they escaped Nazi Europe, with handfuls of them reaching various ports in Asia, including the Philippines. The majority of Mirrer exiles relocated to the US and Palestine at war's end, establishing campuses in Jerusalem and Brooklyn.

92. Norbert Propper, interview by Larry Lerner for the Survivors of the Shoah Visual History Foundation, Bronx, NY, Jan. 3, 1995, USC Shoah Foundation, video recording.

93. Hartendorp, *The Japanese Occupation of the Philippines*, 1:xiii.

94. Ibid.

95. Propper, interview by Lerner.

96. Meadows, interview by Harris.

97. Margaret Sams, interviewed in *Victims of Circumstance—Santo Tomas Internment Camp*, Lou Gopal, Kawayan Productions, DVD documentary, Sep. 1, 2006.

98. Sasha Weinzheimer Jansen and Sally Harden Rosenberg, interviewed in *Victims of Circumstance—Santo Tomas Internment Camp*, Lou Gopal, Kawayan Productions, DVD documentary, Sep. 1, 2006.

99. Cogan, *Captured*, 208.

100. STIC had seven commandants in three years, eight if you count a dual administration that operated as a team between September 1942 and October 1943. The first five commandants of the eight were civilians mostly with Japanese consular backgrounds: Hitoshi Tomayasu (Jan.–Feb. 1942); Ryozo Tsurumi, a Shanghai merchant (Feb. 1942–Sep. 1943); the team of Akida Kodaki and S. Kuroda (Sep. 1942–Oct. 1943); and the last civilian commandant, Kitaro Kato (Nov. 1943–Feb. 1944). The first Japanese military commandant, JMA lawyer Gonshichi Onozoki, began his service in March 1944, the start of the last year of internment, followed by Lt. Col. Yasunksa Yoshie later in 1944, and the last military commandant was Lt. Col. Juichiro Hayashi, also the last commandant of STIC at the time of its liberation in February 1945. See Ward, "Legitimate Collaboration," 161–80, and Wilkinson, *Surviving a Japanese Internment Camp*, 104–15.

101. Pearson, "Morbidity and Mortality," 990.

102. Wilkinson, *Surviving a Japanese Internment Camp*, 98.

103. Carroll, "The Secret War, Chapter 3," Aug. 21, 1945, sec. 1, p. 6.

104. Frank H. Golay, ed., *The Santo Tomas Story by A. V. H. Hartendorp* (New York: McGraw-Hill, 1964), 10.

105. Hoeflein, in Goldhagen, *Manila Memories*, 64.

106. Norbert Propper, interview by Noel Izon, July 7, 2016, Menton, France, video recording.

107. Ward, "Legitimate Collaboration," 164n8.

108. Carroll, "The Secret War, Chapter 5," Aug. 23, 1945, sec. 1, p. 8.

109. Hannah Kaunitz Entell, interview by Ray Ann Kremer, June 18 and Oct. 8, 1986, Atlanta, GA, OHC 10184, p. 18, Herbert and Esther Taylor Oral History Collection, Cuba family archives for Southern Jewish History at the Breman Museum, Atlanta, GA.

110. Ibid.

111. Carroll, "The Secret War, Chapter 5," Aug. 23, 1945, sec. 1, p. 8.

112. Ibid.

113. Carroll, "The Secret War, Chapter 1," Aug. 23, 1945, sec. 1, p. 1.

114. Ibid.

115. Carroll, "The Secret War, Chapter 5.," Aug. 23, 1945, sec. 1, p. 8.

116. Ephraim, *Escape to Manila*, 121. Ephraim interviewed Rebecca Berman, Königsberg's daughter.

117. George Perry, "The Miracle of a Synagogue in Manila," *Jewish Floridian*, Sep. 23, 1960, sec. F, p. 4. See also "Morton I. Netzorg," *New York Times*, Oct. 22, 1946, 24.

118. Herb Brin, "Cantor Cysner's Survival Story," *Southwest Jewish Press*, no. 4, Oct. 13, 1960.

119. Ephraim, *Escape to Manila*, 94.

120. Ibid., 101.

121. Stevens, *Santo Tomas Internment Camp*, 172–73.

122. Ephraim, *Escape to Manila*, 113.

123. Joseph Cysner to Commandant Japanese Forces Santo Tomas Internment Camp, Manila, Feb. 9, 1943, sent to author by Petra Netzorg, wife of Jock Netzorg, son of Israel Netzorg, Nov. 15, 2004.

124. Ephraim, *Escape to Manila*, 103.

125. Carroll, "The Secret War, Chapter 7," Aug. 25, 1945, sec. 1, p. 6. See also n. 103 for names of the military commandants of STIC.

126. Johansen, *So Far from Home*, 93.

127. Clio Matthews Wetmore, *Beyond Pearl Harbor* (Haverford, PA: Infinity, 2001), 105. See also Stevens, *Santo Tomas Internment Camp*, 428.

128. Carroll, "The Secret War, Chapter 9," Aug. 27, 1945, sec. 1, p. 7.

129. Pearson, "Morbidity and Mortality in Santo Tomas Internment Camp," 1013.

130. Esther Robbins Hutton, *Sojourn: A Family Saga* (Vashon, WA: ESFIR Books, 1997), 151–53.

131. Hershfield, interview by Izon.

132. Charlotte Holzer Bunim, interview by Bonnie M. Harris, June 18, 2006, Lawrence, NY, video recording.

133. Ibid.

134. Ralph Preiss, interview by Bonnie M. Harris, June 17, 2008, New York, New York, video recording.

135. Hoeflein in Goldhagen, *Manila Memories*, 64.

136. Kestenbaum, interview by Izon.

137. Recounted in testimonies of Hans Hoeflein and Charlotte Holzer Bunim.

138. Bunim, interview by Harris.

139. Ricardo Trota Jose, *World War II and the Japanese Occupation* (Quezon City: University of the Philippines Press), 121.

140. Hartendorp, *The Japanese Occupation of the Philippines*, vol. 1, 190–91.

141. "Acts Punishable by Death Listed by Army," *Tribune* (Manila), Jan. 14, 1942, Jorge B. Vargas Museum and Filipiniana Research Center, Quezon City, PI, Jorge B. Vargas Archives, Executive Commission Records Series, EC1, p. 27.

142. Stanley L. Falk, "Douglas MacArthur and the War against Japan," in *We Shall Return! MacArthur's Commanders and the Defeat of Japan, 1942–1945*, ed. William M. Leary (Lexington: University Press of Kentucky, 1988) 7.

143. Jose, *World War II and the Japanese Occupation*, 111–13.

144. Alfred Emmerich, "The Chicken Tree," *Kvutzat Chaverim Newsletter*, p. 16, Purim 1946, Manila, JHSSD Archives, Cantor Joseph Cysner Collection, CJC02.03.

145. Ibid. Alfred Emmerich may have been referring to how the Japanese pronounced the Spanish phrase "cortar la cabeza," which means to cut off the head.

146. Emmerich, "The Chicken Tree," 16–17.

147. Ibid., 16.

148. Edgar Krohn Jr., Klaus Schroeder, and Georg B. Weber, *The German Club Manila* (Makati City: German Club, 1996), 3–10.

149. Ibid., 15–21.

150. Francis Burton Harrison, *The Corner-Stone of Philippine Independence a Narrative of Seven Years* (New York: Century, 1922), 171.

151. Ibid., 180.

152. Krohn, *The German Club Manila*, 41.

153. Ibid., 51.

154. Ibid., 51–54.

155. Ibid., 57.

156. Ibid., 57–58.

157. "Jews Given Stern Warning," *Tribune* (Manila), Jan. 26, 1943, Jorge B. Vargas Museum and Filipiniana Research Center, Quezon City, PI, Jorge B. Vargas Archives, Executive Commission Records Series, EC3, p. 48.

158. Ibid.

159. Joseph Schwarz, "The Jews in Manila under Japanese Occupation," JHSSD Archives, Cantor Joseph Cysner Collection, CJC01.12.

160. Ibid.

161. Griese, "The Jewish Community in Manila," 32.

162. Ephraim, *Escape to Manila*, 124.

Chapter 6. *Peletah*—Deliverance

1. Lipetz, interview by Levin.

2. Jacques Lipetz, "Witnesses" part of a Holocaust remembrance website, created by Cybrary Community, Apr. 25, 1995, https://www.remember.org/witness/lipetz.htm.

3. Ephraim, *Escape to Manila*, 131.

4. Lotte Cassel, "A Personal Experience," *Kvutzat Chaverim Newsletter*, p. 29, Purim 1946, Manila, JHSSD Archives, Cantor Joseph Cysner Collection, CJC02.03.

5. Margit Miedzwinski, "Always Trust in God," *Kvutzat Chaverim Newsletter*, p. 33, Purim 1946, Manila, JHSSD Archives, Cantor Joseph Cysner Collection, CJC02.03.

6. George Perry, "The Miracle of a Synagogue in Manila," *Jewish Floridian*, Sep. 23, 1960, sec. F, p. 4.

7. Jenny Hanna, "A Potato Patch," *Kvutzat Chaverim Newsletter*, p. 30, Purim 1946, Manila, JHSSD Archives, Cantor Joseph Cysner Collection, CJC02.03.

8. Preiss, interview by Harris.

9. Frank Ephraim, "My Personal Experiences," *Kvutzat Chaverim Newsletter*,

pp. 38–39, Purim 1946, Manila, JHSSD Archives, Cantor Joseph Cysner Collection, CJC02.03.

10. Golay, *The Santo Tomas Story by A.V.H. Hartendorp*, 404–5.

11. Ibid., 406.

12. Ephraim, "My Personal Experiences," *Kvutzat Chaverim Newsletter*, p. 39.

13. Manfred Hecht, "My Personal Experience," *Kvutzat Chaverim Newsletter*, p. 31, Purim 1946, Manila, JHSSD Archives, Cantor Joseph Cysner Collection, CJC02.03.

14. Rabbi Joseph Schwarz, "History of the Jewish Community in Manila," JHSSD, Cantor Joseph Cysner Collection, CJC02.04 fldr: "Temple Emil Dedication, 1947."

15. George Perry, "The Miracle of a Synagogue in Manila," *Jewish Floridian*, Sep. 23, 1960, sec. F, p. 4. See also Rabbi Joseph Schwarz, "History of the Jewish Community in Manila."

16. William Craig, *The Fall of Japan: The Final Weeks of World War II in the Pacific* (New York: Macmillan, 1955), 267.

17. Schwarz, "History of the Jewish Community in Manila."

18. Ephraim, *Escape to Manila*, 148. Ephraim accessed documents from the war crimes trial of Yamashita, housed in the National Archives, College Park, MD. See also Benito Legarda Jr., "Manila Holocaust: Massacre and Rape," Presidential Museum and Library, Republic of the Philippines, http://malacanang.gov.ph/75102-manila-holocaust-massacre-and-rape/.

19. Eberly, "Manila? Where? Us?," 62.

20. Margot Cassel, "Members of *Kvutzat Chaverim*—Personal Experiences," Purim 1946, p. 36, Jewish Historical Society of San Diego, Cantor Joseph Cysner Collection, CJC02.03.

21. Bunin, interview by Harris.

22. Ibid.

23. Griese, "The Jewish Community in Manila," 33.

24. William Manchester, *American Caesar: Douglas MacArthur 1880–1964* (New York: Dell, 1978), 482–83.

25. Ephraim, *Escape to Manila*, 167.

26. Ibid., 168.

27. Lipetz, "Witnesses." See also Lipetz, interview by Levin.

28. Ephraim, *Escape to Manila*, 165.

29. Lipetz, "Witnesses."

30. Norman Schanin, *In the Service of My People: Reflections of a Jewish Educator* (New York: Gefen, 2000), 47.

31. Ibid., 48.

32. Ibid., 51.

33. Ibid.

34. Edmund Rosenblum, interviewed by Bonnie Harris, June 15, 2008, West Hempstead, NY, video recording.

35. Schanin, *In the Service of My People*, 52.

36. Cysner, Photographic Collection, JHSSD Archives, Cantor Joseph Cysner Collection, CJC02.

37. Schanin, *In the Service of My People*, 53.

38. Griese, "The Jewish Community in Manila," 35.

39. For more information on this monument, see Pave the Way Foundation, "Philippine Monument in Rishon, LeZion, Israel," n.d., http://www.ptwf .org/index.php?option=com_content&view=article&id=142:philippine-monu ment-in-rishon-lezion-israel&catid=89&Itemid=525.

40. It is recorded in the Mishnah Sanhedrin (*m. San.*) 4:9; Jerusalem Talmud Tractate Sanhedrin (*T. San.*) 37A: "whoever saves a life, it is considered as if he saved an entire world." The Talmud is an authoritative record of rabbinic teachings on Jewish law, customs, and ethics, and it is a central text to the study and practice of rabbinic Judaism.

41. Sylvia Cysner, interview by Bonnie Harris, Jan. 24–25, 2007, Los Angeles, CA, video recording.

42. Ephraim, *Escape to Manila*, 192.

43. The Frieder brothers' families had left the Philippines before December 1941. The Netzorgs, Schachners, and Königsbergs along with others remained.

44. Cysner, interview by Harris, Jan. 24, 2004.

45. Ibid.

46. Ibid.

47. Schwarz to Joseph Cysner, 1939, JHSSD Archives, Cantor Joseph Cysner Collection, CJC01.03.

Conclusion

1. For further discussion of the immigration laws of the Philippines ratified in 1940 and how these new laws affected rescue in the Philippines, see chap. 4.

2. A communiqué from Kenneth Day, owner of land on Mindanao Island where the resettlement plans were to be implemented, to Richard Ely of the Bureau of Insular Affairs in August 1940, offered this comparison of McNutt and Sayre with reference to the refugee rescue issue: "Commissioner McNutt was very keen to see President Quezon's promises fulfilled, and if he were in Manila I am

sure everything would be fixed up before now. Commissioner Sayre, however, had not interested himself actively in this project and apparently will not do so unless the State Department indicates to him that it would like to see matters arranged so that Jews may be admitted, as per Q's promise and that of the State Department." Day to Ely, August 13, 1940, NARA II, Record Group 350, Records of the Bureau of Insular Affairs, General Classified Files 1898–1945, Entry 5, Box 1338, 1914–1945, File #28943-59.

3. In April 2018, a new three-year temporary exhibit opened at the United States Holocaust Memorial Museum in Washington, DC, titled "Americans and the Holocaust." Menachem Wecker, journalist for the *Washington Post*, remarks in his April 22, 2018, review of the new exhibit that "this posthumous makeover for FDR at the museum comes amid a new and contentious wave of scholarship, which promises to change the way people think about the former president's legacy." Wecker goes on to discuss current opposing views on FDR and the creation of the War Refugee Board (WRB) in 1944, relating how some credit FDR for the 200,000 Jews the WRB saved and others accuse FDR for failing to support the creation of the WRB and limiting its funding. Just as the scholarship in chapter 2 of this book maintains that FDR's support for the Evian Conference was meant to deflect political criticisms aimed at his nonchalant attitude toward the Jewish refugee crisis, Wecker's article quotes historian Rafael Medoff as claiming that FDR "established it [WRB] only because of strong political pressure, on the eve of an election year, from the Jewish community, Congress and his own treasury Department." Debates on FDR and the Holocaust rage on. See Menachem Wecker, "Holocaust Museum Rethinks FDR's World War II Refugee Legacy," *Washington Post*, April 22, 2018.

4. See notes 1 and 5 in chapter 4.

Afterword

1. Several interviews were conducted with Sylvia Cysner between 2004 and 2007. Some were recorded only as audio tapes, some as transcribed conversations, and others as video-taped testimonies on January 24, 2004, and January 24–25, 2007. All these sources have been edited into the selected narrative recorded here, only adding short phrases as could be derived from our conversations that helped tie her memories together as they came back to her during our visits together.

BIBLIOGRAPHY

Primary Sources

ORAL HISTORIES: SPEECHES/INTERVIEWS

Bocobo, Jorge. "Jewish Settlement in Mindanao—Address by President Jorge Bocobo to the Jewish Junior League, Mar. 14, 1939." Bocobo Papers, University of the Philippines Main Library, box 1, folder 20.

Bunin, Charlotte Holzer. Interview by Bonnie M. Harris. June 18, 2006. Lawrence, NY. Video recording.

Cysner, Sylvia. Interviews by Bonnie M. Harris. Jan. 2004–Jan. 2007. Los Angeles, CA. Audio and video recordings.

Entell, Hanna Kaunitz Weinstein. Interview by Ray Ann Kremer. June 18 and Oct. 8, 1986. Atlanta, GA. OHC 10184, p. 18. Herbert and Esther Taylor Oral History Collection, Cuba family archives for Southern Jewish History at the Breman Museum, Atlanta, GA.

"Extract from the Speech by Hitler, Jan. 30, 1939." In *Documents on the Holocaust*, 8th ed., edited by Yitzhak Arad, Israel Gutman, and Abraham Margaliot, 132–35. Lincoln: University of Nebraska Press and Yad Vashem, 1999.

Johnson, Henry Sioux. "Living with Dignity: An Analysis of a Questionnaire Survey of Former American Civilian Internees." In *A Stranger in a Strange Land*, by Henry Sioux Johnson. Michael P. Onorato, interviewer and editor. California State University, Fullerton: Oral History Program, 1985.

Kestenbaum, Margot Cassel Pins. Email to Bonnie M. Harris. Dec. 26, 2018.

———. Interview by Noel Izon. June 3, 2016. Jerusalem, Israel. Transcription.

Kranzler, David. Interview by Diane Estelle Vicari. Nov. 8, 1998. *Sugihara*, PBS Documentary. http://www.pbs.org/wgbh/sugihara/readings/kranzler.html.

Lipetz, Jacques. Interview by Nora Levin. July 21, 1988. Transcription USHMM 2-1-46.

Meadows, Martin. Interview by Bonnie M. Harris. June 28, 2006. Washington, DC. Video recording.

Nagler, Joan. Interview by Bonnie M. Harris. Mar. 30, 2006. London, England. Video recording.

Netzorg, Jock. Interview by Michael P. Onorato, Mar. 4, 1987. Transcript: *Jock Netzorg: Manila Memories.* Laguna Beach, CA: Pacific Rim Books, 1987.

Odenheimer, John. Interview by Peter Ryan. Nov. 12, 1997. San Mateo, CA. Video recording. JFCS San Francisco Holocaust Center. 2 Tapes in Collections, USHMM, Accession #1999.A0122.0346, RG-50.477.0346. https://collections.ushmm.org/search/catalog/irn509589.

Preiss, Ralph. Interview by Bonnie M. Harris. June 17, 2008. New York. Video recording.

Propper, Norbert. Interview by Larry Lerner for the Survivors of the Shoah Visual History Foundation. Bronx, NY. Jan. 3, 1995. USC Shoah Foundation. Video recording.

———. Interview by Noel Izon. July 7, 2016. Menton, France. Video recording. Transcribed by Michael Iannelli.

Rosenblum, Edmund. Interview by Bonnie M. Harris. June 15, 2007. West Hempstead, NY. Video recording.

Sams, Margaret. Interviewed in *Victims of Circumstance: Santo Tomas Internment Camp.* Lou Gopal, Kawayan Productions, DVD documentary, Sep. 1, 2006.

Weinzheimer Jansen, Sasha, and Sally Harden Rosenberg. Interviewed in *Victims of Circumstance: Santo Tomas Internment Camp.* Lou Gopal, Kawayan Productions, DVD documentary, Sep. 1, 2006.

MEMOIRS/DIARIES/PERSONAL PAPERS

Berges, Max. "Please, don't worry! Nothing came of it." Center for Jewish History, New York, Leo Baeck Institute Archives, Max Berges Memoir Project, call no. MM8.334, n.d.

Carroll, Earl. "The Secret War of Santo Tomas, Chapters 1–9." *Los Angeles Examiner,* Aug. 1945.

Cogan, Frances B. *Captured: The Japanese Internment of American Civilians in the Philippines, 1941–1945.* Athens: University of Georgia Press, 2000.

Cysner, Joseph P. "Zbaszyn." Oct. 30, 1938. Jewish Historical Society of San Diego Archives. Cantor Joseph Cysner Collection. CJC02.01.

Cysner, Sylvia. Interview. Jan. 24, 2004. Transcription of taped interview by Bonnie M. Harris.

Cysner, Sylvia. Personal papers reviewed and photographed by Bonnie M. Harris. Used with permission of the Cysner family.

Emmerich, Alfred. "The Chicken Tree." *Kvutzat Chaverim Newsletter*. Purim 1946, Manila, JHSSD Archives, Cantor Joseph Cysner Collection, CJC02.03.

Goldhagen, Juergen R., ed. *Manila Memories: Four Boys Remember Their Lives before, during and after the Japanese Occupation*. Exeter, UK: Shearsman Books, 2008.

Farley, James A. *The Jim Farley Story: The Roosevelt Years*. New York: McGraw-Hill, 1948.

Hitler, Adolf. *Mein Kampf*. New York: Houghton Mifflin, 1969.

Hutton, Esther Robbins. *Sojourn: A Family Saga*. Vashon, WA: ESFIR Books, 1997.

Johansen, Bruce E. *So Far from Home: Manila's Santo Tomas Internment Camp*. Omaha, NE: PIBI Press, 1996.

King, William Lyon Mackenzie. "Diaries of William Lyon Mackenzie King." Library and Archives Canada. https://www.bac-lac.gc.ca/eng/discover/politics -government/prime-ministers/william-lyon-mackenzie-king/Pages/diaries -william-lyon-mackenzie-king.aspx.

Korman, Gerd. *Nightmare's Fairy Tale: A Young Refugee's Home Fronts, 1938–1948*. Madison: University of Wisconsin Press, 2005.

Liberman, Yaacov. *My China: Jewish Life in the Orient, 1900–1950*. New York: Gefen, 1998.

Lipetz, Jacques. "Witnesses." Cybrary Community. Apr. 25, 1995. https://www .remember.org/witness/lipetz.htm.

Lucas, Celia. *Prisoners of Santo Tomas*. London: Leo Cooper, 1975.

Nash, Peter. "My German Third Reich Passport Found in Shanghai." Dec. 8, 2012. https://www.passport-collector.com/my-german-third-reich-passport -found-in-shanghai/.

Van Sickle, Emily. *The Iron Gates of Santo Tomas: The Firsthand Account of an American Couple Interned by the Japanese in Manila, 1942–1945*. Chicago: Academy Chicago Publishers, 1992.

Weissler, Max H. "Life Story in the Philippines." Hod-Hasharon, Israel, Dec. 13, 2005.

ARCHIVES/COLLECTIONS/DATABASES

Albert Einstein Archives. Berges File-Correspondence M. L. Berges, 52/524– 52/547. Hebrew University of Jerusalem.

American Jewish Joint Distribution Committee Archives, New York City. JDC Collection 33/44.

Avalon Project. Lillian Goldman Law Library, Yale Law School. New Haven, CT. "Anti-Comintern Pact." http://avalon.law.yale.edu/wwii/tri1.asp.

Chan Robles Virtual Law Library. The Chan Robles Group. The Philippine Independence Act (Tydings-McDuffie Act). http://www.chanrobles.com/tydings mcduffieact.htm#XGNGKLyahA.

Franklin D. Roosevelt Presidential Library & Museum, Hyde Park, NY. Master Speech File 1898–1945.

Ghetto Fighter's Museum Archives. Akko, Israel. Zbaszyn Clippings Collection.

Harry S. Truman Presidential Library & Museum. Independence, MO. Papers of Myron C. Taylor.

Jewish Historical Society of San Diego Archives (JHSSD). San Diego, CA. Cantor Joseph Cysner Collection, CJC01-CJC02.

Jewish News Archive. Jewish Telegraphic Agency (JTA). http://archive.jta.org.

Jewish Virtual Library. A Project of the American-Israeli Cooperative Enterprise. http://www.jewishvirtuallibrary.org.

Jorge B. Vargas Archives. Jorge B. Vargas Museum and Filipiniana Research Center, Quezon City, Philippines.

Lilly Library Manuscript Collections. Indiana University. Bloomington. McNutt Mss.

National Archives and Records Administration, College Park, MD. NARA II, Record Group 59, Intergovernmental Committee of Refugees, Country Files, "Philippines," Lot52D408.

National Archives and Records Administration, College Park, MD. NARA II, Record Group 126, Records of the Office of Territories, Classified Files 1907–1951, "High Commissioner-Administrative General."

National Archives and Records Administration, College Park, MD. NARA II, Record Group 350, Records of Bureau of Insular Affairs, General Classified Files 1898–1945, Entry 5, 1914–1945, Box 1338, File #28943.

National Archives and Records Administration, Washington, DC. NARA I, Record Group 59, General Records Department of State, Visa Division, 811b.55.

National Jewish Welfare Board Collection. "Philippine Islands, 1945," 1–180, American Jewish Historical Society Archives. Center for Jewish History, New York City.

National Library Board, Singapore Government, Singapore, Malaysia. "NewspapersSG" http://eresources.nlb.gov.sg/newspapers/default.aspx.

Politisches Auswärtiges Amt. Archives, Berlin. Film 27–125, Band 49013.

United States Holocaust Memorial Museum Archives, Washington, DC. Isidor Kirshot Donation.

US Immigration Legislation Online. *Immigration Act of 1917*, Feb. 5, 1917. H.R. 10384; Pub.L. 301; 39 Stat. 874. 64th Congress; University of Washington

Bothell Library. 2009. http://library.uwb.edu/Static/USimmigration/39%20
stat%20874.pdf. Washington, DC: Government Printing Office. Statistical
Abstract of the United States, 1929.
Yad Vashem World Holocaust Remembrance Center. Jerusalem, Israel. "Emanuel
Ringelblum's Notes on the Refugees in Zbaszyn." https://www.yadvashem
.org/download/education/units/crystal_7.pdf.

Secondary Sources

Adler, Cyrus. *Jacob H. Schiff: His Life and Letters.* Vol. 1. New York: Doran, 1928.
Akira, Fugiwara. "The Road to Pearl Harbor." In *Showa Japan: Political, Economic,
and Social History, 1925–1989,* vol. 1, edited by Stephen S. Large, 230–38. New
York: Routledge, 1998.
Akira, Iikura. "The 'Yellow Peril' and Its Influence on Japanese-German Rela-
tions." In *Japanese-German Relations, 1895–1945: War, Diplomacy and Public
Opinion,* edited by Christian W. Spang and Rolf-Harald Wippich, 80–98.
New York: Routledge, 2006.
"Anti-Comintern Pact." *The Avalon Project.* Yale Law School, Lillian Goldman
Law Library School. n.d. http://avalon.law.yale.edu/wwii/tri1.asp.
Aronson, Shlomo. *Hitler, Allies, and the Jews.* New York: Cambridge University
Press, 2004.
Ascher, Abraham. *A Community under Siege: The Jews of Breslau under Nazism.*
Stanford: Stanford University Press, 2007.
Bachrach, Susan, and Anita Kassof. *Flight and Rescue.* Washington, DC: United
States Holocaust Memorial Museum, 2001.
Bandiera, Oriana, Imran Rasul, and Martina Viarengo. "The Making of Modern
America: Estimating Migration Flows Using Administrative Records from Ellis
Island 1892–1924." University College London, May 2010. https://editorial
express.com/cgi-bin/conference/download.cgi?db_name=res2011&paper_id
=800.
Bauer, Yehuda. *American Jewry and the Holocaust: The American Jewish Joint
Distribution Committee, 1939–1945.* Detroit: Wayne State University Press,
1981.
———. *A History of the Holocaust.* New York: Franklin Watts, 1982.
———. *My Brother's Keeper: A History of the American Jewish Joint Distribution
Committee 1929–1939.* Philadelphia: Jewish Publication Society of America,
1974.
Bei, Gao. *Shanghai Sanctuary: Chinese and Japanese Policy toward European Jewish
Refugees during World War II.* New York: Oxford University Press, 2013.

Beir, Robert L. *Roosevelt and the Holocaust: A Rooseveltian Examines the Policies and Remembers the Times.* Fort Lee, NJ: Barricade Books, 2006.

Ben-Sasson, H. H. *A History of the Jewish People.* Cambridge, MA: Harvard University Press, 1976.

Bergen, Doris L. *War and Genocide: A Concise History of the Holocaust.* New York: Rowman & Littlefield, 2003.

Bergerson, Andrew Stuart. *Ordinary German in Extraordinary Times: The Nazi Revolution in Hildesheim.* Bloomington: Indiana University Press, 2004.

Blake, I. George. *Paul V. McNutt: Portrait of a Hoosier Statesman.* Indianapolis: Central, 1966.

Bloch, Kurt. "German-Japanese Partnership in Eastern Asia." *Far Eastern Survey* 7, no. 21 (Oct. 1938), 241–45.

Breitman, Richard, and Allan J. Lichtman. *FDR and the Jews.* Cambridge, MA: Belknap Press of Harvard University Press, 2013.

Breitman, Richard, Barbara McDonald Stewart, and Severin Hochberg, eds. *Advocate for the Doomed: The Diaries and Papers of James G. McDonald, 1932–1935.* Bloomington: Indiana University Press, 2007.

Brenner, Michael. *The Renaissance of Jewish Culture in Weimar Germany.* New Haven, CT: Yale University Press, 1996.

Brin, Herb. "Cantor Cysner's Survival Story." *Southwest Jewish Press,* no. 4, Oct. 13, 1960, 1.

Brooks, Barbara J. *Japan's Imperial Diplomacy: Consuls, Treaty Ports, and War in China.* Honolulu: University of Hawai'i Press, 2000.

Browning, Christopher R. *The Origins of the Final Solution: The Evolution of Nazi Jewish Policy, September 1939–March 1942.* Lincoln: University of Nebraska Press / Jerusalem: Yad Vashem, 2004.

———. "Referat Deutschland, Jewish Policy and the German Foreign Office (1933–1940)." *Yad Vashem Studies* 12 (1977): 37–73.

Bureau of the Census, Department of Commerce and Labor. *A Century of Population Growth: From the First Census of the United States to the Twelfth, 1790–1900.* Washington, DC: Government Printing Office, 1909.

Cawthorne, Nigel. *Reaping the Whirlwind: The German and Japanese Experience of World War II.* Cincinnati: David & Charles, 2007.

Cesarani, David. "Book Review: The Myth of Rescue. Why the Democracies Could Not Have Saved More Jews from the Nazis." *English Historical Review* 113, no. 454 (1998): 1258–60.

———. "Port Jews: Concepts, Cases and Questions." In *Port Jews: Jewish Communities in Cosmopolitan Maritime Trading Centers, 1550–1950,* edited by David Cesarani, 1–12. London: Frank Cass, 2002.

Cohen, Naomi W. *Jacob H. Schiff: A Study in American Jewish Leadership*. Hanover, NH: Brandeis University Press, 1999.

Craig, William. *The Fall of Japan: The Final Weeks of World War II in the Pacific*. New York: Macmillan, 1955.

Crowley, James B. "A New Asian Order: Some Notes on Prewar Japanese Nationalism." In *Showa Japan: Political, Economic, and Social History, 1925–1989*, vol. 1, edited by Stephen S. Large, 186–207. New York: Routledge, 1998.

Cummins, Paul F. *Dachau Song*. New York: Peter Lang, 1992.

Delmendo, Sharon. "Ike and the Jews: Was Dwight D. Eisenhower Involved in Jewish Refugee Rescue in the Philippines during the Holocaust?" Unpublished manuscript in author's possession.

Druks, Herbert. *The Failure to Rescue*. New York: Robert Speller & Sons, 1977.

Dwork, Deborah, and Robert Jan van Pelt. *Flight from the Reich: Refugee Jews, 1933–1946*. New York: W. W. Norton, 2009.

Eberly, Annette. "Manila? Where? Us?" *Present Tense* 2, no. 3 (Spring 1975).

Encyclopedia Judaica. Vol. 13. Jerusalem: Keter Publishing House, 1972.

Ephraim, Frank. *Escape to Manila: From Nazi Tyranny to Japanese Terror*. Urbana: University of Illinois Press, 2003.

———. "The Mindanao Plan: Political Obstacles to Jewish Refugee Settlement." *Holocaust and Genocide Studies* 20, no. 3 (Winter 2006): 410–36.

Estorick, Eric. "The Evian Conference and the Intergovernmental Committee." *Annals of the American Academy of Political and Social Science* 203, no. 1 (May 1939): 136–41.

Falk, Stanley L. "Douglas MacArthur and the War against Japan." In *We Shall Return! MacArthur's Commanders and the Defeat of Japan, 1942–1945*, edited by William M. Leary, 1–22. Lexington: University of Kentucky Press, 1988.

Falk, Ze'ev Wilhelm. "Hilfsverein der Deutschen Juden." *Encyclopaedia Judaica*. Accessed July 10, 2019, https://www.encyclopedia.com/religion/encyclopedias -almanacs-transcripts-and-maps/hilfsverein-der-deutschen-juden.

Farley, James. *The Jim Farley Story: The Roosevelt Years*. New York: McGraw-Hill, 1948.

Feingold, Henry L. *Bearing Witness: How America and Its Jews Responded to the Holocaust*. Syracuse: Syracuse University Press, 1995.

———. *The Politics of Rescue: The Roosevelt Administration and the Holocaust 1938–1945*. New York: Holocaust Library, 1970.

———. "Review of David Wyman's The Abandonment of the Jews: America and the Holocaust, 1941–1945." In *FDR and the Holocaust*, edited by Verne Newton, 145–60. New York: St, Martin's, 1996.

Friedländer, Saul. *Nazi Germany and the Jews.* Vol. 1, *The Years of Persecution, 1933-1939.* New York: HarperCollins Publishers, Inc., 1997.

Friedman, Saul S. *No Haven for the Oppressed: United States Policy Toward Jewish Refugees, 1938-1945.* Detroit: Wayne State University Press, 1973.

Gibson, Campbell J., and Emily Lennon. "Historical Census Statistics on the Foreign-Born Population of the United States: 1850-1990." Washington, DC: US Census Bureau, Population Division, Feb. 1999. Working Paper No. 29. https://www.census.gov/population/www/documentation/twps0029/twps0029.html.

Gilbert, Martin. *Auschwitz and the Allies.* New York: Rinehart & Winston, 1981.

Glazer, Sidney. "The Moros as a Political Factor in Philippine Independence." *Pacific Affairs* 14, no. 1 (Mar. 1941): 78-90.

Gleeck, Lewis E. *The American Governors-General and High Commissioners in the Philippines.* Quezon City: New Day, 1986.

Golab, Caroline. *Immigrant Destinations.* Philadelphia: Temple University Press, 1977.

Golay, Frank H. ed. *The Santo Tomas Story by A. V. H. Hartendorp.* New York: McGraw-Hill, 1964.

Goldstein, Jonathan. "Singapore, Manila and Harbin as Reference Points for Asian 'Port Jewish' Identity." *Jewish Culture and History* 7, nos. 1-2 (2004): 271-90. https://doi.org/10.1080/1462169X.2004.10512023.

Goodman, David G., and Masanori Miyazawa. *Jews in the Japanese Mind: The History and Uses of a Cultural Stereotype.* New York: Free Press, 1995.

Gopal, Lou, dir. *Victims of Circumstance—Santo Tomas Internment Camp.* Kawayan Productions, DVD documentary, Sep. 1, 2006.

Griese, John W. "The Jewish Community in Manila." Master's thesis, University of the Philippines, 1954.

Gugin, Linda C., and James E. St. Clair. *The Governors of Indiana.* Indianapolis: Indiana Historical Society Press, 2006.

Hanyok, Robert J. *Eavesdropping on Hell: Historical Guide to Western Communications Intelligence and the Holocaust, 1939-1945.* United States Cryptologic History, series IV, vol. 9. Fort George G. Meade, MD: Center for Cryptologic History, National Security Agency, 2005.

Harris, Bonnie M. "Antisemitism." In *Encyclopedia of Race and Racism*, vol. 1, *A-C*, 135-39. New York: Gale, Cengage Learning, 2013.

———. "The Form and Function of Temple Construction in the Ancient Near East as Evidence of Trans-cultural Religious Exchange." Master's thesis, San Diego State University, 2002.

———. "From Zbaszyn to Manila: The Holocaust Odyssey of Joseph Cysner and the Philippine Rescue of Refugee Jews." PhD diss., University of California, Santa Barbara, 2009.

———. "Die Memoiren des Kantors Joseph Cysner: Ein seltenes Zeugnis der 'Polenaktion.'" Translated by Insa Kummer. In Hamburger Schlüsseldokumente zur deutsch-jüdischen Geschichte, 25.10.2017. Institut für die Geschichte der Deutschen Juden. https://dx.doi.org/10.23691/jgo:article-94.de .vi.

Harrison, Francis Burton. *The Corner-Stone of Philippine Independence: A Narrative of Seven Years*. New York: Century, 1922.

Hartendorp, A. V. H. *The Japanese Occupation of the Philippines*. Vol. 1. Manila: Bookmark, 1967.

Hing, Bill Ong. *Defining America through Immigration Policy*. Philadelphia: Temple University Press, 2004.

Hinman, George Wheeler, Jr. "National Origins: Our Immigration Formula." *US Review of Reviews* 70, no. 3 (Sep. 1924). Reprinted in *Readings in US Government*, by Finla Goff Crawford, 304–15. New York: A. A. Knopf, 1927.

"History." Jewish Welfare Board website of the Jewish Community of Singapore. n.d. https://singaporejews.com/our-community/history.

Houben, Vincent J. H. "Southeast Asia and Islam." *Annals of the American Academy of Political and Social Science* 588 (July 2003): 149–70.

Ikle, Frank William. *German-Japanese Relations, 1936–1940*. New York: Bookman Associates, 1956.

Iriye, Akira. "The Failure of Military Expansionism." In *Showa Japan: Political, Economic, and Social History, 1925–1989*, vol. 1, edited by Stephen S. Large, 208–29. New York: Routledge, 1998.

Jansen, Marius B. *The Making of Modern Japan*. Cambridge, MA: Belknap Press of Harvard University Press, 2000.

Jones, Francis Clifford. *Japan's New Order in East Asia: Its Rise and Fall, 1937–45*. New York: Oxford University Press, 1954.

Jose, Ricardo Trota, ed. *World War II and the Japanese Occupation*. Quezon City: University of the Philippines Press, 2006.

Kaiser, David E. "Germany and the Origins of the First World War." *Journal of Modern History* 55, no. 3 (Sep. 1983): 442–74.

Kaplan, Marion A. *Between Dignity and Despair: Jewish Life in Nazi Germany*. New York: Oxford University Press, 1999.

———. *Dominican Haven: The Jewish Refugee Settlement in Sosua, 1940–1945*. New York: Museum of Jewish Heritage, 2008.

Karnow, Stanley. *In Our Image: America's Empire in the Philippines*. New York: Ballantine Books, 1989.

Katz, Jacob. *From Prejudice to Destruction: Antisemitism, 1700–1933.* Cambridge, MA: Harvard University Press, 1980.

———. *Out of the Ghetto: The Social Background of Jewish Emancipation, 1770–1870.* Cambridge, MA: Harvard University Press, 1973.

Kotlowski, Dean J. "Breaching the Paper Walls: Paul V. McNutt and Jewish Refugees to the Philippines, 1938–1939." *Diplomatic History: The Journal of the Society for Historians of American Foreign Relations* 33, no. 5 (Nov. 2009).

———. *Paul V. McNutt and the Age of FDR.* Bloomington: Indiana University Press, 2015.

Kranzler, David. "The Japanese Ideology of Anti-Semitism and the Holocaust." In *Contemporary Views on the Holocaust,* edited by Randolph L. Braham, 79–108. Dordrecht: Springer Netherlands, 1983.

———. *Japanese, Nazis, and Jews.* Hoboken, NJ: KTAV Publishing House, 1988.

Krohn, Edgar, Jr., Klaus Schroeder, and Georg B. Weber. *The German Club Manila.* Makati City: German Club, 1996.

Laffer, Dennis Ross. "The Jewish Trail of Tears: The Evian Conference of July 1938." Master's thesis, University of South Florida, 2011. https://scholarcommons.usf.edu/etd/3195/.

Landau, Ronnie S. *The Nazi Holocaust.* Chicago: Ivan R. Dee, 2006.

Legarda, Benito, Jr. "Manila Holocaust: Massacre and Rape." Presidential Museum and Library, Republic of the Philippines. http://malacanang.gov.ph/75102-manila-holocaust-massacre-and-rape/.

Lemay, Michael, and Elliot Robert Barkan. *US Immigration and Naturalization Laws and Issues.* Westport, CT: Greenwood, 1999.

Loebl, Herbert. *Juden in Bamberg: Die Jahrzehnte vor dem Holocaust.* Bamberg: Verlag Fränkischer Tag, 1999.

Lorenz, Ina. "Die Jüdische Gemeinde Hamburg 1860–1943: Kaiserreich—Weimarer Republik—NS Staat." In *Die Juden in Hamburg: 1590 bis 1990,* edited by Arno Herzig, 77–100. Geschichte der Juden in Hamburg 2. Hamburg: Dölling und Galitz, 1991.

Manchester, William. *American Caesar: Douglas McArthur 1880–1964.* New York: Dell, 1978.

Markovits, Andrei S., Beth Simone Noveck, and Carolyn Hoefig. "Jews in German Society." In *The Cambridge Companion to Modern German Culture,* edited by Eva Kolinsky and Wilfried van de Will, 86–109. Cambridge: Cambridge University Press, 1998.

Marrus, Michael R. *The Unwanted: European Refugees from the First World War through the Cold War.* Philadelphia: Temple University Press, 2002.

Martin, Bernd. *Japan and Germany in the Modern World*. New York: Berghahn Books, 1995.

Maurer, Trude. "Die Anweisung der Polnischen Juden und der Vorwand für die Kristallnacht." In *Der Judenpogrom 1938: Von der Reichkristallnachtzum Voelkermord*, edited by Walter H. Pehle, 52–73. Frankfurt am Main: Fischer Taschenbuch Verlag, 1988.

Maxey, Fred. "Mindanao—Island of Hope." In *The Development of Mindanao and the Future of the Non-Christians*, 10. Manila: Institute of Pacific Relations, 1938.

Melzer, Emanuel. "Relations between Poland and Germany and Their Impact on the Jewish Problem in Poland (1935–1938)." *Yad Vashem Studies* 12 (1977): 193–230.

Meyer, Beate. "Das Schicksaljahr 1938 und die Folgen." In *Die Verfolgung und Ermordung der Hamburger Juden 1933–1945*, edited by Beate Meyer, 25–32. Freie und Hansestdt Hamburg: Landeszentrale fuer Politische Bildung, 2006.

Miller, William H. *Picture History of British Ocean Liners, 1900 to the Present*. New York: Courier Dover, 2001.

Milton, Sybil. "The Expulsion of Polish Jews from Germany, October 1938 to July 1939." In *Leo Baeck Institute Year Book XXIX*, 169–74. London: Martin Secker & Warburg, 1984.

Moore, Bob. "Book Review: The Myth of Rescue: Why the Democracies Could Not Have Saved More Jews from the Nazis." *German History* 17, no. 2 (Apr. 1, 1999): 309–11.

Morse, Arthur D. *While Six Million Died: A Chronology of American Apathy*. New York: Random House, 1968.

Mosse, Werner E. "Albert Mosse: A Jewish Judge in Imperial Germany." *Leo Baeck Institute Year Book* 28 (1983): 169–84.

Müller-Wesemann, Barbara, and Sophie Fetthauer. "Raphael Broches." In *Encyclopedia of Persecuted Musicians of the Nazi Era*, edited by Claudia Maurer Zenck and Peter Petersen. Hamburg: University of Hamburg, 2007. https://www.lexm.uni-hamburg.de/object/lexm_lexmperson_00002396.

Muramatsu, Michio, and Frieder Maschold, eds. *State and Administration in Japan and Germany*. Berlin: Walter de Gruyter, 1996.

Nakano, Satoshi. "The 'Windfall' Revenue Controversy, 1937–1941: A Perspective of Philippine Commonwealth History." Apr. 5, 2008. http://www.quezon.ph/wp-content/uploads/2008/04/commonwealth-funds-windfall-debate.pdf.

Nalty, Bernard C., ed. *War in the Pacific: Pearl Harbor to Tokyo Bay*. London: Salamander Books, 1991.

Neff, Robert R. "The Early Career and Governorship of Paul V. McNutt." PhD diss., Indiana University, Bloomington, 1963.

Newton, Verne W. *FDR and the Holocaust.* New York: St. Martin's, 1996.

Nicosia, Francis R. *The Third Reich and the Palestine Question.* London: I. B. Tauris, 1985.

Olejniczak, Wojciech, ed. *See You Next Year in Jerusalem: Deportation of Polish Jews from Germany to Zbaszyn in 1938.* Zbaszyn-Poznań: Fundacja TRES, 2012.

Otte, T. G. "Great Britain, Germany, and the Far Eastern Crisis of 1897–8." *English Historical Review* 110, no. 439 (Nov. 1995): 1157–79.

Pasachoff, Naomi, and Robert J. Littman. *A Concise History of the Jewish People.* Lanham, MD: Rowman & Littlefield, 1995.

Pearson, Emmet F. "Morbidity and Mortality in Santo Tomas Internment Camp." Reprinted from *Annals of Internal Medicine* 24, no. 6 (June 1946): 990. American Historical Collection, Rizal Library, Ateneo de Manila University.

Penkower, Monty Noam. *The Jews Were Expendable: Free World Diplomacy and the Holocaust.* Urbana: University of Illinois Press, 1983.

Perry, George. "The Miracle of a Synagogue in Manila." *Jewish Floridian*, Sep. 23, 1960, sec. F, p. 4.

Polenberg, Richard. *The Era of Franklin D. Roosevelt, 1933–1945.* New York: Palgrave Macmillan, 2000.

Porter, Catherine. "Ambitious Plans for Mindanao Announced." *Far Eastern Survey* 7, no. 23 (Nov. 1938): 273–74.

———. "An Independent Philippines and Japan." *Far Eastern Survey* 6, no. 8 (Apr. 1937): 83–88.

———. "Philippine Immigration Restrictions Arouse Protest." *Far Eastern Survey* 9, no. 10 (May 1940): 120–21.

Pulzer, Peter. *Jews and the German State: The Political History of a Minority, 1848–1933.* Detroit: Wayne State University Press, 2003.

Purcell, L. Edward. *Immigration.* Social Issues in US History Series. Phoenix: Oryx Press, 1995.

Read, Anthony, and David Fisher. *Kristallnacht: The Unleashing of the Holocaust.* New York: Peter Bedrick Books, 1989.

Rhymes, Edward. *When Racism Is Law and Prejudice Is Policy: Prejudicial and Discriminatory Laws, Decisions and Policies in U.S. History.* Bloomington, IN: Author House, 2007.

Rigg, Bryan Mark. *Hitler's Jewish Soldiers: The Untold Story of Nazi Racial Laws and Men of Jewish Descent in the German Military.* Lawrence: University Press of Kansas, 2004.

Rodriguez, Eulogio. "The Economic Development of Mindanao." *Commonwealth Advocate* 4, nos. 10–11 (Nov.–Dec. 1938): 13–14.

Rohde, Saskia. "Synagogen in Hamburger Raum 1680–1943." In *Die Juden in Hamburg: 1590 bis 1990*, edited by Arno Herzig, 143–75. Geschichte der Juden in Hamburg 2. Hamburg: Dölling und Galitz, 1991.

Rosen, Robert N. *Saving the Jews: Franklin D. Roosevelt and the Holocaust.* New York: Thunder's Mouth, 2006.

Rubenstein, Richard L., and John K. Roth. *Approaches to Auschwitz: The Holocaust and Its Legacy.* Louisville, KY: Westminster John Knox Press, 2003.

Rubinstein, William D. *The Myth of Rescue: Why the Democracies Could Not Have Saved More Jews from the Nazis.* New York: Routledge, 1997.

Sakamoto, Pamela Rotner. *Japanese Diplomats and Jewish Refugees: A World War II Dilemma.* Westport, CT: Praeger, 1998.

Saul, Eric. "US Diplomats Who Aided Jews." Institute for the Study of Rescue and Altruism in the Holocaust (ISRAH). n.d. https://www.holocaustrescue.org/us-diplomats-who-aided-jews/.

Schanin, Dr. Norman. *In the Service of My People: Reflections of a Jewish Educator.* New York: Gefen, 2000.

Schulzinger, Robert D. *The US Diplomacy Since 1900.* New York: Oxford University Press, 1998.

Schwab, Gerald. *The Day the Holocaust Began: The Odyssey of Herschel Grynszpan.* New York: Praeger, 1990.

Seekins, Donald M. "The First Phase of United States Rule, 1898–1935." In *Philippines: A Country Study*, edited by Ronald E. Dolan, 27–37. Washington, DC: Federal Research Division of the Library of Congress, 1993.

Shirer, William L. *The Rise and Fall of the Third Reich: A History of Nazi Germany.* 3rd ed. New York: Simon & Schuster, 1990.

Skya, Walter A. *Japan's Holy War: The Political Ideology of Radical Shinto Ultranationalism.* Durham, NC: Duke University Press, 2009.

Smith, Neal. *American Empire: Roosevelt's Geographer and the Prelude to Globalization.* Berkeley: University of California Press, 2003.

Sorkin, David. *The Transformation of German Jewry, 1780–1840.* Detroit: Wayne State University Press, 1999.

Sottile, Joseph P. "Imperial Japan and the Axis Alliance in Historical Perspective." In *Japan in the Fascist Era*, edited by E. Bruce Reynolds, 1–48. New York: Palgrave Macmillan, 2004.

Spang, Christian W., and Rolf-Harald Wippich, ed. *Japanese-German Relations, 1895–1945: War, Diplomacy and Public Opinion.* New York: Routledge, 2006.

Statistical Abstract of the United States. Washington, DC: Government Printing Office, 1929.

Stevens, Frederic Harper. *Santo Tomas Internment Camp: 1942–1945*. New York: Stratford House, 1946.

Stille, Ben. *Imperial Japanese Aircraft Carriers, 1921–1945*. Oxford: Osprey, 2006.

Strauss, Herbert A. "Jewish Emigration from Germany: Nazi Policies and Jewish Responses." In *Leo Baeck Institute Year Book XXVI*, 343–409. London: Martin Secker & Warburg, 1981.

Szpilman, Christopher. "Fascist and Quasi-Fascist Ideas in Interwar Japan, 1918–1941." In *Japan in the Fascist Era*, edited by E. Bruce Reynolds, 73–106. New York: Palgrave Macmillan, 2004.

Takefumi, Terada. "The Religious Propaganda Program for Christian Churches." In *The Philippines under Japan: Occupation Policy and Reaction*, edited by Ikehata Setsuho and Richardo Trota Jose, 215–39. Quezon City: Ateneo de Manila University Press, 1999.

Tipton, Elise. *Modern Japan: A Social and Political History*. New York: Routledge, 2002.

Tokayer, Marvin, and Mary Swartz. *The Fugu Plan: The Untold Story of the Japanese and the Jews during World War II*. New York: Paddington, 1979.

Tolischus, Otto. "Rublee Questions Schacht on Plan." *New York Times*, Jan. 12, 1939.

Tomaszewski, Jerzy. *Auftakt zur Vernichtung*. Translated by Victoria Pollmann. Osnabrück: Fibre Verlag, 2002.

———. "The Zbaszyn Stop." In *See You Next Year in Jerusalem: Deportation of Polish Jews from Germany to Zbaszyn in 1938*, edited by Wojciech Olejniczak, 71–84. Zbaszyn-Poznań: Fundacja TRES, 2012.

Trevor, John B. "An Analysis of the American Immigration Act of 1924." *International Conciliation 202*. New York: Carnegie Endowment for International Peace, 1924.

United States Holocaust Memorial Museum. *Holocaust Encyclopedia*. Washington, DC. Kindertransport. http://www.ushmm.org/wlc/en/article.php?ModuleId=10005260.

Walk, Joseph. *Das Sonderrecht für die Juden im NS-Staat: Eine Sammlung der gesetzlichen Massnahmen und Richtlinien, Inhalt und Bedeutung*. Heidelberg: Müller Juristischer Verlag, 1981.

Ward, James Mace. "Legitimate Collaboration: The Administration of Santo Tomas Internment Camp and Its Histories, 1942–2003." *Pacific Historical Review* 77, no. 2 (May 2008): 159–201.

Ward, Robert DeCourcy. "Our New Immigration Policy." *Foreign Affairs* 3, no. 1 (Sep. 1924): 99–110.

Weinberg, Gerhard L. *Hitler's Foreign Policy, 1933–1939.* New York: Enigma Books, 2005.

Weiner, Rebecca. "Portugal Virtual Jewish History Tour." Jewish Virtual Library, American-Israeli Cooperative Enterprise. n.d. https://www.jewishvirtuallibrary .org/portugal-virtual-jewish-history-tour.

Wilkinson, Rupert. *Surviving a Japanese Internment Camp: Life and Liberation at Santo Tomas, Manila, in World War II.* Jefferson, NC: McFarland, 2013.

Winch, Donald, and Patricia K. O'Brien, eds. *The Political Economy of British Historical Experience, 1688–1914.* New York: Oxford University Press, 2002.

Worden, Robert L. "The Rise of the Militarists." In *Japan: A Country Study,* edited by Ronald E. Dolan and Robert L. Worden, 55–60. Washington, DC: Federal Research Division, Library of Congress, 1992.

Wyman, David S. *The Abandonment of the Jews: America and the Holocaust, 1941–1945.* New York: Pantheon Books, 1984.

———. *Paper Walls: America and the Refuge Crisis, 1938–1941.* Amherst: University of Massachusetts Press, 1968.

Xin, Xu. "Jewish Diaspora in China." In *Encyclopedia of Diasporas: Immigrant and Refugee Cultures Around the World,* edited by Carol R. Ember, Mervin Ember, and Ian A. Skoggard, 153–64. New York: Springer, 2004.

Yad Vashem. "Kristallnacht." https://www.yadvashem.org/odot_pdf/Microsoft %20Word%20-%206461.pdf.

———. "Ringelblum, Emanuel." https://www.yadvashem.org/odot_pdf/Micro soft%20Word%20-%205830.pdf.

———. "Emanuel Ringelblum's Notes of the Refugees in Zbaszyn." In "But the Story Didn't End that Way." http://www1.yadvashem.org/download/educa tion/units/crystal_7.pdf.

Yahil, Leni. *The Holocaust: The Fate of European Jewry, 1932–1945.* New York: Oxford University Press, 1991.

Yegar, Moshe. *Between Integration and Secession: The Muslim Communities of the Southern Philippines, Southern Thailand, and Western Burma/Myanmar.* New York: Lexington Books, 2002.

Young, Daniel. "American Colony and Philippine Commonwealth 1901–1941." *Welcome to the History of the Philippines, Pearl of the Orient Seas.* Edmonton University of Alberta. n.d. http://www.ualberta.ca/~vmitchel/fw5.html.

Ziedenberg, Gerald. *Blockade: The Story of Jewish Immigration to Palestine.* Bloomington, IN: Author House, 2011.

Zucker, Bat-Ami. *In Search of Refuge: Jews and US Consuls in Nazi Germany, 1933–1941.* London: Vallentine Mitchell, 2001.

INDEX

Note: Page numbers in italics refer to illustrations.

NEW PERSPECTIVES IN

SOUTHEAST ASIAN STUDIES

*Dead in the Water: Global Lessons from the World Bank's
    Hydropower Project in Laos*
Edited by Bruce Shoemaker and William Robichaud

*The Social World of Batavia: Europeans and Eurasians
    in Colonial Indonesia,* second edition
Jean Gelman Taylor

Everyday Economic Survival in Myanmar
Ardeth Maung Thawnghmung

Việt Nam: Borderless Histories
Edited by Nhung Tuyet Tran and Anthony Reid

Royal Capitalism: Wealth, Class, and Monarchy in Thailand
Puangchon Unchanam

Thailand's Political Peasants: Power in the Modern Rural Economy
Andrew Walker

Modern Noise, Fluid Genres: Popular Music in Indonesia, 1997–2001
Jeremy Wallach